D0897705

Volume 1

Critical Studies on
Black Life and Culture

Advisory Editor
Professor Charles T. Davis, Chairman
Afro-American Studies, Yale University

Assistant Advisory Editor
Professor Henry Louis Gates, Jr.
Afro-American Studies, Yale University

Charles T. Davis

BLACK IS THE COLOR OF THE COSMOS

Essays on Afro-American Literature and Culture, 1942–1981

Charles T. Davis

Edited by
Henry Louis Gates, Jr.

Foreword by
A. Bartlett Giamatti

GARLAND PUBLISHING, INC. ● NEW YORK & LONDON
1982

Library of Congress Cataloging in Publication Data

Davis, Charles T. (Charles Twitchell), 1918–1981.
  Black is the color of the cosmos.

  (Critical studies on Black life and culture;
v. 1)
  "A bibliography of the writings of Charles T.
Davis": p.
  Includes index.
  1. American literature—Afro-American authors—
History and criticism. 2. American literature—
20th century—History and criticism. 3. Afro-
Americans in literature—History and criticism.
I. Gates, Henry-Louis. II. Title. III. Series.
PS173.N4D38 1982   810'.9'896073   80-9042
ISBN 0-8240-9315-1   AACR2

Printed on acid-free, 250-year-life paper
Manufactured in the United States of America

For Jeanne

For permission to reprint previously published material: "Black is the Color of the Cosmos" originally appeared as the Introduction to *On Being Black: Writings by Afro-Americans from Frederick Douglass to the Present*, ed. Charles T. Davis and Daniel Walden (New York: Fawcett Publishers, 1970), pp. 13–39. Reprinted by permission. "The Slave Narrative: First Major Art Form in an Emerging Black Tradition" from *The Slave Narrative*, ed. Charles T. Davis and Henry Louis Gates, Jr. (New York: Oxford University Press, 1983 [forthcoming]). Reprinted by permission. "Paul Laurence Dunbar" from *American Writers: A Collection of Literary Biographies*, Supplement II, edited by A. Walton Litz. Copyright © 1981 by Charles Scribner's Sons. (New York: Charles Scribner's Sons, 1981) Reprinted with the permission of Charles Scribner's Sons. Review of *The Harlem Renaissance* by Nathan I. Huggins, *American Literature* (March 1973), 138–140. Copyright 1973, Duke University Press (Durham, North Carolina). "Jean Toomer and the South: Region and Race as Elements within a Literary Imagination," *Studies in the Literary Imagination*, 7 (Fall 1974), 23–37. Reprinted by permission. "Robert Hayden's Use of History." *Modern Black Poets*, ed. D. Gibson (Englewood cliffs, N.J.: Prentice-Hall, Inc., 1973), pp. 96–111. Reprinted by permission. "From Experience to Eloquence: Richard Wright's Black Boy as Art," *Chant of Saints: A Gathering of Afro-American Literature, Art and Scholarship*, ed. Robert B. Stepto and Michael S. Harper (Urbana: University of Illinois Press, 1979), pp. 425–439. Reprinted by permission. "The Heavenly Voice of the Black American," *Anagogic Qualities of Literature*, ed. J. Strelka (University Park and London: The Pennsylvania State University Press, 1971), pp. 107–119. Arthur P. Davis, "William Roscoe Davis and His Descendants," *The Negro History Bulletin* 13 (January 1950), 75–89, 95. Reprinted by permission.

Contents

Foreword

I first met Charles Davis when first he and Jeanne and their sons came to Yale, and we spoke, that first time, of his work on the poets he loved. The last time we spoke, not very long ago, we again spoke of his work—of the book he could see completed, of the volumes now done, of the essays he was finishing—and of so much else besides. Because while Charles's work has the poets and the profession at its core, it embraced worlds as well—of people and plans and purposes. He was always connecting, which is why, while I often saw him in repose, I never saw him still. Like a great artist, he was always making a pattern with his life and we were always finding a place in that design. He never imposed on you, he summoned you out of yourself. Charles never bid you be his loyal friend; once you met him, you could choose no other course. To be with him or around him was an education in how to be faithful to the best you could possibly be. He brought out, effortlessly, the best you had, and like everyone else I loved him for it and loved that gift in him.

His conversation was strong and sinewy and very keen. In parking lots, in the Department, downtown, at the Afro-American Studies office, in the College, at tables in various dank haunts favored by undergraduates; on street corners, at dinners, in committee meetings, on orals boards, at the Bowl: we talked. And as I traveled around the country, I heard Charles's voice in other voices, for he knew innumerable people and was known throughout America and Europe—for his contributions to scholarship, for his high standards as a professional and as a man, for his leadership in countless ways—as critic, teacher, editor, trustee, academic statesman, counsellor, administrator; as thinker about how best to bring people to think justly and well. But for all the issues he shaped, the problems he solved, the force he applied, the people he fashioned, the ever-pressing purpose of his conversation was civility. He taught everyone who came to him or came near him—the students young and old, the young colleagues, the peers and fellow barons in his far-flung profession, the people in the street—he taught them all what it was to live in a city, that is, to live together in humane commerce and just community with each other. He was urbane; his urbanity was much deeper than his instinctive courtesy, his intelligence, his wit, his ability to turn a handsome phrase, his endless patience, his unfailing, wakeful wisdom. His urbanity went deep, to the root of the word and of the man. It was his essence. He was a city builder, a man of passion and conviction who included, who brought people and brought them together, and who made them do better for being with each other than any one of them could have done alone. He built cities, human commonwealths, wherever he was—in the English Department, in the Afro-American Studies Program that he made the best in the country, in Calhoun College, in the University, throughout our country. No good idea was beyond his reach or his embrace. And no person was either.

Charles enriched this institution, and ennobled it, because he knew so well what it is for. He knew that Yale is both an idea and a place of many individuals, and because he had such a clear and candid vision of both the idea and the individuals, he knew how the people could be connected, to each other, and to the greater idea. He made an irreplaceable and immortal contribution to this University because he constantly connected people with ideas— that ongoing act of connecting was the aim and the majestic success of his conversation, of his work, of his life. Charles was all of a piece and by his presence he made us whole. It is an extra- ordinary achievement, achieved by an extraordinarily good and gifted man, whose like I had not met before and do not expect to meet again.

These are the things I wish to say in tribute to Charles, and two more things, things that I will always remember and that tell us of the quality of the man. I will always remember his laugh, that rich and subtle laugh, that knew so much of what the world could do and which healed so much; and I remember that af- firmative, positive, life-giving way he had of saying "That is right." Charles knew what was right and he had the courage and the confidence to say so and thus to make it so. And because of his courage and his confidence, it is a more just world, and we are all forever better able to say with him "that is right" and to know what it means and thus to make it so in our lives.

A. Bartlett Giamatti
April 11, 1981

Preface

It is, of course, an honor for a colleague to be entrusted with the editing of another colleague's work. It is an even more profound honor when that colleague has been one's professor. That this book is published posthumously only makes more poignant the gesture of editing.

During the last decade, Charles Davis trained a generation of critics and scholars of Afro-American literature whose central concerns are matters of language. He taught his graduate students to eschew the expressive realism of literary theories which see the text essentially as a complex vehicle by which the critic arrives at some place *anterior* to the text, such as the author's ideology or especially his or her sense of a supposedly transcendent "racial consciousness," a literary sense of the fact of blackness in Western culture, a presence which somehow is thought to precede its expression, anterior to and independent of the text itself. But he also taught his students to avoid both the naiveté and the internal contradictions of the New Criticism, especially its biological metaphor of "organic wholes," as well as what he firmly thought to be the antihumanism of structural and poststructural critical discourse. Davis taught his students to use the rigorous methods of reading developed by all of these schools, but to avoid their jargon and their own "mythologies"—their self-justifying theoretical frameworks. He did this not only because he believed strongly in the integrity of the self (even though he thought most ideas of the self and its relationship to a discourse to be much too simplistic), but also because he realized that a theory of criticism is *text-specific*, that is, it is determined by the texts one reads, in a fundamentally direct relation. Critics of Afro-American and African literature, he maintained, must be fluent in the languages of criticism, but ultimately must speak their own tongue.

Charles Davis and I completed the editing and organization of these essays, written from 1942 to 1981, just two weeks before he died. Although his critical method evolved during this forty-year period, he was satisfied that the structure of this book allowed the reader to study both one critic's comprehensive statement on the shape of the Afro-American literary tradition, and also one critic's experiences with several schools of critical practice. Both functions struck Mr. Davis as of equal importance.

Without the support of a number of people, this book would not have been printed. The receipt of a Rockefeller Humanities Fellowship and the conferring upon him by Yale President A. Bartlett Giamatti of the John Musser Chair of American Literature in 1980 made it possible for Mr. Davis to devote the last seven months of his life to writing. Paul Wright, a gifted scholar and our former Editor at Garland Publishing, enthusiastically urged Charles Davis to collect his scattered essays. Kimberly W. Benston, John W. Blassingame, and Robert Burns Stepto keenly and avidly read the manuscript. Sharon Adams and Gwendolyn Williams typed several drafts of key, unpublished chapters. Mary Lang McFarland and Darby Tench, Mr. Davis's Research Assistants, known affectionately as "Charlie's Angels," checked footnotes, quotations, and references. On behalf of this group of Charles Davis's friends, let me say that these efforts were mere labors of love.

Henry Louis Gates, Jr.

Charles T. Davis and the Critical Imperative in Afro-American Literature

Writing in the "Introduction" to the Rinehart edition of Edgar Allan Poe (1950), W.H. Auden perceptively discusses the necessarily complex and problematic relation between a writer's life and his works. "If the muses could lobby for their interests," Auden begins, "all biographical research into the lives of artists would probably be prohibited by law, and historians of the individual would have to confine themselves to those who act but do not make—generals, criminals, eccentrics, courtesans, and the like, about whom information is not only more interesting but less misleading. Good artists—the artist *manqué* is another matter—never make satisfactory heroes for novelists, because their life stories, even when interesting in themselves, are peripheral and less significant than their productions." Auden here speaks of the creative writer, but the seminal critic, we know, is every bit the artist, the creative mind. Writing some thirty years after Auden, Fredric Jameson, in a major essay on the problem of the subject in Jacques Lacan, qualifies criticism's taboo on the function of biography: "it should be observed that, where the older biographical criticism understood the author's life as a context, or as a cause, as that which could explain the text, the newer kind understands that 'life,' or rather its reconstruction, precisely as one further text in its turn, a text on the level with the other literary texts of the writer in question and susceptible of forming a larger corpus of study with them." It is Jameson's sense of the nature of biography that is of interest here, since, to draw upon Auden's terms, Charles T. Davis both "acted" and "made." And while it is for his theory of Afro-American literature that he will be judged, his reconstructed life serves as an emblem, a parallel text as it were, of the evolution of his literary criticism, collected in this book and written from 1942 to 1981.

I

Charles Twitchell Davis was born April 29, 1918, and died March 25, 1981. He was a descendant of William Roscoe Davis, born a slave in 1812, who by all accounts* was both remarkably proud and intelligent. Indeed, it was at William Roscoe Davis's insistence that the American Missionary Association sent General Samuel Chapman Armstrong to Virginia to found Hampton Institute in 1868.

Don Andrew Davis, William Roscoe Davis's grandson, was Charles Davis's father. He served as the Business Manager and Comptroller of Hampton Institute, his alma mater. He also served as the Chairman of the Executive Committee of the National Business League. Charles was a second son, of three children.

Charles Davis attended public schools at Hampton, and received his collegiate training at Dartmouth College. He was graduated from Dartmouth in 1939, with an A.B., summa cum laude. During his years at Hanover, New Hampshire, he majored in English, achieved election to Phi Beta Kappa during his junior year, and became during his senior year a Dartmouth Senior Fellow, bringing a special freedom to audit courses at the College, if he wished, and to undertake an independent project. Although denied a Rhodes Scholarship because of his race, he won at graduation the Fred D. Barker Graduate Fellowship, which he took to the University of Chicago, where he matriculated for a Master's degree under the direction of the Committee on the History of Culture. At Chicago, he was awarded two Julius Rosenwald Fellowships and completed work on the Master's early in 1942, just in time to enter the U.S. Army. His Master's essay was on black rhetorical writing from about 1910 to 1920, completed under the supervision of Professor Napier Wilt of the Department of English and Professor Avery Craven of the Department of History.

He entered the U.S. Army as a private, attended Officer's Candidate School of the Adjutant General's Department, and received subsequently assignments as a Classification Officer and

---

Atlantic Monthly, November 1861, pp. 626–640; *American Missionary,* October 1861, pp. 244, 246, 248.

as a Personnel Consultant in America and in Europe. He received an honorable discharge from military service in 1946, with the rank of Captain.

He reentered graduate school at New York University in 1947 after writing two plays which did not survive the hazards of Broadway inspection and remained unproduced. He received a Ph.D. in American Studies in 1951, after completing a thesis on the dramatic works and interests of William Vaughn Moody, E.A. Robinson, Percy MacKaye, and Ridgely Torrence. He taught at Washington Square College of New York University from 1948 to 1955, serving as Teaching Assistant, Instructor, and Assistant Professor in the Department of English. Though his special commitment during these years was to American Literature, his more important contribution was serving as Chairman of the Honors Program.

After the publication of *Walt Whitman's Poems* in 1955, with Gay Wilson Allen as co-author, Charles Davis became an Assistant Professor of English at Princeton University. When he began his appointment, Senator John Stennis threatened to withdraw his son and to protest loudly Princeton's selection of its first black Professor. The administration of President Fleming Henry Norris, however, stood firmly for academic freedom, and the august Senator from Mississippi retreated. There, Davis taught an upper-level undergraduate course in the English Romantic Poets, a graduate course in Bibliography, and ran precepts in Victorian and Modern Poetry. His editions of works by E.A. Robinson, Walt Whitman, and Lucy Larcom appeared during those years. Also while at Princeton, he served as Visiting Lecturer at Rutgers University and at Bryn Mawr College.

He moved to the Pennsylvania State University in 1961 as an Associate Professor of English. There he taught undergraduate and graduate courses in American Literature, directed Master's and Ph.D. theses, and served for a brief period as Chairman of the Freshman English Courses. He was promoted to Professor in 1964. During the period of student unrest in the late sixties, he became Chairman of the Senate Committee on Student Affairs, an active advisory group that recommended and implemented needed changes in university government and dormitory life, serving to ease tensions on campus. As a consequence of involvement with students, especially black students, he gave in 1968 the first course in Afro-American Literature ever given at the University, recovering an academic interest that he had not cultivated since his days at the University of Chicago. The same impulse led him to publish an anthology of works by black writers (*On Being Black*), which was introduced by an essay seeking to present an account of the development of black literature. During his stay at Penn State, he participated actively in organizations and conferences away from State College. He was a member of the Advisory Council of the American Literature Section of the Modern Language Association, the Executive Council of the College Section of the National Council of Teachers of English, and a member of that organization's Commission on Literature. He was a Fulbright Professor in Italy during 1966–67, teaching American Literature at the University of Turin, and he went to India in 1969 to lecture on Whitman in connection with the sesquicentennial celebration of his birth in 1819. He taught an undergraduate course and a graduate seminar at Harvard University during the summer term, 1966.

In 1970, he accepted an appointment at the University of Iowa as Professor of English and Chairman of the Program in Afro-American Studies, then in an early stage of development. He supervised there the organization of a well-integrated and solid curriculum and secured the appointment of key instructors in literature, history, sociology, and other fields. An innovation at Iowa which was especially successful was the Summer Institute for Teachers of Afro-American Studies. With the assistance of Robert Corrigan, now Provost of Humanities at the University of Maryland, he ran two Institutes, one on Richard Wright and another on W. E. B. Du Bois. While at Iowa, he taught American Literature on the undergraduate and graduate levels and gave courses as well in Afro-American Literature.

Charles Davis came to Yale University in 1972 as Professor of English and Chairman of Afro-American Studies. He was responsible for offering undergraduate and graduate courses in American Literature, and supervised dissertations and undergraduate and graduate tutorials. Under his Chairmanship, the Afro-American Program expanded both in terms of the number of courses offered and in the number of students taking them. The Program has been cited for excellence by several national newspapers, journals, and news periodicals and has served as a model for other institutions to follow. He organized a graduate curriculum leading to a Master's degree in Afro-American Studies, which began in 1978, and he brought to Yale its first B.A. program in African Studies, which convened in 1980. In 1973, he became Master of Calhoun College, one of the twelve Colleges at Yale. He served on committees for the National Council or on the Advisory Council of the American Literature Section of the Modern Language Association, the Executive Council for the American Studies Association, of the Society for the Study of Southern Literature, and the Executive Board of the English Institute and the Humanities Center at Research Triangle, North Carolina. He was also on the Board of Trustees of Spelman College, Atlanta, Georgia, and on the Visiting Committee for the Department of English at Harvard. He taught in the Salzburg seminar in Austria during the summer of 1973, offering a course on modern black literature in America. During the 1976–77 academic year he was Scholar-in-Residence at the Bellagio Study and Conference Center and was a Fellow at the Center for Advanced Study in Behavioral Sciences at Stanford; in 1980, he was a Fellow at the Aspen Institute, and received in that year a Humanities Fellowship from the Rockefeller Foundation during which he completed this book; edited a seminal collection of essays on *The Slave Narrative*, to be published by the Oxford University Press; completed with Michel Fabre the definitive bibliography of the Richard Wright canon, to be published by G.K. Hall; and completed the research for his two-volume literary history, *The Shaping of the Afro-American Literary Tradition*, for the Yale University Press. He also was the Advisory Editor for "Critical Studies on Black Life and Culture," published by Garland Publishing.

II

"No scholar has told adequately the dramatic story of
the black tradition, and I wish to tell it."
—Charles T. Davis, 1975

Charles Davis, as a scholar-critic of Afro-American literature, was most concerned, as Kimberly Benston writes of Lionel Trilling, with "the self in its relation to society"; in Davis's instance, with the black rhetorical self and its complex relation both to the larger American artistic and political culture and simultaneously with that self's direct or ironic relation to the myriad manifestations of the Afro-American cultural matrix. Bringing to bear on his close readings of black literature the three cardinal requisites of the critic—a splendid memory; a profound sense of intertextuality, of how a discrete text echoes, extends, and tropes other, somehow kindred texts; and a practiced skill at decoding figurative language, never mistaking a sign for its referent, and never diminishing either the distance or the arbitrary relationship between the two—Charles Davis, in all of his critical writings from 1942 to 1981, concerned himself with how a black text *means*, both in its immediate cultural and literary context and in ours.

It is good to return here to Auden's suggestive essay on Poe (1950), and to his discussion of Poe as critic. "Poe's critical work," Auden argues,

> like that of any significant critic, must be considered in the literary context which provoked it. No critic, however pontifical his tone, is really attempting to lay down eternal truths about art; he is always polemical, fighting a battle against the characteristic misconceptions, stupidities, and weaknesses of his contemporaries. He is always having, on the one hand, to defend tradition against the amateur who is ignorant of it and the crank who thinks it should be scrapped so that real art may begin anew with him and, on the other, to assert the real novelty of the present and to demonstrate, against the academic who imagines that carrying on the tradition means imitation, what modern tasks and achievements are truly analogues to those of the past.

Writing as he did about black literature essentially between 1969 and 1981, Charles Davis defined his principal task as a critic as to mediate between, on the one hand, the black "amateurs" and "cranks" who, especially in the Black Arts movement which he critiques here again and again, thought of their work as a literary Topsy, which, without antecedents, "jus' grew," and, on the other hand, both the hostile white critical academy too willing to dismiss much of black literature as one-dimensional, hate-inspired dogma or shoddy imitation of "the tradition" as well as those black critics unable or unwilling to "place" black writing properly

in its thoroughly American and integrated "text-milieu."* It is
even fair to say that it was the political fervor generated as Black
Power that led Davis to write about black literature once again,
after a hiatus since his Master's thesis at the University of Chicago
in 1942, during which time Edwin Arlington Robinson and Walt
Whitman were the especial focus of his scholarly concern. Mediate between these forces he did, always gracefully, always intelligently, always deftly, defining in the process the truly complex
nature of the Afro-American literary tradition.

It is the contours of this literary tradition that Davis defines
here, in a collection of his published and unpublished essays and
reviews written over a period of forty years. A companion volume
to his two-volume *The Shaping of the Afro-American Literary
Tradition* (forthcoming, Yale University Press), *Black is the Color
of the Cosmos* allows us to examine the process of the unfolding
of an idea of a literary tradition, both in theoretical essays as well
as in more practical criticism. Although these essays are organized
thematically, we have dated them so that some sense of Davis's
chronological development as a critic remains intact.

The essays are divided into three sections. The first, "Theories
of Black Literature and Culture," includes three essays written in
1969 and 1970, those crucial years in the academy and in the
country of widespread student protest against racism and the
Vietnam War, increasingly visible repression of the Black Panther
Party for Self-Defense, and the birth of Black Studies programs
from Harvard and Yale to junior and community colleges. The
Black Arts movement, the cultural reflection of the epiphenom-
enal Black Power movement, dominated most aspects of both
public cultural consumption and of definitions of the black literary tradition then battling its way rather noisily into the hereto-
fore Anglo-American literature curriculum. Davis's essays written
at this time, especially "The American Scholar, the Black Arts,
and/or Black Power," afford an unusually meaningful glimpse of
one traditional scholar's responsible resolution of the question of
the relationship that these two traditions bore in common. Always critical of attempts to force rhetoric to do the necessary work

---

*This phrase was first used by Geoffrey Hartman in *Criticism in the Wilderness*
(New Haven: Yale University Press, 1981).

of the imagination, after Yeats, "The American Scholar" remains after a full decade the seminal essay on the idea of the black tradition and its multi-cultural heritage. "Black Leadership as a Cultural Phenomenon: The Harlem Renaissance," written in 1977, not only expands upon Davis's definition of the ironic nature of "blackness" as a metaphysical concept, but also includes his remarkably perceptive "inversion" typologies of *fin-de-siècle* America's racist ideology and the Harlem Renaissance's curious response to that racism. These essays comprise a compelling unit on the trope of blackness within the Afro-American literary tradition, a sustained theory of black literature.

Part II of this book is called "The Structure of the Afro-American Literary Tradition," and includes close readings of genres and writers in the tradition, from the slave narratives and Paul Laurence Dunbar to the Harlem Renaissance, Jean Toomer, and his most accomplished heir, Robert Hayden. From the theoretical discourse of Part I, the essays in Part II explicate in ever closer detail the specific usages of literary language upon which, finally, all ideas of a literary tradition must rest. "Prose Literature of Racial Defense, 1917–1924: A Preface to the Harlem Renaissance and Its 'Text-Milieu'" not only reveals in massive detail the evidence on which the typology found in "Black Leadership as a Cultural Phenomenon" is based, but also employs a broad notion to "text" to *site* the body of writing that rather self-consciously and grandly thought of itself as part of the tradition and its whole. The essay, written in 1942, remains the single most apt explication of the "textual context" in which Renaissance writing arose.

Part III, "On Wright, Ellison, and Baldwin," brings to bear on the fictions of these three seminal influences in the Afro-American narrative tradition a series of close readings of their fictions as they relate both to other fictions generally, and to the fictions created by each other. More than most formalist critics, Davis here insists upon Richard Wright's essential role as craftsman, directly antecedent to Ralph Ellison, whose *Invisible Man* Davis suggests remains the classic black fictional text. From the most general theoretical basis, then, to these close readings of Wright, Ellison, and Baldwin, *Black is the Color of the Cosmos* defines a theory of literature, and then demonstrates its precise shape in critical practice.

III

Davis's theory of black literature deserves some comment here. What is most curious about it, in one striking sense, is the sustained meditation on the trope of blackness which provides its foundation. Perhaps this is not so very surprising, given his extensive scholarship on the American Romantics, especially on Poe, Whitman, Emerson, Melville, Hawthorne, and Twain. What *is* surprising, however, is that these received and creative renderings of the trope of blackness as a trope of absence, in Davis's theory of black literature become what Kimberly Benston calls a trope of presence. As he writes in the first essay of this volume, originally published in 1970, and echoing James Weldon Johnson's preface to *The Book of American Negro Poetry* (1922), "Awareness of being black is the most powerful and the most fertile single inspiration for black writers in America. It is ironic that blackness, for so long regarded as a handicap socially and culturally, should also be an artistic strength. Consciousness of blackness has brought an especial intensity to the statement of theme, as in Ralph Ellison's *Invisible Man*; a distinction and a beauty to language, evident in the poems of Langston Hughes; and unusual ways of rendering scene, as observed in the work of Jean Toomer." Blackness, then, for Davis formed not only the great and terrible subject and object within the black literary tradition, but also became, in its most sublime manifestations, a fundamental structuring principle as well. This two-pronged definition of the tradition, accounting for both theme and structure, remained for Davis consistently the basis of his theory of literature. As he summarizes these ideas in the same essay, "All writers arrive at a reconciliation of a sense of tradition and a sense of difference. For nearly all black writers in America that sense of difference was the recognition of blackness. For nearly all, but not all. Being black was less important to Charles Chesnutt than it was for James Baldwin. But for most, blackness was the spur, the barb, or the shirt of pain that moved the artist to achieve distinction."

From this identification of blackness itself as a priority, Davis then gives us in outline a reading of the Afro-American literary tradition, and a summary of themes that he develops in fine detail throughout this book. Davis begins the tradition with the slave narratives, those autobiographical accounts of black bondage that proved so popular between 1831 and 1865. Above all, for Davis, the growth of a free black population in Northern urban areas, reflected by the establishment of black-owned and edited newspapers after 1827, was the precondition for the birth of a distinctly *Afro-American* literature. (See "The Slave Narrative: First Major Art Form in an Emerging Black Tradition.") The slave narratives, Davis argues, were in fact one extended mode of discourse, so similar in theme and structure that their underlying typology can readily be isolated:

> There was, preeminently, the escape, presented not simply as a successful, if physically exhausting, flight but accompanied often by instances of treachery on the part of other slaves and outbursts of cruelty on the part of vindictive masters. Always we discover the pathetic picture of the black family in slavery: the father, absent or unknown or possessing an identity to be mysteriously alluded to; the mother, denied access to her children or limited to infrequent and unsatisfying nocturnal visits; the son, sold early into a life of hard labor; the daughter, often victimized by the lust of the slave master or subjected to the caprice and spite of the women of the slave master's family. The tales are full of floggings by overseers and masters, betrayals, broken promises, frustrated attempts to acquire education, religious and secular. Although much is made of the cruelty and general inhumanity of the system, no point is made more often or more forcefully than the fact that the cruelty and inhumanity are practiced by people who say they are Christians. The pretension and the hypocrisy are objected to as much as the brutality and the shabby and penurious treatment.

It was not until 1979 that another scholar even attempted to expand upon this catalogue of shared narrative characteristics.

From the slave narratives, Davis turns to an assessment of four crucial voices of the turn of the century. Of Dunbar, whose work Davis did so much to resurrect from negative and superficial judgments of the Black Arts critic, Davis writes with balance and perception:

> Dunbar, too sensitive and too intelligent to be satisfied with the limitations of dialect verse, aspired to be known for the poems

written in unbroken English. But the truth is that these poems rarely rose above the conventional platitudes and sentiments which were somehow more acceptable given the exotic background of the plantation and the racy rhythms of the Negro dialect. There was no denying Dunbar's fine ear for dialect phrasing and his accurate sense of the ludicrous, the pathetic, or the picturesque episode. He was enormously popular, but it was a popularity that pained rather than pleased the artist. The poems of Dunbar most interesting today are not the dialect verses, nor the many sentimental effusions in proper English, so much a part of Dunbar's age, but the lines that directly reveal the poet's discomfort with his blackness, with the role that he felt somehow fated to play. Dunbar died young, only thirty-four, at the height of his fame, when many Americans, both black and white, were reciting with a great delight: "Dey had a gread big pahty down to Tom's de othah night." Perhaps, had he been granted more time, Dunbar might have come closer to achieving the ideal of the poet that he cherished.

To Chesnutt, he accords that rare distinction of defining for his successors the very possibilities of black narrative discourse, which certainly became shared and repeated structures until Ralph Ellison published *Invisible Man.* "In spite of Chesnutt's deficiencies," Davis writes,

> his achievement in fiction is superior to that of any other Negro artist until the time of the Harlem Renaissance, which brought new definitions of the Negro and the phenomenon of blackness, and new techniques. . . . Chesnutt is a front runner in writing very nearly all of the kinds of Negro fiction that became popular in the twentieth century, if these "kinds" are defined thematically: the narrative using superstitions and folk materials, the story of the Negro's adjustment to urban living, the account of the life of the Negro in the South, the shocking description of the distortion of reality that leads to a lynching, and the record of the trials of the light-skinned Negro who passes.

Relating Chesnutt's fictions to the fierce rhetorical war between W.E.B. Du Bois and Booker T. Washington at the turn of the century, Davis cleverly measures the philosophical distance between these two leaders in terms of their ideas and uses of language: Du Bois's "language—his rhetorical devices and his imagery—

came from the style of the late English Romantics. In some ways the confrontation of Washington and Du Bois was inevitable. After all, the nineteenth century, as we see it through the eyes of Carlyle, Ruskin, and Arnold, had difficulty meshing its parts: its science and its faith; its technology and its literature." It is this attention to language, and explicit comparisons with the nineteenth century, which most aptly characterize Davis's critical method.

Between Du Bois and Washington, rhetorically at least, Davis sees Du Bois's influence as formidable, determining to a large extent the idea of itself that the New Negro Renaissance held. He writes, for example, that

> The Renaissance accepted, first, Du Bois's notion of cultural pluralism. An American Negro could explore his blackness, dramatize it, and describe its roots, and still remain safely within the general frame of an American civilization. And Du Bois anticipated many of the passionate interests of Renaissance artists: in Africa, viewed as the motherland and thought to provide a spirit and a tradition of the emotions quite different from the backgrounds of other Americans; in the spirituals, as products of an authentic folk art, representing one of the great native cultural developments in America.

The Renaissance, throughout Davis's writings, assumes the role of a watershed, from which the critic can "read" the tradition backwards to the slave narratives, and forwards, if you will, to the Black Arts movement, culminating as it did a full century's thought on the nature and function of black literature. It does not surprise us that Davis defines Afro-American modernism, with the publication in 1940 of Richard Wright's *Native Son*, against the received definitions of blackness upon which Wright both drew and redefined.

Davis reads Wright's work as fundamental to the Afro-American tradition not only because of Wright's indisputable abilities as a craftsman, but perhaps even more because Wright altered drastically the very forms of narrative expression even *possible* to contemplate. Few writers, in any literary tradition, occupy such a seminal space. Few critics explicate Wright's role with so much care. "Wright provided a new definition for blackness," Davis maintained, and every subsequent writer who returned to older, simpler definitions did so with reluctance or embarrassment or from a questionable nostalgia. Wright made blackness a metaphysical state, a condition of alienation so profound that old values no longer applied. Only the Existential group that welcomed him warmly in France had the proper terms for the native American phenomenon that Bigger became. Blackness was no longer a set of stereotypes connected with the old plantation, nor was it the primary self with roots in Africa, the South, or the West Indies, which the Harlem Renaissance had discovered; blackness was the disturbing, complicated, ambiguous creation of contemporary civilization.

Wright's great insight, then, was that the trope of blackness as an absence could be drawn upon as an emblem of the state of contemporary, alienated everyman, consistent in every way with the philosophy of Existentialism that generated so much energy and attention in France.

Wright's renderings of blackness, moreover, were of such magnitude and import that both Ellison and Baldwin had to react against them before they could clear a narrative space for themselves. As Davis critiques this complex relationship of influence:

> Ellison thinks of blackness as a state of the soul accessible to all. Baldwin considers blackness to be a mark of pain and hardship which whites can share or sympathize with, but for Baldwin blackness is the sign of admission to a rich, ancient, and elemental tradition—and we have the sense that admission is restricted to blacks. In this way, Baldwin is much closer to the Harlem Renaissance than is Ellison. There is something in the echoes of Old Testament oration, the vestiges of Biblical landscapes, and the simplified disposition of complex moral problems found in *Go Tell It on the Mountain* that is reminiscent of Toomer's racial memories of a noble past, Cullen's imaginative tours of Black Africa, and McKay's visions of a warm, colorful tropical island.

Above all, it is these three writers of fiction through whose works Davis defines a black literary tradition, and especially it is their ideas of blackness by which Davis sketches the shape of the tradition.

IV

Davis identified blackness as the recurring and controlling trope of the Afro-American literary tradition precisely when the Black Arts movement was at its most fully developed and pervasive point of influence (1969). Just four years later, the movement's two central theorists, Larry Neal and Amiri Baraka, had developed new critical positions which were, if not precisely inimical to the tenets of the Black Arts, then at least major qualifications of the aesthetic principles elaborated upon in their anthology, *Black Fire*, a title meant to echo a short-lived periodical of the Harlem Renaissance called simply *Fire!!* In 1970, Neal published an essay called "Ellison's Zoot Suit," in which he effectively supplanted Wright with Ellison as the model for black artists to write after. By 1973, in a more radical shift, Baraka began the apparently painful metamorphosis of himself from a black cultural nationalist into a Marxist, a major transformation, indeed. Davis's searching critique of the Black Arts movement, written in these years between 1969 and 1972, certainly helps us to understand the nature and limitations of that energetic literary movement as perhaps no other critical analysis has been able to.

At the annual gathering of the Modern Language Association in 1969, Davis, in a lecture he called "The American Scholar, the Black Arts, and/or Black Power," told his fellow university professors of English, not an especially radical lot, that

> . . . the validity of the artistic conceptions supporting the New Breed is questionable, providing a most unstable foundation for artistic efforts. We are justifiably suspicious [of the Black Arts movement] when we discover that nearly 200 pages of *Black Fire*, a book of 650 pages of text, are given over to rhetoric, to manifestoes, denunciations, appeals, proclaiming the birth of the Black Arts and the need for Black Power. Our temptation, after so much instruction, is to dismiss the movement. If we should do so, we should be wrong, because its importance rests elsewhere. It is in the emotional energy that has gone into the formulation of programs and into the commitment of serious artists to the black aesthetic. It is also in the genuine response of many Negroes to the Black Arts—some of them, indeed, never touched before by art of any kind. I have in mind especially the interest of black youth—the spirited young men and women

who have added to the general distrust of the adult world, so current these days, a special animus that comes from the identification of that world as white.

In that same address, he observes the "Americaness" of the movement:

> Now the black artists say that they are interested only in a black audience, in inspiring the black masses to action. By this they mean, of course, a basically nonliterary audience, one not corrupted by the inhibitions, the limitations, the hang-ups of white society. There is no doubt that many people, not only the young, living in black city ghettoes and rural slums have been untouched by arts of any kind, and the most effective initial approach to them may be through the emphasis on a common or shared blackness. But this notion of a great mass audience of pure listeners or readers and potential pure believers may turn out to be a fanciful abstraction—like the anticipated mass audiences of the 1930s, the dream of the informed and cultivated workers who would rise from the oppressed classes. We suspect, finally, that a black audience is not very different from a white audience, for better or for worse—nor should we expect it to be. The two audiences share most elements in our culture— assumptions, aspirations, ideals, rewards—the latter, certainly not equally. The historical fact is that the creation of a purely black audience is not possible without negating primary responses. To insist upon an exclusively black relationship is as destructive as is the artist's devotion to the rigid standards and themes of black nationalism.

Such a judicious evaluation of the movement by a scholar of Davis's standing was the first of its kind before the MLA. Despite his support, however, Davis qualified his endorsement with a stern and, in retrospect, prophetic warning:

> . . . Larry Neal designates seven criteria for a black culture: mythology, history, social organization, political organization, economic organization, creative motif, and ethos. The intention is to liberate the black man completely from the repressive standards and values of the society, to reject an inferior status in fact and in symbol, and to achieve a black brotherhood. I am reminded, more than a little, of Whitman's program in 1860. Recall the celebration of sex and brotherhood, the confident

announcement of the arrival of a new human being and a new city of love, the construction of a new mythology based on the perfect equality of the sexes, the affirmation of the evolutionary process, and the implication that Eden was at hand—if not today, tomorrow. Remember the sexual violence that pervades Whitman's system of references, the freedom—license, some called it—of his vocabulary. But above all, let us remember that Whitman's great poetry in 1860 occurred when programs suddenly disintegrated in *Calamus* when the call for brotherhood aroused homoerotic impulses and a strangling death wish, both fusing to supply powerful substance to which Whitman with difficulty gave form. What is clearly stronger than color—black or white—is the disposition toward Romanticism in America. A significant number of Americans still hold to the conviction that art can remake reality.

Davis then criticizes the movement's absence of memory:

> The Black Arts, apparently brash, iconoclastic, frightening in their cultivation of violence, are a thoroughly American phenomenon—indeed, the wedding to Black Power is the consequence of an old seduction involving art and the rigid programming of human intelligence—and art has always suffered. It is perhaps sanguine to hope that those practicing the arts will develop an awareness of the models that have appeared before. A sense of connection would help. Studying American precedents would be a tonic for both the art and the humanity of the artist. Yes, humanity, too, because the human condition is enriched with the sharing of experience. At this crucial moment, we should view the emergence of black consciousness and the Black Arts with sympathy, understanding, and hope: with a range of favorable sentiments that we need not—indeed, should not— reserve for Black Power. The phenomenon we see is one we have seen before. Once again, in American literary history, Adam rises, "early in the morning," with limbs quivering with fire. This time, true, Adam is black. But the cultural situation of the artist remains unchanged.

It is curious to read this essay in 1981, long after both the Black Arts and Black Power movements have become footnotes to the history of the sixties. The crux of Davis's critique was that "the Black Arts have become indistinguishable from Black Power."

This confusion, he argued, was untenable, especially since he saw the Black Arts movement as a potentially major force in the redefinition of a truly comparative American literature. The problem with the marriage of Black Power with the Black Arts, he contended, was a problem of poetics, of aesthetic principles of criticism, without which poetry withers into rhetoric: "Nothing troubles more than the tendency—in many ways, perfectly natural given our recent history—to evaluate literature in terms of power, to pass judgment upon a poem or a play or a story in terms of its imagined contribution to the creation of a black community." Black Power, Davis advocated boldly, must be supplanted with "a framework, partly aesthetic and partly historical." Contrasting the Black Arts movement with its ironic namesake, the "Black Humor" movement, which had been preoccupied with its own antecedents, its relation to other aesthetic movements, and even speculative projections upon its own future, Davis judged the Black Arts harshly: "It is as if history and aesthetic criticism were suddenly erased by the sweep of a damp rag across a blackboard."

Davis sought in his critique to defend the movement from its unthinking attackers in the academy, but also to teach the writers something of their movement itself. His appeal, made simultaneously to both halves of his audience, was an appeal for historical perspective as well as the poet's desires for artistic excellence: "No art," he writes, "that restricts and reduces human sympathies can boast of humanizing the cold world, nor of providing for the true disciple a human condition that satisfies the full range of his instincts and intelligence." The problem with the movement's idea of itself was its unconscious historical model, the "mistaken model" of the proletarian art of the 1930s, complete with its myth of "a great mass audience of pure listeners or readers and potential true believers [which] may turn out to be a fanciful abstraction—like the anticipated mass audiences of the 1930s, the dream of the informed and cultivated workers who would rise from the oppressed classes." The Black Arts' manifesto, *Black Fire*, edited by Neal and Baraka, most clearly embodied these mistaken ideals: "There is in it a statement of intention, rather than achievement, a program, rather than the ordered, deeply felt experience that is art." Nevertheless, a most positive aspect of the group is to be found "in the emotional energy that has gone into the formation of programs and into the commitment of serious artists to the Black aesthetic." Few movements generate such energy. Yet the sources of this energy were, if not precisely dubious, then at least somewhat naive. "Much of the emotional power generated by the Black Arts comes from the sense of newness. The movement claims no Western ancestors; the single allegiance, other than that to a black audience, is, perhaps, to the Third World, and this only tenuously. Acquiring a black consciousness is a little like being born again. Everything in the world is changed. . . ."

Following the determination of the movement's malaise, Davis makes his boldest, and most subtle, rhetorical move: he defines the Black Arts' historical precedents: the Harlem Renaissance and the nineteenth-century great American Romantics, Poe, Melville, Twain, and, from our century, even Faulkner: "the black strain in our home-grown Romanticism that steadfastly refuses to die. The Black Arts, black magic in literature, preceded by a wide margin any thought of Black Power." Moreover, "What is clearly stronger than color—black or white," he concludes, "is the disposition toward Romanticism in America. A significant number of Americans still hold to the conviction that art can remake reality," a claim never demonstrated by historical practice. Davis's final judgment of the Black Arts helps us to understand its brief life and prompt demise.

> In short, the Black Arts offer a brilliant illustration of a paradox that is general: on the one hand, there is the desire to reject all previous interpretations of history, all earlier artistic performances, the desire to experience the exhilarating sensation of beginning from scratch to build a new tradition. This deep impulse in the young derogates and inhibits the exercise of critical faculties that have served in the past to refine and to enrich original expression. On the other hand, there is the desperate need to find models with which to identify and principles to follow, so long as these do not come from a time too far removed from the present. Recent history is the only history that is respectable; the only heroes are those who died yesterday, not the day before.

The search to define black "critical faculties . . . to refine and to enrich original expression" occupied Davis's attention throughout the seventies. His most provocative solution to this quandary he defines in a short, but pregnant, essay called "Black Literature and the Critic," which he wrote in 1972. The black critic's struggle, he writes, is not primarily with the literature itself, but with the creators of the literature whose attitudes toward the academic critic are, at best, myopic. "A period of intensive creative activity fashions its own criticism, selecting elements from the principles and the practice of the past, altering and adding to these as a consequence of the practice of the present. One thinks of the example of the *Lyrical Ballads,* with the preface that shaped critical responses for the century that followed its publication, or of Eliot's *The Sacred Wood* appearing in the same year, 1920, during which his second volume of poems was published. . . ." The challenge to the black critic of arriving at appropriate principles of literary criticism, however, is not the critic's problem; the problem lies elsewhere: "The curious situation in which black literature finds itself today is not the consequence of the failure of criticism but the result of a deep disbelief in all forms of the critical performance. Ours is a time when the critic tends to be scorned because he is considered a part of the white establishment. He is a slave of a decadent Western rationalism, the 'white thing' that all blacks must reject."

Having "solved" this problem by naming it, Davis proceeds to define the "bilingual" method by which black texts are to be explicated.

> For every black work, there is a double history. . . . We have, of course, the tradition of American letters, that continuity in form and ideas that contributed much, say, to the shape of Chesnutt's art, as it did to that of his contemporaries, Howells, Cable, Aldrich. But beyond this there is the hidden tradition, the rich and changing store of folk forms and folk materials, the advantages of a dialectical tongue, with a separate music of its own, and the background of rituals, learned responses, and wisdom that grew from a community given an amount of homogeneity through isolation and oppression.

It is this "double history," the double textual history of each black text, through which the critic must read the work at hand. In the process, the critic serves both to create another chapter in the history of the Afro-American literary tradition, while concomitantly redefining the shape of the larger *American* tradition within which the black unfolds. Above all else, the critic bears this responsibility to the writer: "No black writer of excellence can deny his blackness. If he is shrewd, he will manage a tight chemical equation for his talents, choosing those elements in the general tradition that accommodate best with the ore of his native genius. The role of the critic is to analyze the alloy, to affirm it when it works (that is, organizing successfully the varied talents of the writer), to deplore it when the compound seems loosely joined or lacking in force or grace. *It is not the critic's right to restrict the range of the artist, because he understands how complicated the creative process is* [emphasis added]." It is this set of principles of criticism, whether the critic of black literature thinks of himself as a formalist, a Marxist, a structuralist, or a poststructuralist, with which the major advances in black criticism occurred during the latter half of the 1970s.

The "touchstone" of Davis's idea of literary history was, invariably, the Harlem Renaissance, which serves for him as an emblem both of Black Abolitionism and of the Black Arts movement. It is fair to say that Davis's central interest in the tradition was the Renaissance, starting with his first major work on black literature, his M.A. thesis completed in 1942 at the University of Chicago and printed below. The final essay in this book's first and theoretical section is ostensibly a study of the idea of leadership that obtained during the Renaissance. In fact, however, the essay contains a startlingly perceptive typology of both turn-of-the-century racism, epitomized by Thomas Dixon's *The Leopard's Spots* and *The Clansman* and D.W. Griffith's film version of *The Clansman, Birth of a Nation* (about which Davis writes, "never has a more inventive movie technique been lavished upon a foundation so shoddy"), and the Renaissance's "inversion" of this racist typology. The essay's ostensible attention to the nature of black leadership, although illuminating, enables Davis to reveal the Renaissance's most subtle tensions, tensions which qualified from its start its stated aims of political liberation through the realms of "art."

He who aspires to a role of leadership in the black community must, of necessity, confront in public that which the poet confronts only privately: the fact of blackness.

Even being black is different for the leader. For the poet, the discovery of blackness begins as a complication of consciousness, one for which his education as an artist in America has not prepared him. What begins as the painful awareness of difference or rejection becomes for the artistic imagination raw matter of unparalleled richness. Not so with the black leader who tends to take a dramatic posture of some kind on the defining characteristic which is the most important condition of his life. This fact speaks most eloquently not so much for the obsession or narrowness of black leaders, but for the pathology of a society which places a greater value upon the color or caste barriers than it does upon widely publicized traditions of democracy or individualism. It happens, then, that the emergence of a black leader frequently begins with the publication of his attitude toward his racial identity rather than the assertion of religious or philosophical principles or the announcement of controlling ideas on economics or history or the positing of political or artistic manifestoes. If we look for the documentation of difference, we might compare the starting point of the journey of the imagination that is *Cane* by Jean Toomer, the Chicago sketch entitled "Bona and Paul," with the first essay by Du Bois in *The Souls of Black Folk*.

From this general observation, Davis next discusses the remarkably self-conscious manner by which the leadership of the Harlem Renaissance defined the principles of the "New Negroes" and the "Renaissance" meant to contain them.

What was the achievement in leadership of the Renaissance movement? It opposed the derogatory propaganda about blacks that had flooded America for three decades after the demise of Reconstruction. Thomas Dixon and others had maintained that blacks were without culture, close to the ape on the evolutionary scale and therefore incapable of any education other than vocational, hypersexed, and without responsibility. The Renaissance leaders inverted these misguided assumptions. They maintained that there was a rich black culture in Africa standing unrecognized by the white and that vestiges of it were present in America, in spirituals, folk narratives, dreams, and race memories. They rejected the excesses that evolution had brought into being in America—that is to say, a sterile technocratic culture—and they maintained that blacks would bring a warmth, a closeness to nature, an affirmation of basic emotions that would supply compassion for the Anglo-Saxon machine. They rejoiced in the sexual superiority of blacks, even if it is not so, and they pointed to the adherence of blacks to their own codes of morality, often different from those of whites, to deny the charge of irresponsibility. Now some of these claims were no more true than the derogative charges of the racists, but they served the purpose of supplying dignity and a connection with the past for many Afro-Americans, no matter what their class status was. Black was beautiful, for the first time in the United States.

As Davis concludes of this series of ironic reversals, of what Kierkegaard defines as the process of negative freedom, "What we observe here is amazing. The technique of response to racist attacks is *inversion*—quite literally to make that which was considered bad, good; and that which was considered good, bad. It is argument through distortion of the profoundest kind, through a set of grotesques, if American middle-class values are accepted as cultural norms. We can say, perhaps, that the Harlem Renaissance was disinterested in more obvious forms of leadership, as [Alain] Locke has suggested; it was deeply involved *in creating the cultural climate from which a new leadership could emerge* [emphasis added]." Ultimately, however, the scholar must assess the place of the Renaissance in literary history by careful readings of the texts it created and heralded. Here, Davis is at his most insightful:

> We should be troubled by the prospect of replacing one set of distortives by another. The fact is that there was not much more evidence supporting the mythology of the Renaissance than there was behind the racist assumptions of Dixon and Stoddard. Cullen wrote about Africa without the benefit of direct contact with African life, and, as a consequence, the images in his poetry arouse memories of vivid pictures from poems by Coleridge and Blake, and his rhythms, at times conventionally primitive, might just as well come from the Finnish epic, *The Kalevala*, that inspired the meter of Longfellow's *Hiawatha*, as from the African drum beat. The recollections of the Southern experience, though moving and occasionally lyrical, are hopelessly entangled with another literary convention, the pastoral, the creation of the city man dissatisfied with what is happening at home rather than knowledgeable about what goes on in the land of his ancestors—Georgia or Florida or Virginia or Jamaica or Panama. The folk tradition was a solid and an apparently endless produc-

tive resource, though the Renaissance artists, except for Hughes and Hurston, tended to view this heritage with a certain amount of condescension.

The Harlem Renaissance failed, Davis concludes, because it did not find its *voice*. The essays collected here all share this critical attention to the details of language, rather than intent or effect. These essays reveal the workings, through four decades, of one critic's splendid mind upon nearly the whole of the Afro-American literary tradition. With their publication, Davis's place as a major scholar is secure. The posthumous publication of *Black is the Color of the Cosmos* complements the publication of other major works by Charles Davis, including "Paul Laurence Dunbar," by Charles Scribner's Sons (1981), *The Slave Narrative: Texts and Contexts* (Oxford University Press, 1982), and, in two volumes, *The Shaping of the Afro-American Literary Tradition* (Yale University Press, 1983, 1984). The second volume of this latter work contains Davis's history of the Harlem Renaissance, the scope of which he indicated in a review published in 1973: "What is badly needed," he writes, "is a serious history of the Harlem Renaissance, revealing its sources, defining its leading ideas, covering adequately the interrelated contributions of music, the visual arts, folk material, and experimentation in language and literature, tracing in an orderly fashion the development of the movement, and assessing, finally, its permanent impact upon American life." It is the successful response to this set of concerns that most fittingly emblematizes Charles Davis's collected works as the works of a seminal literary scholar-critic.

Henry Louis Gates, Jr.
New Haven, April 21, 1981

I
Theories of
Black Literature and Culture

Black is the Color
of the Cosmos

Awareness of being black is the most powerful and the most fertile single inspiration for black writers in America. It is ironic that blackness, for so long regarded as a handicap socially and culturally, should also be an artistic strength. Consciousness of blackness has brought an especial intensity to the statement of theme, as in Ralph Ellison's *Invisible Man*; a distinction and a beauty to language, evident in the poems of Langston Hughes; and unusual ways of rendering scene, as observed in the work of Jean Toomer. Being black is not all. The American black writer has worked in the American tradition, using it to the extent of his skill and understanding. In the days of slavery that skill was severely limited, as we should expect, for black people, except for the fortunate few who were granted freedom, were cruelly exploited and systematically denied education and cultural advantages. It is a miracle that George Moses Horton, born a slave in North Carolina and freed finally by an occupying Union Army, wrote a line, and we should be more than politely sympathetic when that line is imitative of Lord Byron's, with the posing and the excess that are all too familiar. The same Byronic distortion is to be found in the early poems of Edgar Allan Poe, a fact which does not make the disease respectable but demonstrates, rather, that it was American. All writers arrive at a reconciliation of a sense of tradition and a sense of difference. For nearly all black writers in America that sense of difference was the recognition of blackness. For nearly all, but not all. Being black was less important to Charles Chesnutt than it was for James Baldwin. But for most, blackness was the spur, the barb, or the shirt of pain that moved the artist to achieve distinction.

Historians can begin American literature with the founding of the first sizeable English settlement, at Jamestown in 1607, though some critics might quibble about whether an English translation of Ovid's *Metamorphoses* by a nobleman residing briefly in the colonies is one of the cornerstones of an American tradition. Beginnings are, at best, uncertain even when there is a literate population to mark progress. The first sizeable settlement of

3

blacks in the English colonies occurred when Dutch traders brought to Jamestown in 1619 slaves collected from the West African coast. The artistic activities of these early blacks are entirely lost in obscurity. Slavery acted to erase the memories of an old culture and not to set the foundation of a new. Presumably vestiges of the African past remained—in song, dance, tales told in slave quarters, work done by hands. Possibly a few slaves (the phenomenon of Horton makes this real and not fanciful) mastered a foreign language sufficiently, despite the blight imposed by the "peculiar institution," to scratch down a few verses or a phrase from a sermon. In the enlightened North, where a slave might gain his freedom, attend school, learn an occupation, marry, and acquire property, Lucy Terry, as early as 1746, described an Indian raid:

> August 'twas, the twenty-fifth,
> Seventeen hundred forty-six,
> The Indians did in ambush lay,
> Some very valient [sic] men to slay,
> The names of whom I'll not leave out. . . .

Surely versification of this quality was to be found everywhere in the colonies, among whites and the few literate blacks. We must thank the happy compulsion of New England to keep records for the survival of the first poem written in America by an author identifiably black, as a document in the history of Deer-field, Massachusetts. We find a somewhat more proper beginning for a tradition of black verse in America in Jupiter Hammon's "An Evening Thought: Salvation by Christ with Penetential Cries," published on Christmas day, 1760, and in Phillis Wheatley's "On the Death of Rev. Mr. George Whitefield," published in 1770; Christian piety marks the work of both pioneer poets. Whereas Hammon's technique was restricted to the conventions of a Wesley hymn (conventions that came naturally to a fervent Methodist, who may have done some preaching around Lloyd's Neck on Long Island), Phillis Wheatley's was more varied. She was well schooled in the devices of neoclassic verse. Her efficient use of the heroic couplet, richness of allusion to figures and episodes in classical mythology, and shrewd intermixing of topical or contemporary matter and the stuff of the poetical are impressive, though somewhat frigid. She published *Poems on Various Subjects, Religious and Moral,* in London in 1773, a little more than a hundred and twenty years after the publication of *The Tenth Muse Lately Sprung Up in America* by Anne Bradstreet, also published in London. Among the tributes to friends and famous people; the discourses on Imagination, Recollection, and Friendship; the admonitions to "man ungrateful" and Harvard students—all standard fare of the eighteenth century, and all convincing testimonies of the emergence of facile talent— no poem moves us so much as one of her direct references, infrequent in her work, to her blackness:

> 'Twas mercy brought me from my *Pagan* land,
> Taught my benighted soul to understand
> That there's a God, that there's a *Saviour,* too:
> Once I redemption neither sought nor knew.
> Some view our race with scornful eye—
> "Their color is a diabolic die."
> Remember, Christians, Negroes black as Cain
> May be refined, and join th' angelic train.

Hammon knew of and admired Phillis Wheatley. In a sense, they offer works that, linked, constitute the beginning of a tradition in black verse, if it is somewhat loosely defined. They appear finally to be fortunate accidents, expressions, black, by the way, of the great creative energy of American pietism.

The Abolitionist cause was another matter. Freedom was the rallying cry for many black poets of the early nineteenth century. The writer's commitment was deep and personal, and it tended to provide an organizing principle for life as well as for art. Frances E.W. Harper and James M. Whitfield worked in organizations opposed to slavery; Whitfield, further, believed in the desirability of the colonization of black people outside of America. George Moses Horton, though a slave in North Carolina, wrote poems about his deep yearning for liberty. So poignant were two of these that they were reprinted in William Lloyd Garrison's *Liberator.* The spirit of the day is best seen not in the poetry but in the prose—in the impassioned appeals to the conscience of America, made on platforms and in the columns of Abolitionist periodicals, and, above all, in the slave narratives that caught so thoroughly the imagination and the sympathy of the people.

The slave autobiography was a useful propaganda tool and an art form. So valuable did it become to the cause that "lives" of escaped slaves were occasionally fabricated rather than recorded with accuracy. It is significant that stylization had proceeded to the extent that the contents of a slave narrative could be predicted and, of course, reproduced. Authentic narratives were often published with an extensive amount of external documentation in the form of letters from former associates (including, often, slave masters) and testimonials from respected friends or sponsors. Also, truth was asserted with what seems to us to be excessive internal documentation: the names of associates and their places of residence; the time, to the day, of arrivals and departures; and the detailed description of the method of escape (except when the information was considered to be valuable to the slave-holding enemy, as it is in *Narrative of the Life of Frederick Douglass*).

The slave narratives, though uneven in quality, offered many of the same elements. There was, preeminently, the escape, presented not simply as a successful, if physically exhausting, flight but accompanied often by instances of treachery on the part of other slaves and outbursts of cruelty on the part of vindictive masters. Always we discover the pathetic picture of the black family in slavery: the father, absent or unknown or possessing an identity to be mysteriously alluded to; the mother, denied access to her children or limited to infrequent and unsatisfying nocturnal visits; the son, sold early into a life of hard labor; the daughter, often victimized by the lust of the slave master or subjected to the caprice and spite of the women of the slave master's family. The tales are full of floggings by overseers and masters, betrayals, broken promises, frustrated attempts to acquire education, religious and secular. Although much is made of the cruelty and general inhumanity of the system, no point is made more often or more forcefully than the fact that the cruelty and inhumanity are practiced by people who say they are Christians. The pretension and the hypocrisy are objected to as much as the brutality and the shabby and penurious treatment.

From these familiar elements Frederick Douglass fashioned his *Narrative* (1845). The superiority of his tale to others rests not upon the fact that the elements are more vivid here or that they exist here in greater abundance; indeed, Douglass offers fewer of them than Henry Bibb does, say, or Solomon Northup. The *Narrative*, for example, provides no details about Douglass's escape and few about his family situation. The difference is in the emphasis upon the psychological. We sense the importance to young Douglass of "manhood," the status of being a free man in the society, and we experience with him his growing abhorrence of his condition of forced servitude. We participate in the gradual expansion of his intellectual and cultural horizons and feel satisfaction with the first signs of a general public response to his talents. Perhaps just as important as the record of Douglass's development is his shrewd observation of the psychological effect of the institution of slavery upon white owners. Slavery corrupts Sophia Auld, whose simple good nature drew initially from Douglass, the newly acquired slave, words of praise at the time that he became a member of the Auld household. The art of Douglass's *Narrative* comes from our sense of the consciousness of the narrator. Simplicity of language and economy in the use of episodes serve to heighten the intensity that Douglass gives to his preoccupation with the problems of mind and soul. In the *Narrative* blackness becomes closely associated with slavery, a condition found intolerable. A triumph of the account is the fact that Douglass retains his identity and asserts his manhood.

Many of the slave narratives seemed very close to fiction, though their authors hastened to claim that they wrote only truth, verifiable by witnesses, documents, and substantial facts of evidence. Small wonder, then, that one writer of a slave autobiography, William Wells Brown, should turn to the form of the novel in *Clotel; or The President's Daughter*, published in 1853, just six years after the Massachusetts Antislavery Society had issued his *Narrative*. Brown was a leading black advocate of the Abolitionist cause, one so widely known (in Europe as well as in America) and so richly talented that he was considered by many to be Douglass's successor as the outstanding antislavery agent, when Douglass broke with William Lloyd Garrison over the issue of political

participation in 1851. *Clotel* was the first novel published by a
Negro in America. It dealt with miscegenation, a theme made
more sensational because it touched an occupant of the White
House. Yet the matter of the novel, looked at in perspective, seems
to be just a shade more "exciting" (if that is the term) than the
bread-and-butter fare of the slave autobiography. Brown should
have had no difficulty making the transition. The art of the novel
is another matter. Few critics have found much to praise in
Clotel, a rich but largely unstructured collection of incidents
derived from Brown's recollections of slavery and his reading. No
book was more important to Brown than Mrs. Stowe's *Uncle
Tom's Cabin*, the fantastically successful work that served, no
doubt, as an inspiration to Brown.

A more substantial artist was Charles W. Chesnutt, whose
work in fiction began to appear at the end of the nineteenth
century. Art, in this connection, meant the technique of fiction
practiced by those writers who published regularly in such magazines as the *Atlantic Monthly, Century, Harper's,* and *Scribner's.* It
was not a high art, if we take our standards from the criticism of
Henry James, but it represented the dominant tradition in American fiction from the 1870s to a point well beyond the turn of the
century. The characteristics of the art were urbanity, fluency,
detachment, curiosity about a life removed from that of the cultivated narrator (almost invariably supplied), concern for moral
issues (though these may be offered in a new guise), and a certain
winking familiarity with a middle-class audience with enough
education, money, and leisure to buy and to read the *Atlantic*
with some regularity. Chesnutt joined the company of artists like
George Washington Cable, Bret Harte, Thomas Nelson Page, and
Joel Chandler Harris when Thomas Bailey Aldrich, in 1887,
accepted for the *Atlantic Monthly* "The Goophered Grapevine."
There was no way to tell that the author of the tale was a Negro,
so well had Chesnutt mastered the conventions of his form. He
was not to be distinguished from James Lane Allen, Kate Chopin,
Grace King, and others rising to prominence in the nineties.
Indeed, it was a fact not generally known for a dozen years, until
the publication of *The Wife of His Youth* (1899), when James
McArthur of the *Critic* discreetly described Chesnutt as one who
"faces the problems of the race to which he in part belongs."

Blackness, "in part," became Chesnutt's most important theme. True, *The Conjure Woman*, his first volume, published in 1899, did not deal with the problems of mixed blood, but *The Wife of His Youth*, which also appeared in 1899, began the stories of the color line, of the trials of "passing" for white, of the problems of recognition and identity, and of aspirations for achievement in middle-class society. Blackness, so muted and so confused with whiteness, supplied matter for Chesnutt's novels: *The House Behind the Cedars* (1900); *The Marrow of Tradition*, perhaps his best novel (1901); and *The Colonel's Dream* (1906). In these we find Clotel, Brown's octoroon, grown up and made more convincingly human, and placed against a social background drawn with the care of a scrupulous lawyer, which is precisely what Chesnutt was in Cleveland, Ohio. There is more art in Chesnutt's short fiction; the novels show less control and tend to slide into melodrama. The uncertainty in structuring a novel was a weakness of many American writers of fiction at the time, Henry James and William Dean Howells excepted. *The Grandissimes* (1880) by George Washington Cable was not nearly so successful as his earlier exotic tales, *Old Creole Days*; or somewhat later, Hamlin Garland's novel *Rose of Dutcher's Cooly* (1895) was much inferior to his *Main-Travelled Roads* (1891), the memorable sketches of harsh farm life in the Middle West. In spite of Chesnutt's deficiencies his achievement in fiction is superior to that of any other Negro artist until the time of the Harlem Renaissance, which brought new definitions of the Negro and the phenomenon of blackness, and new techniques. Certainly Martin Delany's *Blake; or The Huts of America* (1859), the second novel written by an American Negro, and Frances Harper's sentimental *Iola Leroy* (1892) are much inferior to Chesnutt's work. And none of the four novels by Paul Laurence Dunbar (*The Uncalled*, 1898; *The Love of Landry*, 1900; *The Fanatics*, 1901; *The Sport of the Gods*, 1904) approaches Chesnutt's work in the knowledge of the details of social background and in the mastery of the art of telling a tale. Chesnutt is a front runner in writing very nearly all of the kinds of Negro fiction that became popular in the twentieth century, if these "kinds" are defined thematically: the narrative using superstitions and folk materials, the story of the Negro's adjustment to urban living, the account of the life of the Negro in the South, the shocking description of the distortion of reality that leads to a lynching, and the record of the trials of the light-skinned Negro who passes.

Aldrich accepted Chesnutt's first story, and Howells greeted warmly the poems of Paul Laurence Dunbar, expressing his sentiments in a commendatory preface to *Lyrics of Lowly Life* (1896), Dunbar's third volume. These seemed to be hopeful responses of the American tradition to the talents of the black writer. For Dunbar, Howells's well-intentioned praise, which brought him instant recognition as a national literary figure, was as much a trap as a gratifying tribute. Dunbar became known as a writer of dialect verse, the creator of poems like "The Party," only one step removed from the strut of the blackfaced comedian in the minstrel show, and "At Candle-Lightin' Time," full of domestic pieties and nostalgic memories of good times in the old slave cabin. Dunbar, too sensitive and too intelligent to be satisfied with the limitations of dialect verse, aspired to be known for the poems written in unbroken English. But the truth is that these poems rarely rose above the conventional platitudes and sentiments which were somehow more acceptable given the exotic background of the plantation and the racy rhythms of the Negro dialect. There was no denying Dunbar's fine ear for dialect phrasing and his accurate sense of the ludicrous, the pathetic, or the picturesque episode. He was enormously popular, but it was a popularity that pained rather than pleased the artist. The poems of Dunbar most interesting today are not the dialect verses, nor the many sentimental effusions in proper English, so much a part of Dunbar's age, but the lines that directly reveal the poet's discomfort with his blackness, with the role that he felt somehow fated to play. Dunbar died young, only thirty-four, at the height of his fame, when many Americans, both black and white, were reciting with a great delight: "Dey had a gread big pahty down to Tom's de othah night." Perhaps, had he been granted more time, Dunbar might have come closer to achieving the ideal of the poet that he cherished.

At the end of the nineteenth century two Negro leaders faced the problems of blackness with a directness that no poet and no writer of fiction had displayed up until that time. Frederick Douglass died in 1895, and the mantle of leadership was disputed by Booker T. Washington and W.E.B. Du Bois. They faced a time of crisis, the most serious since the Civil War. All over the South and in many areas in the North the race was losing ground. Disenfranchisement, Jim Crow legislation, losses in economic as well as social standing signaled the fact that American institutions were making rigid and official the position of the Negro as a second-class citizen. The problem was most dramatic in the South, where the threat of lynching and other forms of naked violence complemented the segregationist thrust of the law. Washington, facing the grim Southern prospect from the educational institution that he had founded at Tuskegee, counseled conciliation of the whites and offered industrial education as a way out for beleaguered blacks. He held the dream of a property-owning, thrifty, middle-class, black population practicing Christian virtues and progressing inevitably up the ladder of success. He deemphasized, at times derided, higher education and advised preparation for voting rather than demanding immediate acquisition by blacks of the right to vote. He had the confidence of the Social Darwinist that merit and diligence would receive recognition and the conviction of the pietist that his course was the right one.

Du Bois, in 1900, believed as deeply as Washington did in character and economic independence. He could not accept any restrictions placed upon the education of the Negro, and he was too much aware of what black people owed already to higher education—especially to those teachers who were the products of such education in the public schools, academies, and even the industrial schools—to ever look upon industrial education as a general educational panacea good for all Negroes. Moreover, Du Bois, a professor at Atlanta University, in the urban rather than the rural South, did not see how economic advancement could be protected without the possession of full civil and political rights. Then there was the not-so-subtle question of manhood. Of what importance was economic progress if the black man were denied dignity as a human being? To have access to public accommodations, to use the library, to have a berth on the Pullman car, to buy a house where he could afford to do so, to vote, to drink from the public water fountain in the municipal park? Du Bois chose the valley of the Housatonic in New England, not the red clay of

Georgia, as a burial place for the infant son he loved dearly because he found intolerable the thought of the South as a permanent resting place for the child.

Relations between the two leaders were amicable until 1903, at the time of the publication of *The Souls of Black Folk*, in which Du Bois included an essay critical of Washington. After this, bitterness increased. The supporters of Du Bois deplored the influence of the Tuskegee "machine," its screening of all political appointments of Negroes in the Republican administrations of Presidents Roosevelt and Taft, and its control of the sources of money given to private Negro educational institutions in the South. The supporters of Washington accused the learned professor of being envious of Washington's success and of desiring to be white, not black. Beyond the surface noise of charge and countercharge there were interesting fundamental differences separating the two men. We have the sense of the confrontation of two quite different parts of the American nineteenth century. *Up from Slavery* (1901), Washington's eloquent autobiography, is a record of the success of a self-made man, who combined hard work and Christian virtue—indeed, equated the two. Like Ben Franklin, Washington identified his own career with that of a larger group (in Franklin's case, with the people of a new country; in Washington's, with the Negroes in America) and he displayed Franklin's appreciation for material things. Washington, moreover, believed deeply in the new industrial society and sought to insure for a black labor force a place in the New South that Henry Grady and Joel Chandler Harris sought to forge with Yankee capital. He was a cultural phenomenon, after his speech at the Atlanta Exposition in 1895, wholly approved by progressive and forward-looking financial and political leaders in the North and the South. Du Bois, on the other hand, represented the intellectual, humanistic, and literary side of the nineteenth century. Washington had graduated from Hampton Institute and had proceeded immediately to spread the Hampton idea of work and Christian piety. Du Bois, after graduation from Fisk in Nashville, Tennessee, went on to Harvard to take a Ph.D. in history and to Germany during his doctoral study. He had William James's belief in cultural pluralism and something of George Santayana's extraordinary versatility. He was a historian, a sociologist, a poet, a novelist, a master rhetorician, and an editor. He returned from Germany at the end of the century convinced that the methodology and the wisdom of the social sciences could solve most of the problems saddling the American Negro, and he had the hope that responsible, well-trained leadership, provided by the "talented tenth," could give a new shape to the life of the black man. His language—his rhetorical devices and his imagery—came from the style of the late English Romantics. In some ways the confrontation of Washington and Du Bois was inevitable. After all, the nineteenth century, as we see it through the eyes of Carlyle, Ruskin, and Arnold, had difficulty meshing its parts: its science and its faith; its technology and its literature.

As the twentieth century progressed, the future seemed clearly with Du Bois, not with Washington. Washington's national influence waned after 1909 and very nearly disappeared when a Democrat, Woodrow Wilson, occupied the White House in 1913. At the same time the associates of Du Bois were launching a powerful new movement, the National Association for the Advancement of Colored People, dedicated to achieving for Negroes full participation in the American democracy. The NAACP created two tools that it found to be very useful in the years to come—*The Crisis* magazine, edited by Du Bois, for disseminating information and mobilizing public opinion, and the legal assistance program. It seemed possible then that a black American would eventually assume his rightful place within the structure of the whole and that a black cultural contribution might find a general acceptance and an ultimate understanding in the minds of white Americans. Blackness did not seem, then, to be a bar that defied hurdling, but by 1940 Du Bois was to think that it was, given the continued existence of the American capitalist system. And by 1960, we discover, oddly, the reappearance among black militant groups of attitudes associated with Washington: the desirability of two societies, one black and the other white, with limited cooperation between them, and the belief in black economic enterprise as being a foundation for other forms of advancement (we recall that Washington founded the National Negro Business League). The great debate continues, without the leaders who posed the issues initially, and it is presented now in terms likely to confound both. We see in the career of W.E.B. Du Bois the frustration and the disillusionment of the American Negro best equipped by nineteenth-century education for success in the twentieth century. Like Henry Adams, Du Bois found that old standards of value and excellence were not adequate.

Du Bois's ideas made a substantial contribution to the first cultural movement involving American Negroes. This was the Negro Renaissance—or the Harlem Renaissance, as it is sometimes called, after the area that was the cultural center—which was formally announced by Alain Locke, professor of philosophy at Howard University, in an issue in 1925 of the *Survey Graphic* magazine. The Renaissance accepted, first, Du Bois's notion of cultural pluralism. An American Negro could explore his blackness, dramatize it, and describe its roots, and still remain safely within the general frame of an American civilization. And Du Bois anticipated many of the passionate interests of Renaissance artists: in Africa, viewed as the motherland and thought to provide a spirit and a tradition of the emotions quite different from the backgrounds of other Americans; in the spirituals, as products of an authentic folk art, representing one of the great native cultural developments in America.

The spirit of the Renaissance was, in one way, very different from the heritage of Du Bois. Locke insisted that the American Negro no longer needed to regard himself as a problem; he was free now to develop as a person and as an artist without the restrictions of political controversy. For the first time the names of artists make up a sizeable list and do not intrude strangely into a roll call of white artists, as did the names of Dunbar and Chesnutt. The names are those of young artists, all touched in some way by the aesthetics of the movement and all stimulated by each other's achievement and aspiration.

Perhaps the most exciting discovery, according to members of the movement recalling its beginnings, was Jean Toomer. *Cane*, published in 1923, was a wholly new thing—a unified book, consisting of poems and tales of varying length. Toomer, stirred by his experience as a teacher in Georgia, redefined the South in a way not recognizable in the works of Du Bois. The South became the region of memory, where the black man once lived close to the soil, which harbored vestiges of his racial past and moved him to creative expression. The strange beauty of his songs, found incongruously in the brooding terror imposed by white oppression, mocked the more superficial and less satisfying works associated with the adjustment in the Northern cities. Toomer pointed to the defects of the machine society in America and offered as therapy the unified vision of a way of life fast disappearing. "Kabnis" in *Cane* is a long tale in which a modern Negro seeks to reconcile his Northern education and the unexpected primitive strength that he finds in the black people of rural Georgia. It is an agonizing exploration of the problem of identity, so familiar in later works by Ellison and Baldwin. Toomer inverts the stereotypes associated with blackness; the ignorant black peasant, fearful of whites and content with a subordinate status as a sharecropper or a tenant farmer, becomes a holder of mysteries and the possessor of a rich organic relationship with nature.

The nostalgia of Claude McKay was less complicated. Born in Jamaica, he recalled in his poetry and his fiction the simpler tropical beauty of his native land, preferable to the cold and hostile cities of America. In other works McKay celebrated jazz music and the dance he found in Harlem, unique Negro contributions to the urban scene. Countee Cullen, who achieved distinction as a poet while yet an undergraduate at New York University, sang eloquently in "Heritage" of his allegiance to an African past. The Africa he imagined was nothing that demanded documentation by research or firsthand experience. It was a sensual, pagan approach to a lush, violent reality, one entirely opposed to the civilized Christian present, which was supported by reason rather than emotion. Langston Hughes used his fine ear for speech rhythms to catch the nuances of jazz and the blues and to incorporate the sounds of real talk. He too sensed the double allegiance of the black man, restricted now to the sordid city but suggesting in moments of ecstasy and excitement ties to a nobler, more beautiful past. There is the hope in some of Hughes's poems, "Our Land," for example, that life here might be transformed by warmth, love, and joy—qualities intimately associated with black rather than white culture. James Weldon Johnson used the form of the evangelical sermon in *God's Trombones* (1927). This was a marginally literary structure to which black preachers in the rural South and in storefront churches in cities South and North brought imagination and energy. Johnson captured the imagery, the colorful simplification of Biblical stories, the sense of a congregation thoroughly enraptured, and the repetitive, incantatory rhythms of the sermon without the use of dialect, with the limitations that had caused such pain to Dunbar. Johnson knew well that the colloquial tone could be suggested by a phrase here and there or a deliberate departure from proper grammatical usage. The full range of the Negro dialect—with the danger of suggesting, inevitably, either humor or pathos—was not needed.

Many of the writers of the Renaissance—Toomer, McKay, Cullen, Hughes, Johnson, and Arna Bontemps—wrote both fiction and poetry. Some brought highly developed skills only to fiction. Rudolph Fisher, as alert as was Langston Hughes to the spoken word in Harlem, wrote stories about the adjustment of the black man to life in the city. Zora Neale Hurston, like James Weldon Johnson, made rich artistic use of folk materials, in novels about her native Florida. Eric Walrond recreated life in the Panama of his birth, emphasizing the violence, the confusion, and the exotic color and dropping the benign tropical haze that seemed to pervade McKay's West Indian scenes.

The Negro Renaissance was not a movement that touched the common people. Its sacred places were the salon, held often in the homes of well-to-do Negroes in Harlem, and the cabaret. It is no accident, of course, that lower-class black folk in New York were involved in Marcus Garvey's United Negro Improvement Association, a movement that paralleled, in some ways, the Renaissance. Garvey planned to resettle American blacks in West Africa, and he proposed to do this through a black shipping company and on black ships, using black capital. Although the schemes of the UNIA led finally to bankruptcy, the allegiance to Garvey and to the general goal of black separatism lingered in the minds of many of the frustrated true believers, to emerge with force again in movements like that of the Black Muslims in the 1940s and 1950s.

The Depression killed the Renaissance, as it put an end to the Jazz Age. Harlem was hit harder than other sections of New York City by unemployment and general financial distress. The cabarets closed. No one spoke any longer of the special joy, the primitive grace, the unique culture that could be found in Harlem. Blackness in the 1930s often meant dislocation, sickness, unemployment, and general misery; writers who in the twenties found some publishing houses and some periodicals receptive to their manuscripts found great difficulty now in securing publication.

Richard Wright emerged as a writer in the middle of the Great Depression. Though born in Mississippi, where, with short stays in Arkansas and Tennessee, he spent his childhood and youth—brilliantly recorded later in *Black Boy* (1945)—Wright lived during the years of his young manhood in the Chicago ghetto. He knew blackness both as the caste system of the Deep South and as patterns of exclusion, segregation, and deprivation in the urban North. James Baldwin wrote in 1951 that *Native Son* (1940), Wright's first published novel (*Lawd Today*, written earlier, appeared in 1963, three years after Wright's death), was the "most powerful and celebrated statement we have yet of what it means to be a Negro in America." It may still be in 1970. It is a book that makes both whites and blacks uncomfortable. Whites are moved to the point of being offended, because they are asked to accept responsibility for the pathological society that has created Bigger Thomas, Wright's young Negro murderer. Mr. Dalton, the father of the white girl who is Bigger's first victim, is both a do-gooder (with a strong interest in Negro improvement) and a slum landlord, and in the latter role a prime force in making Bigger what he is. And what he is, is what blacks object to. Bigger is a monster. He begins as a bully, a coward, a loafer, and a would-be small-time hoodlum and within a day becomes the murderous black "ape" that the Chicago papers call him. Blacks resist identifying with so unattractive a character. Increasing the stir caused by the novel at the time of its publication was a highly effective dramatic adaptation of it, written by Wright and the playwright Paul Green in 1941, with Canada Lee performing memorably as Bigger.

Native Son is in the rich American tradition of naturalistic fiction. Impressive models for Wright's effort existed in Theodore Dreiser's *An American Tragedy* (1925) and James Farrell's *Young Lonigan* (1932), the latter of which described a section of Chicago just a few blocks south of Bigger's haunts. Though the naturalistic novel as written in America seldom presented a model for structure, Wright, despite tradition, organized his material in *Native Son* with extraordinary care. "Fear," the first book of the novel, covers one day in Bigger's life, and "Flight," the second book, something less than forty-eight hours more. There is in both an impressive achievement of economy and pacing; the tremendous acceleration of action in "Flight" is very nearly breathtaking. One is reminded here of Leopold Bloom's day, in *Ulysses*, rather than of elements from American fiction at the time—unless William Faulkner provided inspiration for Wright.

Wright departs from naturalistic models in the matter of language, too. He was no doubt influenced by Gertrude Stein in this area, as Sherwood Anderson and Ernest Hemingway had been before him. We are reminded in *Native Son* of Gertrude Stein's "Melanctha," which Wright greatly admired; we think of her elimination of words relying for meaning on anything other than sense experience; of her attention to the demands of a controlling primitive consciousness; of her magnifying of action; of her use of incremental repetition.

In addition, we must remember that Wright was a Communist when he wrote *Native Son*, though an odd and perhaps uncomfortable one, even then. As a Communist, he accepted the naturalistic view that environment shapes character, that the shape of the world helps to form Bigger. And it is no coincidence in the novel that Max, the Communist lawyer, dominates the third and final book, "Fate." It is Max, not the church, nor the family, nor the philanthropic liberals, who acts as the sole agent in humanizing Bigger, in civilizing the "ape." And yet the final book escapes becoming the "party line." It is Max who opens communications with the sullen, withdrawn Bigger, but in doing so he opens a Pandora's box, releasing ideas and impulses totally beyond his competence—or that of his Party—to reckon with. Bigger, moved to unfamiliar thoughts by Max's attention, insists that his murders were good. They have led him to a sense of freedom from the restrictions of the ghetto—however transient a freedom; they have gained him the attention of the society that had ignored him previously, however frenzied and hate-filled that attention might be. The change in Bigger is so dramatic that one can almost call it a (secular) "resurrection"—but Max is not prepared for Bigger's existential rebellion, and instead of a conversion to Max's vision of a world of brothers, we see a Bigger completely absorbed in a devastating nihilism.

The third book of *Native Son* has been criticized for many things: for too much attention (in Max's speeches) to communist propaganda; for too great a change in Bigger's character with too little preparation in advance for his long, confidential exchanges with Max; for too heavy-handed and pretentious a handling of symbolic devices (well integrated elsewhere); for too much talkiness. For whatever the reasons, in the third section we have a falling off in tension and a violent shift in language and tone. Exciting as they are, Bigger's rejection of Max's vision and his discovery of his identity are not adequate compensations for a loss of artistic control. Bigger's last powerful act is not artistically prepared for, and though his attitude toward the murders is consistent with his nature, we are unable to accept his own comprehension of that nature and the newly acquired ease with which he articulates his problems.

Despite the flaws in the last section, however, *Native Son* was a watershed in terms of the acceptance of Negro authors. For the first time a black writer gained national attention without the usual special introductions or condescending qualifications and references to a special tradition. The book was a selection of the Book-of-the-Month Club, and it collected an impressive number of serious critical notices, matching the attention given to a new work by Faulkner or Hemingway. Nothing like this had ever happened before. Ralph Ellison and James Baldwin, who followed Wright in gaining national recognition, were inevitably to be compared with Wright by the critics; perhaps more important, Ellison and Baldwin measured themselves against Wright. But nothing that Wright wrote after *Native Son* caused the sensation created by the publication of that novel, not even the fine autobiographical sketch *Black Boy* (1945), more poignant and more evenly written than *Native Son*. Wright left permanently for Europe in 1947 and ceased to be, from that time on, a major influence in American letters, though he haunted the minds and the imaginations of all black writers in America.

Wright provided a new definition for blackness, and every subsequent writer who returned to older, simpler definitions did so with reluctance or embarrassment or from a questionable nostalgia. Wright made blackness a metaphysical state, a condition of alienation so profound that old values no longer applied. Only the Existential group that welcomed him warmly in France had the proper terms for the native American phenomenon that Bigger became. Blackness was no longer a set of stereotypes connected with the old plantation, nor was it the primitive self with roots in Africa, the South, or the West Indies, which the Harlem Renaissance had discovered; blackness was the disturbing, complicated, ambiguous creation of contemporary civilization.

Ralph Ellison makes a gracious acknowledgment of his indebtedness to Wright in one of the essays in *Shadow and Act* (1964), a collection of pieces written between 1945 and 1964. Wright had steered young Ellison to the prefaces of Henry James, the letters of Dostoyevsky, the fiction of Joseph Conrad, and the criticism of Joseph Warren Beach, and Wright had suggested to Ellison that he write his first book review and undertake his first short story. Moreover, the aspiring Ellison recalls that Wright had encouraged a commitment to both writing and criticism. Ellison did not say so, but Wright may have given him the theme for his great novel, *Invisible Man* (1952), winner of a National Book Award and one of the outstanding achievements of modern fiction. That theme emerges in the flawed third book of *Native Son*, when Bigger begins to speculate on his identity and attempts to come to terms with his own blackness. It is developed fully in *Invisible Man* and given a range undreamed of in the earlier novel; there Ellison provides us with a puzzling, ambiguous metaphysical definition of blackness:

> I am invisible, understand, simply because people refuse to see me. Like the bodiless heads you see sometimes in circus sideshows, it is as though I have been surrounded by mirrors of hard, distorting glass. When they approach me they see only my surroundings, themselves, or figments of their imagination, indeed, everything and anything except me.

The narrator of *Invisible Man* pursues misleading distortions of himself through a great part of American culture. The South, in the first section of the novel, offers traditional and degrading patterns of black accommodation to white supremacy and traditional forms of black leadership. There are echoes here of the brutal episodes of the slave narratives and of the humiliating rituals in Wright's *Black Boy*. At the same time we listen again to the great debate between Washington and Du Bois, while our naïve narrator, in his desperate effort to follow the path of the Founder (bearing a strong resemblance to Washington), frantically seeks to avoid the issue that Du Bois had insisted was basic, that is to say, the possession of manhood. In the North, in the second section, the narrator is introduced to urban living in New York City, to the machine, and to technological culture. The paint factory is just as frustrating as the Negro state college in the South. The rhetoric of the school president, which humiliates the young man and threatens to brainwash him, is succeeded by the menacing possibility of a prefrontal lobotomy, discussed by the doctors in the company infirmary. The third section of the novel is concerned with the young narrator's adventures in the Brotherhood, an organization devoted to reforming the society according to principles derived from a science of history and displaying no slight resemblance to the American Communist Party. Here once again the narrator experiences the familiar pattern: the sense of great expectations, the initial success, the suffering of trial and betrayal, the discovery of inhumanity in the institution to which he has given his allegiance, and the ultimate feeling of frustration and defeat. The narrator discovers no satisfactory home for a black man. His solution is to withdraw from society, to retreat to the subterranean chamber he has discovered by chance during a Harlem riot. In his hole he orders his experiences in his mind, adjusts to his blackness, and prepares to emerge again into the upper world, with the problem of invisibility half solved, the half involving his own naïve and inadequate attitudes. The world, he knows, will go its own way.

The ambitious scope of the novel does not restrict its stylistic virtuosity, which moves from naturalism to impressionism to surrealism, as Ellison noted in an interview in the *Paris Review* (Spring 1955). The dream sequences are as compelling as the "straight" episodes, and at times the two are mixed, since nothing seems more unreal than the incidents occurring in the real world. We exist temporarily in a world populated by types—Negro dupes, indifferent whites, enduring blacks, respected models, and demonic philosophers—all creatures of the consciousness of the narrator. Running through the novel are literary references (especially to the poems of T.S. Eliot) and musical references; indeed, we are invited in the magnificent "Prologue" to view the whole novel as a kind of blues, on blackness. Finally, the novel is ironic: a black Horatio Alger, with good intentions, energy, loyalty, and better-than-average intelligence, moves not upward, but downward—to failure, doubt, and nightmare. Perhaps the triumph of Ellison's novel is that it leads all of us, white and black, to acknowledge blackness as the invisibility that is a function of a predatory, dehumanized, mechanized society.

The essays in *Shadow and Act* serve to point up the problem of the Negro artist, but they are perhaps more rewarding as an analysis of Ellison's own resources. What stands above many things that he cites is his access to folk materials: the heritage in tall tales, hunting yarns, and homely versions of the classics and the memory of a variety of musical experiences—the songs of blind preachers and blind blues artists, the improvisations of musical groups in a shoe-shine parlor, and the mountain melodies of white junkmen.

James Baldwin also uses this material brilliantly in *Go Tell It on the Mountain* (1953), his first novel; sermons, hymns, spirituals, recollections of camp-meetings and conversion experiences provide the raw substance for a fine work of art. Ellison makes of blackness both a physical state (involving eating, working, loving) and a *metaphysical* condition. Baldwin is equally sensitive to the details of the physical life of blacks, but in *Go Tell It on the Mountain* he also explores the *religious* dimension of blackness. We walk in two worlds in *Go Tell It on the Mountain*; one is Harlem, in the neighborhood of 135th Street and Lenox Avenue (and by recollection of the characters the rural South), and the other is the valleys, plains, and mountains of the Bible. If Ellison's novel is essentially an inspired picaresque tale (like Twain's *Adventures of Huckleberry Finn*), with a hero who fails to understand his role until near the end of the work, Baldwin's is a fable, constantly playing with archetypes and Biblical analogues.

The substance of Baldwin's novel is the conversion of John. John is no ordinary fourteen-year-old black. He is intelligent, sensitive, and virtuous—intended clearly not only to become a saint in the Church of the Fire Baptized, but a leader and a prophet, here and in greener pastures beyond. John's difficulty, in terms of conversion, is his hatred of his stepfather, Gabriel, who has rejected him. And Gabriel is no ordinary man but a fallen prophet, desiring a return of his old glory and a lineal descendant who will carry on the work that he has not completed. What troubles Gabriel is John's illegitimacy; he stubbornly persists in placing his hopes in his own legitimate son, already wise in the ways of the world and yearning for the pleasures of the damned. John is reduced to the threshing-floor—literally, the floor of the church where the agony of conversion is most acute—in the final brilliant section when he substitutes his heavenly father for his earthly one and when hate eases. The commencement of a new relationship with Gabriel now seems possible. In this section of the novel a shift from Old Testament references to those of the New Testament symbolizes the general movement toward hope.

Baldwin resolves the problem of ordering his novel impressively. The bulk of the novel consists of the confessional prayers of the saints—present or would-be. We hear three: those of Florence, Gabriel's older sister, who in her final sickness returns to the church to become reconciled with her childhood and her family; Gabriel, who desires full restoration to God's grace and thinks he has seen a sign of his redemption; and Elizabeth, Gabriel's wife, who is torn apart by the ambition of her husband and her love for her first child, the illegitimate John. In the third and final part of the novel, "The Threshing Floor," which describes John's experience of conversion, musical references, Christian symbols, phrases picked up from the prayers of members of his family, recollected experiences, and the dust of the floor of the Church of the Fire Baptized contribute to a sequence that is overwhelmingly realistic in portraying John's suffering and release. No doubt this amazing account depended greatly on Baldwin's own memories of a childhood in an evangelical church and of a career as a child preacher. John is touched by God's toe, and we are witnesses to a psychological and spiritual change that rarely finds an adequate expression in words.

Ellison thinks of blackness as a state of the soul accessible to all. Baldwin considers blackness to be a mark of pain and hardship which whites can share or sympathize with, but for Baldwin blackness is the sign of admission to a rich, ancient, and elemental tradition—and we have the sense that admission is restricted to blacks. In this way, Baldwin is much closer to the Harlem Renaissance than is Ellison. There is something in the echoes of Old Testament oration, the vestiges of Biblical landscapes, and the simplified disposition of complex moral problems found in *Go Tell It on the Mountain* that is reminiscent of Toomer's racial memories of a noble past, Cullen's imaginative tours of Black Africa, and McKay's visions of a warm, colorful tropical island.

Baldwin has been a far more prolific writer than Ellison, whose second novel has been eagerly anticipated for many years. In Baldwin's other novels, notably *Giovanni's Room* (1956) and *Another Country* (1962), the problem of blackness is confused with the equally puzzling problem of homosexuality; both rejected groups, the blacks and the homosexuals, are shown as having emotional resources that can serve to humanize the world. By the sixties, Baldwin had become increasingly impatient and shrill about the cruel inadequacies of American society. A shift to a more explicit rhetoric is felt in his novels, and is revealed plainly in his essays, where his rhetorical gifts are unquestionably brilliant, so impressive that they have overshadowed the fictional talent displayed best in *Go Tell It on the Mountain*. His books of essays— *Notes of a Native Son* (1955), *Nobody Knows My Name* (1961), and *The Fire Next Time* (1963)—have startled America. He has demanded, more and more insistently, that America must change and that Americans must learn to love each other without concern for color or race.

Black poets since the Harlem Renaissance, like black writers of fiction, have responded to the developments in the general American literary tradition as well as to problems about their racial identity. As American poets, they were sensitive to the vast amount of experimentation in verse that was especially associated with the second and third decades of this century. But if we can say of Ellison and Baldwin that they had thoroughly assimilated the technical innovations of Faulkner and other original stylists of the day, we cannot trace so dramatic an influence with the poets. Nowhere among the black poets do we find the enthusiasms of a young Hart Crane, who, learning his trade as a poet in the 1920s, passionately followed Ezra Pound and T.S. Eliot in their revolt against Victorian poetic traditions. Instead, Negro poets accepted the revolution in American verse occurring after 1912 (the date of the founding of *Poetry: A Magazine of Verse*) more gradually and selectively, partially because of their preoccupation with blackness.

We tend to forget how broad and how diverse the American poetic revolution was. Langston Hughes, for example, does not relate to Pound or Eliot or Stevens or Crane—all totally foreign if not hostile to his talent—but, rather, to the imagists, to H.D. (Hilda Doolittle) and Amy Lowell. The spare line, the sharp, uncluttered visual images, the concentration upon objects, without rhapsody or elaboration, are all marks of the Imagist school. Hughes by the 1930s had developed a simple, lyrical style that served him well until his death in 1967. Hughes's fine ear, his sense of spoken language, and his racy colloquialism are all his own, and the envy of many a more orthodox Imagist.

Sterling Brown, on the other hand, was attracted to the poetry of Carl Sandburg. Nowhere is this more evident than in Brown's "Strong Men," with an epigraph from Sandburg's verse: "The strong men keep coming." Brown admired in Sandburg's work, no doubt, the deep affection for the people, the knowledge and abundant use of folk matter, the simple, repetitive style, with the heavy emphasis upon action words. Actually, many of Brown's poems are sensitive, precise, and forceful renderings of folk materials, with condensed and often witty narrative lines, and these, we suspect, owe more to countless hours of listening to folk ballads, songs, lyrics, and jokes than to any poetry revolution, out of Chicago or London.

Margaret Walker's impassioned "For My People," with its long prosaic lines and its details lifted whole from a dusty, smelly life, is as close to Sandburg as anything written by a Negro author. Both Melvin B. Tolson and Owen Dodson are more eclectic, and we sense in their work a much fuller assimilation of the techniques, devices, and tone of modern poetry. Tolson has an affection for myth, a preoccupation with the large theme, a love of the learned allusion, a delight in ironic effects that we associate with Pound and Eliot. Dodson's interests are more lyrical, and his poems celebrate love and art with an intensity that reminds us of works by Cummings and Stevens.

Robert Hayden and Gwendolyn Brooks are thoroughly within the modern tradition. They have forged their own styles in a manner to suggest a mastery of the influences at work in form, language, and theme since 1912. They are without the self-consciousness that we sometimes feel in Tolson, whose poems sometimes seem too imitative of Pound's *Cantos*. And they are without Dodson's nostalgia, the echoes of the nineties, of late Victorian decadence, that we find in a poem like "Drunken Lover."

Robert Hayden has developed skill both in handling historical themes—which he dramatizes and explores fully, in terms of his own intellectual and spiritual values—and in offering witty, perceptive descriptions of colorful features of Afro-American life. The first talent is the more impressive, perhaps, because no other contemporary black poet has this special ability. "Middle Passage" deals with the slave trade, presenting episodes involving sickness, slave factories, and mutinies clearly based on careful research. The term "Middle Passage" has a dual meaning: it refers, of course, to the terrible journey made by black slaves to America in the festering holes of slave ships, and on a higher plane, it is a voyage through death to life, a trial that "transfigures" many. In the poem, three distinct voices are effectively counterpointed. One is that of an objective, intelligent observer who is moved, occasionally, to prophecy or to prayer; a second is that of a member of the crew of the slave ship, who offers a record in the form of an entry in a ship's log, or a deposition, or a reminiscence; and the third, the most ambitious voice of all, is the conscience of the slave trader, hinting at the real state of his soul. The whole poem is a moving experience that approximates a racial memory seen in perspective. We understand why Hayden was given the Grand Prize for Poetry at the First World Festival of Negro Arts, held in Dakar, Senegal, in 1965.

Gwendolyn Brooks has Emily Dickinson's ability to make fine poetry from the details of domestic life, though Miss Dickinson's house and garden were in Amherst, Massachusetts, and Gwendolyn Brooks writes of an apartment house in Chicago and the streets below it. Even in "The Chicago *Defender* Sends a Man to Little Rock," on the integration of Central High School, we sense the power of Miss Brooks's domestic metaphor. Her poetry consistently displays a controlled point of view, a precise diction, and an exciting power to associate unlikely images. Her skills are lyric, narrative, and rhetorical.

Gwendolyn Brooks has suggested that the racial element is "organic" to a black artist's work, by which she probably means that blackness is woven into the texture of a black artist's reactions even when the subject of his art is not racial. Robert Hayden would probably agree, though he resents any tendency to limit a black poet to racial themes. Both would doubtless bristle at the thought that their work has been judged by critical standards different from those applied to other Western artists.

But that is what LeRoi Jones now proposes be done. Having assimilated the modern Western tradition in poetry, Jones is moved by anger and impatience to turn his back on Western civilization, which he calls a "white thing." His anger represents the culmination of resentment that has built up since the days of the Harlem Renaissance.

Langston Hughes is moved to say in "Harlem," a poem on the section of New York City that he had celebrated earlier:

> Here on the edge of hell
> Stands Harlem—
> Remembering the old lies,
> The old kicks in the back,
> The old "Be patient"
> They told us before.

But Jones is determined to have no more of the "old lies" and has given to blackness the most ambitious definition yet. For him and for his followers blackness in the sixties meant a new system of aesthetics, entirely opposed to Western aesthetics, with emphasis upon improvisation and folk roots. This poses an interesting problem. As we have seen, the great achievements in black American art have always been a fusion of elements in the general tradition (neither exclusively white nor black, by the way) and qualities of spirit and resources of experience associated with being black in American society. Ellison's *Invisible Man* and Gwendolyn Brooks's poems offer examples of such successful merging. So too, by the way, does Jones's "The Death of Nick Charles." We wonder if it is necessary to deny the father to affirm the mother. Actually the question may be not one of desirability but one of possibility. The black man in America is so thoroughly a part of the American tradition that even his forms of revolt tend to follow well-tried paths.

Black militants look beyond aesthetics to the prospect of a black community and, ultimately, of a black nation. For them art is wedded to politics, black literature to black power. Art has never prospered as a consequence of such a wedding, as Americans who lived through the 1930s know clearly.

No black artist writing today can afford to ignore today's black revolution. It means, among other things, a great expansion in the black reading audience to include people never before touched by art of any kind. It means, too, an intensified interest in all phases of the life of black people in America. There is no doubt that LeRoi Jones has contributed much to both developments, undeniably important to black artists, old and new. The danger, of course, rests in the creation of a new straitjacket for literature, a new set of dogmas which will be ultimately destructive of talent. We view with considerable interest, then, the promising writers of the early seventies—William Kelley, James Alan McPherson, David Henderson, for example. Whatever happens, we can expect that blackness will continue to operate as a creative element, neither as a mark of shame nor as a badge of honor, in the literature of this country.

1970

The American Scholar,
the Black Arts, and/or Black Power

The Black Arts are an issue in the present crisis in America. It makes little difference where you locate the crisis—on the campus or in the streets of our cities—the issue remains. The American, whether he is a student attending a university or its president, whether he is a citizen of a city or its mayor, cannot avoid reckoning with new intellectual pressures that threaten in their most extreme expression to overthrow traditional values in an abrupt and barbarous way. Adding to the necessity for attending to the Black Arts is the confusion of artistic disciplines and political and economic strength. The Black Arts have become indistinguishable from Black Power. Indeed, some black militants insist that no art is black unless it serves the objectives of those believing in Black Power. What was a relationship between two plainly different things becomes suddenly, by alchemical transformation, an equation. The society has responded in a manner to support the confusion. Universities have ignored the need for the study of the literature of the American Negro for years, with a complacency unruffled by periodic explosive contributions from a Wright or an Ellison or a Baldwin or a Jones. But when Negro Literature became Black Literature, complacency was succeeded by rapt attention. What has changed is not Wright or Ellison or Baldwin—perhaps only Jones, in a direction not helpful to his art; what is added to the official view of many educational institutions is the apocalyptic vision of what Congressman Adam Clayton Powell used to call "Marching Blacks," at a time when there were few. Now at a time when there are more, literature, because it is wedded to power, commands an audience unimagined before.

I am pleased, quite frankly, with some of the consequences of the marriage. Certainly, the new, greatly expanded audience, both black and white, for Afro-American literature is a gratifying sight, especially to scholars and students who have sought to make the study of American Literature something other than the great tradition from Hawthorne to Robert Lowell. I am disturbed by other consequences. Nothing troubles more than the ten-

dency—in many ways, perfectly natural given our recent history—
to evaluate literature in terms of power, to pass judgment upon a
poem or a play or a story in terms of its imagined contribution to
the creation of a black community. It is a little like comparing the
art of John Updike and that of Jacqueline Susann by counting
and classifying the erotic episodes in *Couples*, say, and *The
Valley of the Dolls*. I do not need to be told that sex is power, too,
and with us to stay. What is urgently needed now is a sober
evaluation of the new literature written under the stimulus of the
black aesthetic. In short, I am demanding a divorce—a separation,
at the very least—for the Black Arts (specifically, the art of literature) from Black Power. I wish to replace Black Power as a
context by supplying a framework, partly aesthetic and partly
historical, that is more traditional. I do this, not because I am old-
fashioned or because I am on the wrong side of thirty, but because
genuine connections exist linking the Black Literature of today
with the artistic achievement of the past.

First, I must explain why it is that I have to engage in a critical
act that would be obvious and expected, given a cultural situation
that approximates the normal. A few years ago the phenomenon
of "Black Humor" (not related by blood line to the Black Arts,
but connected, rather, by spiritual ties and qualities of mood and
atmosphere) received exhaustive examination by the critics. I look
in vain in the discussion of the Black Arts for the same preoccupation with sources, the same attention to comparisons with movements both within and without the American cultural tradition,
the same concern for historical perspective and speculative projection. I do not find them. Instead, I encounter inevitably the
themes of Black Power. It is as if history and aesthetic criticism
were suddenly erased by the sweep of a damp rag across a blackboard. The answer, of course, is the simple fact that our cultural
climate is not normal. We exist in a situation of emergency, then,
and art does or does not relate to the moment of crisis. Whether or
not I wish to, I have to begin with a description of the crisis, the
general outline of which is as familiar to you as it is to me.

On campuses too numerous to mention, where there is a
Douglass Society, or an Afro-American group, or a Black Student
Union, and where there are cooperating chapters of S.D.S. or
White Liberation Fronts, the demand has been made by petition,

by sign, by demonstration for Black Literature, Black History, Black Anthropology, Black Economics—indeed, the full range of the Black Arts. What is wanted is an Instant Black Curriculum, to be organized often, in the most ambitious projections, into Afro-American programs and Afro-American institutes. The interest in the Black Arts is not tangential or peripheral to the main thrust of the student revolution. It stands at the center of the turbulence, like the eye of the hurricane, exemplifying, in a remarkably pure way, the desperate need of the contemporary student for a relevant tradition and for a dignity that grants him the responsibility and the authority of manhood. In short, the Black Arts offer a brilliant illustration of a paradox that is general: on the one hand, there is the desire to reject all previous interpretations of history, all earlier artistic performances, the desire to experience the exhilarating sensation of beginning from scratch to build a new tradition. This deep impulse in the young derogates and inhibits the exercise of critical faculties that have served in the past to refine and to enrich original expression. On the other hand, there is the desperate need to find models with which to identify and principles to follow, so long as these do not come from a time too far removed from the present. Recent history is the only history that is respectable; the only heroes are those who died yesterday, not the day before.

The sense of emergency exists not only in American universities but in American society as well. In the black ghettoes of American cities the issue is, if anything, clearer. Militant leaders no longer base their pleas for change upon the integration of blacks and whites, upon the implementation of constitutional decisions, upon the fulfillment of the American dream. They speak of a black culture, separate and distinct from a decadent society which they call white. The Black Arts will provide a substructure for a new black consciousness, black schools, black institutions, a black economy, and, finally, indeed, a black nation. The dream of Marcus Garvey has acquired strength and overall popular support that it never possessed in the 1920s. And it has moved some distance from some black artists, a few black intellectuals, a sampling of black technicians, people equipped to offer orientation and direction and to supply the know-how to achieve limited goals. Indeed, it is just possible this time that the Black

Star Line will not founder in a sea of futility and economic chaos.

We should make the point that the situation of blacks in the inner city resembles, in many ways, that of all urban citizens caught in a condition of poverty. The difficulty is that more blacks suffer in the city than do other racial or ethnic groups, and they suffer more. It is hard to say to a black boy living in the Bedford-Stuyvesant ghetto that he deserves a better art, when, before his exposure to the Black Arts, he had been untouched by art of any kind. Yet, it must be said. We understand why he should be attracted to an art devoted to the objective of improving his lot in life and restructuring the damaged image of self. No doubt there is a stage in his development when the aesthetics and the mythology of separation offer the only support that is available to him. But they offer no permanent relief. No art that restricts and reduces human sympathies can boast of humanizing the cold world, nor of providing for the true disciple a human condition that satisfies the full range of his instincts and intelligence. My hope is that the Black Arts will develop, profiting by a truer perspective than that afforded by Black Power. I say "truer" because the Black Arts, like the White Arts, have come from our general Western tradition (where else?), an extension of those skills and disciplines developed first in Egypt, the Near East, and Greece, a tradition, to my best knowledge, neither exclusively black nor white.

The primary meaning for the "Black Arts" is obvious, though it must be stated. The phrase describes the culture of black people. Specifically, in our own society, it stands for the culture of the American Negro, to use a descriptive tag now much out of favor, since it arouses in the minds of many, black and white, unpleasant associations of inferior status. There is another meaning that is equally apparent. I refer to the tradition of magic, diabolism, and incantation that covers practices as diverse as *Voudoun* and alchemy and invests authority in figures as different as ju-ju man, Goody Cloyse, and Doctor Faustus. In this context, the Black Arts emerge from the dark, evil side of our natures, offer concrete expression to secret and forbidden impulses, and supply satisfaction that is exotic and intense. Commonly found in manifestations as removed in time as Salem witchcraft and *Rosemary's Baby* is an opposition to established values, frequently religious and social. If the establishment is Western culture, as it is for the new wave of black artists, we have a point of correspondence that is not simply academic. One black critic, Larry Neal, lines out the form of this opposition in a recent issue of *The Drama Review* with disturbing lucidity: "The motive behind the Black aesthetic is the destruction of the white thing, the destruction of white ideas, and white ways of looking at the world."[1] And LeRoi Jones, the Merlin of the movement, has written in full awareness of the secondary associations of "blackness":

> We are unfair
> And unfair
> We are black magicians
> Black arts we make
> in black labs of the heart
>
> The fair are fair
> And deathly white
>
> The day will not save them
> And we own the night.[2]

Let me offer some preliminary comments that may help us in arriving at a new phenomenon. The first observation that must be made is that the Black Arts, considered in any pure sense, have very little meaning for the bulk of the creative achievement of the American Negro. For all the talk of cultural imperatives and national goals, black artists wrestle with their problems in the same old way, adopting techniques and altering themes in light of their own experience, and both have come to them from a Western tradition not dead, but alive and kicking. A second observation, equally necessary, is that what we have in literature as being representative of the new wave is, unhappily, not very good. If we take the new anthology *Black Fire*, edited recently by LeRoi Jones and Larry Neal,[3] as an early harvest, we have reason to wish for more. There is in it a statement of intention, rather than achievement, a program, rather than the ordered, deeply felt experience that is art. Talent we discover without doubt, but it survives with difficulty in a setting defined by revolution, anticipated political and economic power, and crystallizing concepts of black aesthetic theory. The problem is not simply a reliving of the cultural situation of the 1930s, when proletarian art served the class struggle. It requires no scholar's perspective to say that the result of that commitment was not memorable art. Indeed, the point is drama- tized by the simple fact that we see on every hand a fulfillment of the brave beginnings of the 1920s, in poetry, fiction, and criticism. What survives from the thirties is a mistaken model, accepted with passion and without criticism by the leaders of the Black Arts movement in the 1960s.

The problem of the unholy alliance of the Black Arts and Black Power is more serious than the issue of a wrong-headed choice. Art has survived bad models in the past—and will again. Edward Margolies, in a valuable study, *Native Sons*, has described the danger well. He documents the deterioration in much of Jones's recent writing, the loss of depth and sensitivity, as nation- alistic ideals have become stronger, replacing artistic principles. Margolies notes that Jones's poetic style has become "a destruction of syntax, order, and sense—as if somehow to write may be an expression of hostility."[4] In short, the desperate effort to get rid of the "white thing" moves toward the destruction of self. The black magician succeeds not so much in destroying the hated white civilization as he does in vulgarizing his own skills. What is threatened, at last, is Jones's identity as an artist, his ability to move an audience, either black or white.

Now the black artists say that they are interested only in a black audience, in inspiring the black masses to action. By this they mean, of course, a basically nonliterary audience, one not corrupted by the inhibitions, the limitations, the hang-ups of white society. There is no doubt that many people, not only the young, living in black city ghettoes and rural slums have been untouched by arts of any kind, and the most effective initial approach to them may be through the emphasis on a common or shared blackness. But this notion of a great mass audience of pure listeners or readers and potential pure believers may turn out to be a fanciful abstraction—like the anticipated mass audiences of the 1930s, the dream of the informed and cultivated workers who would rise from the oppressed classes. We suspect, finally, that a black audience is not very different from a white audience, for better or for worse—nor should we expect it to be. The two audiences share most elements in our culture—assumptions, aspirations, ideals, rewards—the latter, certainly not equally. The historical fact is that the creation of a purely black audience is not possible without negating primary responses. To insist upon an exclusively black relationship is as destructive as is the artist's devotion to the rigid standards and themes of black nationalism. I must say, in all honesty, that I find it increasingly difficult to distinguish between black reactions and white reactions. When a colleague of mine attended a concert by James Brown recently, he discovered that race was not a significant factor in determining the depth of response: white college students seemed to be just as excited as the black ones. Though race had little importance here, age did, alas, to judge from his tempered reaction.

We reach now a delicate stage in this investigation. How *are* we to assess the Black Arts? Measured by ordinary scholarly yardsticks, the phenomenon is so far hardly impressive. But we cannot measure without sampling, without examining carefully the achievement in the art that most concerns us as students of literature. Here we must limit our discussion to only those works officially claimed by the black artists themselves. It is convenient, then, to use the anthology of Afro-American writing, *Black Fire*, published last year. Our first impression is that the new departures that we find here are not a matter involving innovations in form; the allegiance is, in general, to the main tradition of American letters, though there are some new departures in the plays, especially in the street dramas. Novelty appears in the themes, in ideas that run counter to the accepted notions of our society.

I say "novelty" with some hesitation because the same themes are repeated often in the works of the black artists. Yet these ideas are new to those of us unfamiliar with the general system of thought that informs the art. The full range of that thought appears in the poems—the fiction and the drama are more restricted in this way. The repetition of ideas makes possible a more risky enterprise—generalization, even classification, perhaps even the suggestion of something approaching an order in the approach of the artists to reality.

One pervasive idea is contempt for the existing social and economic system because it opposes life. It dehumanizes and kills—as Calvin C. Hernton maintains in "A Black Stick with a Ball of Cotton for a Head and a Running Machine for a Mouth":

Will it be like this, Charlie
In life's other solidified enterprise?
Stiff in the strut of the dead
Dituminous shirt,
Carbonic boots and spider web,
Cling to our flesh more fierce
Than instinct.

We are a stampede of late supplicants
Who have found no love in swaddling clothes
But the mummy of a worthless radiator
In a cold tenement.

Oh. Charlie! When we have crossed under this death.
Paranoid cells explode rural areas of the psyche
Will it be the same in life's other formaldehyde
Metropolis? (p. 210)

There is power in the rhetoric and the imagery here, but both have the strength of parody. The wind that sears the mechanical desert of Calvin Hernton comes from T.S. Eliot's dead land, his cactus land. The question, as originally put, appears in "The Hollow Men":

Is it like this
In death's other kingdom
Waking alone
At the hour when we are
Trembling with tenderness
Lips that would kiss
Form prayers to broken stone.

Now, parody, especially good parody, which this is, is an art in itself, but it cannot claim to be an art nourishing the roots of a new black culture.

Related to the dissatisfaction with society is the sense of acute despair that overwhelms sensitive black men and women, the victims of an unfeeling system. Sonia Sanchez, in "summary," states the problem:

no sleep tonight
not eve after all
the red and green pills
i have pumped into

> my shuttering self or
> the sweet wine
> that drowns them.
> >   this is
> a poem for the world
> for the slow suicides
> in seclusion.
> somewhere on 130th st.
> a woman, frail as a
> child's ghost, sings. Oh,
> >   Oh what
> can the matter be? Johnny's
> so long at the fair. (p. 252)

I find this to be direct, touching, and intimate.

All of the black artists herald the awakening of a new racial consciousness, and many say that this maturity can be sustained only by violence. Few, it is true, are quite as direct as Marvin E. Jackmon is, in "Burn, Baby, Burn":

> Tired, sick and tired
> Tired of being sick and tired
> Lost. Lost in
> The Wilderness of white America.
> Are the masses asses?
> Cool. Said the master
> To the slave, "No problem.
> Don't rob and steal, I'll
> Be your driving wheel."
> Cool.
> And He wheeled us into
> >   350 years of black
> Madness—To hog guts,
> Conked hair, Quo Vadis
> Bleaching Cream,
> Uncle Thomas, to Watts
> To the streets, to the
> >   Killllllllllll. . . . . .
> >   Boommmmm. . . . . .
> >   2 honkeys gone. . (p. 269)

And nearly all would support the sentiments of David Henderson in "Keep On Pushing (Harlem Riots/Summer/1964)":

> Lenox Avenue is a big street
> The sidewalks are extra wide—three and four times
>   the size of a regular Fifth Avenue or 34th
>   Street sidewalk—and must be so to contain the
> unemployed vigiling Negro males, the picket lines
> and police barricades.
> Police Commissioner Murphy can
> muster five hundred cops in fifteen minutes.
> He can summon extra
> tear gas bombs, guns, ammunition
> within a single call
> to a certain general alarm.
> For Harlem
> reinforcements come from the Bronx
> Just over the three-borough Bridge
>   a shot   a cry   a rumor
> can muster five hundred Negroes
> from idle and strategic street corners
>   bars   stoops   hallways   windows
> Keep on pushing. (p. 239)

These poets glorify the contributions of the black subculture of America. Lance Jeffers maintains:

> My blackness is the beauty of this land,
> my blackness
> tender and strong, wounded and wise,
> my blackness (p. 273)

There are numerous tributes—too many to count—to Negro jazz musicians—John Coltrane, Ornette Coleman, Billie Holiday, Charlie Parker, Lester Young, even rhythm and blues quarters. Oddly, whatever happened to Duke Ellington or Art Tatum or Jimmie Lunceford, the musical giants of my youth? What is admired especially is the quality of improvisation in the music, the imaginative resistance to structure and convention. It is no less admirable that many of these talented musicians found it difficult to adjust to society. One such tribute is Walt Delegall's "Psalm for Sonny Rollins":

> This vibrant, all-embracing, all pervading
> sound which bleeds from vinylite veins
> Of my record, steals into the conduits of my heart

Forces entrance into the sanctuary
Of my soul, trespasses into the temple
Of my gonads. In a life-span while, I am
Absorbed into the womb of the sound.
    I am in the sound
    The sound is in me
    I am the sound. (p. 278)

This strange language—a mixing of the technological and the
organic, the prosaic and the religious, is not entirely new to
American poetry. We are reminded of the second part of Hart
Crane's famous poem "For the Marriage of Faustus and Helen."

The culture hero of the movement who surpasses all others is
not a musician: he is Malcolm X, a holy martyr, on the road to
beatitude. Perhaps the most impressive, certainly the most detailed, poem of praise to the slain leader of the Black Muslim
movement is Larry Neal's "Malcolm X—An Autobiography."

I hustler. I pimp. I unfulfilled black man
bursting with destiny.
New York City Slim called me Big Red,
and there was no escape, close nights of the smell of death.
Pimp. hustler. The day fills these rooms,
I am talking about New York. Harlem,
talking about the neon madness.
talking about ghetto eyes and nights
about death protruding across the room. Small's paradise.
talking about cigarette butts, and rooms smelly with white
sex flesh and dank sheets, and being on the run,

talking about cocaine illusions, about stealing and selling.
talking about these New York cops who smell of blood and
        money.
I am Big Red, tiger vicious, Big Red, bad nigger, will kill.
    (pp. 315–316)

But there is rhythm here, its own special substance:

I hear Billie sing, no good man, and dig Prez,
        wearing the Zoot
suit of life—the porkpie hat tilted at the correct
        angle. (p. 316)

Malcolm's conversion to the Muslim faith is recorded in this fashion:

> To understand is to surrender the imperfect self
> For a more perfect self.
> Allah formed brown man, I follow
> and shake within the very depth of my most imperfect being.
> And I bear witness to the Message of Allah
> And I bear witness—all praise is due Allah! (pp. 316–317)

Now there are some ideas in the black poetry which I have not referred to: the high position of the black woman, often victimized by white men and betrayed by black men in the past; the renewed contact with the African heritage, found in frequent allusions to witch doctors and ju-ju men, lost kingdoms and a forgotten way of life, nobler and happier. The ambition of all of the members of the group can best be summed up by LeRoi Jones, who announces at the end of the poem "Black Art":

> We want a black poem. And a
> Black World
> Let the world be a Black Poem
> And Let All Black People Speak This Poem
> Silently
>
> Or LOUD. (p. 303)

I must say a word, not loudly, about the fiction that has grown out of the movement. It is undistinguished. It resembles nothing so much as the fiction of the proletarian writers of the thirties—in the obvious insistence upon political programs and in the tendency to reduce characters to types.

The drama is not so simply assessed. True, it does not possess the ideas, the range of allusion and reference that we have found in the poetry. On the other hand, it has had the benefit of a surer craft. The best of the playwrights, LeRoi Jones and Ed Bullins, impose an impressive economy upon their art. Their work is highly symbolic and, at the same time, deeply sensitive to language, to nuances of the spoken voice. It is revolutionary drama, building on concepts that we have already explored and displaying, perhaps, more than a little indebtedness to Bertolt Brecht. Imagination touches many of the elements of the theater—scene, sound effects, lighting. It is possible that the interest in street dramas, the short sketches designed for a black audience gathering, say, at the corner of 125th Street and Seventh Avenue in Harlem, has enriched the talent of these artists. Jones has already demonstrated his mastery of the medium in a play that preceded the official birth of the Black Arts, *Dutchman,* and nothing he has done since has come close to the explosive force of that work. Bullins, in *How Do You Do,* demonstrates that he can work imaginatively within the very tight ideological and technical restrictions of the emerging black theater. But even here, though there is force, there is a narrowness in the statement (pp. 595 604) of theme that may ultimately be damaging.

The achievement of the new movement, looked at in perspective, is so far uneven, except for the poetry of David Henderson and Sonia Sanchez possibly, and a scattered set of dramas by Bullins and one or two other black playwrights. Moreover, the validity of the artistic conceptions supporting the New Breed is questionable, providing a most unstable foundation for artistic efforts. We are justifiably suspicious when we discover that nearly 200 pages of *Black Fire,* a book of 650 pages of text, are given over to rhetoric, to manifestoes, denunciations, appeals, proclaiming the birth of the Black Arts and the need for Black Power. Our temptation, after so much instruction, is to dismiss the movement. If we should do so, we should be wrong, because its importance rests elsewhere. It is in the emotional energy that has gone into the formulation of programs and into the commitment of serious artists to the black aesthetic. It is also in the genuine response of many Negroes to the Black Arts—some of them, indeed, never touched before by art of any kind. I have in mind especially the interest of black youth—the spirited young men and women who have added to the general distrust of the adult world, so current these days, a special animus that comes from the identification of that world as white.

Much of the emotional power generated by the Black Arts comes from the sense of newness. The movement claims no Western ancestors; the single allegiance, other than that to a black audience, is, perhaps, to the Third World, and this only tenuously. Acquiring a black consciousness is a little like being born again. Everything in the world is changed, even the special place that mother occupies in our hierarchy of sentiments: mother flunks again, as she has been doing steadily since 1920. More immediately evident is the alteration in the tastes of the New Breed—in friends, music, clothes, hair styles. It is possible for one of the editors of *Black Fire* to say: "We can learn more about what poetry is by listening to the cadences in Malcolm's speeches, than from most of Western poetics."[5] The statement is as false as it is brash. Malcolm was many things to many people, no doubt—Elijah, Joshua, Mohammed, Cicero—but never Aristotle.

But are the Black Arts new? If we as objective critics can demonstrate that there are Western precedents for the new phenomenon, we may have less difficulty in coming to terms with it, and, perhaps more important, we can urge the artists to claim and to profit from a tradition rightfully theirs. This is to assume that history can teach. And I cling to this idea, despite the insistence of the young today that wisdom is the property of postadolescence, vanishing in the desert of middle age.

The Black Arts recall another movement, the Harlem Renaissance, that flowered in the 1920s and lived until it was killed by the Great Depression. The high priest of that movement was Alain Locke, Professor of Philosophy at Howard University, who announced the coming of the Renaissance and illustrated its achievement in the March issue of the *Survey Graphic* in 1925. The two movements have much in common. Both are international. Locke considered the American Negro as the advance guard of African peoples in contact with twentieth-century civilization, while present nationalists speak at times of their loyalty to the Third World. Both define the unique central contribution of the Negro, emphasizing in the documentation music and folk arts. Both tend to deal in character types—that is to say, to isolate certain personality traits as being especially desirable or as belonging uniquely to the Negro. Locke's New Negro understood that his nature emerged from a tradition of "humor, sentiment, imagination, and tropic nonchalance,"[6] which was not destroyed by American slavery. Contemporary "black consciousness" builds similarly on qualities of personality—rather different ones, however, since a premium is placed upon a militant resistance to assimilation. Still, the personality patterns in both instances highlight primitive virtues, the ability to sense emotional rather than intellectual truth. Both movements assume the burden of rehabilitating the race in terms of world prestige, correcting the low opinion of the black man established originally by the institution of slavery.

The differences between the movements are marked too. The Harlem Renaissance was essentially a phenomenon restricted to the literary salon, the academy, and the cabaret. It did not touch the people—indeed, it did not extend with any certainty beyond the city limits of New York, Philadelphia, and Washington. The Black Arts seek now to build upon close ties connecting the artist and black people. The Renaissance was not overtly political. Locke wished to present the Negro as a human being rather than as a problem or a formula; he hoped to liberate the Negro from moral debate and historical controversy. The Black Arts, we are told, accept Black Power and contribute to the political and economic revolution that is coming and to the black nation of the future. And, finally, the Harlem movement, though glorifying in the primitive, in the heroes of Claude McKay and Jean Toomer, did not engage in black magic. It did not oppose the full range of moral, religious, and social values to be found in our world. It did not call for arson and murder as necessary steps toward the achievement of complete freedom. It did not see artistic expression as a substitute for physical violence, as a channel for the festering hate that this society has created in the minds and souls of all black people. Indeed, the Harlem Renaissance envisioned Negro art as a force complementing and enriching the dominant white culture. In the minds of some ambitious prophets, the black arts would humanize the white machine society. Du Bois's pluralism, announced in *The Souls of Black Folk*, seemed entirely possible. A man could be both black and American. The Black Arts of today deny that this is possible.

The black magician now wishes to destroy the America that he knows, a "white thing." This posture is new; it is, perhaps, the most distinctive feature of the Black Arts. Yet there are precedents even for this position, coming from the American tradition that is so thoroughly despised. In this connection, Leslie Fiedler supplies a provocative idea in his treatment of the Negro and the development of American Gothic in *Love and Death in the American Novel*. Fiedler says of *The Narrative of Arthur Gordon Pym*:

"Poe's novel is surely the first which uses gothicism to express a peculiarly American dilemma identifying the symbolic blackness of terror with the blackness of the Negro and the white guilts he embodies."[7] Now the natives of Tsalal are never identified specifically as being Negroes, though they are jet black and are given other Negroid characteristics such as "thick and woolen hair" and "thick and clumsy lips."[8] Certainly, the models for the inhabitants of this region in Antarctica are the black slaves in Poe's own state, Virginia. Pym makes an amazing discovery about the dark followers of Too-Wit. They are not the cheerful, incompetent, faithful menials who populate the pages of sentimental fiction about the South and live still amazingly in the imaginations of some Americans; they are instead devious, beyond the wildest expectation of Poe's narrator, and malignant, beyond his power to describe. They destroy all the members of the crew of the *Jane Guy*, except for Pym and a companion, who survive largely by accident, rather than by reliance upon intelligence and ingenuity. There is not a dash of white applied at any point in the description of these benighted primitives; even their teeth are black. In this context, blackness does stand for unknown and indescribable terrors, a malice defying powers of explanation by a civilized man, and an energy totally beyond the measurement of science (and, lest we forget, Pym has become a scientist, true, without benefit of a degree).

Fiedler discovers a tradition for blackness so defined—identified invariably with the Negro and presented always as a force taxing, if not exceeding, human understanding. There is Babu, in Melville's *Benito Cereno*, entirely outside of the experience of Captain Delano and different from any conception that emanates from Delano's simple good nature. There is the Negro blood in Roxana and in Valet de Chambre in Twain's *Pudd'nhead Wilson*, a blackness so deep that Roxana maintains that it has possessed the soul of her son—a white man to the society around him. And the line does not cease with Twain, but is cultivated, with typical virtuosity, by Faulkner when he creates Charles Bon in *Absalom, Absalom!* and Joe Christmas in *Light in August*.

Let me suggest what surely must be obvious now. The potency of the black magic of present-day practitioners is not anything out of Africa, or Haiti, or Trinidad. It comes out of the American nineteenth century, the black strain in our home-grown Romanticism that steadfastly refuses to die. The Black Arts, black magic in literature, preceded by a wide margin any thought of Black Power. There is something familiar, too, about the impulse to construct programs, and there are lessons to be learned from earlier fusions of art and power. Larry Neal designates seven criteria for a black culture: mythology, history, social organization, political organization, economic organization, creative motif, and ethos.[9] The intention is to liberate the black man completely from the repressive standards and values of the society, to reject an inferior status in fact and in symbol, and to achieve a black brotherhood. I am reminded, more than a little, of Whitman's program in 1860. Recall the celebration of sex and brotherhood, the confident announcement of the arrival of a new human being and a new city of love, the construction of a new mythology based on the perfect equality of the sexes, the affirmation of the evolutionary process, and the implication that Eden was at hand—if not today, tomorrow. Remember the sexual violence that pervades Whitman's system of references, the freedom—license, some called it—of his vocabulary. But above all, let us remember that Whitman's great poetry in 1860 occurred when programs suddenly disintegrated in *Calamus* when the call for brotherhood aroused homoerotic impulses and a strangling death wish, both fusing to supply powerful substance to which Whitman with difficulty gave form. What is clearly stronger than color—black or white—is the disposition toward Romanticism in America. A significant number of Americans still hold to the conviction that art can remake reality.

The Black Arts, apparently brash, iconoclastic, frightening in their cultivation of violence, are a thoroughly American phenomenon—indeed, the wedding to Black Power is the consequence of an old seduction involving art and the rigid programming of human intelligence—and art has always suffered. It is perhaps sanguine to hope that those practicing the arts will develop an awareness of the models that have appeared before. A sense of connection would help. Studying American precedents would be a tonic for both the art and the humanity of the artist. Yes, humanity, too, because the human condition is enriched with the sharing of experience. At this crucial moment, we should view the emergence of black consciousness and the Black Arts with sympathy, understanding, and hope: with a range of favorable sentiments that we need not—indeed, should not—reserve for Black Power. The phenomenon we see is one we have seen before. Once again, in American literary history, Adam rises, "early in the morning," with limbs quivering with fire. This time, true, Adam is black. But the cultural situation of the artist remains unchanged.

The Black Arts will never prosper as long as aesthetic judgments are dictated by the desire to achieve political goals. I have spoken of Whitman in 1860; I might use just as well Richard Wright in 1940. Though officially a Communist, Wright refused to adjust the conclusion of *Native Son* to fit the orthodox sentiments of his Party. I am reminded of the great length of time intervening between the publication date of the book and the date of the review in *The Daily Worker*. The allegiance to art, to the integrity of Bigger Thomas, to the human truth of Bigger's tragic situation, was too great to permit distortion. It is my hope that the Black Arts will come of age, free themselves from the reductive standards of Black Power.

Eliot warned us in "Gerontion," nearly a half century ago, that history cannot teach modern man because his corruption is so complete. I should like to think that Eliot was wrong, that teachers can listen and learn from each other, and even from their students; and that students will admit that their elders have something sensible and worthwhile to say and consider the futures of the young the most precious legacy in our time. I hope too that black artists will derive lessons from history and cease hankering after the false gods and leap to the true. In this way, in this way only, will the Black Arts mature, the Black Fire be tempered, trimmed so that the flame will endure.

1969

Notes

1. Larry Neal, "The Black Arts Movement," *The Drama Review*, 12 (Summer 1968), 30.
2. Ibid., p. 31.

3. LeRoi Jones and Larry Neal, eds., *Black Fire: An Anthology of Afro-American Writing* (New York: William Morrow and Co., Inc., 1968). Quotations from the anthology will be cited in the text.

4. Edward Margolies, *Native Sons: A Critical Study of Twentieth-Century Negro American Authors* (Philadelphia and New York: J.B. Lippincott Company, 1968), p. 194.

5. Larry Neal, "An Afterword," *Black Fire*, p. 653.

6. Alain Locke, *The New Negro* (New York: Albert and Charles Boni, 1925), p.5.

7. Leslie A. Fiedler, *Love and Death in the American Novel* (New York: Stein and Day, 1975), pp. 391–430.

8. Ibid., p. 398.

9. Neal, "The Black Arts Movement," p. 33.

Black Literature and the Critic

This is not the day for the old-fashioned critic—historical, analytical, linguistic—nor should it be. A period of intensive creative activity fashions its own criticism, selecting elements from the principles and the practice of the past, altering and adding to these as a consequence of the practice of the present. One thinks of the example of the *Lyrical Ballads*, with the preface that shaped critical responses for the century that followed its publication, or of Eliot's *The Sacred Wood*, which appeared in the same year, 1920, that his second volume of poems was published (the one containing "Gerontion" and the Sweeney poems). The curious situation in which black literature finds itself today is not the consequence of the failure of criticism, but the result of a deep disbelief in all forms of the critical performance. Ours is a time in which the critic tends to be scorned because he is considered a part of the white establishment. He is a slave of a decadent Western rationalism, the "white thing" that all blacks must reject. We should point out, to assume for the moment the much maligned role of the detached critic, that even a casual critical examination reveals how much the impassioned denunciations of "whitey" depend upon traditional rhetorical forms and conventions. Marvin Jackmon's cry in "Burn, Baby, Burn," "2 honkeys gone," states, no doubt, a desirable end, but it is not an artistic innovation of staggering significance. There is more artistic merit in the rhyming slang that precedes this news, but even this echoes a derogatory form of social comment that has erupted in Cockney and in other vigorous dialects all over the Western world. Jackmon has written:

> Are the masses asses?
> Cool. Said the master
> To the slave, "No problem,
> Don't rob and steal, I'll
> Be your driving wheel."

We are reminded of the lyrics of songs by the Beatles or the eloquence of Brendan Behan's companions within the walls of Borstal prison. The literature of revolution requires little critical sophistication, and the most inflammatory utterance is likely to seek the assistance of stale and hackneyed verses. Too long two revolutions have been confused, and the consequence has been the dismissal of the critic. The point is that art is one way of recording the revolutions that occur in the imaginations of men, the surer way, as Yeats well knew. Change in the social order is another—a good deal more risky and, on the whole, much less satisfying, as Baraka's *The Slave* points out. Happily, we do not need to sacrifice one (revolution) for the other; and it is possible, though difficult, to cultivate both simultaneously. If we believe still in the excellence of art, we need the critic. This is no time for him to take down his sign and go a'fishing. There is more business than ever at his door, if he has the wit to understand the new product that he is asked to inspect and the new tools that are required for his special performance. It is fashionable today to deny the historical context for the work of art. The young say that history corrupts, that the only heroes are those who died yesterday, not last week. The fact is that if we reject our true history, we are faced with the necessity of fabricating one that fails to relate fully to life and, for us, more important, fails to supply a valid system of references for art. I am reminded of the foreword of a new book of poems just received from a fine black poet, Michael S. Harper, *Song: I Want a Witness*:

> When there is no history
> there is no metaphor;
> a blind nation in storm
> mauls its own harbors
> sperm whale, Indian, Black,
> belted in these ruins

Perhaps more to the point is the story of Malcolm X's reform in prison. The key to his resurrection was the acquisition of a historical framework—one entirely new to him. He learned from Elijah Muhammad's teachings about Yacub's history, the extraordinary narrative that accounts for the creation of the world, the appearance of the original man, black, of course, the corruption of the world by Yacub's experiments in eugenics, resulting in the devil race—a bleached-out strain, all-white. The fact is, then, that history of some kind is necessary—and if it is not inherited or discovered, it is made, of whole cloth, if nothing else serves.

The historical context for black art is fearfully complicated, true, a fact that in itself suggests the simplistic advantage of fabrication. Facing what passes for a true history is hard enough for the black artist, especially when that history has excluded blacks for years. I think of the problems of Charles Chesnutt in the 1890s, a writer who desired to use the facts of recent Southern history and who had inherited a view of the plantation system shaped by the backlash of Reconstruction—a view we have only just got around to revising substantially. One of the stories in *The Wife of His Youth*, "The Passing of Grandison," builds on what was assumed to be the good life on a generally enlightened plantation in Kentucky. The incorruptible slave, Grandison, was exposed to life in the North, the rhetoric of Abolitionists, the abuse of black freedmen, and the temptation, even, of a forced excursion to Canada itself, Beulah-Land, no less. Grandison, despite these trials, returns to his master. He turns out not to be the happy idiot that we think him to be. After a period of basking in his master's best graces, Grandison disappears, but this time with his whole family. When Grandison passed, all Grandisons passed, and with him, perhaps, even the idea of the faithful Grandison. What is at stake here in this amusing tale, told in the most sophisticated manner of the genteel tradition, is an alternate approach to history—one nourished by the slave narratives and by the memories of ex-slaves. Osofsky has suggested in a collection of slave autobiographies, entitled *Puttin' On Ol' Massa*, that the slaves survived by mastering techniques of deception, subterfuge, and dissimulation. Indeed, far from being an idiot, Grandison passes with honors in the special skills demanded of him.

For every black work, there is a double history of another sort as well. We have, of course, the tradition of American letters, that continuity in form and ideas that contributed much, say, to the shape of Chesnutt's art, as it did to that of his contemporaries, Howells, Cable, Aldrich. But beyond this there is the hidden tradition, the rich and changing store of folk forms and folk materials, the advantages of a dialectical tongue, with a separate music of its own, and the background of rituals, learned responses, and wisdom that grew from a community given an amount of homogeneity through isolation and oppression. Take another tale of Chesnutt's—this time "The Goophered Grape-vine," the first entry in a collection of pieces called *The Conjure Woman*, published in 1899. The envelope for the story has all of the characteristics of genteel fiction—we have a sophisticated, knowing, perhaps somewhat condescending observer who discusses the adventures of two cultivated Northerners, of somewhat more than modest means, seeking to locate in the South. All of this seems rather familiar, including the discreet interest in quaint local customs and the accurate reporting of what is seen and heard. What is different is old Julius McAdoo's account of the goophering, the hexing, the bewitching of the vineyard which the Northerners wish to purchase. There is, then, an inner core of the tale told in dialect controlled entirely by Julius's superstitions and beliefs, the source of which is not genteel precedents but black folklore.

The context of every work of black art is an interaction, then, a kind of working equilibrium between elements often identified in Spiller, Thorp, Johnson, and Canby and elements far less easily defined. Tolson, in *Harlem Gallery*, sounds much like Pound, as we would expect him to if he has chosen to follow the mythical rather than the meditational variant of our modern American poetic tradition. But there is another tradition at work here, fortunately, in the humor, the love of vulgar excess, the swinging rhythms, and the folksy faculty for self-derogation. Thank God Tolson has heard often

> . . . a dry husk of locust blues
> descend the tone ladder of a laughing goose,
>   syncopating between
> the faggot and the noose:
>   "Black Boy, O Black Boy,
>   is the port worth the cruise?"

The use of divergent materials is better seen, perhaps, in Robert Hayden's poem "Runagate Runagate." Note the plain statement of the slaveholder, resembling something from *John Brown's Body* of Stephen Benét, a work that influenced Hayden a great deal, then listen to the echoes of the spirituals. No black writer of excellence can deny his blackness. If he is shrewd, he will manage a tight chemical equation for his talents, choosing those elements in the general tradition that accommodate best with the ore of his native genius. The role of the critic is to analyze the alloy, to affirm it when it works (that is, organizing successfully the varied talents of the writer), to deplore it when the compound seems loosely joined or lacking in force or grace. It is not the critic's right to restrict the range of the artist, because he understands how complicated the creative process is. It was Jean Toomer's discovery of his blackness that made him an artist, a fact made clear in his letters, but the discovery was richly prepared for by already developed attitudes toward language, culture, and a sense of the endless depths of his own psyche. Behind Toomer, in this sense, is the discussion of the place of the machine culture of the 1920s. The conjunction produced an entirely new thing in 1923— *Cane.*

Among the pieces of excess baggage that many contemporary writers have discarded these days is the New Criticism. Authors, black and white, have turned against a narrow formal analysis that sought to isolate the work of art from history and to place it in a glass case so that it would not be touched by irreverent hands. The warm nexus between a people and its art, so deeply cherished by Whitman, William Carlos Williams, and Ginsberg, and so loudly announced by black militant artists, especially those in the drama, was not anything that this form of criticism took into account. I am old enough to be cynical about the extravagant claims for the powerful influence of any work of art upon a mass audience. I remember too well Whitman's frustration when, at the height of his early enthusiasm, he imagined that he might offer a program that would remake his countrymen in a new land. But that is not what is important about the nexus. The importance rests upon the flowing into the artist's consciousness of new materials never before considered appropriate for a proper art. The people make their mark in this way, breaking up the conventions of the poetical, so ably defined by Leavis in *New Bearings on English Poetry,* that are nourished by a restricted formal analysis. As good a critic as John Crowe Ransom exhibited perhaps too much an affection for the tight structure and the well-integrated rhetoric which the New Criticism could always demonstrate with a marvelous clarity when he admitted to favoring Donne over Shakespeare as a poet. What is at stake in Ransom's choice may be the infusion of matter defying easy ordering, matter that often has a source in popular culture.

Much recent black literature has deliberately sought to incorporate folk materials, if we may apply that term to the varied matter that rises from the customs, mores, attitudes, and life patterns of black people. Analysis of some kind seems necessary for a black art that displays this bent, if the art is to improve and if it is to succeed in touching deeply the large, essentially unsophisticated, audience that is the object of so much attention. There are few models for formal analysis here. The New Criticism was content to deal with the lovely ballads of the Scottish border and little else that smelled of popular origins, largely because it could read the ballad in terms of the dynamics of the lyric. There were no successful critical procedures for sprawling organisms like Whitman's "Song of Myself," partly because anticipated audience reaction was so much a part of the rhetoric of the whole, from the "Trippers and Askers," badly in need of the right training, to the "eleves" (if I may pronounce that Whitman barbarism) in mid-curriculum, to the joyous athletes all set to go into spiritual huckstering on their own.

Much new research has brought fresh perception to those art forms that retain vestiges of origins in the culture of ordinary people. I refer especially to the discoveries of Parry and Lord revealing the probable source of the epic in the oral tradition of the people, as it is to be seen developing even today in Yugoslavia. Many of the apparently arbitrary literary conventions of the epic may be explained by the assumptions that the teller of the tale makes about his audience and by the devices which he uses to hold the attention of an always distractable listening public. This discovery points to a method that could conceivably have enormous value in constructing rewarding analytical approaches to many contemporary works.

If we can isolate and define a form in folk culture, we have a model that does not rely upon the more rarefied conventions of a literary tradition. I am thinking not merely of the epic but also of other verbal structures like the folk sermon. Bruce Rosenberg, a well-trained folklorist and medievalist, has given such a recognizable and definable shape to the folk sermon in *The Art of the American Folk Preacher,* so that it is possible to use that form as a basis for critical commentary. There is no doubt that a considerable part of the energy that we observe in the use of the form in Johnson's *God's Trombones*, Baldwin's *Go Tell It on the Mountain*, and Ellison's *Invisible Man* comes from associations and echoes of the finely honed rhetoric of the old Black Preacher, as he chants at the height of his frenzy the words of God. Rosenberg cites the Reverend Shegog in Faulkner's *Sound and the Fury* as a carefully imitative and skilled practitioner of the folk art, but black literature displays so many examples of the use of the sermon as a controlling device for art that Shegog seems to be an odd case, a sport. The most brilliant exploitation of the artistic counterpart of the folk form is to be found in *Go Tell It on the Mountain*, in which Baldwin not only reproduces some moving sermons in the body of his novel but also shapes the whole novel as a reaction to a sermon, from which we collect odd bits and pieces as the consciousness of his characters projects them as platforms for memory.

Actually, the structural function of folk art is nothing new to those who are familiar with the Harlem Renaissance and its experimentation in verbal techniques. No one was more skillful or resourceful than Langston Hughes was in following the pattern of the blues with its inflexible metrics and its unvarying rules about the repetition of key statements in the lament. And Hughes was just as scrupulous about giving a shape to jazz, with choruses that change ever so little as they are repeated and with improvised solos that are frequently identified with the flights of fancy of the speaker-observer.

> Oh, silver tree!
> Oh, shining rivers of the soul.
>
> In a Harlem cabaret
> Six long-headed jazzers play.
>
> A dancing girl whose eyes are bold
> Lifts high a dress of silken gold.
>
> Oh, singing tree!
> Oh, shining rivers of the soul!
>
> Were Eve's eyes
> In the first garden
> Just a bit too bold?
> Was Cleopatra gorgeous
> In a gown of gold?

> Oh, shining tree!
> Oh, silver rivers of the soul!
>
> In a whirling cabaret
> Six long-headed jazzers play.

Nor should we forget the virtuous rendering that Sterling Brown gives to that old spiritual "When Saints Go Ma'chin' Home," catching the quality of the original, before it became the property of every New Orleans–type band that has migrated North all the way from New Jersey to Fifty-Seventh Street. Brown's genius in using folk materials is not limited simply to the activity of reconstruction, accomplished with remarkable accuracy in "When Saints Go Ma'chin' Home." The work song "John Henry" offers a source of strength for a troubled poet in "Strange Legacies" as he meditates upon injustice in his own time:

> John Henry, with your hammer;
> John Henry, with your steel driver's pride,
> You taught us that a man could go down like a man,
> Sticking to your hammer till you died.
> Sticking to your hammer till you died.

> Brother,
> When, beneath the burning sun
> The sweat poured down and breath came quick
> And the loaded hammer swung like a ton
> And the heart grew sick;
> You had what we need now, John Henry,
> Help us get it.
> So if we go down
> Have to go down,
> We go like you, brother,
> 'Nachal' men . . .

And "Sporting Beasley" goes further, presenting an example of the folk imagination actively at work in transforming the objects within the immediate sight of the poet:

> Good glory, give a look at Sporting Beasley
> Strutting, Oh my Lord
>> Tophat cocked one side his bulldog head,
>> Striped four-in-hand, and in his buttonhole

A red carnation; Prince Albert coat
Form-fitting, corset like; vest snugly filled,
Gray morning trousers, spotless and full flowing,
White spats and a cane.
Step it, Mr. Beasley, oh step it till the sun goes down.

These two dimensions of Brown's art foreshadow the experimentation in the use of folk matter occurring in black literature today.

As we think of appropriate and relevant critical approaches to contemporary black literature, we are reminded that we have never dealt adequately with the innovative genius of the Harlem Renaissance—though this state of affairs is not Alain Locke's fault. We are partly to blame, then, for the ignorance of the young, because our criticism of this extraordinary movement has scarcely moved beyond minimal competence. I must add that the recent book by Nathan Huggins has helped very little.

No single aspect of contemporary black writing has been more controversial than language. My middle-class friends, less tolerant than I am, are turned off by the string of obscenities or profanities (if these terms still have meaning) to be found often in poems and stories. Actually, this is not a black phenomenon, but a general hang-up of our times, when our intellectual fascination has transferred itself from the heart to the naming of anatomical parts below. What is black is the special virulence in the language reserved for "whitey" and "whitey's world." This characteristic of diction is so commonplace that it requires no documentation. It obscures something which is intrinsically much more interesting: Black English—that is to say, the language of lower-class blacks. This has become in recent years a selected medium for a number of experimental black writers. An earlier form of the language is to be found in the dialect verse written, much of it, at the end of the nineteenth century. This leads me to note in passing that dialect verse, traditionally dismissed as a limited and pejorative representation of black people, has never been adequately examined. I know enough to say that James Weldon Johnson was wrong when he said that dialect had only two stops, humor and pathos. Used with the full pressure of black folk sources, the dialect poem moves from low entertainment, with the smell of the tent and blackface of Sambo, to art. Modern-day black diction has

urban rather than country roots. Ishmael Reed shapes, in *The
Free-Lance Pallbearers*, a unique combination of Black English
and a battering array of satirical and symbolic references that
emanate from a critical view of modern American society. Listen
now to Elijah Raven, who confides in the hero, Bukka Doopeyduk,
his newly acquired opposition to Sam, the dictator of the strange
country, resembling America, in which they live:

> "But Elijah!" I persisted. "It was only a few weeks ago that
> you were saying familiar things like 'Hello' or 'Hya doin'' or
> 'What's happening, my man.' Sometimes even slapping the
> palm of your hand into mine."
> "That was last week. I have rejuvenated myself by joining
> the *Jackal-headed Front*. We are going to expose SAM, remove
> some of these blond wigs from off our women's heads, and
> bring back rukus juice and chittlins. You'd better get on the
> right side, brother, because when the deal goes down, all the
> backsliding Uncle Toms are going to be mowed down. You
> hear? Every freakin', punkish Remus will get it in the neck,
> Doopeyduk."

Words respond to experimentation in the arts that are not
literary. We should recall the revolution in language initiated by
Gertrude Stein. That imaginative expatriate, intrigued by the
experimentation that she saw in Post-Impressionist art, especially
in Cubist painting, sought to introduce into fiction the method of
the visual arts. In short, Stein eliminated the narrative line, the
story, in her fiction, concentrated upon states of consciousness
and feeling, and abhorred all words that suggested cerebration
and intellectual activity. It was a language of no adjectives and
few adverbs, one that relied heavily upon progressive verbs because they communicated immediacy, and upon incremental
repetition. The consequence was something like the Cubist preoccupation with the essential forms in reality, and it brought into
being an economic, sensuous diction so much admired by Ernest
Hemingway that he had to deny vigorously that he had ever
learned anything in the Stein household. Presumably Gertrude
and Ernest gossiped about mutual friends while Miss Toklas
exchanged cooking recipes with Hemingway's wife, Hadley.

Linguistic influences follow the shape of the culture. It is the
musical analogue that has captured many of the black poets and

novelists of our day. Not since Whitman has the English language been so close to music in America. We recall Whitman's arias, his imitation of the soaring songs of birds, his recitatives, the contrasting hortatory elements, and his orchestration of themes and sounds to approach a musical composition. Whitman loved Italian opera and never missed the opportunity to hear his favorite singers, especially Alboni. Black poets Michael Harper and David Henderson follow John Coltrane—and to a lesser extent Miles Davis—in the cultivation of the long, fragmented, natural prose line, the attention to realistic details polished to precision, the reliance upon unconventional syntax and upon a voice with a volume that is preferably *fortissimo* and a tempo that is often *presto*. The opening poem of Harper's *Dear John, Dear Coltrane*, bearing the title "Brother John," displays these characteristics:

> Black man:
> I'm a black man;
> I'm black; I am—
> A black man; black—
> I'm a black man;
> I'm a black man;
> I'm a man; black—
> I am—
>
> Bird, buttermilk bird—
> smack, booze and bitches
> I am Bird
> baddest nightdreamer
> on sax in the ornithology-world
> I can fly—higher, high, higher—
> I'm a black man;
> I am; I'm a black man—
>
> Miles, blue haze,
> Miles high, another bird,
> more Miles, mute,
> Mute Miles, clean,
> bug-eyed, unspeakable,
> Miles, sweet Mute,
> sweat Miles, black Miles;
> I'm a black man;

> I'm black; I am;
> I'm a black man—
>
> Trane, Coltrane; John Coltrane;
> it's a slow dance;
> it's the Trane
> in Alabama; acknowledgement,
> a love supreme,
> it's black Trane; black;
> I'm a black man; I'm black;
> I am; I'm a black man—

You should note that Harper's lines pay tribute to two other black musicians as well—Charlie Parker and Miles Davis.

I began this discussion by maintaining that we must establish a clear and a clean distinction between political revolution and a revolt in the arts. I did so to get rid of what I may call now the "honky-tonks"—the simple-minded and simplistic identification of putting down whitey and screaming that Black Is Beautiful is high art. But nothing in literature is clean or pure, or, perhaps, black or white, to be somewhat more fanciful. I suggested earlier that possessing a commitment to both types of revolution was possible—indeed, not necessarily bad. I wish to go further now. There is no question that disaffection with contemporary society in an artistic sensibility that is serious and sophisticated encourages experimentation in form. Now political revolution builds on this type of disaffection, but the important point, clearly, for our purposes is not the birth of an activist, but the liberation from traditional ways of thinking that precedes the making of new commitments. What counts is not the shape of the new Jerusalem but the unleashed, explosively creative imagination that is required to conceive of it. Black literature has been conservative, on the whole, in regard to form—even during the period of the Harlem Renaissance in the 1920s, when experimentation in our general American tradition seems to have been the rule rather than the exception. I am reminded of the indebtedness of Wright and Ellison, the most able of all black writers of fiction, to political revolution, to a flirtation with communism which, like chicken pox, left scars but ushered in the maturing of a healthy talent. I would suggest that the climate of political revolution recently has provided just the emotional charge to push a considerable number of gifted artists into bold and rewarding experimentation.

The black theater provides the clearest case of the influence of political revolution. Baraka, in *Dutchman,* and Bullins, in *The Gentleman Caller,* through the urgency of their political message, are pushed to adopt a spare expressionism that is deeply moving. The evidence is to be seen elsewhere too, and in other forms. David Henderson turns his back upon the drift of much modern poetic practice to offer the facts, statistics, and details of mundane reality which Whitman cherished so much, and, in "Keep On Pushing," with more than a little of Whitman's skill in suggesting tension, motion, and a sense of a developing action of heroic proportions. And Ishmael Reed, in *The Free-Lance Pallbearers* and *Mumbo-Jumbo,* carries the tradition of the grotesque, the most exciting recent development in American fiction, a step further. We have here the indeterminate, chance-ruled world of many of the great novels of the fifties, and we see the effects of indeterminacy upon scene, character, and overall structure.

My task here has been to suggest new ways to practice an old office. I advocate the revision of traditional critical functions that are historical, analytic, and linguistic. I do so because the old methods do not fully describe the creative revolution that is taking place in the black world around us, and I call for a critical performance that does just that. I have not mentioned other critics of black literature in this discussion, though it is obvious from the principles that I have established that I consider much of this labor to be inadequate, though it may be well-intentioned. I hasten to say that we can learn something from inadequate criticism so long as it is accurate on its own terms. What is intolerable is error. Last year, when lecturing at the University of Illinois, I asked a black youth in the audience what he thought of *Cane* by Jean Toomer. His response was that *Cane* was "like an integrationist-type thing," and my reaction was to tell him in the most forceful way that the lecture platform permits that he had not read the book. The student confused a development in Toomer's life, after the writing of *Cane,* his decision to be white, not black, with the substance of the work of art. As we have said before, *Cane* came into being because Toomer discovered his blackness; the identification with black people created at that given moment an artist of a very high order.

Error can occur in high places as well as low. Not long ago Larry Neal, recently a much valued colleague at Yale, wrote in one of the many manifestoes in *Black Fire*: "We can learn more about what poetry is by listening to the cadences in Malcolm's speeches, than from most of Western poetics." I wish to say quickly that Larry Neal would not make this statement today, and I do him an injustice to quote him. But his remark has an especial value for me because I recall once discussing with him the possibility of his giving a course in Black Revolution—and he refused, saying that he was now interested exclusively in aesthetic problems. As we have seen earlier, there is a kind of truth in the Neal comment. Now I admire Malcolm, too, as Augustine, Joshua, Mohammed, Defoe, Cicero, perhaps, but never as Aristotle. And I am not about to abandon Aristotle—nor should you. I wish to amend the tradition that has flowed from him—to force an adjustment to the realities of history, form, and language in the black world, seek an appreciation for a music, indeed, for a literary performance, that is off as well as on the beat.

The black literary tradition exists. Indeed, it has never been more open and more vital. The openness comes not from the lack of artistic models but from the fact that new models have been used, coming from folk materials and from nonverbal strains of the black tradition where blacks have traditionally excelled. The vitality has political roots, in the past, a function of the general acquisition of status by blacks, and psychological roots, with the release of submerged portions of the psyche. What is offered now to the new black writer is a tradition unusually rich, like that of the Irish early in the twentieth century, waiting to nurture the imagination and to sustain the impulse to create.

1973

Black Leadership
as a Cultural Phenomenon:
The Harlem Renaissance

To make a leader black, to distort for a moment a phrase from the well-known Countee Cullen poem, is the proposition that this essay considers. It offers as many problems today as it did for Cullen when he considered the dilemma of possessing a dark skin in a white world. The problems are different, however, involving not only the accident of racial identification but the making of the leader as well. Now Cullen assumed that the speaker of his poem had the stuff that poets are made of, the rare combination of sensibility, high purpose, and expressive power that coalesces infrequently in our philistine world. But we cannot identify a leader with such reassuring confidence; often he or she tends to look like the rest of us, warts and all. The difference is that he or she has followers, not many necessarily, but some. A poet can be a poet—and a good one—with no readers to speak of, aside from a few professors and students at Berkeley, Cambridge, New Haven, or Princeton, or a few little old ladies living in Brooklyn Heights or on Edgecombe Avenue. The existence of a leader requires a social dimension, if not a cultural one, because the birth of a leader is a consequence of a dynamic, sometimes mysterious human relationship.

Even being black is different for the leader. For the poet, the discovery of blackness begins as a complication of consciousness, one for which his education as an artist in America has not prepared him. What begins as the painful awareness of difference or rejection becomes for the artistic imagination raw matter of unparalleled richness. Not so with the black leader, who tends to take a dramatic posture of some kind on the defining characteristic which is the most important condition of his life. This fact speaks most eloquently not so much for the obsession or narrowness of black leaders, but for the pathology of a society which places a greater value upon the color or caste barrier than it does upon widely publicized traditions of democracy or individualism. It happens, then, that the emergence of a black leader frequently begins with the publication of his attitude toward his racial identity rather than the assertion of religious or philosophical principles or the announcement of controlling ideas on economics or history or the positing of political or artistic manifestoes. If we look for the documentation of difference, we might compare the starting point of the journey of the imagination that is *Cane* by Jean Toomer, the Chicago sketch entitled "Bona and Paul," with the first essay by Du Bois in *The Souls of Black Folk*.

Our attitudes toward black leaders have been conditioned, inevitably, by prevailing views in the American society; we approach all aspirants for leadership with a certain ambivalence. De Tocqueville in *Democracy in America*, published in the 1830s, described this curious tendency in our culture. We have, on the one hand, an intense interest in affairs of state, even in the gossip of the marketplace, which takes the form of animated discussion and a willingness to give ourselves to panaceas of various kinds, whether free land or free silver or, after a great deal of twisting and turning of the mind, free blacks. On the other hand, we are deeply distrustful of leaders with abilities superior to our own, especially if they operate from principles not readily accessible to us. This means that the more substantial leadership in America is that which has emerged from needs and desires felt deeply by the common people, though these feelings may be largely amorphous or barely articulated. Americans have been drawn less to leaders inspired by a cosmic vision of life or wedded to a comprehensive design for an improved society, than to those more facile. To check how this tendency works within a black context, we should look at an odd leadership competition presented by the 1920s. Many blacks then were attracted to Marcus Garvey and the United Negro Improvement Association because they discovered an immediate, if not wholly valid, response to basic needs in a new urban setting for community, status, and economic independence. Few blacks were moved to accept Du Bois's vision of Pan-African cooperation expressed in an impressive series of conferences held during the years immediately after World War I. His was a cosmic vision.

The temptation always in any discussion of black leadership is to restrict attention to politics. This preoccupation is wholly understandable given the importance of legal status and civil rights in the history of American blacks. But the result is a form of tunnel vision, extracting one color from the full range of the spectrum. It is the merging of several forms of leadership that accounts for the almost unparalleled influence of Booker T. Washington at the turn of the century. What Washington offered first in 1881 was an educational philosophy, industrial training, buttressed by a Christian piety that had been acquired at Hampton. Rarely in American history have pedagogy and morality been so thoroughly intertwined, perhaps not since the seventeenth century. Washington in the 1890s urged upon uneasy blacks in an unstable and often depressed economy a program that stressed self-sufficiency, and the cultivation of services, and the mastery of the techniques of agricultural and industrial production. His thought led to the founding of the National Negro Business League. Political influence followed other forms of leadership— educational, moral, economic, social—and Washington's power in this final category achieved its zenith in the administrations of Theodore Roosevelt and William Howard Taft. The point here is that leadership achieves expression in patterns that pay little attention to conventional restrictions of field, area, or discipline.

The myths about black leadership are legion, encouraged no doubt by the unhappy legacy of Washington's success. This was the conviction held by both blacks and whites for many years after 1900: that there was one black man who could carry the burden of the race. This was the one with whom the President would wish to consult, or the one that Northern philanthropy and the foundations could trust, or the one who developed techniques for extracting money from parsimonious, if not hostile, legislatures. Closely related to the favored one is the popularity of published works bearing titles like "What the Negro Thinks" or "What the Negro Wants." It has been a long time now, a generation anyway, since such simplicity has had much credibility. Nevertheless, though we are far removed from the Washington precedent, we retain, in some measure, the belief in the appearance of the great black man.

Not all of the intriguing stories about black leaders stem from the post-Washington obsession with the representative race man.

Indeed, if we place this matter in perspective, we see that the notion of *the* black spokesman is a vestige of the nineteenth-century affection for the great man, for the hero who imposes his will and his personality upon the society. Part of the mythology, perhaps the most fascinating part, is the tradition of the trickster character that comes to us from the folk narratives of the slave plantations. The most sophisticated folklorists tell us that these narratives have identifiable African sources, so we have no real sense of their age. They formed a part of the African heritage that was adapted to and shaped by the immediate necessity for survival under the distressing conditions of slave life in this country. There is much attention here to what I shall call the trickster-leader, who embodies a long tradition that stretches from Brer Rabbit to Rinehart, the man of many faces in Ellison's *Invisible Man*. His strength is based upon meeting "The Man" (Zora Neale Hurston has said that The Man in some folk tales at times becomes God, who seems never to be far away in any case) and taking his measure. The trickster's devices are dissimulation, deception, and disguise, and they form, as the slave autobiographies confirm, the necessary equipment for any potential slave leader who would instruct his followers in a protected spot in the woods or the swamps or plan to make his escape North to the Beulah-Land.

This bundle of tales, some of them tall, no matter about the source, assumes the same unchanged basic reality. Black life exists under conditions determined by a dominating, indifferent, if not hostile, white society. Advantages, indeed survival at times, depend upon those blacks who have perfected techniques of apparent accommodation and skill in making special pleas. We tend to assume now that we are far removed from the obligation to adjust in old ways to a context defined by naked white power, but we have recently found an echo of the old dispensation in a theory considered by sophisticated white critics such as David Potter. This context, true, is more intellectual and more dignified, but we can recognize a familiar landscape. Black leadership, it is maintained, is a function of white necessity. That is to say, as I understand it, that the larger American society manipulates (perhaps too strong a word), *uses* its black component to achieve changes that are desirable for all members. The implications of this claim are extraordinary, and not, by the way, wholly derogatory, though any group bearing the record of abuse which blacks have in this country cannot avoid being alarmed at yet another instance of exploitation, even for objectives ultimately benign.

We can think of several important moments in American history for which the theory of white necessity would appear to have some relevance. There is the period from the 1830s through the 1850s, which is marked by the feverish activity of black and white Abolitionists. This is a time when black leadership afforded the most useful instrument to purge America of a shameful institution, slavery, wholly incongruous in Western society in the nineteenth century. Douglass, Brown, and their talented associates were indispensable tools in making America respectable. The assumption would be that the black Abolitionist served not merely the conscience of a few enlightened preachers from New England but the conscience of most Americans, who realized by the 1850s that human bondage was revolting and looked for a way, preferably an easy one, to rid the state of slavery.

Or let us entertain a second illustration, this one closer to our own time and separated from the first by somewhat more than a century. America suffered in the 1960s from a social structure grown too rigid to permit the upward mobility of members of minority groups in significant numbers; from institutions, educational and financial, committed to serving a favored population, except for token representation given to groups without status; from a tenor of life chilled and depersonalized by an unthinking commitment to middle-class conventions; and from a widely accepted value system that ignored the basic needs of many Americans and ruthlessly exploited the natural resources that are the heritage of all Americans. The blacks and the young of all races addressed themselves to these problems. But it was especially the blacks, the ones suffering most from American inadequacies, who forced the issues, demanding a more open social system with more opportunities for the traditionally deprived, creating their own black institutions to offer alternatives to the cold structures so much abhorred, and cultivating a native black tradition, in large part hidden before, more sensitive to human, emotional needs and more aware of the intimate and multiple connections linking man to his natural world.

Who has profited from the black leadership that stood at the center of the profound upheaval of nearly a decade ago? Blacks have, certainly, more in the way in which they look at themselves than by any tangible advantage achieved. But it is America ultimately that has been richly rewarded, with its new awareness of the gold to be found in its ethnic groups and of the delicacy and tenderness that mark the relationship between one person and another and between all people and the earth which nourishes us.

A final example of the symbiotic connection between white needs and black leadership is, perhaps, the most obvious one. It is certainly the one most cited to illustrate the point. Some critics stop just short of saying that the Harlem Renaissance was a white creation. Nathan Huggins is careful to point out that money from white patrons supported two prominent authors of the movement, Hughes and Hurston, during a part of the Renaissance decade; that white intellectuals introduced black authors to publishers downtown and urged the publication of their works; that whites flocked uptown, above 125th Street nightly, hungry for jazz and blues and frequenting nightclubs that few blacks could afford to attend, even if permitted to enter. There is no doubt that the Renaissance served as therapy for a white urban population, weary of the horror and responsibilities of World War I, appalled by the pattern of American life that flourished in the administrations of Harding and Coolidge, and sustained by the sense that the economy was committed to an unending upward spiral. But to say that the Renaissance is a white thing is a cruel statement, only partly true—cruel because it discounts the aspirations of hard working black artists who sought to interpret and to present black life with an honesty and a newly broadened imagination, and partial because it ignores the consciousness of black folks and the often dramatic changes to be observed there.

What applies to the Harlem Renaissance applies also to black Abolitionism and, more recently, to the black revolution of a decade ago. The whole truth requires us to think not only of the general American response, the white reaction to black leadership, but of the shift in the attitudes of blacks who have followed and sustained the action of their leaders. Consideration of white necessity has invited a larger conception of the function of black leadership. We are forced to think less of individual leaders, evaluating their success or their failure, praising them for their integrity or their commitment or damning them for their excesses, to be measured either in hubris or in sensual appetite, and to think more in terms of movements of the mind, changes in the way the self is defined or the society is to be approached or the culture is to be weighed. If we look at the leadership of the Harlem Renaissance in this way, we must conclude that it achieved an astounding success. It is superficial to declare, as Huggins does, that the Renaissance is a failure because it did not produce political leadership that would give direction to black hopes. What is needed to document this point is the careful examination of what the Renaissance truly did achieve in the large cultural context which must offer a framework for any accurate approach to black leadership. We must remind ourselves that we are not concerned now with the critical approval of books published, or the number of copies sold, or the exhibitions held by a painter or a sculptor, or the number of discs cut by the race's record companies. Though these facts are important, they serve only to document a movement that touched all black people, a change in consciousness that made "black" something different from what it was before.

Let us be clear how we propose to look at the Renaissance in terms of the problem of leadership. For our purposes, we are not interested in the activities of individuals in the political area at that time, important as they are. For the moment, we shall put aside the day-to-day engagement of three officers of the National Association for the Advancement of Colored People—W.E.B. Du Bois, the influential and many-talented editor of *The Crisis*, and the two courageous field secretaries of that organization, James Weldon Johnson and Walter White. And as we do this, we should recall that Jessie Fauset gave important service as well to *The Crisis*. We are not concerned either with the leadership role of the National Urban League, with an economic rather than a political or legal orientation. Charles Johnson was the able editor of *Opportunity* magazine, and he enlisted the services of Countee Cullen, Eric Walrond, Sterling Brown, and other literary figures. Nor shall we weigh how the more radical leadership contribution of *The Messenger* group, allied to the American labor movement through an activist tradition stemming from Eugene Debs, George Schuyler, Theophilus Lewis, and A. Philip Randolph, examined the events of the day with a consistently disapproving eye and reported what they saw in the broad satire and lively language made popular by the editors of the *American Mercury*, H.L. Mencken and George Jean Nathan. It is not a matter of immediate relevance to document the early political career of Claude McKay, an editor of *The Liberator* magazine, the personal organ, more or less, of that colorful revolutionary Max Eastman, who espoused his own brand of freewheeling communism, to become anathema to Mike Gold and his Stalinist comrades. No, we are interested in the leadership achievement of the Renaissance as a whole, as a movement, the contribution that is intimately related to artistic activity.

One other bit of cautionary advice is required. The art that has most significance for us is the more experimental and more advanced practice of perhaps a dozen figures, those who felt keenly in various ways that their work formed a part of an emerging coherent mythology. We should note quickly that many very competent artists fail to qualify in this respect—among them Jessie Fauset, Nella Larsen, Walter White, and W.E.B. Du Bois, except for *Dark Princess*, when the austere editor yielded momentarily to the temptations provided by the more radical young. But Toomer, McKay, Hughes, Johnson, Rudolph Fisher, Countee Cullen, Arna Bontemps, Hurston, and Sterling Brown most certainly do qualify. Closely connected with their work is the practice of musicians, painters, and sculptors who were moved by similar ideas about Africa, about the value of life in the South, about the importance of the folk tradition, and about the superior merit of man's emotional life, as opposed to his intellectual pretensions. And not to be forgotten, too, is the extraordinary critic blessed with an apparently infinite capacity to absorb artistic experience, Alain Locke, who attempted, imperfectly finally, to organize and to codify it all.

What the Renaissance really means requires a recall of popular notions held by many Americans, perhaps most Americans, in the three stormy decades before the emergence of the Renaissance.

We know something of the erosion of Negro rights and privileges in America that occurred in the 1890s and in the early years of the twentieth century. It involved voting rights, public accommodations (including the use of libraries), public parks, public transportation, housing facilities, and, not to be forgotten, public toilets and public drinking fountains. What is often forgotten today is the powerful white supremacist rhetoric, pseudointellectual and apparently authoritative, that sustained the oppression of black citizens. Many of the names of these champions of white civilization and white honor have been forgotten, but even today we can expect a mild response from a reference to Thomas Dixon's work, especially *The Leopard's Spots*, and Lothrop Stoddard's *The Rising Tide of Color*. From Dixon's novel came the movie masterpiece *Birth of a Nation*; never has a more inventive movie technique been lavished upon a foundation so shoddy. But we cannot evade the fact, though we should like to do it, that a part of the popularity of the movie was dependent upon the wide acceptance on the part of the American people of Dixon's assumptions. The rhetoricians presenting the necessity for protecting a white civilization had done their work well.

What were Dixon's assumptions? It is important to know, because black intellectuals reacted not only to the excesses of *The Leopard's Spots* but to the basic pretensions to truth that prompted these excesses. Let us reconstruct these in the list that follows:

1. Change "white" to Anglo-Saxon and assert that civilization is being carried by the Anglo-Saxon race, now being threatened by hordes, black or yellow. There was always a convenient German scholar lurking in the background ready to prove that the cherished democratic assembly came from an obscure convocation of Teutonic warriors.

2. Say that the black man is lower on the evolutionary scale and cannot be expected to participate in civilization on a level of equality. Biological factors prevent him from ever offering a contribution—after all, science is science, even when reduced to making generalizations from statistics about head size or test scores. History has offered numerous examples of the destruction of the seats of higher culture by barbarians, and America must be careful to avoid the fate of Rome, which by some enormous leap

of the historical imagination is to be considered a frontier or precursor of Anglo-Saxon culture.

3. "Lower" means closer to the animal state. The black is more of an animal than the white man. For that reason, he is sexually superior to the white man, who is more refined. Moreover, the almost automatic object of the lust of the black man is the white woman, who must be protected at all costs.

4. "Lower" also means that the black man lacks the sense of responsibility demanded of a fully mature human being in our society. Every Southerner knows that a black person must be treated like a child, that he or she cannot be trusted with food or valuables in the big house, that he cannot maintain a stable household and function as a responsible father or mother. No doubt, "mammies" are different.

5. What counts for these white theoreticians is "history." The life of a black man is worth less than that of a white man because *history* is carried by the white race. Acts of violence are unfortunate but they may be necessary to protect the integrity and the future of the race.

Now Du Bois and Washington had sought to deny the validity of these bizarre assumptions, to confront them directly. They asserted that the American black man could measure up to the white man's standards and had contributed already to Western civilization, but rhetoric could not do the job of art, as Du Bois and Yeats well knew. Art touches the emotions from which these shoddy projections spring, the fears, doubts, and insecurities generated when a half-educated provincial faces the formidable challenge of technology and supersensual power.

The Renaissance, looked at from the point of view of this racist assault, becomes a fascinating, if not outrageous (in that distortion is extreme) phenomenon. Now what were the assumptions of the Renaissance? Say instead:

1. There is a rich black culture that stands unrecognized beside the white, evident in the emotional associations surrounding the spirituals or in the intimations of Africa that come in dreams, race memories, or flights of fancy. Characteristically, those intimations do not arouse the vision of an early republican democracy, but of kingdoms, priests, and noble lovers.

2. The idea of progress or of evolution is faulty. The emotional side of man has been neglected in the mad rush toward a more perfect technology. What is desirable is harmony with one's self, with one's community, and with nature. More primitive societies than our present one offer models that we should follow. Look to Africa, the West Indies, or, if we wish, to Mexico and the vestiges of Indian culture in New Mexico.

3. Yes, the black man is closer to the animal state than the white man is, but this proximity is good. The black affirms the senses, lives a fuller, richer life, has an opportunity for happiness unavailable to a white man. Yes, too, the black people are better lovers and can give and receive more satisfaction than their fairer and less gifted brothers and sisters.

4. The life of the vagabond, as McKay has pictured it in *Home to Harlem* and in *Banjo*, is desirable, superior. It makes possible the full enjoyment of the senses. We can discard the restricting, dehumanizing conventions of middle-class society, as baggage hindering the birth of a free spirit.

5. Finally, what counts for the black participants in the Renaissance is not "history" or the "future," or a place in a neon sun, but life, its richness and its variety. Every bit of life is precious and must be nourished.

What we observe here is amazing. The technique of response to racist attacks is *inversion*—quite literally to make that which was considered bad, good; and that which was considered good, bad. It is argument through distortion of the profoundest kind, through a set of grotesques, if American middle-class values are accepted as cultural norms. We can say, perhaps, that the Harlem Renaissance was disinterested in more obvious forms of leadership, as Locke has suggested; it was deeply involved in creating the cultural climate from which a new leadership could emerge.

The questions suggested by this achievement are many, and we should face them directly. What strikes us forcefully initially is that the political commitments of the individual leaders are very different from what I have described as the intellectual thrust of the Renaissance. Communism, libertarian or Stalinist; socialism of the Debs, or of the more genteel Du Bois, vintage; reformist Republicanism in many shapes that would seem to have little in common with a set of principles and beliefs that verge upon an elegant primitivism. We are tempted to say that for Renaissance artists their real life was not something attached to the duties and responsibilities of prosaic life, but was rather that other, richer existence within the realm of art.

We should be troubled by the prospect of replacing one set of distortives by another. The fact is that there was not much more evidence supporting the mythology of the Renaissance than there was behind the racist assumptions of Dixon and Stoddard. Cullen wrote about Africa without the benefit of direct contact with African life, and, as a consequence, the images in his poetry arouse memories of vivid pictures from poems by Coleridge and Blake, and his rhythms, at times conventionally primitive, might just as well come from the Finnish epic, *The Kalevala*, that inspired the meter of Longfellow's *Hiawatha*, as from the African drum beat. The recollections of the Southern experience, though moving and occasionally lyrical, are hopelessly entangled with another literary convention, the pastoral, the creation of the city man dissatisfied with what is happening at home rather than knowledgeable about what goes on in the land of his ancestors— Georgia or Florida or Virginia or Jamaica or Panama. The folk tradition was a solid and an apparently endless productive resource, though the Renaissance artists, except for Hughes and Hurston, tended to view this heritage with a certain amount of condescension.

Actually, what saved the Renaissance was exactly what the ardent racist thinks, and artists claimed, they had in their pockets —history. The artists of the Renaissance, more intelligent, more sensitive, and more compassionate, had made the right guess. Research in art history has demonstrated to everyone's satisfaction the continuity in black civilization and has singled out for special attention the linkage existing between blacks in America and blacks in Africa. Increasing discontent with the machine age and a mounting dismay at the consequences of nuclear fission and the menace of nuclear war have led to an affirmation of the values of community and a renewed affection for the planet earth. The folk tradition, only dimly known, in the 1920s, by black artists and intellectuals, prospers, affording models for life and for art. Its exploration, now an industry constantly expanding, confirms the right of folk knowledge to stand beside formal history, science, and art as one of the pillars of civilization. The cantankerous grandmother of Reed's *The Free-Lance Pall-bearers* may yet receive a Ph.D. in *Hoodoo*, supported by government funding resembling the benefits of the G.I. Bill.

Much has been made of the middle-class orientation of the Renaissance. This is to confuse rhetoric and art and suggest erroneously that art is somehow limited by its class origins. This is simply not so. We do not need to be day-laborers to love the blues nor business executives to recite *God's Trombones*. The achievement of the Renaissance has changed all blacks, a phenomenon in leadership that is impressive, and that achievement lives still, as a resource for newly emerging leaders to turn to, even when they do not trouble to acknowledge their indebtedness.

We have moved, then, from a speculative discussion of black leadership as something attached to charismatic individuals to leadership as the function of a movement, as something over-shadowing individual efforts, no matter how thoughtful or sin-cerely motivated. It would be a mistake to ignore the individual. We should look, then, for a resolution of some sort. When we examine our experience, we discover that those black leaders who remain with us are those who ride the crest of the wave of forces bringing changes in attitude and in social structure. We remember King because he dramatized the failure of the nation to humanize itself through the accepted procedures of law and government and articulated first the great revulsion against institutional sterility that overwhelmed us after his death, and we remember him even though we do not know what he saw at the top of the mountain. And we learn still from Baraka, who understood that it was not enough to make finely wrought rhetoric from that revulsion. Instead, he was attacking the apparently inevitable rot in our cities by organizing a genuine community on the shards, broken pots, and vermin of urban culture. He would do so by forcing blacks to discover what he sees to be their genuine roots and to accept their obligations to each other. And he has come now to see that malignant neglect in a still basically affluent society must be excoriated by a commitment to Marxist economic principles forcing a redistribution of wealth, not apparently attainable in any other way. Indeed, work, community organization, and renewed faith in one's past and in one's future seem insufficient in a volatile and capricious economy to provide the essentials for life. We look forward with confidence to the time when projecting a new society will offer, as it did for Yeats, a system of references for superb poetry. Meanwhile, his views foreshadow the emergence of new attitudes toward city life, a new sense of the need for a national commitment to sustain the cities, and a new necessity to think of communities in the city, organized societies sufficiently small for people to discover their identities, control their destinies, and express their love.

On the other hand, Malcolm is less important to us. We recall him with affection and keep his memory alive, not so much for his leadership, but because he has written one of the great auto-biographies of the twentieth century, a genuinely original combination of the *Confessions* of St. Augustine, a rogue's tale worthy of any eighteenth-century picaro out of Defoe, a record of re-making self and society through work and virtue best exemplified previously in our literature by Benjamin Franklin.

Some black leaders have yet to receive the public recognition they deserve. Richard Wright is one. I think not so much now of the writer in his Communist young manhood, or in his anti-Communist phase, or in his period of association with Sartre at Paris in seeking to bring into being the Rassemblement Démocratique Revolutionnaire, as a viable Socialist alternative for people disenchanted with both capitalism and Russian communism. I refer now to the prophetic author who wrote *Black Power* and *White Man Listen!* in the 1950s. Wright saw clearly the staggering problems faced by the leadership in the new African nations. He emphasized the necessity both for coming to terms with the Western enlightenment and for retaining ties to African customs and African institutions; he deplored the excesses of capitalism and tribalism; and he predicted the emergence both of Nyerere in Tanzania and Idi Amin in Uganda. Had he been listened to more attentively there would be more Nyerere's and no Amin. Wright's leadership, like Baraka's and King's, was based upon understanding developing social forces and employing all of the resources of rhetoric and organization to guide the flow of history into channels that are constructive and life-giving.

I said at the outset of this essay that our problem was the study of the phrase: "To make a leader black." To answer this quandary, we are obligated to study with all of our intelligence and compassion how the changing forms of blackness and the changing status of blacks in the world shape the leader.

What was the achievement in leadership of the Renaissance movement? It opposed the derogatory propaganda about blacks that had flooded America for three decades after the demise of Reconstruction. Thomas Dixon and others had maintained that blacks were without culture, close to the ape on the evolutionary scale and therefore incapable of any education other than vocational, hypersexed, and without responsibility. The Renaissance leaders inverted these misguided assumptions. They maintained that there was a rich black culture in Africa standing unrecognized by the white culture and that vestiges of it were present in America, in spirituals, folk narratives, dreams, and race memories. They rejected the excesses that evolution had brought into being in America—that is to say, a sterile technocratic culture—and they maintained that blacks would bring a warmth, a closeness to nature, an affirmation of basic emotions that would supply compassion for the Anglo-Saxon machine. They rejoiced in the sexual superiority of blacks, even if it were not so, and they pointed to the adherence of blacks to their own codes of morality, often different from those of whites, to deny the charge of irresponsibility. Now some of these claims were no more true than the derogatory charges of the racists, but they served the purpose of supplying dignity and a connection with the past for many Afro-Americans, no matter what their class status was. Black was beautiful, for the first time in the United States.

You will notice that there is a pendulum that describes the kinds of leadership for blacks, an oscillation between individual action and group action. If you glance over the pages of black history, you will observe that from 1830 to 1860, leadership came from a talented group of antislavery orators and writers like Douglass, Brown, Remond, Bibb, and Delany. The forty-year period from 1865 to 1905 was the Golden Age of the black spokesman: Frederick Douglass until 1890 and then Booker T. Washington, who in turn was succeeded by Du Bois (from 1906 into the 1920s) providing guidance for a black elite, whom he insisted must be responsible to the black masses. In the twenties, the Renaissance movement absorbed and redirected Du Bois's writing and his energies, and he made an enormous contribution, both artistic and critical, to the image of the New Negro. The Depression years, despite the persistent Communist appeal to the black masses, which was largely ignored, produced once again individual leaders of distinction: A. Philip Randolph, with a background in the labor movement and Socialist politics, and Robert Russa Moton, the conservative bearer of the mantle worn by Booker T. Washington. Martin Luther King and Malcolm X, exemplifying once again the radical and conservative split that goes back perhaps to Du Bois and Washington, mobilized black people in the 1950s and 1960s and fell victims to a new age of terror that seems to mark for assassination all charismatic leaders in our time. King and Malcolm X were harbingers of a new group endeavor, the Black Nationalist revolution of the 1960s and early 1970s. Blacks are now at sea, with signals of leadership emanating from neither strong individuals or defined groups. The only spokesman with any authority today is Jesse Jackson, and he has much to teach us. The new pattern seems to be regional or local rather than national, organized around specific needs that may or may not be common to other areas. What we should look forward to now is not the emergence of a single leadership group but groups, responding to soaring unemployment figures for blacks, welfare cuts, discrimination in industry and the labor unions, miserable schooling and housing conditions, and applying pressure upon political leaders, public service administrators, and officials in public education. Not in the near future will there be another King or Malcolm X or Du Bois or Washington or Douglass. Instead, I welcome such real and speculative developments as Operation Bread Basket, A New York for All New Yorkers, San Francisco, the Rainbow City, anticipating there the recognition of all of the many cultural stands in the Bay area.

Beyond the oscillation between individual and group leadership patterns, we see a bold and, indeed, a noble progress of blacks in America. Until 1876 freedom was the absorbing issue for black leaders; after that date until 1910 economic survival and racial identity were prime problems. Du Bois and the Renaissance documented that blacks had made a rich cultural contribution to America and come from a unique cultural tradition. Through the thirties, the forties, and the early fifties the struggle for political equality absorbed all energies. After 1954 the battle about equality covered the whole spectrum of American life—challenging failure in interpersonal relationships, subtle forms of economic discrimination, and long-accepted patterns of exclusion. Respect was demanded: if not as a friend and neighbor to be understood and loved, then as an enemy to be hated and feared.

Many misguided people tend to measure progress in terms of political appointments. Carter has boasted that he has filled more positions with blacks than any other President, and Nixon, before him, made a similar claim. The fact is that these appointments have done nothing to improve the basic inferior condition of blacks. Patricia Harris and others become absorbed within the administrative bureaucracy and lose whatever touch they have had with folks on Georgia Avenue in Washington, D.C., or 125th Street in New York. One bright black journalist called for a moratorium on black appointments so that the national administration could attend to basic issues, without hiding behind the most recent scintillating "first" for a black politician. I do not quite agree with my journalist friend, but he has a point. Appointments must not obscure the reality of unemployment, sickness, misery, and frustration. The job that I have in mind for regional and community groups is to point the finger of blame where it belongs in the society and to insist upon and assist in the construction of a better neighborhood and, indeed, a better world.

The good work is there for us all to do, and our reward may be not another black Senator from Massachusetts but the sense that we have gained in compassion, love, and dignity, those human virtues that are neglected all too much in a fragmented, interest-haunted society. To make a leader black absorbed our attention thus far. My purpose is grander—that is to say, to make all of you black, if not in race, then in sympathy and understanding. America will not fulfill its destiny, or even maintain its health or equilibrium, unless it does so. Go now and pursue your proper work.

1977

II

The Structure of the Afro-American Literary Tradition

The Slave Narrative:
First Major Art Form
in an Emerging Black Tradition

The Afro-American literary tradition, at its moment of birth, married rhetoric and art, though artistic achievement for David Walker was an aftereffect if not an afterthought. He had sought to impose upon a powerful overflow of ideas and passion the shaping influence of respected models easily available to him from contemporary American and Afro-American culture. He succeeded far beyond anyone's expectation, perhaps even his own, because argument rarely leaps the barrier that separates ordinary exposition from the dramatic eloquence of Thomas Paine and W.E.B. Du Bois, the structured expression of ideas that only can be called art. The obstacles are fewer and less formidable for the slave narrative, the primary literary form practiced by blacks in the three decades following Walker's *Appeal*. The autobiography and the biography of the fugitive slave combined story with propaganda, and where there is a tale to be told, there is a likely chance for the creation of art. It is true that few of the narratives remain memorable as achievements of the imagination, but some do, and these survive to have an enduring effect upon the shape of the tradition of black expression in America.

The immediate background for the emergence of slave narratives was the shift in attitude in the opponents of slavery. The old-style reformer of the gradualist school with membership in the local society promoting colonization for freed blacks gave way to a new breed of radical activist. The reasons for change are many and complex. Certainly important would be the disillusionment with the American Colonization Society, but beyond this would be the growth of communities of free blacks in the North, the increase in Southern and Northern investment in the slave economy, and the hardening of the statutes and the sanctions that locked the black slave into a condition of permanent servitude. Walker's *Appeal* and the Nat Turner insurrection in the summer of 1831 tended to eliminate a middle ground of polite discourse and largely church-centered debate on antislavery issues, participated in by both Northerners and Southerners. Gone was the eighteenth-century dream that slavery would somehow wither away, and gone too was the atmosphere of sweet reason that some Northern intellectuals studiously cultivated. William Ellery Channing, the famous Unitarian minister, wrote to Daniel Webster in May 1828, extending to Southerners the sympathy of Northerners in achieving a solution to the problem of slavery: "We consider slavery as your calamity, not your crime, and we will share with you the burden of putting an end to it."[1] But this sentiment was not to anticipate the events of the next few years. William Lloyd Garrison founded *The Liberator* in 1831 and published during the next year a vigorous attack on the American Colonization Society. A year later the American Anti-Slavery Society held its first meeting in Philadelphia. The new reformers cared little for the qualms of conscience of uneasy slaveholders; they stood for immediate and unconditional emancipation. The Society possessed too a new constituency, largely excluded from the Colonization group, Northern blacks, who took the place in the new movement of the Southerners who were attracted to the old.[2]

One ambition of the American Anti-Slavery Society had special significance for the development of black literature. The Society aspired to organize grass-roots support, and it sought vigorously for ways and means of doing so. The most efficient instruments in mobilizing sentiment, it was discovered, were the victims of the slave system, ex-slaves who had gained their freedom and who lived now, often in some danger, in the North. The practice commenced in the 1830s of using blacks at antislavery gatherings to tell the story of life under the yoke in the South, and an important complement to the performance on the platform was the publication of a paperbound pamphlet or modest book, often costing as little as twenty-five cents,[3] making the experience in bondage available to a larger audience. The value of these accounts is best stated by John Greenleaf Whittier, who edited and wrote the "Preface" for the *Narrative of James Williams, an American Slave*: "But . . . for a full revelation of the secrets of the prison-house, we must look to the slave himself. The in-

quisitors of Goa and Madrid never disclosed the peculiar atrocities of their 'hall of horrors.' "[4]

Though they cared little for matters of tradition, the activists
of the 1830s gave new life to an old form. Charles Nichols reports
that the genre of the slave narrative began in 1703 with *Adam
Negro's Tryall,* written by John Saffin, a well-known colonial
author, who was moved to respond to Samuel Sewall's antislavery
tract *The Selling of Joseph.*[5] Saffin was white, but other writers
who cultivated the genre in the eighteenth century were black,
Briton Hammon, John Marrant, and Gustavus Vassa. There were
not many accounts of this kind published during the century, and
in general they possess no claim to artistic distinction. This is not
true of *The Interesting Narrative of the Life of Olaudah Equiano,
or Gustavus Vassa, the African,* published in London in 1789. The
modern editor of *The Narrative,* Paul Edwards, reports that eight
British editions and an American volume were printed during
Equiano's lifetime (probable date of death was 1797), and ten
were published posthumously, including translations into Dutch
and German. It is, perhaps, suggestive that an American edition
appeared in 1837.[6] Though Equiano's story is far superior to
many of the accounts appearing in his own century and later, it is
separated in fundamental ways from the Afro-American tradition
and from the nineteenth-century narratives.

Equiano considered himself to be English, not American, or
indeed what would be thought of in the mid-eighteenth century
as a colonial. His phrase of self-identification during his years of
wandering was "almost an Englishman."[7] Crucial to understanding *The Interesting Narrative* is the recognition that Equiano had
two homes rather than one: first, the charming valley of Essoka in
Eboe, loosely connected with the Kingdom of Benin, and, second,
"old England," deeply yearned for while he was forced to labor in
the West Indies. The fact is that Equiano spent all of his years as a
slave (except for journeys elsewhere with his master) in the West
Indies, and these years account for a relatively modest portion of
the narrative as a whole. Indeed, more attention is given to
Equiano's precarious existence as a free black. Many of the
adventures are trials of body and spirit at sea, in which un-
predictable elements, sea battles, and sea explorations are prominent. Incompetent and unscrupulous sea captains represent rather

more of a danger than do evil and sadistic slave masters. It would seem that *The Interesting Narrative*, looked at strictly, is neither an Afro-American work nor a slave narrative, though a part of the whole consists of memories of enforced servitude in the West Indies. And that part may account for the American edition in 1837.

Equiano's narrative was very different from the American slave autobiographies and biographies of the nineteenth century in style and manner of telling, as well as in matter. Edwards has commented in the "Preface" to an abridgment of *The Interesting Narrative* that the hero resembles Gulliver as he desperately sought to adjust himself to the enlarged perspective in Brobdingnag and Robinson Crusoe in his intense preoccupation with economic and moral survival. We do not need to accept that slavery is Equiano's desert island[8] in order to sense the strong eighteenth-century character of the tale. Not only were the realities of black slavery more urgent and brutal for the nineteenth-century author, but the literary traditions that touched these stories demanded a radically altered technique. *The Interesting Narrative* is a respected forerunner of the slave accounts that began to appear in the 1830s; it is also a remote one, which did not impose upon its successors precedents that might be followed.

Thousands of slave narratives appeared after 1831, when the opposition to slavery became a crusade. They were printed as separate volumes or as important contributions to the columns of Abolitionist periodicals. The determination of authorship is a problem in this vast flow of printed matter. Charles Nichols does not doubt that "most of the narratives were produced with the aid of the antislavery men of Boston and New York, and contain literary, ethical and sentimental elements added by white ghost writers and editors."[9] Yet some, certainly, were untouched by extensive editorial assistance, a fact prominently acknowledged by the author's phrase on the title page, "Written by Himself." And it happens that the accounts that have greatest artistic merit are marked by this claim—but not all of them. Perhaps the most wretchedly told tales carried this announcement of authenticity too, though what is authentic for the historian is not the same as what is true, or certainly what is valuable, for the student of literature.

The point is made clearly by the *Narrative of James Williams.* When this account appeared in 1838 and when copies of it were circulated in the area of Alabama where Williams had worked as a slave, the Alabama *Beacon* claimed that Williams's story was false, an assertion supported with vigor by a number of slave-holders in the state. Even the American Anti-Slavery Society admitted the likelihood that it might have been duped, withdraw-ing the book from sale for a time.[10] At the same time, no one questioned the Quaker integrity of John Greenleaf Whittier when he described his role as a recorder of dictation, as a secretary who was responsible for the accurate reproduction of the words of the narrator: "The Editor is fully aware that he has not been able to present this affecting narrative in the simplicity and vivid fresh-ness with which it fell from the lips of the narrator. He has, however, as closely as possible, copied his manner, and in many instances his precise language. THE SLAVE HAS SPOKEN FOR HIMSELF. Acting merely as his amanuensis, he has carefully abstained from comments of his own."[11] What was in question was Williams's facts; no one denied that Williams had uttered them or that they had emerged, without outside provocation or distortion, from his own imagination. The integrity of the story as Williams's own remained intact, something reassuring for a man of literature who wishes to comment upon a truth or a skill that requires no external validity, though the historian may doubt and express dissatisfaction. Even the essential accuracy of the Williams story was reaffirmed, despite disagreement about details, since the Anti-Slavery Society offered it again for sale, doing so, as the editor of a recent issue of the account maintains, "because of its dramatic description of slave life."[12]

The problems raised by the *Narrative of James Williams* emphasize the importance of art. Though art, even the art of the slave narrative, is a synthesis of many influences, it comes pri-marily in this instance from the power of the impression of black life under bondage, an intensity that is related less to the heaping up of atrocity upon atrocity than to the unity of the story, the sense of development and fulfillment that occurs within it, and, to an extent, the appropriateness of the language in which it is told. These are qualities that editors, finally, can only preserve and not supply, as Whittier's comment so eloquently states. And there is no reason to believe that other amanuenses of the slaves, Lydia Maria Child, Edmund Quincy, and Samuel Eliot, all, like Whittier, persons of integrity, were any less sensitive to the artistic strength of the tales they recorded.

Much of the scrupulousness of the editors came from something other than the recognition that a moving story of slave life cannot really be well fabricated by a writer who has not thoroughly absorbed or responded deeply to the facts of black reality, and that normally the ability to construct such a tale is possessed only by those who speak from direct experience—but not always, as Harriet Beecher Stowe demonstrated, substituting for experience the careful and selective assimilation of the narratives of others.[13] But that is to go a step beyond the range of the art which is being presently defined, a movement into a more sophisticated expression to be taken as well by William Wells Brown and Frederick Douglass. The editors of the period were interested essentially in effective propaganda, though they respected art. They knew that the cause of freedom would suffer from fraud or even the appearance of fraud, and they insisted upon the publication of documents, letters, and reports of investigating committees supporting the character of the authors and the accuracy of their recollections. Moreover, they were scrupulous about indicating the extent of editorial contributions, describing their services with precision, in such areas as spelling, punctuation, chapter formation, and the like.

Authenticity was no guarantee of artistic merit. A case in point is *A Narrative of the Adventures and Escape of Moses Roper from American Slavery*. The Reverend Thomas Price, D.D., remarks in the "Preface" that *A Narrative* is Roper's "own production, and carries with it internal evidence of truth."[14] Indeed, it does. The account has no chapter divisions; the whole story bears the subtitle "Escape from Slavery." Roper's tale consists of a countless number of escape attempts, so many that it is difficult to separate one from another, and so similar that they lose force in the telling. Each departure from bondage, after an initial attempt when Roper was thirteen or fourteen,[15] was succeeded by a progressively more fiendish punishment. The appalling accumulation of atrocities on the part of slaveholders is unequalled anywhere else in the literature, describing such experiences as Roper's receiving five hundred lashes, working with twenty-five pounds around his neck, performing the office of a horse in dragging a heavy barrow to the cotton field, being chained to a female slave, hanging by his hands from a machine regularly used for packing and pressing cotton, losing his nails from his fingers and his feet in the course of deliberate torture.[16] And the list of horrors continues through the record of events occurring on other plantations, including a suicide, a forced confinement in a box overnight after the unfortunate slave had received a generous dose of castor oil and salts, and a forced roll down the hill in a fiendish contraption consisting of a hogshead with nails protruding into its interior.[17] Roper adds that there are things best left unsaid, but he seems not to have neglected many. Yet despite this chamber of horrors the sense of the degradation and corruption of the slave society is somehow muted because these atrocities are not placed in a context that has meaning or that demands from us great sympathy. The narrative lacks an effective principle of order and a center of feeling or consciousness to force awareness of the depth of depravity to which the slaveholders have sunk. What is absent is art; instead of development and unity there are repetition and disjunction. No more need be said about the first of these faults, and the second is best seen in the pious conclusion, in which Roper expresses an unconvincing affection for the country that has refused him the status of a domestic animal: "Whatever I may have experienced in America, at the hands of cruel task-masters, yet I am unwilling to speak in any but respectful terms of the land of my birth."[18] Extraordinary horror is succeeded by even more extraordinary Christian compassion, and neither is moving.

The force of the slave narrative is directly related to art displayed in its telling. The tale that survived conveyed an intense and unified impression of the life of the slave, one that was republished frequently. Some sense of a rough evaluation of the narratives in terms of popularity rather than artistic merit may be had from this comment by the editor of the *Narrative of the Life and Adventures of Henry Bibb*: "Of the many narratives that preceded Bibb's, three were outstanding. *The Narrative of James Williams* (1838) gained notoriety because it was fictitious; the *Autobiography [Narrative of the Life] of Frederick Douglass* (1845) was so well received that it was translated into most European languages, and the *Narrative of William Wells Brown* (1847) sold so well that it went into four American editions and one English edition within two years."[19] These are cases, even the doubtful one of James Williams, in which popularity does follow the display of art, and not even the claim of fabrication can stimulate in the long run the persistence of reader interest. Leaving the Williams narrative aside for the moment, we can find substantial reasons in the remaining three tales for their distinction, and we can say, finally, that in the achievement of Douglass, Brown, and Bibb the slave narrative fused effectively the qualities of rhetoric and art.

The three narratives are very different, though they resemble each other in following clearly understood principles of organization. They display unity and power, offering in varied ways authoritative pictures of the barbarity and inhumanity of the slave system, though without the excesses of cruelty and sadism so lavishly distributed through Roper's autobiography. The sense of the brutal world of the black slave is projected through a growing intelligence that recognizes gradually the need for freedom and for community and that learns the value of dissimulation in order to achieve this end. All three narratives display the virtues that Benjamin Quarles attributes to Douglass's account, sensitivity in the "descriptions of persons and places" and "ability to mingle incident with argument."[20] It should be added that no recollection by a slave quite matches Douglass's in its power to suggest the special character of place, incorporating the significant details of land, water, work, and social organization on large and small plantations on the Eastern Shore of Maryland. In the three autobiographies there is an awareness of audience, to which are attributed principles of morality and religion, an affection for family and home, and a belief in the healthy influence of work and sobriety, though little or no firsthand knowledge of the slave system. Quarles, in describing Douglass's ideas about his readers, might be referring also to Brown and Bibb: "He [Douglass] did not propose to speak to Negroes exclusively; he wanted all America, if not all the world, for his sounding board."[21] What surfaces again, as with David Walker, is the assumption of the presence of a mixed group of readers: the blacks look to the author as a spokesman and truth-teller and the whites find an educator and a persuasive voice forcing them to take seriously a problem they might otherwise ignore.

Though the details in the slave stories are often quite similar, so much so that a devoted reader of the narratives might accurately anticipate what might follow from page to page, the impression left by Douglass, Brown, and Bibb is that of entry into a unique world. Each author had his own approach to oppression, separate and different from others, and each abandoned the effort to present the institution of slavery in any comprehensive way in favor of concentrating upon and developing what was important to him.

For Douglass it was the growth in his intellectual competence, the increase in his yearning for freedom, and the search for a community in which he could achieve an amount of self-realization. These objectives he pursued against a most unpromising background. He had no education aside from three sessions in a sabbath school at St. Michael's in Maryland, broken up by Christian slaveholders, who considered a slave's literacy to be dangerous and potentially subversive, even though the point of the instruction was to learn to read the Bible. There was no encouragement for Douglass to seek freedom. No one in his immediate family was free, and anything other than rigid conformity with the wishes of the master or overseer might be punished. His introduction to the penalty suffered by those who disobeyed was being awakened as a child at dawn by the shrieks of an aunt who was being beaten for her interest in a slave who lived on a neighboring plantation. The master had his own reasons for this act of excessive cruelty, and these did not bear inspection. The prospect for Douglass's discovering a community that might sustain and nourish him was similarly bleak. Douglass never knew his father and he saw his mother no more than four or five times.[22] Indeed, he was deliberately separated from his mother as an infant. There are in the *Narrative* few references to other members of his family, though these are made more of in a later account of this early period of his life.[23] He began life, we are told, without the "ties that ordinarily bind children to their homes," and he was moved to say in recollection in 1845: "My home was charmless, it was not home to me. . . ." As a consequence, Douglass welcomed his departure for Baltimore to serve a new master, even though he was leaving at a tender age, "between seven and eight years old,"[24] the area of his birth and early childhood.

An exciting development grew from these meager beginnings. Douglass learned his ABC's from his mistress in Baltimore before she discovered from her husband that correct behavior toward slaves frowned upon such instruction. He managed to continue his learning to read by bribing with bread willing young white scholars and poring over a copy of *The Columbian Orator,* which he purchased in 1831. Acquiring the skill to write was no less difficult. It began with the challenge of the initials on pieces of timber at a Baltimore shipyard where he worked, advanced to copying italics in *Webster's Spelling Book* and competition with more knowing school boys, and continued with the filling of the spaces in the discarded copybook of the son of his master. All signs of progress had to be hidden, of course, since writing, like reading, was a skill of mystery and power that was denied a slave. The single event that made this all possible was his departure for Baltimore, remembered in later years as the manifestation of a kind providence in his life.[25]

Douglass charted with equal care the growth of the need to be free, though the desire seems always to have been with him: "From my earliest recollection, I date the entertainment of a deep conviction that slavery would not always be able to hold me within its foul embrace. . . ." Baltimore was of great importance in this respect too because it was here that Douglass learned a trade, calking at a shipyard, and became equipped subsequently to hire out his time through an arrangement with his master. He experienced just enough of the existence of a free man and of an independent worker to wish for the real thing and not the poor counterfeit article: ". . . whenever my condition was improved, instead of its increasing my contentment, it only increased my desire to be free. . . ." The crisis moment in his feelings about liberty occurred not in Baltimore but back on the Eastern Shore, when Douglass was assigned to a small plantation operator named Covey for the purpose of being broken. But this was not to be. It was Douglass who whipped Covey, after suffering six months of harsh and capricious treatment, and the ex-slave recalled the triumph as "the turning-point in . . . [his] career as a slave," as the spark that "rekindled the few expiring embers of freedom, and revived within . . . [him] a sense of [his] own manhood."[26]

A home and a place within a community were aspirations to be satisfied last within the *Narrative*. Douglass received intimations of the value of participating in black community life during a year spent on the plantation of his most liberal master on the Eastern Shore. There he taught sabbath school to slaves with fewer advantages than he possessed, doing so, of course, in the face of a general prohibition placed upon activities of this kind and memories of an earlier failure. The young teacher persevered despite the risks, and, in later years, recollected the effort with affection: "The work of instructing my dear fellow-slaves was the sweetest engagement with which I was ever blessed." Other substantial satisfactions of this kind were not to be had in bondage. After his departure from Baltimore, Douglass pursued more directly his search for home in its broadest sense. He was married in New York and was introduced later by Nathan Johnson into the spirited black community of New Bedford. The sign that announced his arrival in an environment giving him human dimension was a change of name—no longer "Bailey," identified with slavery, or "Johnson," with flight, but "Douglass," to be associated with new prospects and new life. Douglass discovered *The Liberator* in New Bedford, a challenge for his hard-won literacy and an inspiration ("My soul was set all on fire"), and through it he gained admission to an even wider community of the antislavery crusade. How prophetic was the remark made quite early in the *Narrative* about the mystery attached to "abolition" and "abolitionist,"[27] when he was struggling to learn to read and to write! The three intertwined threads of Douglass's story achieve a satisfactory design almost simultaneously at the end of the *Narrative*: an intellectually mature and free man stands at last in New Bedford, in his own home, in a black community that welcomes him, and in a broader family of committed reformers that will inspire him to do noble work.

If Douglass's story can be called a work in the "heroic fugitive school of American literature,"[28] Brown's would carry a tag indicating something quite opposed to the heroic. There is precious little heroism in Brown's slave world, and bold strokes against oppression are not conceivable. Douglass triumphed over the wicked system, largely through the strength of his own will and intelligence; Brown escaped from slavery almost by accident, since he was beset by hypocritical and sadistic masters and overseers, lustful and deceitful slave drivers, and treacherous blacks. He encountered only two good men. One, the editor Lovejoy, though destined to become a martyr to the cause of abolition outside of the limits of this narrative, was helpless to protect Brown from a punishment that was cruel and undeserved, and the second, Wells Brown, was the fugitive's savior, though he might just as easily have been the self-righteous agent who would return the desperate runaway to bondage.[29] Edmund Quincy, one of the leaders of the fight against slavery, observed, "It is a terrible picture of slavery,"[30] and he should know, since he had recorded and reviewed a number of such accounts as an Abolitionist editor. The author of the "Preface" of the original edition, J.C. Hathaway, put his reaction to Brown's account more dramatically: "This little book is a voice from the prison-house, unfolding deeds of darkness which are there perpetrated."[31]

Two organizing principles give shape to Brown's *Narrative*. The first is the gradual growth of the desire to escape from slavery, a development which resembles Douglass's in that it relates more to the acquisition of intellectual maturity and sophistication than to any sharp change in oppressive conditions. Brown followed Douglass also in making the leap for freedom when he was serving a relatively benign master, Captain Enoch Price, a steamboat owner and commission merchant, not a brutally oppressive one. The second principle, the one referred to by critics with some frequency,[32] is the exposure, by accident, of course, but with the appearance of system, to all aspects of the peculiar institution, on the plantation and in the city; in the border states and in the deep South; and on the road, including travelling with a slave coffle on land and working on a riverboat carrying the human cargo from St. Louis to New Orleans. Small wonder that Quincy would tell Brown: "Your opportunities of observing the workings of this accursed system have been singularly great."[33] And the consequence of such a comprehensive review was the discovery of corruption and inhumanity everywhere in the slave culture.

Early in the *Narrative*, Brown admitted that his hope for liberty was tempered by a sense of obligation to his family. But the family was a fragile unit, a mother and seven children, no two of whom had the same father. Disruption came to the family when Brown was still young. He recalled that his master sold his mother and all of her children, except him, to different persons in St. Louis, and he commented on the event as a cause of "great unhappiness." Despite this separation, Brown remained close to his mother and to his sister, whom he refused to leave in bondage. After his sister was sold to a slaveowner bound for Mississippi, Brown made an abortive effort to achieve an escape to Canada with his mother, but the failure of this attempt resulted only in his mother's sale and departure for New Orleans, with the prospect of a hard life and an early death on a cotton, sugar, or rice plantation. These bitter experiences increased Brown's desire for freedom, to the point that the slave willingly accepted the hazards of winter when he undertook finally to make his escape.[34]

In Brown's account, there is neither the record of education achieved despite great difficulties nor the discovery of a rudimentary community life among blacks in slavery, both of which we see in Douglass's *Narrative*. Education for Brown is wholly a matter of survival, learning the ways of the master and the slave driver so that he might profit by that knowledge. There is no community to join nor prospect of one on the point of appearing, since trust in another human being is entirely unthinkable on the part of a slave: "The slave is brought up to look upon every white man as an enemy to him and his race; and twenty-one years in slavery had taught me that there were traitors, even among colored people."[35]

The Brown *Narrative* offers a careful unveiling of one facet after another of the business of owning, working, transporting, and selling slaves, and the accumulation of Brown's observations and experiences, all described in a calm and reserved manner, creates a picture of slavery in the South of unparalleled ugliness. The story includes a record of life on plantations in Kentucky and Missouri, where Brown was a house boy and a field hand; an account of residence in St. Louis, where he worked both within a household and for business establishments when his time was bought from his master; and recollections of travel on the Mississippi, Missouri, and Ohio Rivers and to the farms and villages that lie along them, as an assistant to a slave driver and as steward on a riverboat. Acts of brutality against slaves are to be observed everywhere, beginning with witnessing the beating of his own mother by an overseer for the offense of arriving late in the fields, an ominous inauguration. The atrocities mount relentlessly: a slave woman dies as a consequence of a whipping; one black man is burned at the stake, and another is drowned in the Mississippi—acts of violence committed for trivial, capricious, or unknown reasons. Though ingenious punishments abound in Moses Roper's narrative, they move us less than do the more ordinary and apparently routine penalties for slave misbehavior that appear in Brown's tale because the recorder here is not an incorrigible runaway who would not stay put, no matter what the seriousness of the menace to body and life, but a sober, responsible observer, who performed tasks assigned to him with care and efficiency. Brown exploded the myth of slavery as a benign institution in the border states: "Though slavery is thought by some to be mild in Missouri, when compared with cotton, sugar and rice growing states, yet no part of our slaveholding country is more noted for the barbarity of its inhabitants than St. Louis."[36]

Slavery was cruel, barbaric, and inhumane everywhere in the South. The system encouraged the satisfaction of the lowest emotions in the dominant whites: lust, as exhibited by the slave driver intent upon seducing the quadroon girl in his charge; sadism, in the outraged man who bought a slave coachman whose carriage had splashed mud on him simply to inflict exorbitant and excessive punishment upon his victim; duplicity, as displayed by the master who sold a slave boy down the river and informed the slave's family subsequently that the boy had died of yellow fever. Not the least of the vices was something less dramatic—a callousness to the feelings of other humans when the problem was one involving only convenience: a slave driver separated a small child from its mother because he was irritated by the child's crying.[37]

There was no protection for blacks in the system. Spiritual fortitude, intelligence, responsibility, and Christian virtue were of no help save to bring a few more dollars at the auction block. Innocence could not survive, and the stoutest of female hearts could not withstand seduction. Nor was there protection in physical strength, as the story of the breaking of Randall, a mighty slave, demonstrated all too clearly.[38] Frederick Douglass's successful defiance of the overseer Covey would be impossible in Brown's world.

No part of the South was untouched by the diabolical system, from Senator Benton and a doctor of divinity with a local reputation for learning and piety to the poor whites scratching out a living on the sandy hills. No white man in the South was a good master, a flat denial of a possibility projected in *Uncle Tom's Cabin,* and no one, white or black, had integrity. Corruption extended to Brown himself, who, threatened with punishment, deceived a black free man who received the whipping that was intended for Brown; and the sad comment on this act when it is recollected is not to be challenged: "This incident shows how it is that slavery makes its victims lying and mean. . . ."[39] And the judgment applies to all who live within the region where slavery was sanctioned. Slavery corrupts the whole South and parts of the North where the institution is respected, and it appears to corrupt totally all persons involved in the vicious system. Brown has made art from a sober, careful documentation of depravity, and he has used well a style that is distinguished for its simplicity and stark economy. It requires no great step to move from the *Narrative* to *Clotel,* Brown's novel and the first ever published by an American black,[40] in which the blight of the institution extended to the White House itself.

Though the narratives of Douglass and Brown are quite different from each other, both are far removed from that of Henry Bibb. In some ways the stories of Douglass and Brown are similar in kind and seem to profit from the same general sort of inspiration; both present the struggle of talented individuals in resisting the slave power, which threatens in one instance to deprive the hero of the development of his intellectual abilities and his achievement of manhood, and in the other to corrupt the humanity of the hero and to rob him of any expectation of a better moral life. The stress in Bibb's story is not upon self-realization of the individual but upon the protection of the family and the home. Bibb is concerned with domestic virtues that are either minimized or ignored by Douglass and Brown. It is true that Douglass did marry at the end of his story, but only after freedom had been secured. Even then the home in New Bedford is subordinated to the discovery of two larger communities, that of the blacks in the city and that of the Massachusetts Abolitionists.[41] The wife of his last master proposed to arrange a marriage for Brown with an available female slave within the household, but he recognized this as a trick to keep him in bondage and resisted it successfully, first by deception and then by flight.[42] There are no diverting details of courtship in slavery in either account, but these are important to Bibb, who recorded with accuracy the progress of passion. In short, Bibb's narrative has its own special ordering principle, one that is well understood and pursued with success.

Quite early in his recollections, Bibb outlined the nature of the conflict which stands at the center of his story: "And I believed then, as I believe now, that every man has a right to wages for his labor; a right to his own wife and children; a right to liberty and the pursuit of happiness; and a right to worship God according to the dictates of his own conscience."[43] Though slavery denies the validity of all such "rights" for those held in bondage, the two that the narrative turns on are the "right to . . . wife and children" and the "right to liberty," which become for Bibb irreconcilable. He could not achieve both, though he exhibited much energy and imagination, and suffered great hardship in order to try to do so.

Bibb's story divides itself into two parts. A short early section describes courtship, marriage, and a brief period of happiness; a much longer division of the whole presents Bibb's vain efforts to rescue from slavery his wife and daughter. The culmination of the action is not the hero's liberation from bondage, because Bibb made good his escape from slavery no less than three times, but his acceptance that his wife and daughter would be forever lost to him.

The preparation for marriage offers a progress that seems familiar, with only its occurrence within the institution of slavery contributing an element of strangeness. Bibb initially resisted involvement with the attractive slave girl Malinda, but he could not control his passion for her: "I suffered myself to be turned aside by the fascinating charms of a female, who gradually won my attention from an object so high as that of liberty; and an object which I held paramount to all others." He overcame massive opposition to achieve his romantic desire—the resistance of his mother, who thought him too young; of his mother-in-law, who thought him too poor; of his master, who feared the loss of his farm products to a wife and her offspring; and of other male slaves, who desired Malinda for themselves. He defied the lack of legal sanctions for a slave marriage by giving his complete faith to an informal and improvised ceremony: "Clasping each other by the hand, pledging our sacred honor that we would be true, we called on high heaven to witness the rectitude of our purpose."[44] The romantic venture seemed destined for success when Bibb was sold to Malinda's master and when a beautiful baby girl was born.

Bibb was moved to escape from slavery for reasons old and new. His old aspiration was not dead; his desire remained for liberty, that "high" object which he rejected for marriage. Even more serious was a disturbing consequence of life with Malinda. Bibb discovered that he could not bear witnessing inflicted upon his wife the "insults, scourgings and abuses, such as common to be inflicted upon slaves." He left his wife and daughter on Christmas day carrying "all the love of home and birth-place which is so natural among the human family."[45]

Bibb in subsequent years made continued and untiring efforts to recover what was "natural" for other Americans. He was not deterred by initial failure, and he returned a second time to rescue his family, only to suffer capture himself. Nor did he give up when the family was sold south to a cotton planter on the Red River in Louisiana, who mouthed Christian platitudes and practiced cruelty and brutal exploitation in the treatment of his slaves. A final attempt came to nothing, and Bibb was flogged, placed in irons, and removed permanently from his family. He was sold to a company of Southern sportsmen who, despite their questionable morality, were persuaded by Bibb to make an offer for his wife and child, but the pious cotton planter, possessing less compassion than the gamblers, rejected the offer. And in December 1840, exactly five years after his first leap for freedom, Bibb was forced to leave his family, never to see his wife or his child again.[46]

The desire to free his family lingered in Bibb's mind for another five years. During that period he escaped once more, found employment in Perrysburgh, Ohio, received a little education in Detroit, and joined the Abolitionist crusade to tell the story of "sufferings and adventures, connected with slavery." In 1845, he returned to the South again to seek news of his family, and he discovered then that his wife had been living in a state of adultery with her master for three years.[47] After a decade of commitment to protecting the institution most cherished by American culture, Bibb abandoned hope for the recovery of his original family. Though there are atrocities in his story that bear comparison in cruelty and barbarism with anything in the narratives by Douglass and Brown, the essential force of Bibb's attack on slavery rests in the destruction of the domestic happiness of people who might be the reader's neighbors, so much do they share sentiments, values, and aspirations. The power of Bibb's tale is here, and its art comes from the ordering of the familiar details of the slave accounts to point up the pathetic battle of a virtuous and loving family against the overwhelming opposition of the slave system.

Bibb married again, as he faced bravely a profound disorder which he could not control, and the terms that apply to the new wife lack the fervor of those describing the old: ". . . a bosom friend, a help-meet, a loving companion in all the social, moral, and religious relations of life." Receiving this portion of belated happiness prompted an observation about the new wife that generalized about the sad fate of Malinda: "She [the new wife] is to me what a poor slave's wife can never be to her husband while in the condition of a slave; for she [the slave wife] can not be true to her husband contrary to the will of her master. She can neither be pure nor virtuous, contrary to the will of her master."[48]

So unique is the art in each of the narratives of Douglass, Brown, and Bibb that we are likely to overlook the many qualities which they hold in common. These are primarily the facts that describe reality for many slaves: birth at a time which cannot be precisely determined and without the presence of a father; early separation from the mother; hard labor from dawn to dark with little food or clothing and few conveniences in the slave cabin; introduction to the brutality of slavery by witnessing the flogging of a female relative; sexual abuse of slave women by masters, overseers, and slave drivers; exposure to severe punishments for trivial offenses; justified fear of being sold down river, to the cotton, rice, and sugar plantations of the deep South; denial of education, often of religious instruction as well; restriction of movement by patrollers and a demeaning system of passes; lack of legal sanction for marriage; use of bloodhounds to capture runaway slaves; possession by the master of complete dominion over the slave, with the power to maim and to kill with impunity; exploitation of the skills of slaves who are hired out without the expectation of receiving pay of any kind; and a wide range of sadistic punishments that were reserved for runaway slaves, involving flogging, confinement, and the use of irons. It is only the art of telling that accounts for our sense of the vast differences in atmosphere, characterization, and action that separates one tale from another.

One form of shared matter that enriches all three narratives is the documentation with some care of the customs of a unique black folk life. Of the three writers, Bibb supplies most details and Brown least. Bibb described various forms of conjuration, involving bitter root, powders, cow manure, red pepper, hair, and even the bone of a bullfrog; and he reported sadly that none of the rituals and devices of tricking and witchcraft worked, either to prevent a flogging or to attract a girl.[49] Douglass consulted a conjurer to secure protection from punishment, and relied, with no success, upon the powers of a certain root,[50] and Brown sought the advice of a fortune-teller before he made his leap for freedom.[51] Bibb referred to the dance "pat juber" and commented, not without criticism, on slave participation in leisure moments in singing, wrestling, fighting, butting, jumping, running, and drinking whiskey.[52] Douglass had much to say about the plaintive melodies of the wild slave songs, conveying often not joy or simple delight but despair which found relief in music, and he commented, as well, on the sports, fiddling, dancing, and drinking that were the distractions ("gross fraud," Douglass says) for the slave at Christmas time.[53] Though there is not much material of this sort, it has an importance beyond the space it occupies. Its presence suggests that blacks, despite intimidation, oppression, and deprivation, had a shared life only dimly seen by the master and the overseer. We catch here only the low hum of an existence that is made up of traditional responses to basic needs, but that hum provides a valuable perspective for the brutal stories that attract the center of our interest.

The intense impression of black suffering that endures in the autobiographies of Douglass, Brown, and Bibb accounts, finally, for neither the popularity of these narratives nor, perhaps, for many of the characteristics of their art. For answers to these problems we must look elsewhere, indeed to the general American tradition to which black writers responded, either consciously or unconsciously. A life story like an argument acquires shape from inherited precedents, so deeply embedded in the enveloping culture that they are assumed without comment rather than adopted with a full sense of their influence. We get a clearer perception of what these precedents were by looking at the slave narratives that were discovered to be fictitious or partly fictitious because in them we see the design of the author's work that is not compromised by an obligation to record accurately life experience. This is why the narratives of Archy Moore[54] and James Williams have a certain fascination for us.

The Slave: or Memoirs of Archy Moore is a novel written by Richard Hildreth, better known for his later work in American history,[55] published in 1836 with an advertisement from the alleged editor which read: "It is sufficient for me to say, that I received it, with an injunction to make it public."[56] Receiving was in fact writing; Hildreth constructed the tale during a period of residence in Florida for reasons of health. It may be inaccurate still to say that he manufactured the work from whole cloth since there is evidence of a close observation of plantation life, but Hildreth was not Archy, who existed only in the mind of the author. There was a real James Williams, as we know, and what remains a question is whether or not he experienced in fact all of the acts of oppression and the adventures which he claimed. The two tales, representing truth or fiction or, perhaps better stated, truth *and* fiction, had an impressive vogue, as the prefatory notices of modern reprints of the slave narratives have accurately maintained.[57] Their popularity, clearly, involved something other than truth—rather, indeed, patterns of taste and artistic conventions that had won widespread acceptance in the culture well beyond the heat of political controversy.

Though the passion that moved Hildreth was undoubtedly the hatred of slavery, the form of his novel came from the sentimental fiction of his day. The novel, despite its impressive documentation of the declining state of the plantation economy,[58] is essentially a pathetic story of frustrated love. Archy and Cassy, notwithstanding their slave origins, were acceptable figures in a contemporary romance because they were creatures of sensitivity, honor, and high breeding.[59] They met, fell in love, married, and gave birth to a son. They seemed well on the way to enjoying the blessings of a happy home, despite the restrictions of the slave system, when disruption occurred. The arch-villain of the piece was their common father, Colonel Moore, a distinguished Virginia aristocrat, who displayed an unnatural affection for his lovely daughter Cassy. Though there seemed to be no objection in the novel to a blooming and fertile love joining a half brother and a half sister, there was, understandably, much expressed horror at the Colonel's intention to make his daughter his mistress, by force if necessary.[60] Archy was sold and drifted from one plantation to another until he escaped from bondage. During this period there was one happy reunion for the family, which was all too brief. The villain forcing the new separation was not another lecherous plantation owner with Colonel Moore's tastes, not a person at all, but the system. Hildreth showed that a Southern plantation, aside from an exception here and there, was an unprofitable economic venture, condemning slaves to a precarious existence no matter what good intentions had been expressed by masters and mistresses.[61]

Hildreth extracted ideas from the tradition of sentimental fiction and contributed with his art to a shift occurring within it. The sentimental novel underwent, during the sixty-one years separating the publication of Susannah Rowson's *Charlotte: A Tale of Truth* (1791) and Harriet Beecher Stowe's *Uncle Tom's Cabin* (1852), a transition that might be called the domestication of the genre. Ola Elizabeth Winslowe describes the change as a stripping off of "layer after layer of romance and moonlight from the literature of the average woman reader," assisting her "to plant her feet solidly on the American earth. . . ." Responsibility for shaping new tastes is attributed to the editor of the influential journal *Godey's Lady's Book*, Sara Josepha Hale, the novelist Catherine M. Sedgwick,[62] and a few other talented literary women, among whom would be included Lucy Larcom and Harriet Beecher Stowe. Women were more prominent, no doubt, in effecting this transformation, but men like Richard Hildreth made a contribution too. In the year after Catherine Sedgwick published *The Linwoods*,[63] in which careful description of life on a New England farm and of the mundane troubles of a New York family divided in its loyalties during the Revolutionary War stands beside the melodramatic coincidences, midnight excursions, and meditations on the destructive power of a broken heart, Hildreth "discovered" and issued Archy's tale, offering the same mixed bag of old lace and homespun.

The domestication of the genre brought a change in the structural elements of the novel. More and more documentation of background came now from the facts of common life—from the farms, the cities, the mills, and, indeed, the plantations. The American home became a center of attention and an object to be admired and protected. Novelists paid tribute to family contentment and the virtues of togetherness involving parents and children, avoiding the glorification of transcendent love demanding the sacrifice of all else. They adjusted familiar formulas that provided a basis for characterization. Hildreth, as we have seen, had no trouble attributing to Archy and Cassy high birth, elevated moral standards, and enduring loyalties despite their status as slaves. His approach to character definition resembled strongly that followed by Henry Bibb as he represented his relationship with his beloved Malinda and by Brown in *Clotel*.

An element of the sentimental novel that resisted change more strongly was event. Writers did not quickly relinquish the reliance upon coincidence, dramatic confrontation, and a rough scale of justice in which sins are paid for and virtues rewarded. Hildreth, though constructing a slave biography, did not neglect these conventions, so important in sentimental fiction. Archy and his loyal slave comrade, Thomas, in this spirit executed the brutal overseer who had whipped to death Thomas's wife, and they experienced together not the qualms of conscience of murderers but the "lofty feelings of manhood vindicated, and tyranny visited with a just retribution. . . ."[64]

One overall pattern for action Hildreth found to be especially useful in *The Slave*. Many novels in the sentimental tradition displayed a development offering a period of early happiness followed by an unforeseen catastrophic disruption and brave attempts to recover the innocence or the purity or the pleasant world that had been lost. Within the altered Hildreth perspective early bliss became childhood and marriage within the cultivated surroundings of a plantation in a border state. Disruption came from an abuse or an excess sanctioned by the slave system—the lust or the cruelty or the indifference of a master or a mistress and the collapse in the economy of the plantation. The inevitable consequence of disruption was the division of the slave family and the sale of its members to different owners in the deep South where conditions were hard and life cheap. Memories of lost happiness and intolerable oppression moved the efforts to secure freedom, and though these were ultimately successful, the full dimension of original delight was never recovered. Archy, at the end of his story, was a free man of wealth, culture, and position, but he mourned still the loss of Cassy and his son.[65]

The precedent provided by Hildreth's successful application of the formulas of sentimental fiction to the slave question was too strong to be ignored. It is likely that Henry Bibb and other ex-slaves in organizing and expressing their recollections of their life in slavery were touched by it. Bibb's *Narrative* seems especially close to *The Slave*. It is not simply a matter of the cultivated hero and heroine, already noted, but the emphasis upon home and the glorification of domestic virtues. There is the pattern of action too of happiness experienced and lost early and the record of extraordinary attempts to recover it. The sense of balance so peculiarly a characteristic of sentimental fiction is to be found also in the way Bibb's second marriage is justified and in his devotion to the antislavery cause. He would be the protector of the Christian family and denounce its destruction by slaveholders.

Though the facts of Bibb's *Narrative* are certainly true, offered with rich support from letters and a report by a respected committee of investigation, the shape these facts are given owes something to the influence of sentimental fiction. Contemporary publications, in reviewing Bibb's story, commented frequently on the apparent conflict. The *True Wesleyan* made the point: ". . . did we not know the author, and know from the best proof that the book is a true narrative, on reading it we should pronounce it a novel." The *New York Tribune* echoes this judgment in almost the same terms: "His [Bibb's] book has the attraction of a romance, though there was no romance in his sufferings."[66] We confront a phenomenon which is not uncommon, the power of art to condition memory or, more accurately, the way the memory records past experience, and we see once again a fusion of black life and American literary conventions, a fusion that moves readers much beyond the power of a simple report of the hard life in bondage.

The narratives by Douglass and Brown, though shaped essentially by a tradition quite different from the sentimental, contain some elements that suggest a trace of indebtedness. There is the moment on a summer Sunday when Douglass, a slave unhappy and restive under Covey's tyranny, looked at the boats sailing on the Chesapeake Bay and poured out a complaint which might appropriately come from the hero of a sentimental novel: "You are loosed from your moorings, and are free; I am fast in my chains, and am a slave! You move merrily before the gentle gale, and I sadly before the bloody whip! You are freedom's swift-winged angels, that fly around the world; I am confined in bands of iron! O that I were free!" There is no other romantic apostrophe of this kind in Douglass's story, but this one was important and functional, providing a background for the resistance to Covey's barbarous treatment. It is not then entirely surprising that the ex-slave should adopt the name "Douglass," a consequence of the impression made upon the consciousness of a New Bedford friend by *The Lady of the Lake* by Sir Walter Scott,[67] a work cherished by American readers with an affection for the sentimental.

The touch of the sentimental is to be found in Brown's autobiography too, though there are no apostrophes to the Mississippi River or to the steamers that made their way from New Orleans to St. Louis. Instead there are snatches of verse that appear throughout the *Narrative*, like the poem that reconstructs the emotions of a black slave mother when she is deprived of her baby. We find yet another echo of the sentimental novel which is more subtle, the emphasis upon a sense of balance based upon moral values. We are struck by the righting of supposed wrongs and by the payment of debts freely confessed as we move toward the conclusion of the *Narrative*. Brown favored woman's rights, an appropriate response somehow for the debt he owed to the white woman who fed him when he was a fugitive and to his mother, not to mention serving as a form of expiation for the sense of guilt which he felt for escorting slave women South as an assistant slave trader. In connection also with his contribution to the commerce in slaves, Brown informed us that he assisted a great number of fugitives in their successful escape to Canada, some sixty-nine in 1842, we are told. Brown embraced the temperance cause[68] and in his so doing we are reminded that he had observed the intoxicated behavior of passengers on the riverboats where he worked as a waiter and as a steward. All of these details are facts of life surely, but they have the neatness of fiction, and once again we must admit that the two are closer than we customarily suppose them to be.

The narratives of Douglass and Brown reflect the influence in large part finally of a tradition far removed from the sentimental. They resemble more the *Narrative of James Williams, an American Slave* than they do Hildreth's novel *The Slave*. In doing so they have responded more deeply to a religious than to a secular heritage.

Whittier's record of James Williams's recollections takes us to a form of religious opposition to slavery that had roots in the eighteenth century and which shaped in a way not to be denied the spirit and the tactics of the antislavery radicals of the 1830s. We touch through Whittier and Williams the itinerant Quaker minister John Woolman, who expressed his sense of the evils of slavery in Friends meetings up and down the East coast from New England to North Carolina and in England as well as in America, for a generation, from 1743, a year after he experienced an uneasiness of soul about the peculiar institution,[69] to his death in 1772. Though he wrote two influential essays on the problem, *Some Considerations on the Keeping of Negroes*, published in Philadelphia in 1754, and *Considerations on Keeping Negroes, Part Second*, printed in the same city in 1762,[70] Woolman exerted a greater force for reform in small groups of Friends, in which he faced directly Quakers of opposing views. From his remarkable *Journal* we gather that he was very persuasive in this context, even though, frequently, his was the only voice declaring the holding of slaves to be a sin. Participation in Friends meetings was often followed by individual conferences with slaveholders.[71] Always the emphasis in his work for God was upon giving testimony only when Woolman was deeply moved to render it and receiving it in the same spirit. What emerges from the *Journal* is an authentic voice, mild, insistent, and totally committed. Yet behind Woolman's quiet way was a sense of powerful urgency: "Many slaves of this continent are oppressed, and their cries have reached the ears of the Most High! . . . Should we now be sensible of what he requires of us, and . . . neglect to do our duty in firmness and constancy . . . it may be that by terrible things in righteousness God may answer us in this matter."[72]

The line connecting Woolman's thought and ministry to the leaders of the Abolitionist movement of the nineteenth century is clear and direct. Phillips P. Moulton, Woolman's modern editor, maintains that the influence came through Benjamin Lundy, a Quaker disciple, who published the paper *The Genius of Universal Emancipation* and who, in turn, "inspired William Lloyd Garrison to devote his life to the cause."[73] Woolman's influence shaped the methods of the reformers as well as their ideas, moving them to think in terms of persuasion and to rely upon meetings in small groups which encouraged testimony, confession, and ultimately conversion. Woolman bore partial responsibility, no doubt, for Garrison's strong prejudice against political action. There was no loss among the later Abolitionists of a sense of urgency; it was increased, indeed, and nowhere is it more clearly evident than it is in Whittier's "Preface" to Williams's *Narrative*, where it is given a form of poetic expression not found in the *Journal*: "The world will see it [American slavery] as God has always seen it; and when He shall at length make inquisition for blood, and His vengeance kindle over the habitations of cruelty, with a destruction more terrible than that of Sodom and Gomorrah, His righteous dealing will be justified of men, and His name glorified among the nations, and there will be a voice of rejoicing in Earth and in Heaven."[74]

It is tempting to say that Woolman's ideas came of age in the 1830s. The period was a time of anxieties about the coming apocalypse, forebodings much intensified by David Walker's *Appeal* and Nat Turner's insurrection. America, in fact, had not recovered fully from the convulsive emotional upheaval that had erupted shortly after the turn of the century, a wave of evangelism called the Second Great Awakening. A million Americans, it was said, dressed in ascension robes in 1833 in preparation for the descent of the sword of an angry God. The refuge provided by a small group of Christians committed to prayer, testimony, and conversion proved to be a strong attraction for many disturbed by the signs of the times, and the Abolitionist societies of the 1830s offered just the haven for the pious who saw slavery as an over-whelming plague upon the land.

Williams's *Narrative* must be seen against the background of the gathering of the faithful. His story then is a former slave's lengthy testimonial of his exposure to the hardships and the cruelty of slavery. At the conclusion of a tale crammed with references to beatings and murders caused by the slightest sign of resistance on the part of the helpless slave, Williams made the following appeal, unthinkable without a reasonably precise sense of his audience: "Oh, if the miserable men and women, now toiling on the plantations of Alabama, could know that thousands in the free states are praying and striving for their deliverance, how would the glad tidings be whispered from cabin to cabin, and how would the slave mother, as she watches over her infant, bless God, on her knees, for the hope that this child of her day of sorrow might never realize, in strife, and toil, and grief unspeak-able, what it is to be a slave!"[75]

Certain formal characteristics develop naturally from the cultivation of the method of telling a tale. The strength of a testimonial depends upon the sense of authenticity which the narrative projects. Fictional effects, though pleasing, are to be avoided in general, though even the most scrupulous of truth-tellers may find this hard to do. The narrator demands from his audience its complete belief, and to fulfill expectations his voice should be not only credible in terms of education and experience but consistent. The style of such a slave narrative may be expected to be simple and direct, with a tendency to emphasize facts and details of action rather than sentiments or observations that are intellectual or even general in nature. Archy Moore was never bound by such restrictions, but James Williams was.

The slightest variation in Williams's voice would invite challenge from Southern and Northern detractors, and this is not to take into consideration the facts of his story, which were indeed questioned. Williams had to display just the amount of knowledge that would be appropriate for a house slave on a well-to-do plantation owned by a Virginia family of some cultivation and distinction, a problem for the recorder-editor Whittier as well, who was fully aware of the difficulties. Moreover, time in the tale had to be accounted for with precision. For the primary audience, the convinced Christians already committed to the cause of abolition, rigor of this kind was, perhaps, less important than the voice that testified, but not so for the extended audience, those readers who might be converted and who looked upon such testimony with indifference, if not skepticism, initially. There is nothing fuzzy about the record of Williams's experience. Despite questions which were raised subsequently about the details of the life of the slave in Alabama, we receive a clear and apparently authoritative description of Williams's career. We know the facts about James: he was born in 1805, married in 1822, sent to Alabama as a slave driver in 1833. He made the break for freedom in 1837 and he arrived in New York City on January 1, 1838. Perhaps the very appearance of absolute accuracy annoyed slaveholders more than anything else and moved the campaign to discredit the account. Whittier and his friends, if they took the long view, should have had ambivalent feelings about this form of proslavery questioning since the challenge created a wider readership for the Williams narrative than it would otherwise have had, but there is no evidence that they were anything other than deeply disturbed by the possibility that Williams was not quite what he appeared to be. An ex-slave should not fabricate his sufferings, even though the fabrications might be true in general to the tenor of slave life in the deep South.

It seems likely that Southern doubt about the truth of the Williams account resulted in a new form of external documentation, to accompany the emphasis upon inner consistency and a precise ordering of events in time. The 1840s witnessed the emergence of elaborate prefaces or appendices for slave narratives, not simply the publication of assurance from editor-recorders. We now see letters from respected people with national and international reputations, recovery claims issued by irate slaveowners demanding the return of ungrateful and irresponsible slaves, reports of investigating committees, and odd documents, even at times irrelevant ones, that supply overwhelming proofs of the existence of actual persons, identifiable places, and infamous practices, laws, and customs.[76]

Though documentation, internal and external, became a constant element in the slave narratives, at times, even, an annoying or distracting one, it had less importance in moving readers than the authority and the integrity of the *voice* of the narrator. The voice itself was not simply the gift of God. It was a possession refined and honed by the performance of an ex-slave in recounting his experiences at antislavery meetings, before a group collected, no doubt, by the local Abolitionist society, often in churches in small towns in New England, New York, and the Midwest. Many authors of the slave narratives had had the chance to tell their stories again and again, perhaps beyond their ability to count the occasions, before they were recorded. Frederick Douglass first rose to speak of his life in halting, emotion-packed sentences in August 1841 at an Abolitionist meeting on Nantucket island.[77] After this memorable initiation, he was engaged by the Massachusetts Anti-Slavery Society to travel the reform circuit with the great men of the movement, William Lloyd Garrison and Wendell Phillips. He had the experience of telling his story over a period of four years before the publication of the *Narrative* in 1845. Brown, as early as 1843, was a lecturing agent for the Western New York Anti-Slavery Society, and in this capacity he had repeated the story of his life many times during the four years that preceded the appearance of his *Narrative* in 1847. William Farrison, Brown's biographer, thinks that the idea of writing the autobiography was conceived in New York, stimulated probably by the publication of Douglass's *Narrative*.[78]

The autobiographies of Douglass and Brown, unlike Bibb's, relied heavily upon the background of oral performance. Bibb's justification for publishing his life story was wholly different; he insisted on the novelty of his account, despite his appearance on many antislavery platforms. He anticipated the challenge from his audience: "My answer is, that in no place have I given orally the detail of my narrative; and some of the most interesting events of my life have never reached the public ear."[79] The narratives of Douglass and Brown share, then, certain stylistic qualities. Both are told in a language almost self-consciously simple and in a manner that is, on the whole, restrained. Individual tensions appear within each, forms of reaction against stylistic restraints. Douglass moved toward an open expression of outrage against slaveholders, Brown toward the pointing up of dramatic ironies produced by the slave system. Above all, the tone was pious, reflecting the confidence of the authors in their approaches to the

Christian faith. In manner and in matter what was written resembled Williams's *Narrative*; that is to say, a record of public truth-telling, stripped of intimate personal details, that would be appropriate as testimony before a sympathetic group possessing outstanding religious and moral standards.

Yet despite the religious context, the narratives took the character and the personality of their authors. Douglass described a condition of intense deprivation—of food, clothing, family, education, even the rudiments of Christian training, and prospect of a fulfilling life within a community, all disadvantages which the Christian hero with great effort could overcome. Brown dramatized the vulnerability to corruption of every person, high or low, touched by the slave system, and he expressed no confidence in change, not to mention redemption, short of the intervention of divine grace. Both deplored the hypocrisy of Southern Christianity, calling attention to the need to purge the church of self-righteous sinners, proclaimed to be the worst kind.[80] Douglass and Brown were preoccupied then with religious themes, matter which they managed to integrate skillfully into the apparently straightforward accounts of their lives. A part of the popularity of their stories may come from the fact that this melding of the religious and the secular was an old New England habit, if not to say an American compulsion.

There is much about the slave narratives that is reminiscent of an earlier set of tales involving the experience of Indian captivity. One characteristic they hold in common, aside from the obvious preoccupation with forced confinement in an alien society, is their great vogue. *The Sovereignty and Goodness of God, Together with the Faithfulness of His Promises Displayed: Being a Narrative of the Captivity and Restauration of Mrs. Mary Rowlandson,* originally published in Boston in 1682, was widely read for a century and a half, undergoing reissue in Boston well into the nineteenth century. A preface to an edition of 1930 states the case accurately: "No book of its period in America can boast equal evidence of enduring public favor with this work of a comparatively uneducated Lancaster goodwife. . . ."[81] Mrs. Rowlandson did more than write a popular book; she initiated a genre, since the publication of many accounts of captivity followed, often with the support of such influential Puritan divines as Cotton

Mather.[82] Richard Slotkin in *Regeneration Through Violence* claims that of the four narrative works that became best-sellers in the early eighteenth century, three were captivity narratives; the fourth, to be expected, was *Pilgrim's Progress.*[83]

Slotkin constructs an intriguing theory accounting for the vogue and having, conceivably, important implications regarding the wide audience for the slave narratives. He finds in the captivity tale a form of symbolic drama, a representation of the Puritan view of colonization in New England. The essential meaning of the ordeal of captivity for the Puritan rested upon this simple analogy: "The sufferer represents the whole chastened body of Puritan society; and the temporary bondage of the captive to the Indian is dual paradigm—of the bondage of the soul to the flesh and to the temptations arising from original sin, and of the self-exile of the English Israel from England. . . . The captive's ultimate redemption by the grace of Christ and the efforts of the Puritan magistrates is likened to the regeneration of the soul in conversion." Puritan ministers, intellectuals, and men of letters seized the new matter eagerly for their own purposes, for use in revival sermons, as evidence for philosophical and theological demonstrations, and as models for literary entertainment of a sober kind. Typical in many ways was Cotton Mather's employment of the narrative of Hannah Dustin's escape from captivity as the basis for a series of revival sermons delivered in 1694.[84] Later, well into the eighteenth century, Jonathan Edwards relied upon imagery derived from the Indian captivity tales to give dramatic power to the most disturbing, perhaps, of all revival sermons, "Sinners in the Hands of an Angry God."[85]

The descendants of Mather and Edwards found in the recollections of an escaped slave the symbolic drama discovered earlier in the Indian captivity tales. Garrison and his colleagues saw the condition of slavery as a great sin that corrupted the land, and they considered the suffering of the individual slave an ordeal that should be shared by all Christians desirous of purifying their souls. Each break for freedom by a slave was the operation of God's grace, a sure sign that liberation would come in time to all of the suffering slaves of the South and that a purging would come inevitably to a wayward and blighted America. Garrison responded to the news of the Nat Turner insurrection with a cry of triumph: "What we have long predicted . . . has commenced its fulfillment. The first step of the earthquake, which is ulti-mately to shake down the fabric of oppression, leaving not one stone upon another. . . ."[86] Another aspect of Garrison's view of the symbolic drama that was to be seen in the life of the ex-slave was his stout opposition to paying slaveholders to prevent them from hounding fugitives in the North, a practice thought to be trafficking with the Anti-Christ. This attitude is reflected in William Wells Brown's initial refusal to sanction negotiations by Edmund Quincy and other Boston friends for the purchase of his freedom from Brown's last master, Enoch Price: "God made me as free as he did Enoch Price, and Mr. Price shall never receive a dollar from me or my friends with my consent."[87]

There is, doubtless, no conclusive answer about how much the extension of an old Puritan analogue contributed to the popu-larity of the slave narrative. Its appeal in the small towns and villages of the North where Calvinism died slowly suggested that this notion had some basis in fact. In addition, old habits of mind could find reenforcement in fresh anxieties about the prospect of an apocalypse, anxieties based upon signs of God's intention other than those embodied in slave insurrections and slave es-capes.

Douglass and Brown brought authoritative documentation to one part of this symbolic structure of the nineteenth century, evidence of the hell that American slavery was, degrading and corrupting all people that it touched. Brown approached more closely the necessity for a total reliance upon God's grace; his salvation, like Mary Rowlandson's, seemed to depend upon out-side interference; Brown's benevolent Quaker, Wells Brown, re-sembled the efficient negotiator for Mrs. Rowlandson's libera-tion, the Puritan John Hoar of Concord, Massachusetts.[88] There is abundant evidence too of Douglass's awareness that his free-dom was fated, a firm part of God's design: "From my earliest recollection, I date the entertainment of a deep conviction that slavery would not always be able to hold me within its foul embrace; and in the darkest hours of my career in slavery, this living word of faith and spirit of hope departed not from me, but remained like ministering angels to cheer me through the gloom. This good spirit was from God, and to him I offer thanksgiving and praise."[89] In short, the pious demonstrations of God's presence in the affairs of men and women were to be found here in these testimonies, available for use by ministers of the cloth like Garrison and Phillips and their many followers in the North.

The fact not to be forgotten is that it is the art of the narratives of Douglass, Brown, and Bibb that moved their readers. The echoes reverberating from the religion of an earlier America and from sentimental fiction of the day were elements of their craft, shrewdly assimilated to give force and an increased range of reference to the facts of particular lives. This mixture of black slave realities and American forms of expression stirred an army of readers before the Civil War and gave to Harriet Beecher Stowe the ammunition which she needed to fire the blast that brought ever closer the conflict between the North and the South. Perhaps Lincoln exaggerated, but not by much when we consider the background for *Uncle Tom's Cabin*, the preparation to be found in the slave narratives. The slave autobiography in a few hands became impressive art, lingering since the 1830s in the imaginations of creative blacks and a few whites. It is not surprising then that it should provide a basis for a more sophisticated art of the time and that it should stand as a vestige of a not-to-be-forgotten past in the memories of such writers, otherwise dissimilar, as Booker T. Washington, Richard Wright, Ralph Ellison, Malcolm X, and Ishmael Reed.

1979

Notes

1. Quoted by Quarles in *Black Abolitionists*, p. 11. Letter written May 14, 1828, in *The Works of Daniel Webster*, ninth edition (Boston, 1856), V, 367.
2. Quarles, *Black Abolitionists*, p. 18.
3. Charles H. Nichols, *Many Thousand Gone: The Ex-Slaves' Account of Their Bondage and Freedom* (Bloomington and London: Indiana University Press, 1974), p. xii.
4. James Williams, *Narrative of James Williams, an American Slave* (Boston: Isaac Knapp; New York: American Anti-Slavery Society, 1838. Reprint. Phila-

delphia, Pa.: Rhistoric Publication No. 215 in Afro-American History Series, ed. Maxwell Whiteman, 1969), p. xvii. The *Narrative* was dictated to Whittier.

5. Nichols, pp. ix–x.

6. Paul Edwards, ed., *Equiano's Travels, His Autobiography* (London and Ibadan: Heinemann Educational Books, Ltd., 1969), p. viii.

7. Ibid., p. 43.

8. Ibid., p. xvi.

9. Nichols, p. x.

10. Maxwell Whiteman, "Introduction," *Narrative of James Williams*, p. [2] of "Introduction."

11. John G. Whittier, "Preface," *Narrative of James Williams*, pp. xviii–xix.

12. Whiteman, "Introduction," *Narrative of James Williams*, p. [2].

13. Mrs. Stowe had read the *Life of Josiah Henson, formerly a Slave, Now an Inhabitant of Canada. Narrated by Himself*, which appeared in Boston in 1849, and profited by the editorial skills of Samuel A. Eliot. She depended also upon *American Slavery As It Is: Testimony of a Thousand Witnesses* (New York, 1839), compiled by Theodore Weld.

14. (Philadelphia, Pa.: Merrihew and Gunn, Printers, 1838. Reprint. Philadelphia, Pa.: Rhistoric Publication No. 236 in Afro-American History Series, ed. Maxwell Whiteman, 1969), p. 5. First published in London, 1837.

15. Ibid., p. 15.

16. Ibid., pp. 18, 17, 19, 20, 48, 49.

17. Ibid., pp. 60, 51, 24.

18. Ibid., p. 88.

19. Maxwell Whiteman, "Henry Bibb, Determined Fugitive" (Introduction), *Narrative of the Life and Adventures of Henry Bibb, An American Slave, Written by Himself, with an Introduction by Lucius C. Matlac*, Third Stereotype Edition (New York: Published by the Author, 1850. Reprint. Philadelphia, Pa.: Rhistoric Publication No. 204, 1969), p. [1] of Introduction. First published in 1849.

20. Benjamin Quarles, "Introduction," *Narrative of the Life of Frederick Douglass, an American Slave. Written by Himself* (Cambridge, Mass.: The Belknap Press of the Harvard University Press, 1967), p. xvii. First published in 1845.

21. Ibid., p. xix.

22. Douglass, *Narrative*, pp. 85, 29, 24.

23. In *My Bondage and My Freedom* (New York and Auburn: Miller, Orton and Mulligan, 1855).

24. Douglass, *Narrative*, pp. 53, 52.

25. Ibid., pp. 58, 65–66, 70–71, 56.

26. Ibid., pp. 56, 132–139, 133, 104.

27. Ibid., pp. 114, 151, 153, 69.

28. Quarles, "Introduction," *Narrative of the Life of Frederick Douglass*, p. xvi.

29. William Wells Brown, *Narrative of William W. Brown, A Fugitive Slave, Written by Himself*, 2nd Edition, Enlarged (Boston: Published at the Anti-Slavery Office, 1848. Reprint. Reading, Mass.: Addison-Wesley Publishing Co., 1969), pp. 9, 44.

30. Cited by Larry Gara, "Introduction," *Narrative of William W. Brown*, p. ix, from a letter from Edmund Quincy to Caroline Weston, July 2, 1847, in the Weston Papers, Boston Public Library.
31. J.C. Hathaway, "Preface," *Narrative of William W. Brown*, p. xxv.
32. Letter from Edmund Quincy, Esq., to William W. Brown, July 1, 1847, in prefatory matter for Brown's *Narrative*, p. xxiii.
33. Ibid.
34. Brown, *Narrative*, pp. 1, 7, 10, 34, 42.
35. Ibid., p. 42.
36. Ibid., pp. 2, 8, 9, 25, 8.
37. Ibid., pp. 18, 8, 26, 19.
38. Ibid., p. 3.
39. Ibid., pp. 37, 23.
40. *Clotel; or, the President's Daughter: A Narrative of Slave Life in the United States, With a Sketch of the Author's Life* (London, 1853).
41. Douglass, *Narrative*, pp. 146, 148–153.
42. Brown, *Narrative*, pp. 39–41.
43. Bibb, *Narrative*, p. 17.
44. Ibid., pp. 33, 39–40, 38.
45. Ibid., pp. 42, 47.
46. Ibid., pp. 134–149.
47. Ibid., pp. 178, 188.
48. Ibid., pp. 191, 191–192.
49. Ibid., pp. 23–30.
50. Douglass, *Narrative*, p. 102.
51. Brown, *Narrative*, p. 40.
52. Bibb, *Narrative*, p. 23.
53. Douglass, *Narrative*, pp. 36, 106–107.
54. Richard Hildreth, *The Slave: or Memoirs of Archy Moore* (N.p.: John H. Eastburn, 1836. Reprint. Upper Saddle River, N.J.: The Gregg Press, 1968).
55. Richard Hildreth, *History of the United States*, 6 vols. (New York, 1849–52).
56. Hildreth, "Advertisement," *The Slave*, p. [iii].
57. The note entitled "Richard Hildreth" in *The Slave* asserts that the novel is "an abolitionist classic second only to *Uncle Tom's Cabin* in its inflammatory effects on Northern opinion . . ." (p. x), and the preface to Bibb's *Narrative*, cited before, states that Williams's story is "outstanding."
58. See Hildreth, *The Slave*, I, 164–165.
59. Archy says: ". . . both on the father's and the mother's side, I had running in my veins, the best blood of Virginia—the blood . . . of the Moores and the Randolphs!" (*The Slave*, I, 19).
60. Hildreth, *The Slave*, I, 53–54.
61. Ibid., II, 55–58.
62. "Books for the Lady Reader, 1820–1860," in *Romanticism in America*, ed. George Boas (Baltimore: The Johns Hopkins Press, 1940), p. 108.
63. *The Linwoods: or, "Sixty Years Since" in America*, 2 vols. (New York: Harper & Brothers, 1835).

64. Hildreth, *The Slave*, II, 117–118.
65. Ibid., II, 162.
66. Reviews quoted in Bibb, *Narrative*, p. 206.
67. Douglass, *Narrative*, pp. 96, 148.
68. Brown, *Narrative*, pp. 19–20, 48, 49.
69. *The Journal and Major Essays of John Woolman*, ed. Phillips P. Moulton (New York: Oxford University Press, 1971), p. 33.
70. Ibid., pp. 198–237.
71. A typical entry in the *Journal* suggesting Woolman's methods is recorded after a visit to Rhode Island in 1760: "We had five meetings in Narragansett and thence to Newport. . . . In several families in the country where we [Woolman was accompanied by another Friend, Samuel Eastburn] lodged, I felt an engagement in my mind to have a conference with them in private concerning their slaves, and through divine aid I was favoured to give up thereto. Though in this thing I appear singular [peculiar, different] from many whose service in travelling I believe is greater than mine, I do not think hard of them for omitting it. I do not repine at having so unpleasant a task assigned to me. . . ." *The Journal and Major Essays*, pp. 107–108.
72. *The Journal and Major Essays*, p. 93.
73. Phillips P. Moulton, "Introduction," *The Journal and Major Essays*, pp. 13–14.
74. Whittier, "Preface," *Narrative of James Williams*, p. xxii.
75. Williams, *Narrative*, p. 99.
76. An example of the range of external documentation is to be seen either in the "Introduction" to Bibb's *Narrative*, pp. i–x, or the "Appendix" supplied for the second edition of Brown's *Narrative*, pp. 54–77.
77. Douglass, *Narrative*, p. 153.
78. William Edward Farrison, *William Wells Brown, Author and Reformer* (Chicago and London: The University of Chicago Press, 1969), pp. 81, 112.
79. Bibb, *Narrative*, p. xi.
80. Douglass wrote in his *Narrative*: "I assert most unhesitatingly, that the religion of the south is a mere covering for the most horrid crimes,—a justifier of the most appalling barbarity,—a sanctifier of the most hateful frauds,—and a dark shelter under which the darkest, foulest, grossest, and most infernal deeds of slaveholders find the strongest protection" (p. 110). And Brown commented, after an abortive attempt to escape: "The men who but a few hours before had bound my hands together with a strong cord, read a chapter from the Bible, and then offered up prayer, just as though God had sanctioned the act he had just committed upon a poor, panting fugitive slave" (*Narrative*, p. 32).
81. Frederick Lewis Weis, "Preface," *The Narrative of the Captivity and Restoration of Mrs. Mary Rowlandson* (Boston: Houghton Mifflin Co., 1930), p. v.
82. Richard Slotkin, *Regeneration Through Violence: The Mythology of the American Frontier, 1600–1860* (Middletown, Conn.: Wesleyan University Press, 1973), p. 96.
83. Ibid.
84. Ibid., pp. 94, 96.

85. Jonathan Edwards, *Representative Selections*, ed. C. Faust and T.H. Johnson (New York: Hill and Wang, 1962), pp. 158–159.

86. *The Liberator*, Boston, September 3, 1831; reprinted in *Documents of Upheaval: Selections from William Lloyd Garrison's The Liberator, 1831–1865*, ed. Truman Nelson (New York: Hill and Wang, 1966), p. 28.

87. Farrison, *William Wells Brown*, p. 238.

88. Rowlandson, *Narrative*, pp. 60–70.

89. Douglass, *Narrative*, p. 56.

Paul Laurence Dunbar

The 1890s was a bleak time for a black poet to debut, as Paul Laurence Dunbar quickly discovered. Indeed, it was a bleak time also for a serious white poet, as E.A. Robinson eloquently testified in his poems and his correspondence. The two poets had something in common. They opposed the rampant materialism that dominated the age, which took the form of corporate mergers, industrial expansion, and a vast increase in the power of the investment banker. Robinson learned his opposition to a crass material culture in part from his instruction at Harvard where he was a special student, from Charles Eliot Norton especially. Dunbar acquired his, no doubt, from the sermons which he heard in a black church in Dayton and from the early development of the instinct of a true poet. Neither Dunbar nor Robinson could express an easy allegiance to Romantic idealism and look with great comfort on a world controlled by businessmen and the industrial tycoon.

The Genteel Tradition, the most powerful force in American letters from 1870 through the 1890s, could. It had adopted a convenient form of Romanticism, a truncated and modified version that stressed ornamental devices, precision of form, and exotic and historical references, but deplored any substantial contact with the real world. An older and more vigorous Romanticism undertook the impossible task of defining what was real in the world and harshly criticized human behavior that did violence to conscience, ignored the ties linking people in the world, displayed ignorance of the potential for spiritual development that existed in everyone. The ideas, shunted aside by Genteel critics, made a Renaissance in American literature that extended from the 1830s through the 1860s. Robinson, in order to save himself as a poet and as a man who was overwhelmed early by domestic tragedy, returned to the older Romanticism and received from it the power that flows from his early poems. Dunbar, on the other hand, knew it only superficially and turned rather to the tradition of the English Romantic poets, from Burns and Keats to Rossetti and Swinburne, which did not inspire him to dig deeply into the matter of his own existence or that of others. Despite the cultivation of impressive skills, rarely do Dunbar's poems in conventional English triumph over the derivative forms, a rigidly proper poetical language, and a set of ideas that in general passes for poetical pieties. Though Nature and the redemption of man never stirred Dunbar deeply, two other subjects did: the struggles of the Negro race and the agony of composition: what to put in a poem, how to write it, especially how to phrase it so that it would be acceptable to a largely white audience. The constraints sound rather Genteel. Indeed, they are, since such periodicals as *The Century, Harper's, Scribner's,* and *The Atlantic* applied inflexibly the standards of a limited Romanticism in the hope of pleasing the large new audience that technological advances in printing had made possible since 1870. A case can be made that the true bastions of gentility in American literature from the 1870s to the 1890s were those magazines with their demands for acceptable, saleable material, not critics like Stedman, Stoddard, or Aldrich. Dunbar made his escape from the prison of gentility in a manner rather different from Robinson's.

There were ways to do this. Robinson, as noted before, became a thoroughgoing idealist, not a half-hearted one, and advanced to the point of treating idealism in dramatic frames that questioned and parodied, through irony, Romantic belief. *Captain Craig* (1902) represents fully this development in Robinson's art. George Santayana and Trumbull Stickney relied upon a tradition not English, the classical. The consequence is an economic art, frequently on enduring classical themes, that was free of the cant, artificiality, and poetical debris that a century of Romanticism, despite its glories, had accumulated. Another form of escape from a stifling poetic influence was more domestic and more immediate. James Whitcomb Riley, Frank Stanton, Will Irwin, and others turned to dialect verse. The advantage of doing so is quite obvious —a fresh language closer to real speech and a likelihood of discovering a poetic matter of importance to Jim and Janie, not the tired conventional themes inherited from Romantic verse. There were hazards, too. Dialect verse by the time that Dunbar discovered it through Riley already had conventions of its own, among them established comic verbal devices, suggesting that making an audience chuckle rather than accuracy of presentation was the more important consideration. It took a keen ear and a responsible sensibility to winnow a true voice out of the "deses" and "doses" of black dialect verse, and the same can be said for excursions into Hoosier and German dialects. Dunbar, not unexpectedly given his background, brought skill to an accurate recording of both black and white dialects, though the black bears a special resonance from living in a black community and exposure to black folk and historical traditions. Another danger for the writer employing dialect is sentimentality, not the well-worn apostrophes and cliches of Romantic verse but the equally deplorable complacent and simplistic distortions of mundane existence. The proposition that life around one had a sweetness, order, and an amusing quaintness was not a bit more satisfying or useful in the 1890s than the idea that life was concentrated in moments illumined by contacts with the ideal, as far removed as possible from the grubbiness of the real world. In black dialect verse, the simplifying and reductive influence came from the Plantation Tradition, the Southern wing of the Genteel, which was nourished in part by the efforts of many Southerners, and Northerners too, to heal the wounds inflicted by decades of conflict and a devastating Civil War. It is no accident that Joel Chandler Harris, the author of tales about Uncle Remus, was a staff writer for the Atlanta *Constitution*, the strong supporter if not the shaper of the New South. Henry W. Grady journeyed North to convince Yankee businessmen that the South was a fertile area for investment while Harris made a winning appeal to the North, and to the South as well, suggesting that slavery was not so bad, indeed quite charming in some of its aspects. Though he is rather too distant from the clank of chains of the slave coffle or the crack of the overseer's whip, Harris did reveal to a nation in the 1880s the power of the black folk tradition.

Dunbar was saved, in general, from the excesses of the Plantation Tradition by his deep consciousness of being black, though other black writers of dialect were not so fortunate. One sobering reality was the fact that his mother and father were ex-slaves. Matilda Dunbar was a slave until the news arrived on her plantation of the Emancipation Proclamation. Joshua, the father, was a plantation plasterer, who recalled even fewer moments of lighthearted happiness than did Matilda. Joshua had escaped by Underground Railroad to Canada and returned later to join the 55th

Massachusetts of the Union Army, the second Negro regiment organized in the North. Paul absorbed the mixed views of his mother toward slavery rather than the more bitter outlook of his father, but he could not avoid hearing in some detail about repressive and cruel aspects of slavery. Such a young man, born in Dayton in 1872, not yet a decade after the War's end, was not likely to accept willingly the saccharine portraits and narratives of the Plantation apologists.

The dialect tradition in verse prospered, in part, because of its close association with journalism. Joel Chandler Harris, who had earned distinction on the Atlanta *Constitution*, was, as the world knows, a successful writer of black dialect, but there were many others, both black and white, who turned their hands to dialect, usually with much less success than that which Harris achieved. The role of the journalist here is not accidental. No doubt, what is involved is a familiarity with the talk of ordinary people, especially those with little education, and a remarkable opportunity to hear stories and verse from provincial regions still untouched by the explosive expansion of the cities. Dunbar was strongly attracted to journalism. The poems that first achieved publication, "Our Martyred Soldiers" and "On the River," appeared in the Dayton *Herald* in June and July 1888; and his first dialect poem, written in a German dialect, not in the broken, colorful language of the Southern black, appeared in 1890 in the Dayton *Tattler*, a newspaper which Dunbar published and edited for the black community in Dayton. "Lager Beer" followed the precedent established in the dialect ballads of "Hans Breitman." Though the admiration for Riley sparked a serious commitment to dialect verse, Dunbar, through his early journalistic ambitions, knew of the journalist's publication of verse in a number of different forms of dialect. As dialect was nurtured by journalists in the 1880s and 1890s, so the Southwestern humor tradition, with its many forms of dialect, from folk talk in Mississippi and Arkansas to the notorious expression of the Pike character in Missouri and points West, was cultivated by editors, feature writers, and reporters for newspapers. Among these writers was one well known, Mark Twain.

The reference to Mark Twain is a reminder that literary works in both verse and prose use dialect. Dunbar's interest essentially was its application to poetry, though he did employ it in narratives that relied upon the Plantation tradition. But it is the verse that reflects Dunbar's serious experimentation in dialect, marking his work as the most successful achievement in America in dialect verse, surpassing the worthy efforts of both James Russell Lowell and of James Whitcomb Riley. Charles Chesnutt, rather than Dunbar, displayed the power of dialect in narrative in *The Conjure Woman* (1899), and he too was troubled with the restraints of Genteel literary principles. Never in *The Conjure Woman* does the full force of the black folk matter touch the reader. Always there is a literary frame provided by an educated observer, who tempers and mutes the energy of the wild black tales that are to be found within. Though Dunbar was to make a substantial contribution to fiction, he did so within the contemporary conventions that govern the prose narrative, which were undergoing in the 1890s, with the emergence of Naturalism, a considerable critical examination. Toward the end of his career, Dunbar was preoccupied with developing his ideas about the novel, evident particularly in *The Sport of the Gods*, and this interest, rather than his outstanding work in poetry, is the one that leads him into the twentieth century. This work of 1902 foreshadows in theme, point of view, scene, and craft the rich development of the modern black novel that receives its next advance in the *Autobiography of an Ex-Coloured Man*, published by James Weldon Johnson a decade later.

A black writer in the 1890s could hope for little support from the general social climate of the time, not simply from the uninspiring literary context. This was the "nadir" in the post–Civil War history of blacks, as Rayford Logan, the distinguished Negro historian, has said. Southern states completed the process of disenfranchising blacks, using devices unheard of before in American politics. Blacks suffered from gross discrimination in education, in money appropriated and in facilities, and one Southern Senator announced his opposition to the support of vocational instruction for blacks, not to mention any vestige of a liberal education. The same bleak situation existed in public accommodations, public transportation, and public libraries. Even the water fountain required protection from black contamination. The effect upon the black economy was drastic too, with a loss in the South of jobs traditionally held in barber shops, blacksmith shops, stables, and catering establishments. The North was no easy haven for ambitious blacks since it acted also to eliminate political appointments, restrict employment, and place limitations upon public accommodations and housing. When Paul Laurence Dunbar was graduated from high school in 1891, after acquiring honors of various kinds, including the editorship of the *High School Times,* he could secure, after a desperate search, a job of running the elevator in the Callahan Rock building in Dayton, little suitable to his tastes and offering little prospect for the development of his literary interests. A coincidence that only hindsight finds significant is that Dunbar's last poem published in the *Times* in the April issue was entitled "Melancholia."

The racial crisis of the 1890s did not frustrate black advancement on several fronts. Black business in the South and the North underwent unprecedented expansion, partly because whites pursuing institutional purity ignored the black market. Insurance companies, retail stores, real estate agencies, emerged and prospered. More pertinent for this discussion, the crisis stimulated writers, who responded in various ways to the new repression. Not since the 1840s and the 1850s, when the archaic institution of slavery provoked the writing of an endless number of slave narratives, sermons, and tracts of protest, had black writers appeared in such abundance.

Dunbar faced then a total cultural environment which was both hostile and challenging. The 1890s came at the end of one of the least rewarding periods in the history of American literature, though there were evidences of constructive ferment—in the interest in real talk rather than the language of the poetical, in the imaginative interpretation of classical themes without the ornate diction of the late Romantics, and in the Counter-Romanticism of Robinson which involved the use of standard Romantic themes as opportunities for irony and parody. Dunbar was born in an age committed to business and industry, and little else, one that cried out for opposition by contemporary artists, as if that mattered. Meanwhile, business tycoons raided Europe for paintings, sculpture, furniture, stairways, parts of cathedrals, and designs for town houses in New York and Chicago and summer residences at Newport. In Dayton, Dunbar was hard put to sustain his writing and to support his mother, and the generosity of white friends like James Newton Mathews, Charles Thatcher, and H.A. Tobey meant much to the young black poet. His situation was not unique. Robinson nearly starved to death in New York in the late 1890s and in the early twentieth century, and he too owed his ability to devote his energies totally to poetry to wise benefactors. Dunbar bore bruises from the crest of the tide of opposition to blacks in America. When success came finally to the young poet, he was viewed as the black exception or as the model for his unfortunate race to follow or as a black singer whose talent came from instinct alone, unconditioned by wide reading and experimentation.

Cultural obstructions for Dunbar should not hide the view of the challenge coming from American society. The most provocative stimulus for Dunbar was racial. It was the new repression emanating from the South, but not confined to it, that produced and inspired many black writers. There were two basic ways for a black writer to express his reaction to his hostile environment. He could protest directly the status of blacks, citing the violation of civil law and the scrapping of the Constitution; the ignoring of human rights, respected by all countries in the West; and the betrayal of blacks in light of their support of the Union in both the Civil War and Reconstruction. Or he could make a case for the black cultural tradition, tracing its roots back to a noble heritage in Africa; investigating the rich folk background in song, tale, jokes, boasts, and artifacts; providing evidence of a rewarding black community life despite the blight of slavery; and celebrating black heroes like Frederick Douglass and valuable white associates who had battled for the cause of freedom for blacks like John Greenleaf Whittier. W.E.B. Du Bois, the many-talented professor at Atlanta University, did both, as *The Souls of Black Folk* (1903) reveals, and offered in addition criticism of Booker T. Washington, the Principal of Tuskegee Institute, for being soft on issues involving human rights, promoting vocational education and derogating liberal instruction, and directing white philanthropy to support the institutions which he certified. Dunbar, on the other hand, tended in his works of art to restrict his interests in the race problem to exploring and using the black cultural tradition, a more indirect response but equally important as the frontal attack. He did write some important articles that dealt directly with the fact of present oppression. "The Race Question Discussed," published in the Toledo *Journal* on December 11, 1898; "The Hapless Southern Negro," which appeared in the Denver *Post* on September 17, 1899; "Is Higher Education for the Negro Hopeless?" printed in the Philadelphia *Times* on June 10, 1900; and "The Fourth of July and Race Outrage: Paul Laurence Dunbar's Bitter Satire on Independence Day," to be found in the New York *Times*, July 10, 1903, do offer effective protest against white discrimination and white atrocities in America. There was never any question about Dunbar's commitment to the welfare of black people or his pride in black achievement, though there were persistent rumors that Dunbar hated his blackness and sought to achieve a reputation as a writer that was without a racial label. Some truth may exist in the second charge, since all great artistic talents desire universal recognition, but none in the first, despite the condescension and occasional humiliation received by Dunbar from indifferent, even well-meaning whites at the very height of his career.

Dunbar emerged as an artist in a difficult and demanding time and his important place in American and Afro-American literatures is a thing to marvel at. What must be considered now is how Dunbar approached his writing and what his art means in terms of a developing Afro-American literary tradition.

An important problem for every writer is finding his own *voice*. "Voice," roughly defined, is a distinctively consistent way of speaking, and it is a powerful instrument in giving a work of art unity and intensity. It involves diction, manner of addressing an audience, range of reference, and ultimately values in describing or weighing reality. Voice has significance in prose, in fiction and in nonfiction, and it is absolutely indispensable for good poetry, in which every phrase must contribute to a developing structure. A writer cannot create a voice out of nothing; it represents, rather, a summary of a life, including the trials of day-to-day experience and reading. Long after he has read a work of genuine artistic merit, a reader will remember the voice that has spoken to him.

The determination is a particularly trying matter for a black writer. This is so principally because of the duality in black life. Du Bois pointed to the two cultures existing within a single black body, one black and one white, and he held that the problem for the Negro was to integrate the two constructively. This is easier said than done, and many black writers have wasted their energies in resolving this dilemma. Though one black writer may lean more toward the white side of the tradition he shares and another toward the black, the fact is that a resolution of some sort is necessary before a voice emerges to order the confusion and to speak with force. Dunbar's problem in discovering an appropriate voice, one that he was never to solve with total satisfaction, stems from his life. That life exposed Dunbar almost equally to the black and white aspects of his Southern Ohio culture. Such a double exposure was shared with the same even distribution of experience by a few other blacks at the time, notably W.E.B. Du Bois, whose early years were spent in Great Barrington, Massachusetts, who expressed first the reality among blacks of a double consciousness.

Dunbar's black credentials are considerable. His parents, Matilda and Joshua, were black without visible intermixture of white blood, a fact that W.D. Howells was to note about the poet in his influential introduction to the *Lyrics of Lowly Life* (1896). Born in 1872, not quite a decade after the Emancipation Proclamation, Dunbar learned about slavery from his mother and father and their friends. His mother talked to him more than his father, and from her the young boy picked up accounts of happy moments in the quarters and an early exposure to poetry, as well as the repressive side of slavery. From Joshua, Paul heard only bitter memories. No doubt in the early years much of his absorption of this background of the period before the War was unconscious. But once Riley, whose poems Dunbar had analyzed with care, had turned him on to the use of dialect, and once Charles Dennis, editor of the Chicago *News-Record*, had suggested that he accept the model provided by the poetry of Robert Burns and apply it to Negro experience, the young poet talked with more purpose to his mother's friends and neighbors, probing them for details of the life in slavery and recording both their tales and their manner of telling them. Dunbar could scarcely discover more authentic sources short of being himself a slave in Ol' Kentuck.

Young Paul was a member of the black community in Dayton. He attended the Eaker Street Methodist Church, where he gave his first public reading, "An Easter Ode," in 1885. A few years later, as a member of the Knights of Pythias, the Gem City Palace Lodge Number Two, Dunbar saw an all-Negro minstrel troupe perform at the Park Theater. He organized his own black dramatic group, the Philodramian, which presented, among other productions, "The Stolen Calf," a play written by him. In his last year of high school, Paul began publishing a Negro newspaper, the Dayton *Tattler*, an ambitious effort sustained largely by his own writing, in fiction as well as poetry. What began with questionable promise in Winter (December 13, 1890) expired after no more than eight issues. The *Tattler* is useful chiefly, not for "The Gambler's Wife," a serialized Western play, or "His Bride of the Tomb," a romance, but for the demonstration of Dunbar's persistent interest in contributing to the advancement of his race. A mature assertion of his commitment to black culture occurred when Dunbar moved to Chicago at the time of the Columbian Exposition. There he met black leaders Ida B. Wells, Hallie Q. Brown, Mary Church Terrell, and, above all, Frederick Douglass, who offered Dunbar a place in the office of the Haiti Pavilion. Of greater significance to Dunbar, he met black artists actively involved in various creative activities. He discussed the problem of writing dialect verse with James Carrothers and James Campbell, published poets and able practitioners but rather closer to the tradition as influenced by plantation pieties than was Dunbar. He met the black musicians Joseph Douglass, a violinist who was the grandson of Frederick, and Harry Burleigh, composer and singer, and the budding dramatists Richard B. Harrison, later God in *The Green Pastures*, and Will Marion Cook. Cook persuaded Dunbar to read at Colored Americans' Day, and he did so, reciting his ode, "Colored Americans."

All of these black associations point to the discovery of a poetic voice that was essentially black. The best evidence of its shaping is to be found in the dialect poems, not all of them, but those that incorporated serious problems like the lack of freedom or the unequal distribution of the world's goods and others that displayed dramatic complexity, frequently tapping rich folk matter in music, dance, and narrative. These developments in art required the presence of an intelligent, sensitive, tolerant, speculative observer or commentator who stood for humane values and their equal application to blacks and whites. Such a voice need not be confined to dialect verse. It appears, though not in its fully developed state, in "Frederick Douglass," a fine poem that suffers somewhat from the imposition of an old-fashioned eighteenth-century rhetoric. In Dunbar's finest volume of poems, *Lyrics of Lowly Life* (1896), which consolidated and confirmed the poetic promise in *Majors and Minors,* published early in 1896, two poems appearing next to each other display qualities of Dunbar's developing voice: "Accountability" and "Frederick Douglass." The emerging voice was never to take shape fully and with an enduring shape because Dunbar was attracted to many ways of speaking, not simply that which was reinforced by his black experience.

Dunbar, in his early years, achieved general success in the Dayton society, apart from the black community. The focus of his accomplishment is to be found in the schools that he attended, all overwhelmingly white. There were few traumas during these years, according to his biographers, and Paul's progress resembles that of any talented white scholar.

Dunbar attended District Schools in Dayton during the elementary years, and he wrote his first poem at age seven. What succeeded elementary instruction in Dayton was Intermediate School, where Paul was the only black in his class. He experienced little difficulty in making white friends, and race posed no barrier to close association with Orville Wright. Dunbar encountered his first great teacher here, Samuel Wilson, possessing many qualities of the poet himself, who read poetry to his class. Paul entered Central High School in 1886, and he proceeded to accumulate an impressive set of honors. He achieved distinction in debating and composition and he published poems in both the *High School Times* and the Dayton *Herald.* Election to the exclusive literary society, the Philomathean, confirmed his high status in his school, and serving as editor-in-chief of the *High School Times* seemed clearly appropriate for a scholar as distinguished as Paul.

Though discrimination prevented Dunbar from finding a suitable job after his graduation from high school, it did not deter him from pursuing diligently his interests in poetry. Legend has it that the black elevator operator at Callahan Rock's building always had a book in his hand. Dunbar's primary literary conditioning in high school was one that gave a great importance to

Romantic verse. This is evident in his early poems in proper English where there are echoes of Wordsworth, Keats, Tennyson, and Rossetti, and also of the Americans Poe, James Russell Lowell, and Whittier. Dunbar studied with particular care the successful practitioners in dialect who were white: Ella Wheeler Wilcox, Eugene Field, Sam Walter Foss, James Russell Lowell, and James Whitcomb Riley. Riley made such a strong impression that Dunbar imitated him in his early poems in dialect: "The Ol' Tunes," "A Banjo Song," "The Old Apple Tree," "The Old Homestead," "An Old Memory." This collection of "olds" points directly to Riley. But perhaps the most explicit example of such imitation is "A Drowsy Day," written from the point of view of meditative old age and using, indeed, Riley's Hoosier dialect. Dunbar had an opportunity to express his admiration for Riley in "James Whitcomb Riley—From a Westerner's Point of View," apparently never published.

White literary associations, publishers, benefactors, and authors were major influences in promoting Dunbar's career. Perhaps the first opportunity for Dunbar to acquire a reputation, extending then not much beyond the city limits of Dayton, was provided by a meeting of the Western Association of Writers. Here he read poems to the convention in June 1892, which attracted the attention of many members, including Dr. James Newton Matthews, who was to become a much-valued benefactor. Certain newspapers were especially interested in Dunbar's work, notably the Chicago *News-Record* and the Toledo *Bee*. One of Dunbar's most significant white benefactors was the foreman of the job printing department of the Press of the United Brethren who accepted *Oak and Ivy*, Dunbar's first volume of poems, without any financial guarantee from the author. The volume appeared in December 1892, just in time to be a Christmas present for his mother, to whom it was dedicated. There were other committed white supporters: Matthews, of course, who wrote a letter about Dunbar to Riley and sent complimentary letters and notices to newspapers; Charles Thatcher, a lawyer in Toledo, who offered to send Dunbar to college; Dr. H.A. Tobey, who did the same, specifying Harvard as the preferred institution and who with Thatcher sponsored Dunbar's second volume of poems, *Majors and Minors* (1896).

Nor were white writers indifferent to his talent. Riley, so much admired by Dunbar, wrote to him in 1892: "Already you have many friends and can have thousands more by being simple, honest, unaffected, and just to yourself and the high source of your endowment." Riley raised here the problem of voice, though his terms were moral rather than literary. George Washington Cable, short-story writer and novelist, whose fame rested upon his portrayal of the behavior of the Creoles in Louisiana, praised Dunbar's work and commented on his pure African descent, a fact which had a special meaning for a Presbyterian who in New Orleans had been surrounded by vestiges of African culture. Ingersoll, the well-known orator and essayist, expressed appreciation for Dunbar's poetry, especially for six poems, all written in conventional English. James Herne, the author of *Shore Acres* and other plays exhibiting the first evidences of substantial realism in the American theater, to whom Dunbar gave a copy of *Majors and Minors* (1896), was the channel to Dunbar's most influential white supporter in the world of American letters. This was William Dean Howells, whose review in "Life and Letters" in *Harper's Weekly* gave Dunbar a national reputation. Howells was concerned as well about the problem of voice, and he sought to define the literary approach that seemed to him to be immensely impressive in Dunbar's verse. The poet, Howells wrote, was "the first man of his color to study his race objectively, to analyze it to himself, and then represent it as art as he felt it and found it to be, to represent it humorously, yet tenderly, and above all so faithfully. . . ." Howells preferred the dialect poems in Dunbar's collection, the "Minors," as Dunbar described them, suggesting problems about the poet's attitude about the use of dialect that were to emerge more fully later in his career. The poem that struck Howells's fancy particularly was "The Party," which opened "vistas into the simple, sensuous, joyous nature of [the Negro] race." One can hardly blame Howells for his choice, but "The Party," though "sensuous," is not "simple," and its dramatic complexity denies that all is joy in Dunbar's heaven of fine food and extraordinary entertainment. Howells offered Dunbar the opportunity that he yearned for and, in addition, some good advice that the poet in subsequent years had difficulty accepting.

The dilemma of one black poet seemed clear in 1896. Dunbar was the product of many experiences, one melting into another, perhaps without great differentiation. But in his creative world he made a sharp distinction between what was black and what was white. Experience determines voice in large measure and Dunbar's had exposed him to black and white associations, manners, and values. This liberal spread is not of much help in arriving at a unique and memorable way of speaking. Dunbar never understood fully that he had to make a decision, though he did agonize about what seemed to be restrictions imposed by his audience. The choice of voice is finally an act of will, and it requires a sense of where a poet's greatest strength lies. Yeats turned to Ireland to discover his natural voice; Eliot to a decadent England, full of intimations of cultural collapse, with a few strands of hope resting in vestiges of Christian doctrine; Robinson and Frost to New England. And where would Dunbar turn? His direction was not clear in 1896, possibly because his choices were so many and he felt no pressure really to sort them out.

A list of Dunbar's options is formidable. The black tradition presented two. The first is the poetry of high rhetoric about noble black themes. In *Lyrics of Lowly Life,* two excellent examples are "Frederick Douglass" and "Ode to Ethiopia." Such a rhetoric is almost impenetrable to the insertion of anything natural, least of all a voice, but Dunbar deserves credit for bringing his own personal values to the tribute to Douglass. Then there is dialect verse, more accessible to the creation of a natural voice. But dialect had its unnatural dangers. One is the language itself, the temptation to follow slavishly the minstrel or the Plantation Traditions. Dunbar offered eloquent testimony on this point, moved, perhaps, by his own involvement with Will Marion Cook's musical show *Clorindy:* "The outlandish, twisted mispronunciations of minstrel darky talk had none of the musical cadence of real Negro speech; it kept the Negro character a clown and a scamp." The second part of Dunbar's statement involves the matter of substance as well. The Plantation Tradition did not trouble to give black people minds worth reckoning with. Negro characters were loyal servants, obedient to the end, the very end; self-indulgent darkies who longed for corn pone and possum and were not above stealing a pig from the tolerant white man in the big house; clowns delighted to engage in antic routines for the amusement of a white audience; and children without any age of maturity, from six months to sixty years, who required guidance and assistance, never a corrupting formal education.

Though there were only two black options, many more came from the white tradition. One hears echoes of an ode by Keats in "Ere Sleep Comes Down to Soothe the Weary Eyes," a Wordsworthian exercise in morality in "The Lesson," a tale of mystery within a strangely animate nature by Coleridge in "The Rising of the Storm," memories of a sonnet by Milton, stressing endurance and patience, in "Not They Who Soar." And the list goes on to include poems that owe much also to the late English and the American Romantics. In this area, the opportunity to choose has overwhelmed Dunbar, and few poems display any imprint of a personal touch that is special and unique. Those in *Lyrics of Lowly Life* that do are worth noting. "The Poet and His Song," "The Mystery," "Unexpressed," "Religion," "The Dilettante: A Modern Type," and "We Wear the Mask" offer much more than the reverberations of a lament by Poe in "Dirge" and "Ione," or the rhetoric of Lowell in "Ode for Memorial Day" and "Columbian Ode," or the sensuous language of the late Romantics in "Song," or the numerous pious expressions of the homeside poets, Whittier and Longfellow, in "The Master Player." Dunbar, in a half dozen poems in the *Lyrics*, seeks a more personal way of talking, probes the experience that he knows, and produces finished, sharply focused poetic statements. The search for the natural voice appears to be easier for Dunbar in dialect verse and the evidence is far richer of success in achievement. The search is clearly not so easy or productive in conventional English verse, and what appears in the *Lyrics* is largely imitative, well done, it is true, and enough to establish the reputation of a lesser poet in the Genteel Tradition, but only imitative finally.

Dunbar does not make the decision that would enhance his stature as a poet. He could not bring himself to perform the act of will, to elect to concentrate upon his strengths and to create the geography, the psychology, and the imagery that must accompany a fundamental artistic decision of this kind. Dunbar's poetic development ends with *Lyrics of Lowly Life*, though he would continue to write poems and would publish three major volumes of verse: *Lyrics of the Hearthside* (1899), *Lyrics of Love and Laughter* (1903), and *Lyrics of Sunshine and Shadow* (1905).

Dunbar devoted his creative energy increasingly to fiction after 1896, but the problem of voice, now a narrative voice, still haunted him. *The Uncalled*, his first novel, was begun in England and finished in the home of Professor Kelly Miller, an outstanding black essayist, at Howard University in Washington, D.C. The novel seems promising because it employs the background of Southern Ohio, which Dunbar knew, and centers on a young man who rejects the "Call," the divine command to become a minister of God, in favor of a more generous and more human form of Christianity without the authority of the cloth. The plot is sufficiently close to incidents in Dunbar's life to capture a few overtones from it, but it is not clearly a story drawn from the author's life, as Alice Moore Dunbar, the writer's wife, claimed at one point. The conflict is far too simple, the sense of a rich town or city life absent, and the approach to a point of view, a way of looking at and saying things, uncertain and fuzzy. The novel has only white characters who act from a superficial or pious motivation, suggesting that the proper tradition of the work was to be found in the religious line in sentimental fiction. The novel for Dunbar was only a beginning, and he would move, though sometimes in a wayward fashion, toward the discovery of a more rewarding matter and a more sophisticated way of approaching it. He succeeded in part in *The Sport of the Gods* in a manner more convincing, perhaps, than in any of his poems.

Dunbar did not in the nineteenth century solve the problem of voice in either poetry or fiction, but he succeeded, despite this, in creating an art that demands high respect and careful critical attention. What Dunbar did achieve requires not only careful examination but the recollection of the special cultural environment of the 1890s from which his work emerged.

Dunbar wrote poems, novels, short stories, articles, dramatic works, and lyrics for songs. It is not possible to do justice to all of his many talents, and it makes sense to concentrate upon the areas of the canon that would establish his reputation as a writer, that is to say, the poetry and the fiction. The poetry divides itself into the verses written in dialect and those written in conventional English, which outnumber those in dialect. The fiction includes both novels and short stories, with the burden of experimentation located in the novel. The short stories document essentially Dunbar's interest in exploiting the Plantation Tradition and represent a phase in Dunbar's general development as a writer of fiction, and these do not deserve, perhaps, separate consideration from the novel.

Dialect verse is a touchy topic still, one that inspires mixed feelings in black intellectuals even today, despite the black consciousness raising that occurred in the 1960s. The reasons are not hard to find. For years dialect was used to derogate and to ridicule black people. The problem is not simply now a matter of the Plantation Tradition and the minstrel stage, alive and well still in the small towns of America, but of witnessing the flow of characters like Stepin' Fetchit, Sunshine Sammy, and Al Jolson in blackface continuing into the twentieth century, insulting misrepresentations sprung from the nineteenth. This sad history makes a critic doubt that serious art can come from a language so consistently employed for one purpose.

James Weldon Johnson, black novelist, poet, diplomat, and political activist, thought not. Though he had used dialect for lyrics for songs presented on the musical stage in New York, he refused to use it in his poetry. He insisted that dialect, though colorful and musical, as he well knew, had too many limitations because of its unfortunate history. Black dialect, according to Johnson, invited two well-established reactions, the pathetic and the humorous, and neither was appropriate, he thought, for serious art. When in 1927 Johnson published *God's Trombones,* those artistic renderings of black folk sermons, he did not use dialect. He restricted himself rather to touches of the colloquial here and there and to imitations of the syntax and the imagery of the black exhorter, but he did not experiment with black dialect. The result in *God's Trombones* is not wholly reassuring because Johnson's work lacks the power and the energy of the exhortation of a genuine black folk preacher, who had never heard of literary reservations about the language that he used and could care little if he had. His responsibility was to his congregation and to God, to whom he spoke directly in moments of spiritual frenzy. The decision to concentrate upon dialect was not to be plainly an easy one for Dunbar, given the pressures from black society and interested white readers. Johnson could not make it and Dunbar was reluctant to do so, though his ear for language was much superior to Johnson's. If a decision was hard in the 1920s, it was much harder in the 1890s, when the Plantation Tradition occupied a central place in contemporary sentimental literature and the minstrel stage was a staple in American entertainment.

Dialect verse appeared first in the work of Southern white writers who achieved humorous effects by using it in light verse or in reproductions of folk narratives. Foremost among these white writers were Irwin Russell, whose poems were published posthumously in 1888; Joel Chandler Harris, who achieved fame for the Uncle Remus tales; Thomas Nelson Page; and A.C. Gordon. Black writers moved into the field too, though often with certain feelings of ambivalence.

The truth is that black writers stood at the point of making a commitment to dialect a decade, at least, before the works of white writers appeared. Frances E.W. Harper, a black poet, offered the substance and the structure of a typical dialect poem in "Learning to Read." The only thing that is lacking is the dialect.

The voice heard in the poem is that of an old ex-slave, Aunt Chloe, who reminisces about a small triumph in her modest career. The scene is the "little cabin," the conventional place for most Americans for happy times on the old plantation. There are the expected references to the Southern black cuisine, "pot liquor," for example, and to black character, noting that stealing is an established practice. Aunt Chloe herself is excessively pious, and her small triumph is the acquisition of glasses without being able to read. She does so because she wants to read the Bible on her own, and she achieves her ambition. All of the elements of a typical dialect poem are here: the sincere and simple narrator, the locale, the jaundiced, tolerant view of black character, the sentimental wish that is acted upon, the food, and the pervasive sense of Christian piety—all but the language, except in touches of dialect.

Frances Harper's poem is clearly not high art, nor are, indeed, very nearly all of the poems in the dialect tradition. But Johnson was wrong. High art could and did come from black dialect, but only under certain conditions imposed by a sophisticated poetic intelligence. Dunbar made high art from dialect, and a few of his contemporaries did so as well, though most turned to more elaborate versions of the Harper formula. Dunbar, though the master of his special craft, was then not alone in practicing it with an amount of distinction.

James Edwin Campbell, a black journalist who had received his education at Miami College (now Miami University), had some of Dunbar's ambitions. Much of Campbell's dialect verse follows the usual pattern, but "Ol' Doc' Hyar" does not. It is a beast fable that has a strange toughness. Instead of possessing a pervasive sentimentality and an abiding Christian piety, the world of "Ol' Doc' Hyar" is amoral, if not immoral. It offers a climate for trickery, if not for downright malevolence. Doc' Hyar practices a form of quack medicine, and Mistah B'ar is his unfortunate victim. The final stanza expresses Doc' Hyar's attitude toward his inadequacies as a physician:

> But de vay naix day Mistah B'ar he daid;
> Wen dee tell Doc' Hyar, he des scratch he haid;
> "Ef pashons git well ur pashons git wu's,
> Money got ter come een de Ol' Hyar's pu's;
> Not wut folkses does, but fur wut dee know
> Does de folkses git paid"—an Hyar larfed low,
>   Dis sma't Ol' Hyar
>   What lib up dar
> Een de might fine house on de mighty high hill!

The lesson that "Ol' Doc' Hyar" teaches the critic is that dialect verse acquires a new power and a distinctive racial energy as it approaches the folk tradition. This is one of the ways by which a routine dialect exercise can become art. Gone are the artificial conventions of the sentimental and the familiar locale with all of its expected associations. Instead there is a fresh, serious view of human behavior (displaced in beasts) that raises uneasy reservations about the drift and the values of current society.

The energy emanating from a black folk culture in the nineteenth century, infinitely richer than the formal tradition, was not lost upon Dunbar, though he could employ the conventions of ordinary dialect verse with a skill that no other writer of dialect possessed. James Weldon Johnson maintained that Dunbar's "When De Co'n Pone's Hot" was superior to Riley's "When the

Frost is on the Punkin," and he is unquestionably right. Johnson points to a superior delicacy in handling nuances of sentiment, the possession of a more musical lilt, and the use of a more deft and more economic technique. But the poem is, nonetheless, thoroughly within the mainstream of conventional dialect verse. The subject is food, good-eating, Southern style. The basic emotion is an excess of sentiment lavished upon a familiar and modest object. The manner is that of high rhetoric—"Tek away yo' sody biscuit"—and the overriding atmosphere is that of Christian piety. What gives this ordinary dialect poem an amount of distinction is the swing of the heptameter couplets and the economic technique, both mentioned by Johnson. In addition, there is imaginative imagery, unusual in dialect verse, based upon incongruous juxtapositions:

> Dey is times in life when Nature
>   Seems to slip a cog and go,
> Jes' a-rattlin' down creation,
>   Lak an ocean's overflow;
> When de worl' jes' stahts a-spinnin'
>   Lak a picaninny's top. . . .
> When de oven do' is opened
>   An de smell comes po'in' out;
> Why, de 'lectric light of Heaven
>   Seems to settle on de spot. . . .

There is substantial hope for a young poet who can offer such startling images.

"An Ante-Bellum Sermon" is rather another matter. It is on a serious topic, freedom from slavery, and it employs the framework of a folk sermon which is preached to a congregation still enslaved. Dunbar uses his form with great skill, staying close to the traditional movement in such a sermon, which is a progress toward truth-telling and the revelation of the words and the wisdom of God. Another characteristic of the folk sermon is the primitive reconstruction of familiar stories in the Bible. In general, what is lost in accuracy is more than made up for by the awesome power that God has assumed and the crushing consequences of His acts. For a short period in "An Ante-Bellum Sermon," the cosmos is located in a shabby cabin a convenient distance from the big house. The substance of the poem is the retelling of the story of the liberation from Egypt of the children of Israel. The complexity of telling is described by the narrator as "a-preachin' ancient" and "talkin' bout today." The trouble is that one line of discourse keeps slipping into another at strategic intervals. This slippage requires continuing admonition from the minister to his congregation: "Now don't run an' tell yo' mastahs/ Dat I's preaching discontent." At the same time, the opportunities for a relationship to "today" abound, extending from:

> Dey kin fo'ge yo' chains an' shackles
> F'om de mountains to de sea,
> But de Lawd will sen' some Moses
> Fu' to set his chillun free.

to:

> Fu' de Bible says "a servant
> Is a-worthy of his hire."
> An' you cain't git roun' nor thoo dat,
> An' you cain't get ovah it. . . .

and:

> We will praise de gracious Mastah
> Dat has gin us liberty. . . .

The "gracious Mastah" is clearly not the one in the big house, who is not prepared to make slaves "citiz-," the word which the minister cannot finish, since it would place him in great danger. Though he pretends not to, the preacher makes a clear case for a lack of justice in his own day; "preachin' " is more powerful than "talkin'," and he ends on a triumphant note with a reference to the inevitable coming of Moses.

"An Ante-Bellum Sermon" is a demonstration of how dialect verse can become high art. It has here a serious theme which is treated with dramatic complexity and subtlety. It relies upon the authority of a folk form, using its particular defining characteristics. It has the benefit of a delicate correlation of dramatic and intellectual movements, and it has the advantage of a narrator whose point of view is apparently objective but who speaks naturally and effectively through character, background, and dramatic movement. This is what dialect verse can be in the hands of a master.

"Accountability" is another demonstration of the successful treatment of a serious idea. The subject matter here is contemporary rather than eternal. Determinism was much on the minds of the intellectuals in the 1890s, and as Dunbar wrote this poem, Frank Norris and others were constructing narratives documenting that a form of natural determinism was the essential reality of existence.

Determinism in "Accountability" is pushed to a humorous and ironic conclusion. The point, in fact, is the irony: a serious world view seen in the perspective of a chicken yard. The poem begins with a tribute to the greatness of God who does not neglect the "alleys" and displays concern for nature and the city, differences in human nature, and all of the happenings in the world. God's comprehensive power must also include the capture by the narrator of "one of mastah's chickens." Revealed in the poem are the limits of determinism, a reservation of intellectual significance, and a disposition by human beings to rationalize their behavior.

"Accountability" has the qualities of "An Ante-Bellum Sermon." It is serious and humorous; it has a dramatic complexity provided by the presence of two value systems, and it has the advantage once more of an intelligent, speculative narrator who orders naturally and without contrivance the movement in the poem. The result is a fine dialect poem, full of somber implications and informed by a meaning that could only come from the common sense and practical wisdom of an oppressed people.

"A Negro Love Song" is on its face a superficial lyric without the probing of accepted assumptions and the dramatic complexity that are to be found elsewhere in the Dunbar canon. It does contain one innovation of Dunbar's that deserves comment, since it enlivens the verse and appears in more highly developed poems. The routine expression of love is placed within the context of what appears to be a dance. The refrain "Jump back, honey, jump back" reminds the reader of this possibility. This repeated phrase has another use: it serves to cut the sentiment, which would otherwise be cloying. Much to be admired, too, but not unusual in Dunbar's poems, is the clarity of structure. It consists of the memory of a man's encounter with a lady; a record of the impression made by the lady upon him; a declaration of love, followed by an overly economic response. The attempt to limit an excess of sentiment represented by the repetition of "Jump back, honey, jump back" is echoed by a conclusion something less than reassuring for the lover:

> Love me, honey, love me true?
> Love me well ez I love you?
> An' she answe'd, "cose I do—"

"When Malindy Sings" is a poem that is more complex than it appears to be. Its power comes from the ultimate frame into which Malindy's music fits, and the strength of Malindy's talent is enhanced by comparisons and sacrilegious domestic distractions:

> Towsah, stop dat ba'kin', hyeah me!
> Mandy, mek dat chile keep still. . . .

Sacrilege is the correct term for these apparently harmless family activities, for Malindy has the power of the folk preacher, for whom, at high points in his sermon, nothing stands between his voice and God's. The folk tradition of black people once again intrudes here in the way that it has done in "An Ante-Bellum Sermon." It affirms that there can be in a special black cosmos, which is both awesome and personal, direct transfers of glory, in word and in song. Not frequently, it is true. But every time that Malindy sings, the faithful and the knowing respond, just as they did when God sent Moses to liberate the Israelites, establishing an expectation in the congregation that He will do so again when sufficiently provoked.

Malindy's song transcends earth and provides an intimation of the eternal life, though the channel of connection is not educated or sophisticated, but simple, intense, and touched by otherworldly power:

> Who dat says day humble praises
>   Wif de Mastah never counts?
> Hush yo' mouf, I hyeah dat music,
>   Ez hit rises up and mounts—
> Floatin' by de hills and valleys,
>   Way above dis buryin' sod,
> Ez hit makes its way in glory
>   To de very gates of God!

Though the great power of "When Malindy Sings" rests in the folk connection with God within a clearly defined black cosmos, the poem has other virtues that are dramatic and thought-provoking. What we hear is one side of a conversation, presumably with Mandy, who lacks the faith, the experience, and the perception of the narrator. Though another voice never breaks the flow of the monologue, Mandy, if she hears at all, acquires an education about the organization of the cosmos, learning how close God is to faithful blacks:

> Let me listen, I can hyeah it,
>   Th'oo de bresh of angels' wings,
> Sof' an sweet, "Swing Low, Sweet Chariot,"
>   Ez Malindy sings.

The comparisons have Dunbar's shrewdness in selection, including white Miss Lucy with her music book and her devotion to practice. She is the only representative from the world of written notes and polite society. The other comparisons are from nature, and these representatives, more sensitive and more understanding than Miss Lucy, simply stop their music when Malindy sings. Fiddlin' man, robins, la'ks, mockin'-bird, and "Folks a-playin' on de banjo" appear in the poem with a lack of differentiation in nature between what is human and what is not.

"When Malindy Sings" calls upon Dunbar's full power: his reliance upon the black folk tradition, his dramatic skill, and, above all, the thoughtful, speculative, humane presence that hovers above the narrator's voice.

Dunbar's virtuoso poem in dialect is "The Party." This may be the most popular poem in black dialect ever written, and an ear attuned to distances can still hear "Dey had a gread big pahty down to Tom's de othah night" floating from high school auditoriums all over America. "The Party" lacks the serious compelling ideas that inform Dunbar's very best dialect poems, unless one considers the cultivation of envy in an enchanted listener a great idea. Great or not, it has a long tradition, originating, no doubt, with Satan. The poem is an extraordinary collection of all of the technical devices in Dunbar's arsenal, and the poet is never again to display his many skills in black dialect with such brilliance and abundance.

"The Party" contains all of the elements of a typical dialect poem. These can be named almost without thought by now: the good times on the old plantation; the humorous antics of blacks as they imitate their betters; the exaggerated and distorted movements associated with the minstrel stage; the emphasis upon simple emotions: hunger, jealousy, pride, all fallible; the racial vulnerability of the preacher, in regard to food and dancing; the broad rhetoric; and the food: white bread, egg pone, roasted shoat, ham, hot chitterlings, sweet potatoes, the entire Southern black cuisine.

More important in generating excitement in the poem is the dramatic frame. The narrator tells his story to someone who has not been lucky enough to be at the party. Since he clearly wishes to arouse the appetites and to encourage envy and frustration in his listener, the narrator may not be above exaggerating what he has seen, heard, and tasted, perhaps not even above departing from the truth. The reader senses the mounting excitement in the captivated listener and also the developing involvement of the narrator in the tale that he is telling. Excitement, indeed, is compounded, not simply doubly, but triply so, if the reader's reaction is counted.

"The Party" offers Dunbar's most skillful use of the dance in his poetry. The movements of the dance and the lyrics both appear here. The relationship between the two is curious since the lyrics come from a high culture not available to the blacks who are dancing and singing. This incongruity is functional since much of the poem deals with the effort of the blacks to imitate their white superiors in both dress and manners. The dance routines appear two times in the poem, but the most revealing sequence is the second, in terms of the basic comparison of white and black societies:

> You know when dey gits to singin' and dey comes to dat ere
>   paht
>   "In some lady's new brick house
> In some lady's gyahden.
>   Ef you don't let me out, I will jump out,
>   So fa' you well, my dahlin'."
> Den dey's got a circle 'roun you, an' you got to break de
>   line. . . .

This sequence suggests a problem beyond imitation. It is the effort of an outsider to join the circle that has been defined wholly in terms of white gentility. Scott Thomas was so anxious to do so that he "lit head fo-most in de fiah/ place right plump. . . ." There is the suggestion of a moral here about racial dignity and pride and the temptations to abandon these virtues for immediate success in white terms, but this matter should not be pushed too far.

What has been presented is the range in form, idea, and technique of Dunbar's best dialect poems. These are works of high art, requiring no condescending introductions. What is the best in dialect verse is the best in Dunbar's whole poetic canon. Nowhere else does the poet display such diversity of technique, subtlety of form, command of folk sources, and a sense of authority over poetic movement. The demanding ordering principle that makes all this wonder possible is *voice*, and the pity is that Dunbar chose to yield to it so infrequently. All Dunbar poems in dialect have his music and his acute sense of what is dramatically appropriate, but no other poem has the power or provides the tug on the imagination possessed by the examples of Dunbar's highest art which have just been examined.

None of the poems in conventional or literary English approaches the magnificence of the great dialect poems. This is so despite Dunbar's mounting reservations after 1896 about the publication of dialect verse. The consequence of the refusal to recognize the sources of his greatest strength appears in *Lyrics of the Hearthside* (1899), Dunbar's first volume after *Lyrics of Lowly Life*. Though Dunbar's technical competence is much present, the volume is dominated by poems written in the high Romantic style which the poet admired so much. The back of the volume has the verses devoted to humor and dialect, and these lack the force of the earlier poems in dialect. Certainly "Little Brown Baby" does. Dunbar appears to have made his decision about where he should place his poetic energies and talents, and it is, for many critics, the wrong one.

The clearest statements of Dunbar's unhappiness about being identified as a dialect poet are in the conversations which the poet had with another black poet, James Weldon Johnson. One exchange occurs in 1901, and Johnson, who had reservations also about the "possibilities of stereotyped dialect," reports.

He said, "You know, of course, that I didn't start as a dialect poet. I simply came to the conclusion that I could write it as well, if not better than anybody else I knew of, and that by doing so I should gain a hearing, and now they don't want me to write anything but dialect."

Johnson records also in his autobiography, *Along This Way*, that five years later Dunbar's attitude remained unchanged and Dunbar commented in the year of his death:

I've kept on doing the same things, and doing them no better. I have never gotten to the things I really want to do.

What those "things" were are unknown, but Johnson guesses that they were long poems, perhaps poems of epic length, about the Negro. This speculation has a relationship, possibly, to *The Sport of the Gods*, which has some of the qualities of a prose epic.

Dunbar's poems in literary English have usually one praiseworthy quality. They are touched by the poet's remarkable skill in metrics and versification. His prosody absorbs with ease complicated metrical structures that are to be found in a period that extends from the sixteenth through the nineteenth centuries in English literature.

These poems divide themselves into three categories. What may be called "imitations" is the first. The term is not quite fair, because Dunbar's very best verses that derive from English and American practice have innovations of substance that are Dunbar's own. Certainly this is true in "Ere Sleep Comes Down to Soothe the Weary Eyes," the first poem in *Lyrics of Lowly Life*, and in "The Haunted Oak," which appeared first in *Century Magazine* in December 1900. A second category is a set of heroic poems that are either tributes to the black race or to individual black leaders like Douglass or Alexander Crummell. A good example of the formal salutation to the race is "Ode to Ethiopia," an early poem that appears in *Lyrics of Lowly Life*. "Alexander Crummell—Dead" is an eloquent memorial for the black clergyman whose religious endeavors touched three continents, America, Europe, and Africa, and it was published by the *Boston-Traveler* on March 22, 1899. A third form of Dunbar's verses in literary English is the personal account of the poet's struggle with writing, acceptance, distortions of meaning, and frustration. These poems have great economy, and they make up for their compression by displaying unusual force. These are unquestionably some of the most moving poems in the Dunbar canon. "We Wear the Mask" and "The Poet" fall here; the first poem is from *Lyrics of Lowly Life* and the second from *Lyrics of Love and Laughter* (1903), where "The Poet" seems somehow to be out of place.

"Ere Sleep Comes Down to Soothe the Weary Eyes" has every appearance of being one of Keats's journeys of the imagination to a realm of peace and an overwhelming sensuous beauty, a place of abundance and satisfaction, haunted only by the near presence of death. The difference in Dunbar's poem is that the journey is through a form of purgatory, not an adventure carried by the hedonistic impulse alone. Instead of a draft of cool wine from the South, the narrator discovers a "base witch's caldron," and the pilgrim is overwhelmed by "griefs and heartaches we have known" that "Come up like pois'nous vapors that arise/ From some base witch's caldron. . . ." As if the memories of the past are not appalling enough, the poet's fancy projects his spirit to a world not known, but offering little comfort:

> To lands unspeakable—beyond surmise,
> Where shapes unknowable to being spring. . . .

Neither past nor future offers the balm, satisfaction, and peace that the poet seeks. He is reduced to his naked, unflattering self in the twilight world:

> But self exposes unto self, a scroll
> Full writ with all life's acts unwise or wise,
> In characters indelible and known. . . .

Not until the "awful self alone" is viewed does sleep come. It is not a sating of the senses but a relief from "sad world's cries," from probing "th'eternal mystery," and from fretting with frustration and with unsuccessful attempts to penetrate the surrounding gloom. Sleep, then, is a release and a blessing and a condition more firmly attached to death than what is revealed in an ode by Keats.

Dunbar has drastically altered the substance of the journey of the imagination, though he does not go quite so far as Poe does in "Dream-Land," in which the narrator finds satisfaction in an underworld less than life, full of distortions and phenomena enduring a minimal existence in a twilight world.

"The Haunted Oak" is equally fascinating with its use of the form of a Border ballad to record the lynching of an innocent black man. The oak responds to the fact that a man has been hanged from one of its boughs, and it does so by rejecting life for the blameless bough that has participated in this atrocity:

> And never more shall leaves come forth
> On a bough that bears the ban;
> I am burned with dread, I am dried and dead,
> From the curse of a guiltless man.

The machinery of the Border ballad is abundantly displayed in "The Haunted Oak"; the familiar metrics, the repetition of phrase, the curse, the ominous and knowing nonhuman phenomena like trees and birds, the violence, and the sense of betrayal. The Border ballad is admirably suited to document a lynching; it has done justice to many a violent deed occurring on the boundary between England and Scotland. One innovation in "The Haunted Oak" is that a tree tells the brutal story. It is a witness tree in the true sense, in that it declares that the souls of all of the apparently respectable participants, the judge, the doctor, the minister, and the minister's oldest son, are in mortal danger:

> And ever the judge rides by, rides by,
> And ever goes to hunt the deer,
> And ever another rides his soul
> In the guise of a mortal fear.

Both "Ere Sleep Comes Down to Soothe the Weary Eyes" and "The Haunted Oak" make impressive use of derivative forms. Old vessels are filled with new wine, and the new is almost as good as the old.

"Ode to Ethiopia" is one of Dunbar's heroic pieces designed to give pride and dignity to black people in America. It employs a pattern of references that comes from the black nationalism of the late nineteenth century, which centered on Ethiopia as the mother of the race. This form of nationalism, a predecessor in some ways to the New Negro Renaissance, stressed a noble African past and expressed confidence in the continuing rise of the black race within the family of nations. There is only one reference to an ancient and noble past in the poem, and that is fairly general:

> Be proud, my Race, in mind and soul;
> Thy name is writ on Glory's scroll
>   In characters of fire.

The immediate past was Dunbar's more pressing concern: "When Slavery crushed thee with its heel,/ With dear blood all gory." He emphasizes the survival of the race during slavery and the display of humanity and tolerance which blacks exhibited after securing their freedom. The final stanza is a rousing affirmation of a glorious future for black people, powerful enough to stir the emotions of all members of the race:

> Go on and up! Our souls and eyes
> Shall follow thy continuous rise;
>   Our ears shall list thy story
> From bards who from thy root shall spring,
> And proudly tune their lyres to sing
>   Of Ethiopia's glory.

"Alexander Crummell—Dead" is a moving tribute to a black leader that presents two contrasting attitudes toward his death. The first is the strong statement that Crummell has deserved his rest because of his many services to his fellow man:

> Back to the breast of thy mother,
> Child of Earth!
> E'en her caress cannot smother
> What thou has done.

The second is an uncertainty about the leadership for black people as a consequence of Crummell's following "the trial of the westering sun. . . ." A set of disturbing questions is posed:

> Who shall come after thee, out of the clay—
> Learned one and leader to show us the way?
> Who shall rise up when the world gives the test?

There are no answers to these queries, reflecting a decision about the conclusion, which gives unexpected strength to the poem. An average tribute would point inevitably to the new heroes who are inspired to follow Crummell's inspiration. Not so here, only the wise advice to the reader—and, amazingly, to Crummell:

> Think no more of this—
> Rest!

"Ode to Ethiopia" and "Alexander Crummell—Dead" explore two forms of heroism. One involves assurance that the black race has done well so far and has every reason to be proud of its history and humanity, and it expresses confidence in a bright future and in a sure path to glory. The second is a more subtle performance. "Alexander Crummell—Dead" accepts the death of a great man, as the title implies, and offers questions about the future. What is impressive is the toughmindedness of the speaker, who points in a general way to Crummell's holiness and his achievements despite opposition but who offers no assurances about what follows him. An approach to the future, the poet says, begins with awareness of loss and shouldering responsibility. "Ode to Ethiopia" glorifies the past and future, and "Alexander Crummell—Dead" stresses, rather, the challenge of the present day.

It is probably a mistake to describe "We Wear the Mask" and "The Poet" as personal poems. They are personal and much more. To be more precise, they describe the problems of a black artist, and these may be projected to define a more general condition shared by many aspiring artists in an unfriendly world.

The "mask that grins and lies" is surely, first, the property of an artist, deriving, no doubt, from the use of masks by actors in classical drama. It hides "torn and bleeding hearts" because exposing an artist's inner reality to a world governed by "human guile" would be pointless, perhaps humiliating. The artist has pride, and he refuses to stoop to test the questionable response of an unsympathetic and unappreciative audience. Christ offers an avenue of last appeal, but the artist fails to receive either hope or balm from divinity. The only sure realities dwindle down to three basic facts: "We sing," because true artists have to, no matter what the world says; ". . . the clay is vile . . .," projecting an unchanged world in which "guile" still governs; ". . . long the mile . . .," suggesting that the time during which this alienated state must be endured is long, very long. But what remains for the artist is his talent and his pride:

> But let the world dream otherwise,
> We wear the mask!

The poem applies with especial force to Dunbar, dramatizing not only the attachment to dialect verse, which he was just beginning to resent, but his attendant roles as a skilled reader of his own poetry and as a model for the race. The pronoun used in the poem is "We," and the poet conceivably here identifies with all black artists performing in vaudeville or minstrel shows, writing for these theatrical productions, or turning out verse and narratives that are acceptable to a genteel audience.

A second level of meaning suggests the participation of the race. All blacks, to survive in the society, must conform to standards that they do not necessarily approve of and learn to play the games and assume the masks that will assure protection and, occasionally, advancement. A further extension of meaning involves everyone. All people living in a shallow and pretentious society, an expression of gentility in an extreme state, wear masks. No one reveals his inner reality fully to another, for the reasons that Dunbar has stated.

It is no wonder that "We Wear the Mask" is Dunbar's best-known poem in literary English. It is a poignant cry of distress calling attention to a pathological condition for which there is no immediate remedy. It has meanings on many levels, ranging from the definition of a personal problem to the inadequacies of the entire society. The particular dilemma becomes, without strain, the property of all readers.

Comparison of "We Wear the Mask" and "The Poet" is revealing. Both poems deal with the same general subject matter: the failure of the world to recognize a distortion of talent, a "mask," in short, and its patent disinterest in the whole body of the poet's achievement or, indeed, the life and the psyche of the artist. "The Poet," however, suffers from the contraction of meaning and reference that characterize so much of Dunbar's verse after 1896. "We Wear the Mask" offers meaning on many levels, but "The Poet" does not. The poem is plainly what it is, with little possibility of extension of reference.

The poet's preferred subject matter is recorded in the poem, though admittedly in terms a little vague. All of them bear the imprint of the ideals of nineteenth-century Romanticism, with no reference to the contemporary pessimism which Dunbar's poem "The Mystery" reflects. The subjects listed are "life, serenely sweet,/ With now and then, a deeper note . . ."; ". . . the world's absorbing beat . . ." which the poet knows, in some mystical way; and ". . . love when earth was young,/ And Love, itself, was in his lays." These are general topics, too general, and one cannot blame the public for desiring something more specific, since it was sated with Romantic lays about life, the world, and Love.

The poet suffers when ". . . the world, it turned to/ praise/ A jingle in a broken tongue." The application to Dunbar could not be more precise, though the poem underestimates his contribution in literary English to exaggerate the world's rejection. What is clear also is that Dunbar has come, in the later years of his career, to place a low value upon his dialect verse.

"The Poet" is a specific statement which has intensity and pathos, but its application is limited, primarily to an assessment of Dunbar's own achievement, and not broad with a cluster of implications and rich associations that touch the world.

Dunbar's verse in conventional or literary English, though varied in quality, offers moments of excitement and power that are surpassed only by the master poems in dialect. The poems examined here suggest the very wide range in Dunbar's literary interests, and though there are individual poems that are memorable and moving, there does not seem to be any focus in his canon in literary English. When one looks at both the dialect and the literary verse, one comes away deeply impressed by what one has seen. True, Dunbar did not attain the highest levels possible for him in the area of his greatest strength and in forms making demands upon the full powers of his fertile imagination, but he accomplished a great deal in destroying stereotypes about black intellectual capacities and appealing to a large audience, both black and white. Dunbar is the first great black poet in America, a fitting pioneer for Sterling Brown, Langston Hughes, M.B. Tolson, Robert Hayden, and Gwendolyn Brooks.

Dunbar's fiction has tended to suffer a form of critical neglect for three reasons. His reputation as a poet has overshadowed his other artistic contributions, and this situation is quite understandable given his exciting career as a poet. Dunbar was considered somehow to be a less effective writer of fiction than Charles Chesnutt, who emerged with him in the 1890s as the first really professional black artist in America. This reservation about Dunbar's fiction requires qualification. Certainly "One Man's Fortunes," "Mr. Cornelius Johnson, Office-Seeker," and "A Council of State," all in Dunbar's most seminal volume of short pieces, *The Strength of Gideon and Other Stories* (1900), deserve to stand by the tales in Chesnutt's *The Wife of His Youth*, published at almost the same time. The last cause for neglect is unquestionably Dunbar's continuing association with the Plantation Tradition, an enduring commitment that fictional experimentation in other areas does not support. There may be a simple answer—money, the sustained desire of the contemporary magazines for this always successful and much-tried fictional staple. It is very likely that Dunbar made a distinction in his mind between Plantation breadwinners and the more daring excursions into social realism and into the social order in black urban communities. In any event, more than half of around one hundred short pieces are tales from the old plantation, more or less furnished with the characters and formulaic plots too well known for repetition. Hugh Gloster, a fine critic of black fiction, can assert with some justification:

> In his short stories . . . Dunbar generally accepts the limitations and circumscriptions of the plantation tradition. Glorifying the good old days in the accepted manner, he sentimentalizes master-slave relationships and implies that freedom brings social misery to the black man. Negro migrants to the North are usually represented as nostalgic misfits. . . .

Gloster is finally wrong, partly because he underestimates the value of Dunbar's attempts to explore social problems in the North and the alienation of the outsider there and partly because he does not fit together the short stories and novels to see how they relate to each other.

The fact is that *The Uncalled* and *Folks from Dixie* were published in the same year, 1898, suggesting that Dunbar was perfectly capable of carrying in his head two quite different structures for fiction. Essentially, they represent two sides of the strong sentimental tradition in America. *The Uncalled* is a novel about a minister, Freddie Brent, an orphan whose foster parent, Hester Prime, forces him to accept a call to undertake divine work which Freddie hears only imperfectly, if at all. Ultimately, Freddie quits the Methodist ministry when his stern superior, Reverend Simpson, asks him to preach a sermon reprimanding a poor fallen woman. Freddie finds an expanded life, joy, and love in Cincinnati, although many critics have said that Dunbar has found nothing to praise in the city.

> I have learned to know what pleasure is, and it has been like a stimulant to me. . . . I have come face to face with Christianity without cant, and I respect it for what it is.

The novel falls into a rather special line of sentimental narratives about the troubled minister, and though there are touches of realism and a few black characters within its structure, *The Uncalled* does not deserve to be classified with the strong realistic novels of Middle Western life, *The Hoosier Schoolmaster* (1871) by Edward Eggleston and *The Story of a Country Town* (1883) by Edgar Watson Howe. Dexter, Ohio, has no complex social dimensions and poses to the minister a simple problem of the restricted as opposed to the expanded life under the umbrella of Christianity. The questions that really disturbed churchmen at the time—science, the corruption of wealth, urban alienation— have no place here.

Folks from Dixie (1898) is essentially a collection of pieces dealing with plantation life, but it is more of a mixed bag than it appears to be. Though there are several tales set in Northern backgrounds, the genuine surprise in the collection is "At Shaft II." This is a story of a miners' strike in West Virginia. Violence occurs when black strikebreakers are introduced into the mine. Blacks battle whites for the possession of the property until the troops arrive and disperse the white strikers. The blacks retain their jobs under the original management of the mine. The significance of the tale is not so much who wins or who loses but Dunbar's willingness to face the vexing problems of a new era and provide a glimpse of a larger and more impersonal system of economic distribution and human relations, in which race plays only a part, and possibly not a dominant one. This discovery of what appears to be an external force larger than life is one that Dunbar is not to forget.

A comparison of the two books suggests that Dunbar chose the short fiction for the launching of trial balloons. The novel is the careful, if not cautious, achievement, restricted by the limitations of the sentimental line of narratives of which it is a part. *Folks from Dixie*, despite its unprepossessing title, offers the radical departure in fictional material, vastly different from anything to be found in the novel.

A similar incongruity exists between *The Love of Landry* and *The Strength of Gideon and Other Stories*, both published in 1900. *The Love of Landry* is more a product of the sentimental tradition than is *The Uncalled*. Both novels have as their main actors white characters. *The Uncalled* dealt with a real problem that had a modest appeal for thoughtful readers. *The Love of Landry* has no problem at all, except to promote the alliance between representatives of two upper-class families. The novel was a product of Dunbar's stay in Colorado, recuperating from tuberculosis, and it poses the question of a difference between Eastern and Western attitudes and Eastern and Western realities. Interest in it extended beyond Dunbar. William Vaughn Moody wrote a play, *The Great Divide*, that probed for more substantial distinctions between Easterner and Westerner, and which was produced with considerable success in New York in 1906. Landry talks of breathing space and a lack of duplicity in the West, and Mildred, who has suffered from general weakness in her constitution, is rejuvenated by her visit to Colorado. A visit becomes a permanent stay since East and West are to be joined in marriage with the place of residence for the couple to be, apparently, in the West. Nothing could be fluffier than this tale, which moves toward seriousness only with the appearance of a black porter.

The Strength of Gideon, on the other hand, contains much more provocative matter. The range of topics is very broad indeed. There are plantation stories emphasizing black fidelity to families of former masters ("The Strength of Gideon"); black wisdom in assisting the families of former masters in accommodating to post–Civil War poverty; and black good sense and faithfulness to other blacks, despite temptations offered by freedom and the North. The collection has, in addition, plantation anecdotes dealing with familiar characters who enjoy favorable turns of fortune so that a bad case is made good. More innovative are the stories about the corruption of blacks by the cities. Perhaps the most compelling of these is "The Finding of Zach," in which a wild young buck is cleaned up and made respectable by the Banner Club so that he can greet the father who has come to New York to see him. Then there are urban anecdotes in which city ways seem either to be better or more honest than country approaches to life. The most impressive pieces by far are Dunbar's explorations of the forms of discrimination in the urban North.

"One Man's Fortunes" presents the brief career as a lawyer of Bertram Halliday who has returned to his home town with a college degree and the idealism of Henley. He is determined to study law, despite the objection of a white friend, Featherton, a lawyer who thinks that the time is not ready. He is hired by Featherton to get out the black vote for his election as a "Christian judge," and fired immediately after the election. Deeply embittered, he decides to go teach in the South. Webb Davis, also a college graduate, a realistic counterpart to Halliday, has prospered by setting up a barber shop and proceeding to engage in local politics.

"Mr. Cornelius Johnson, Office-Seeker" records the frustration of a black candidate for office who arrives in Washington to collect what is due him as a consequence of his efforts in an Alabama election. Optimism is succeeded by doubt and then despair, as Congressman Barker either refuses to see him or delays giving him what he seeks. He is totally crushed by the news that the Senate has refused to confirm his appointment. At the end he is a broken and bitter man.

"A Council of State" is the most ambitious tale in the volume. It describes the successful attempt of Boss Luther Hamilton to prevent criticism of the administration at the Afro-American Convention. His agent and confederate is an intelligent, hard, near-white lady named Miss Kirkman, who "found it more profitable to ally herself to the less important race because she could assume a position among them as a representative woman, which she could never have hoped to gain among the whites." Miss Kirkman packs the convention with pro-administration people, tears up the speech of her fiancé, who wishes to complain about administrative neglect, and defeats the progressive forces.

There is much that is new in these stories; black involvement in urban political power struggles, black insensitivity to other blacks because of ambition or fear of losing status, and black vulnerability to capricious acts of fate, unexpected inconsistencies in character, or the attraction of forms of unrealistic idealism. One no longer talks of the innocent, pleasure-loving blacks in these urban sketches, because innocence has died, and the only ambition worth respecting is power.

The Fanatics is a sentimental novel, using scenes both in Dorbury, Ohio, and on a Virginia plantation. What occurs on a Virginia plantation is predictable, following the familiar pattern of the plantation romance. What happens in Dorbury is something else, since there we find actions for the first time that have had the benefit of experimentation and trial in the short fiction. This new matter is inserted within a sentimental frame and acquires a life of its own apart from the general pattern of reconciliation involving representatives from the North and South in Dorbury after the War, not only long-separated lovers but fathers and sons as well.

The action is predictable, full of emotional crises, declarations of love, denunciations and disowning, transformations and reconciliations. The matter and manner of the novel achieve a distinction above that of the plantation romance only when blacks appear.

Dorbury does not like or accept blacks. These sentiments are shared by both Northerners, who hold blacks responsible for the War, and Southerners, who have accepted them only as slaves. The chapter "The Contrabands" and the one that follows, "License or Liberty," present an explosion in Dorbury when a group of rootless, shifting blacks, shaken from their home environment by the War, arrive in town. There is a violent confrontation in which the blacks stand fast and the leader of the mob, a drunkard, rabble-rouser, and a defiler of the weak, is killed by a new arrival from the South, whose family had suffered insults from Stothard. The only prominent citizen who is sympathetic to the blacks is a white ex-Confederate soldier from a prominent family, Steven Van Doren.

Sympathy does not come from the blacks in Dorbury. They bar the new arrivals from entering their church, and they are apprehensive about their own status, which might be degraded by an influx of ignorant blacks from the South. The regeneration of Nigger Ed, a forlorn black and the town drunk before the War, who performs heroic services on the field of battle and who wins acceptance with respect and love by the whole town when he returns, offers little comfort.

For the first time, Dunbar has introduced into the novel unpleasant matter documenting real problems involving blacks. The description of the black upheaval in Dorbury was accomplished with the same clear-eyed, objective perspective that appears first in the short pieces. Blacks and whites are good and bad, perhaps mostly in-between, and they shape ambitions, high and low, and struggle to achieve them. The plantation mythology has no place here.

Though Dunbar published two other collections of largely plantation tales, they do not figure really in the development of Dunbar as a writer of fiction. *In Old Plantation Days* (1903) represents, if anything, regression, since it records in the familiar style the quaint actions of slaves on Colonel Mordaunt's property, and Colonel Mordaunt presides over the proceedings with appropriate dignity and tolerance. *The Heart of Happy Hollow* (1904) offers, with the plantation tales, more varied items, and the whole collection is an improvement upon *In Old Plantation Days*. *The Heart of Happy Hollow* permits the inclusion, for example, of a shocking story of violence, "The Lynching of Jube Benson." Both collections may suffer from Dunbar's waning energies and the unfortunate progress of the tuberculosis which would cause his death.

The real culmination of Dunbar's achievement as a writer of fiction is *The Sport of the Gods* (1902). The novel incorporates much of the substance and the style that the finest tales have displayed. There are specific points of connection: Dunbar's handling of the problem of a group's ostracism by a town; his knowledge of the many forms of cruel exploitation that can occur in a city; his even-handed view of the presence of good and evil in whites and blacks, except that these properties suffer at times from an amount of vagueness; and his skilled portrayal of the mounting frustration, even rage, in the black psyche. These are matters of substance that are new in a Dunbar novel, but not foreign or alien to the short fiction. *The Sport of the Gods* possesses them all.

Equally important is the approach to character and action, the guiding intelligence that organizes and paces the events within a narrative. The novel has as its narrator a cultivated observer who displays a detached manner and a disposition to point up ironies in the developing action. The voice of the narrator is consistent and unforced; it has the natural authority of someone who knows country and city and has the historical perspective to make informed commentary when it is required. Dunbar clearly shapes in *The Sport of the Gods* a form in fiction that suits his purpose, and he does not respond to the demands of traditional structures. Dunbar's irony, muted in narratives of sentiment, is here in full display.

The first sentence suggests, to some extent, the manner of the whole novel:

> Fiction has said so much in regret of the old days when there were plantations and overseers and masters and slaves, that it was good to come upon such a household as Berry Hamilton's, if for no other reason than that it offered a relief from the monotony of tiresome iteration.

This serves as an introduction to the two large ironic propositions that dominate the novel. The first involves the way of life of the Hamiltons in the years following Emancipation. The plantation romance offers a picture of good times before and after the War, and affirmation comes, apparently, from the favorable situations of Berry Hamilton, who is an old and respected retainer of Maurice Oakley's. What seems good turns vicious and offers a demonstration that the relationship between a former master and a former slave amounts to little, when Oakley falsely accuses Hamilton of stealing money, prosecutes him, sends him to jail for ten years, and turns out his family. None of the traditional

virtues of trust, kindliness, and benevolence are here, just narrowness, vindictiveness, and a lack of charity.

The North does not fare much better. New York, before and
after the War, was regarded as a haven for the homeless and the
oppressed, especially blacks who made their way in recurrent
waves to the city of opportunity and freedom. As Dunbar has
destroyed the Hamiltons' "bower of peace and comfort," he de-
molishes systematically the expectation that New York will be the
Hamiltons' salvation:

> To the provincial coming to New York for the first time, igno-
> rant and unknown, the city presents a notable mingling of the
> qualities of cheeriness and gloom.

This mixed beginning is a preface to a reaction on the part of the
newcomer even less encouraging:

> . . . after he has passed through the first pangs of strangeness
> and homesickness, yes, even after he has got beyond the stranger's
> enthusiasm for the metropolis, the real fever of love for the place
> will take hold upon him. The subtle, insidious wine of New
> York will begin to intoxicate him.

And the expected conclusion follows:

> Then he is hopeless, and to live elsewhere would be death.

Such a city is clearly not the appropriate place for Mrs. Hamilton
and her two children, Joe and Kitty, to seek the comfort and
psychic restoration which they require.

The story of the Hamiltons is a tale of two locales, a small
Southern town and New York City. Berry Hamilton, despite his
twenty years of faithful service in the Oakley household, is accused of stealing money which has actually been gambled away
by the spendthrift, artistic brother of the master of the household,
Maurice Oakley. Berry Hamilton is tried and receives a sentence
of ten years in prison; the rest of the family is turned out of their
comfortable house on the Oakley grounds and suffers hostility
and ostracism by blacks and whites in the town. Fannie Hamilton
and her children make their way to New York where they undergo

a spectacular degeneration. Joe, weak, callow, and much pampered by his parents, becomes a drunkard, a parasite, and a murderer. Kitty, "a pretty, cheery little thing" who "could sing like a lark," goes on the stage and tosses aside her moral instruction with almost the same eagerness that Joe displays. Fannie, the faithful, religious, loving wife, takes another man, with Berry in prison, a man who beats her and dies violently just in time to prevent his murder by the newly released Berry. His liberation is a consequence of the good work of a white reporter, Skaggs, a frequenter of the Banner Club where he encounters Joe, who senses from Joe's drunken babbling that a good story exists for the *Universe*, his paper. Skaggs pursues the sordid story of the Hamiltons to its Southern source and discovers Maurice Oakley's cruelty, his brother Frank's confession, revealing that the money was squandered, not stolen, and Maurice's refusal to acknowledge the confession. The whole affair finds its way to the pages of the *Universe* and Berry receives justice and freedom, at last, but not in time to do much about his shattered family. The elder Hamiltons return to the South and receive a warm welcome and a home from the wife of Maurice Oakley, now repentant and contrite. The couple, broken, humbled, and sad, live in a peace broken only by the shrieks of the mad Maurice Oakley, who, with the public revelation of his shocking behavior and his family's dishonor, has lost his mind.

There is no simple moral for the story. It is certainly not to be found in the general question which the novel poses: "Oh, is there no way to keep these people from rushing away from small villages and country districts of the South up to the cities, where they cannot battle with the terrible force of the strange and unusual environment?" True, the city corrupts, and it is especially hard upon untrained, ill-prepared blacks like Mrs. Hamilton and her children. But there are people of nobility and strength in black New York, to be found especially among the artists. Hattie Sterling, the generous and vulnerable musical comedy singer and dancer who takes up weak Joe, looks at her life and her future with complete realism. Martin, the managing star of "Martin's Blackbirds," impresses his associates by his display of professionalism and integrity. The city, then, does not corrupt all, no more, indeed, than the country, where the standards of a depraved gentility seek to dominate still in a changing world.

Some critics make the claim that *The Sport of the Gods* is a Naturalistic novel. Dunbar offers the suggestion that powerful, impersonal forces are at work in the city, but the suggestion is not really pursued or documented. No more than are the vague references to the "Will" that are scattered throughout the novel. The fact is that there is no overwhelming influence of environment, since possibilities exist for something other than an inevitable degeneration. The Hamiltons suffer their various calamities because of deficiencies of character, not from an impassive Naturalistic fate. There are none of the other trappings of Naturalism: the careful documentation of the total environment, the preoccupation with a design imposed by heredity, and the symbolism.

The Sport of the Gods must be accepted for what it is: a fine, ironic, penetrating novel that offers no easy solutions for anyone, nor easy classification for critics. There are moments of striking realism in the novel, especially in the scenes in the Banner Club, but Dunbar's structure is too mannered, too dependent at times upon accident and upon melodramatic reversals to be called realistic. *The Sport of the Gods* is, in fact, a carefully planned narrative designed to sweep away vestiges of old myths and to encourage honesty in looking at and evaluating reality and an acceptance of self, with all of its deficiencies. There are few triumphs in Dunbar's mature, if slightly cynical, world, and that world has not much to do with Gods. The Gods are, if anything, the symbols of old expectations, unrealistic and without support in fact or possibility, and these creatures of fantasy make sport and play havoc with vulnerable mortals. Protection exists in honesty and maturity. The wise course for the elder Hamiltons is a return to their home in the South, having been deeply wounded by life in the city, and they are able to resume their life there, much wiser than they were before.

The Sport of the Gods is a splendid demonstration of the power of a controlling voice. The wise and completely informed narrator orders the events of the narrative with authority and a newly discovered freedom. He is not deterred from using events because they are realistic or melodramatic, and he is uninhibited in his comments on the action or on the motivation that stands behind the action. He has chosen to give the novel a large perspective, a wide view of the black experience as it undergoes psychic change in the South and the agonies of migration. Dunbar's sweep is not epic, but it is suggestive of a quality of narration just short of that. The triumph of the novel is the triumph of voice. For once, the mature, speculative, objective narrator appears, and that appearance, more than anything else in the novel, is Dunbar's legacy to the twentieth century.

The literary achievement of Paul Laurence Dunbar is important for all black artists who follow him. He made an outstanding contribution in poetry, both in dialect verse and in literary English, even though he never fully sensed where his greatest strength rested. But all poets who use the spoken language of the people as their medium owe Dunbar a great debt, because he stretched dialect to incorporate serious ideas and to achieve new artistic effects. No poet in America has approached his success in this respect. Dunbar stands also as a pioneer in the development of the black novel. The influential work *The Sport of the Gods* has been hailed sometimes as the first black novel to use at some depth an urban background. This may be so, but infinitely more important, this is the first black novel to be ordered by a sophisticated narrator who exercises his freedom to choose and to organize fictional elements from any source. *The Sport of the Gods* is the first well-constructed ironic novel on the black experience with a fictional voice that speaks, with authority and without commitment to a cause, on an important and central event in black history, migration to the cities.

Dunbar's life is so close to the model presented by the Romantic artist that it is difficult to consider him anything other than a creature totally given over to idealism. The artist is born in a modest home in Dayton and he rises in an incredibly short time to fame. He falls in love with Alice Ruth Moore from a picture in a magazine next to a poem of hers. He experiences the hurt of separation from Alice at a time when he receives honors for his literary achievements and more generous payments from publishers. He dies of tuberculosis at a young age, on February 9, 1906. But the aura of high Romanticism is misleading. Dunbar's great accomplishment is his pushing beyond Romantic restrictions and standards, both in his poetry and his fiction. His doing so makes him the beginning, the father, in effect, of black poetry and fiction in the twentieth century. What he has done for blacks he has done for all America, and he will survive in memory as a great, innovative, and brave black artist.

1980

Prose Literature of
Racial Defense, 1917–1924:
A Preface to the Harlem Renaissance

The years 1917 and 1924, not arbitrarily, limit the literary material written by Negroes to be considered in this essay. Two social phenomena give the beginning of the period significance: America's entrance into World War I and the participation of American Negroes in the conflict as well as the migration of Negroes from rural districts in the South to industrialized areas in the North. These major social events have importance because of the consequent fundamental dislocations in the life of the Negro and the necessity for new adjustments. Garvey organized the Universal Negro Improvement Association (U.N.I.A.) in 1917—a modern and extended Back-to-Africa movement, and the first in a series of race riots swept the country that same year. Social phenomena have another significance as well; contemporary writers were unusually absorbed in exploiting their rhetorical possibilities. Simple exposition of social happenings became confused with a literature of justification and defense as the turmoil and dislocation of the period fanned racial resentment to a white heat. The excitement of the period, increasing the concern for protection of the race's good name, stimulated around 1917 a revitalized interest in the controversial essay, perhaps a revival of the principal form by educated Negroes which no similar period had seen since the 1850s, when the antislavery fight absorbed the energies of Alexander Crummell, Frederick Douglass, Charles Remond, William Wells Brown, and Samuel R. Ward, to mention a few names among many. Fiction and poetry also reflected the contention perceptible in the social scene.

The year 1925 marked the formal dawn of the Negro Renaissance and the strengthening of the emphasis upon more form-conscious production. That tendency was what Alain Locke meant when he stated that the Negro was no longer looked upon as a problem but was regarded as a person of human status, capable of creative expression.[1] Negro criticism flowered; William Stanley Braithwaite, James Weldon Johnson, Jessie Fauset, and

Alain Locke emerged as analysts of the new imaginative writings. The heavy emphasis upon form after the period of muddling and contention was accompanied by the crystallization of the concept of the Renaissance, which was equated with certain thought patterns and tendencies in art production. Moreover, to the ardent follower of the movement, the name "the New Negro" was given; Claude McKay indicates that the term was made common language by the Garvey publications.[2] By 1925, these directions in the Negro art world had become so much common property that Alain Locke in the Harlem issue of *The Survey Graphic* (March 1925) could construct what was tantamount to production blueprints for the striving Negro writer and receive the universal approval of a great part of the Negro intellectual world. The thrashing out of ideas broached in that manifesto occurred in the period under consideration, and the preliminary intellectual battles which accompanied their presentation and made them common currency occurred in the major Negro periodicals and newspapers of the day, *The Crisis, The Messenger, Opportunity,* the Chicago *Defender,* and *The Negro World.* Occasionally, controversial matter written by a Negro author found its way into a white periodical. A notable example of this extension of publication was the airing of the Garvey–Du Bois tussle over the question of pan-Africanism by the magazines *Current History* and *Century.*[3]

The Black Milieu

More than 330,000 Negroes moved out of the South and into the North and West during the decade 1910–1920; for the most part, the emigration was crowded into the latter half of the decade, particularly in the years 1916 to 1918.[4] The reasons expounded for the pronounced increase have been many and by themselves constitute no small amount of literature. Ever since the close of the Civil War, the migration of Negroes had been continuous, but largely within the South; yet, there had been a constant and increasing number of Negroes moving to the North. Thus, Benjamin Brawley's statement that "migration had not ceased since 1879"[5] is undeniably true, but not adequate. There began in the spring of 1879 an emigration of Negroes from Louisiana and

Mississippi to Kansas which had the spectacular quality of the War movements. Moses Singleton and Henry Adams were the leaders, and Adams alone was credited with organizing 98,000 blacks.[6] For a time after the Civil War, there were two diverging currents of Negro migration. One was northward from the more Northern of the Southern states, Maryland, Virginia, Kentucky, Tennessee, and North Carolina. The other was a migration southward and westward on the part of Negroes in the lower Atlantic and Gulf states. In 1910, the flow of Negro migrants from Virginia and Kentucky accounted for 56.2 percent of the Southern Negroes living in the North. Thereafter, a change occurred in the nature of the migration; Joseph A. Hill commented that "The migration between 1910 and 1920 reduced the proportion who were born in the two states to 37 per cent." On the other hand, the proportion of Northern Negroes coming from the cotton belt states further south (South Carolina, Georgia, Florida, Alabama, Mississippi, Arkansas, Louisiana, and Texas) "increased from 18.2 per cent of the total southern born Negroes living in the North in 1910 to 40.2 per cent of the total in 1920."[7]

Other characteristics of the movement of black migrants in the second decade of the twentieth century stand out. The size of the migration and the added factor of the overwhelmingly urban direction of the moving people are important. The urban trend among Negroes was not a new phenomenon, but it did assume especial importance when it was evident, as Louise V. Kennedy observes, that "practically all of the migrants to the North went to the cities rather than to rural communities."[8] The percent increase ran into incredible figures for the northeast and north central states. Detroit increased in the decade by 611.3 percent, Cleveland by 307.8 percent, Chicago by 148.2 percent, New York City by 148.2 percent, Indianapolis by 59.0 percent, and Philadelphia by 58.9 percent.

Much of the literature of migration expresses the opinion that the migration was confined to and represented a strictly Negro affair involving long-distance journeys from the deep South to the North. These assumptions are responsible for this extravagant statement of Emmett Scott's: "More than 400,000 Negroes suddenly moved North in the brief period of three years following the outbreak of the first World War."[9] It has been stated, previously, that since the Civil War the greater part of the Negro migrations had been within the South. There was a constant shift from one Southern state to another, an ever-present flux from one county to another and from rural to urban districts. It is significant, then, that in 1920 in the South even those states (with the exception of Kentucky) which revealed in 1920 an actual decrease in Negroes had at the same time an increase in the urban Negro population.[10] The heaviest losers were the rural districts, indicating suffering from both intersectional and intrasectional migration.

Whites shared both the drift toward the Northern urban areas as well as the drift toward the Southern cities. This general statement can be made: the tendency in the Southern urban areas was for the rate of increase of whites in the population to exceed that of the Negroes; in the North, however, the Negroes increased much more rapidly than did the white population. It must be remembered, still, that the rate of increase of whites was often considerable in the Northern urban centers—in Detroit it reached the extraordinary height of 107.0 percent.[11]

Among the immediate economic causes of the migration were the labor depression in the South in 1914 and 1915 and the large decrease in foreign immigration resulting from the World War. Then came the cotton boll weevil in the summers of 1915 and 1916, greatly damaging the cotton crop over extensive areas largely in Louisiana, Mississippi, Alabama, Georgia, and Florida, and threatening to unsettle farming conditions in 1917. There followed the cotton price demoralization and low prices during subsequent years. The usual floods during the summer of 1915 over large sections in practically the same states plagued by the weevil further aggravated the situation. The Negroes, moreover, were generally dissatisfied because of the continual low wages paid in the South in spite of the increasing cost of living. Complementing these important incentives for migration were the lack of credit extended to tenants, their general dismissal because of the hard times, and the closing of some of the commissaries.[12]

There were other specific economic inducements. Declining foreign immigration in addition to the expanding industrial system of the immediate prewar years created an immediate demand for labor, which became even more urgent when America's economy became a war economy. Wages offered to the laborer in the North were double and treble those received in the South.[13]

A dramatic series of causes, whose importance was the subject of much debate, is involved in the emotional reactions of Negroes to the civil, political, and social climate in the South. Several specific grievances stand out among the many lengthy written complaints. Primarily, these were lynching and the threat of physical violence. Emphasized almost as much were the treatment which Negroes received from the courts and guardians of the peace, the disparity in punishment and conviction between whites and Negroes, the discrimination in regard to accommodations for travel, and the fee system by which a fixed amount per head was received by the sheriff for feeding prisoners.[14] There was also the frequent complaint that educational facilities for Negroes were insufficient. Emmett J. Scott made this observation in his monograph, written during the great wave of immigration of 1919:

> Negro parents appreciate this situation because, although admitting that they can tolerate the position to which they are assigned, they do not welcome such an arrangement for their children. For this reason they are not reluctant to send their sons away from home.[15]

All kinds of stimuli were responsible for the impetus given to the movement. Barber shop and grocery store gossip, church meetings, public speakers, personal appeals in the form of letters, the return of successful migrants for brief visits, functioning as living examples of prosperity, labor agents, and the Chicago *Defender* were all influential; the last force—the Chicago Negro weekly—contributed greatly to the movement by its dissemination of statements outlining the urban utopia and criticism of the South. At the beginning of the movement, the circulation of the paper was 50,000; in 1918, it had reached 125,000. Contributing factors also were the scheme of setting definite departure dates (e.g., May 15, 1917) and the circulation of rumors (e.g., the story was current that the Germans were on their way to invade the South through Texas). Finally, there were literary attempts, springing directly from the heart of the movement; poems and songs such as "Bound for the Promised Land," "Farewell We're Good and Gone," "Northward Bound," "The Land of Hope," "Negro Migration," and "The Reason Why" were infectious. Increasing numbers caught the spirit and shared the migration fever.

Scott indicates the religious cast which the migration sometimes took: "The devout and religious saw God in the movement." Elaborate allegory was constructed by the migrating populace to give divine sanction to the violent dislocation in the lives of the black people: "The movement was called the 'exodus' from its suggestive resemblance to the flight of the Israelites from Egypt."[16] These terms were a part of the vocabulary of the migrant: "The Promised Land," "Crossing Over Jordan" (Ohio River), and "Beulah Land." At times, demonstrations took on a spectacular aspect, as when a party of 147 from Hattiesburg, Mississippi, while crossing the Ohio River, held solemn ceremonies to commemorate their freedom.

The Negro did not find the "Beulah Land" when he came North. Some of the desired advantages he found: the new schools, better pay, more apparent personal freedom, and delightful and exotic ways to spend one's money. But there were serious drawbacks: the cold Northern winter, inadequate housing, and the inhospitability of one's neighbors. The tide of race riots, becoming numerous in 1917, shaking both the North and South, broke out with particular violence in East St. Louis, Chicago, and Washington, cities which had been recently the recipients of large numbers of black migrants. The suffering was considerably alleviated as the migration progressed, for those migrants who arrived after the first two or three years of painful adjustment. An editorial in *Opportunity* in 1924 expresses this view of the change in the condition of the newly arrived migrants:

> Beginning about 1919 those who had come in two or three years preceding had gained a substantial economic footing and knowledge of being able to stand the climate and other living conditions.[17]

The assurance which this new security in urban areas gave to prospective migrants in the South was responsible for the development of more systematic migration.

> Frequently whole families or neighborhoods, sometimes with previous arrangements for employment in some of the industrial communities, migrated in a group. A few cases have been recorded of whole church congregations bringing their pastors with them.[18]

Yet there was much food for counterpropaganda designed to keep the Negroes in the South. Particularly acute was the housing situation. *Opportunity* in 1923 makes the statement: "New York, for example, has about 40,000 more Negroes than present buildings can comfortably or even decently accommodate." In Pittsburgh, the Negro home-seekers, it was said, had been forced to retreat to the uninhabitable cliffs, isolated from the city's gas and water supply.[19] Carter G. Woodson indicated many of the evils which were to befall the migrant in the North and predicted frankly: "The North will have a problem." Furnishing a great part of the difficulty would be, in addition to the ever-pressing housing situation, the behavior of irresponsible Negroes and problems of vice, crime, and disease. Health was seen as a great and difficult end to be attained by the newly arrived black populace. "Many of them have been unable to resist pneumonia, bronchitis, and tuberculosis."[20] Other forebodings were heard about the health of the urban Negro not only in regard to his possibilities for survival but with respect to his fertility as well. Joseph A. Hill commented in 1924, six years after Woodson's prediction:

> The birth rate for the Negro, however, remains lower in the North than it is in the South; and it seems fairly evident that the northward migration of the Negroes has retarded the increase of the Negro population.

The writer expressed the hope that these conditions would be temporary.[21] Prediction and comment about health became even more significant in light of the extended arguments on the point of the race's chance of existence in the urban society. Census figures were used to bolster the concept of the "dying race." Extended research into comparative mortality rates and investigation concerning the inroads of the "white plague" were carried out, and the results of the research were used to construct a rhetoric opposed to the philosophy of "inevitable extinction." The fine points in this discussion are reserved for treatment in the discussion of controversial literature below.

Not the least of the troubles of the black migrant was the outbreak of violence and racial riots which swept the urban centers and seemed to form, therefore, justification for the predictions that the good lot of the Negro in the North was only temporary. Trouble began in 1917 with the riots at Chester, Youngstown, and East St. Louis. That at East St. Louis in February took a toll of over a hundred Negroes. A combination of undesirable conditions—distressing congestion among Negroes, a tradition of lawlessness, and a large criminal element—formed a tinder box needing only an overt act of antagonism to touch off the combustion. That came with the strikes in the aluminum ore works. The employers felt reasonably secure in delaying making an agreement with the striking workers, since Negroes were then pouring into the city from the South.[22] At Houston during the same year Negro soldiers clashed with the residents of the town. The year 1919 brought bloody riots in Chicago and in Washington. The riot in Chicago beginning Sunday, July 27, stemmed from a clash of white people and Negroes at a bathing beach which resulted in the drowning of a Negro boy. The subsequent race riot took a toll of thirty-eight lives.[23] There were outbreaks of violence at Longview, Texas, and at Elaine, Arkansas. Governor Brough blamed *The Crisis* and the Chicago *Defender* as primary causes for ill feeling in Arkansas.

This period of upheaval had an important effect upon the literature of the Negro at the time. The Negro was more articulate than ever about the injustices to which he had to submit. The feeling was not only one of resentment but one of belligerent resistance as well. The tradition of writing begun with Booker T. Washington was carried on by William H. Holtzclaw, William J. Edwards, and Robert R. Moton.[24] Emmett J. Scott and Lyman B. Stowe[25] in their biography of Booker Washington had emphasized judicious and optimistic language. The tradition had placed a premium upon the accounts of individual achievements in spite of adversity; it advocated and looked toward greater cooperation between the races, and it talked of the duties and responsibilities which the black man owed his white neighbor. It stood for mediation and harmony. The violence of the day punctured the popularity of this tradition and made acceptable to the masses of Negroes the fighting talk and the impassioned literature of resentment which Du Bois and Monroe Trotter had been writing since the first decade of the century. Brawley expressed the new feeling among the Negroes:

A great spiritual change had come over the Negro people of the United States. At the very time that their sons and brothers were making the supreme sacrifice in France they were witnessing such events as those at East St. Louis or Houston.[26]

The new spirit in literature in its crudest expression was embodied in this statement of Walter White's concerning the Chicago race riot:

One of the greatest surprises to many of those who came down "to clean out the niggers" is that these same "niggers" fought back. Colored men saw their own kind being killed, heard of many more and believed that their lives and liberty were at stake.[27]

Passion was not deleted from the writings by Negroes on this controversial subject until the material of the Chicago Commission on Race Relations appeared in September 1922. The investigators who carried on the research for the study proceeded to their findings with a refreshing objectivity. So profound had been the emotional upheaval that one of the participants wrote of the new work with great and warranted enthusiasm in *Opportunity*:

. . . the Commissioners—men with reputations established apart from any interest in the race question—are serene and agreed in their findings, new convictions and pronouncements, despite the fact that these findings and recommendations mark perhaps the most significant epoch in race relations since Emancipation.

The workers upon the new study were, perhaps, overly aware of the assumption and maintenance of an objective approach. These statements reflect the complete confidence which they had in the objectivity of their vision:

. . . the passion for truth and justice survived over a hundred deliberative sessions and nearly three years of study. . . .

Traditions and taboos backed by centuries of unquestioned acceptance have overshadowed the relations of the races. . . .[28]

The World War constituted a major disrupting factor in the life of Negroes during this period. Nearly 400,000 Negro soldiers served in the United States Army,[29] and black soldiers composed

13 percent of the Army.[30] The emotional upheaval in Negro life caused by the drainage of those men from civilian life was further intensified by a series of incidents which seemed to indicate to many Negroes that the government had no intention, in dealing with its black soldiers, of providing treatment equal to that received by white soldiers or of exacting the same responsibilities. Among the incidents kindling the ill-feeling among Negroes toward the administration of the War were the refusal to call into active service Colonel Charles Young, the only Negro colonel in the regular U.S. Army, the tardiness in supplying a camp for the training of Negro officers, and the Houston riot in August 1917, when Negro troops attacked residents in the town, after much discrimination and petty assault had fanned resentments to a fever heat. Other disturbing occurrences were the narrowly averted race riot at Spartanburg, South Carolina, and Bulletin No. 35, issued to officers and soldiers of the 92nd Division by General Ballou, commanding officer at the division with headquarters at Camp Funston, which requested that Negro officers and soldiers should refrain from attending places of public amusement or recreation if their presence seemed to the white patrons of such resorts as likely to provoke racial friction.[31] General Ballou's bulletin was particularly resented by the Negro press, and many newspapers pronounced the "order" an insult to the Negro race.

A training camp was finally authorized for colored officers by the Secretary of War on May 19, 1917, and soon afterwards the candidates for the commissions set out for Fort Des Moines, Iowa, where they were to undergo training. Complaints did not cease as the war progressed. Woodson states that three-quarters of the 200,000 soldiers sent into action were reduced to laborers and commanded in large part by illiterate white men. Current also among Negroes was the belief that every effort was made to discredit the Negro officers in France with charges of cowardice and inefficiency.[32] There was objection to discrimination in eating quarters in the YMCAs and to propaganda intended to persuade the French to adopt the discriminatory practices of Americans.

The Wilson Administration made several adjustments to handle the problem of the Negro in the War. Emmett J. Scott, Secretary of Tuskegee Institute, was appointed Special Assistant to the Secretary of War on October 5, 1917. George Haynes directed the Bureau of Negro Economics in the Department of Labor. It was Woodson's opinion that the new appointments did little to alleviate the difficult racial situation in the Army.

Robert Moton went to France in December 1918 to look into conditions affecting Negro soldiers. There were at the time rumors concerning the brutal instincts of Negro soldiers, the "unmentionable crime," and the cowardice and inefficiency of Negro officers. Moton found through the investigation of the division reports surprisingly few occurrences of the "crime" and little reservation in the opinion of military men in France in regard to the excellent qualities of the Negro soldiers.[33]

The Negro emerged generally with a splendid record in spite of much adverse propaganda. A section of the 92nd Division, which had not been adequately prepared, proved defective for the conflict when first placed under fire, but the record of the men of the 367th, 369th, and 370th Infantries indicates courage and efficiency of an extremely high order.

The attitude of the Negro public toward the black soldiers emphasized their sacrifice in spite of discrimination, injury, and incidents revealing the hatred and malice of their white fellow citizens. Kathryn H. Johnson expressed the position briefly:

> They summoned with superhuman strength the courage to overcome the galling and heart-breaking discriminations which they had known before they crossed the seas; the open and public discussion as to whether colored men should be allowed to fight; the tragedies of Houston, and the resulting discouragement at Des Moines; the impudence of the commanding officer at Camp Funston [Bulletin No. 35], and the prearranged and infamous plan to discredit colored officers on the battlefields; all this was sufficient to sap their very sap blood before it had a chance to crimson the soil of Flanders Fields.[34]

This is a representative bit of expression indicating the form the complaint of Negro writers often assumed.

An important change in the postwar Negro mind was the flowering of a deep interest in Africa and a tendency to speak in terms of an underlying brotherhood of all the darker races of the earth. Benjamin Brawley placed heavy emphasis upon the effects of the contact of American Negro soldiers with colonial troops and considered, therefore, that "it was not surprising that the heart of the Negro people in the United States broadened into new sympathy with the problems of their brothers the world over."[35] There were other equally significant if not more important causes of the new pan-African impulse. Postwar peace negotiations created Poland, Czechoslovakia, Yugoslavia, Finland, and other small states; and political talk was in terms of the self-determination of races and of the necessity of having national boundaries conform with the geographical limits of a cultural area. The Negro intellectual, too, turned nationalistic and talked of establishing an independent African nation and culture. Alain Locke, soon to function as the major interpreter of the Negro Renaissance, wrote: "But eventually all people exhibit the homing instinct and turn back physically and mentally, hopefully and helpfully, to the land of their origin."[36] Kelly Miller in *The Everlasting Stain* wrote in a similar vein:

> The continent of Africa is under their [the Negroes'] physical dominance and in some blind, half-conscious way it is looked upon as the homeland of this race. . . . No race question can be solved by dealing with scattered fragments, but the essential solution must be effective in the homeland of the race.[37]

Du Bois's guidance and enthusiastic support were responsible for three pan-African Congresses. The first was held under martial law in Paris on February 19–21, 1919. The second was held in 1921 in England, Belgium, and France, and, according to Du Bois, it "began to gather aspects of a real world movement but met difficulties based on particularism and economic jealousy of imperialism."[38] A third Congress in 1924 had as its meeting places London and Lisbon.

There was, however, a vigorous interest in Negro nationalistic movements preceding the pan-African Congresses of the twenties and having its beginnings in the prewar period. In 1917, Marcus Garvey organized in Harlem the Universal Negro Improvement Association, and the first public meeting was held in the Annex of the St. Marks Roman Catholic Church. Garvey had arrived in New York in March 1916, after leaving the Caribbean island of Jamaica. In 1914, he had attempted in Jamaica to found a Negro nationalist and Back-to-Africa movement, but the organization had failed. Claude McKay stated that Garvey had picked up the germ of his idea in London during 1912 and 1913 through association with the Egyptian author Duse Mohammed Ali, who published the monthly *African Times and Orient Review*. Garvey returned to Jamaica just before the outbreak of the War, and, according to McKay, "his head was big with the idea of an African Redemption and Colonization scheme."[39]

After the second organization of the U.N.I.A. in 1917, Garvey outlined a program for a planned Negro economy and began in the first month of 1918 the publication of the *Negro World*, a weekly newspaper, which in a few months established itself as a leading national Negro weekly. The most important of the Garvey economic enterprises was the Black Star Line which was to serve the double function of taking optimistic Negroes back to the homeland, Africa, and becoming a communication link among black people of all lands as well as serving as a lucrative form of investment for Negroes interested in supporting race enterprises. Actually, about eight hundred thousand dollars was squandered on ancient vessels. There was also a Negro Factories Corporation capitalized at one million dollars whose material goods consisted of a few rather negligible grocery stores in Harlem.[40] The first national convention of the movement was held in Harlem in 1920 and a gorgeous show was organized, one which exploited all of the U.N.I.A. creations, the black nobility (Garvey's lieutenants), the Black Cross nurses, the Royal African Legion, and the African Orthodox Church.

Garvey's telegram to President Warren G. Harding after his Birmingham speech in 1921 was evidence of his determination to play a part in national politics, and it reveals also his position on the most electric issue concerning the Negro at that time: social equality:

> All true Negroes are against Social Equality, believing that all Negroes should develop along their own social lines. . . . The new Negro will join hands with those who are desirous of keeping the two opposite races socially pure and work together for the industrial, educational, and political liberation of all peoples.[41]

Opposition crystallized immediately against him, and forming its nucleus was the small but intelligent and influential group of Negroes affiliated with labor and racial movements, plus the N.A.A.C.P. and the Equal Rights Association of Boston. Garvey was arrested in January 1922 on a charge of using the mails to defraud. The prosecution was not rushed, the trial did not begin until the middle of 1923, and it lasted then a full month. Garvey served as his own attorney, but his cause was not helped by his court orations. He was jailed in February 1925, and entered the Atlanta Federal Penitentiary to serve five years. He was released in 1929 and deported to Jamaica.

Garvey's influence over Afro-Americans, native Africans, and people of African descent was vast. His appeal was directly to the lower class, the Southern and West Indian migrants to the Northern centers of industry.[42] The basis of Garvey's attractive power rested in his presentation of a panacea for all problems disturbing the mass mind. An analysis of his speeches and writings indicates how successfully he was able to use a vocabulary readily understood and applauded by the Negro migrant. Garvey's grandiose schemes gave the Negro a glimpse of a colorful future. The whole pan-African and Negro nationalist movement caused an indulgence in utopian thinking to an extent not comparable in race history except possibly in the expression of the vigorous antislavery orations of the 1850s. Not the most uninspired creators of new black worlds—ebon pipe dreams—which were grasped eagerly by the postwar Negro were Du Bois and Locke, differing widely in academic training and in background from the self-educated printer Marcus Garvey.

The stirring question which fascinated the Negro intellectual world during the decade before and the one after the turn of the twentieth century was the Du Bois–Washington controversy. Briefly, Booker T. Washington's idea was that youth should not be educated away from his environment but trained to lay a foundation for the future in his present situation.[43] He was a forceful advocate of industrial education for Negro youth. He considered it necessary to make the masses of Negroes see and realize the necessity and importance of applying what they learned in school to the common and ordinary things of life; to see that education, far from being a means of escaping labor, is a means of raising up and dignifying labor and thus, indirectly, a means of raising up and dignifying the common and ordinary man.[44]

His purposes, as defined in his educational philosophy, were to foster increased economic self-sufficiency and the formation of character. Washington's biographers, Emmett J. Scott and Lyman B. Stowe, have recorded a concise expression in regard to the latter point: "any education is 'low' which does not make for character and effective service." He labored to turn out leaders for his people "wholesale and as fast as possible."[45]

Almost as soon as Booker T. Washington emerged as a leader of the Negro people in the 1890s, opposition to his philosophy and influence crystallized. Resented particularly by the opposing groups was Washington's so-called subservience to the Southern bourbons. It was the conviction of these groups that the first efforts to secure recognition for the Negro must come through agitation for higher education and political equality.[46] Washington was condemned for not taking a more forceful stand on the disenfranchisement of Negroes in the South and accused of being a race traitor, endeavoring to reduce the whole race to menial service. Causing additional resentment among the militant Negroes of the opposition was Washington's personal attitude toward race prejudice, which the Scott and Stowe biography defines with considerable care:

> Very early in his career Washington worked out for himself a perfectly definite line of conduct in the matter of social mingling with white people. In the South he scrupulously observed the local customs and avoided offending the prejudices of the Southerners in so far as was possible without unduly handicapping his work.[47]

This was interpreted as evidence of a stand on the issue of "social equality" and encouragement to other Negroes to be hesitant about insisting upon their civil rights.

Most eloquent in the denunciation of Washington were W.E.B. Du Bois and Monroe Trotter. Organization of the opposition was begun in 1905 with the launching of the Niagara Movement, in which twenty men participated. Both races were represented,

Negro intellectuals being joined by the "remnant of the abolitionists"[48]—Oswald G. Villard, Jane Addams, Moorfield Storey,
Charles E. Russell, Joel E. Spingarn, and Mary W. Ovington.
The founding of the National Association for the Advancement
of Colored People (N.A.A.C.P.) four years later was a continuation of the move toward effective machinery to stimulate action
and opinion which would function as a rebuttal against the
dominant influence of believers in Washington's thinking.

In the heat of the agitation, *The Crisis* magazine was established in 1910 with Du Bois as its editor. As the official organ of
the N.A.A.C.P., it was essentially a magazine of protest; it described infractions of the civil and political rights of the Negro,
and it detailed and at times dramatized the most flagrant of the
infractions. The increasing popularity of *The Crisis* indicated
that the Negro populace was undergoing two significant changes:
primarily, there was a growing sensitivity on the part of many
Negroes to the violation of their "rights." The great jumps in
circulation during the years following 1916 were an indication of
the second important change; the migration and the World War
had increased the opportunities for misunderstanding and friction
between the races, and Negroes, with justification, thought that
racial tension had heightened. *The Crisis* had contributed in a
major way to forming the attitude of righteous defense and grew
more influential as racial relations became less satisfactory during
the early twenties.

An indication of the kind of program *The Crisis* and the
N.A.A.C.P. were boosting in this period was revealed in Du Bois's
editorial comment under the caption "Plain Speech to the South,"
in an issue published in 1920:

> We want to vote
> We want lynching stopped
> We want schools
> We want 'Jim Crow' cars abolished
> We want labor peonage ended
> We want decent conditions of wage and labor and a cessation of
> insult and slander.[49]

A deep interest in securing privileges and in fighting real or
imagined prejudices to the race permeated Negro thinking so

completely that aside from the development of pan-Africanism, the patriotic action which accompanied America's entrance into the War, the social background is packed with dramatic incidents stemming from racial misunderstanding. To the black populace, these were the important social issues of the time. The major incidents of protest in relation to the World War and to the migration have been considered. The race riots were the most violent displays of the dislocations in racial relations. Other manifestations during the postwar period were numerous. There was the Veteran's Hospital squabble which had as a source of contention the objection of Negroes to the staffing of a Negro hospital at Tuskegee with white doctors and white nurses, since the South refused to accept a biracial arrangement. There were to be colored helpers; as Du Bois stated the situation: "colored nurse maids for each white nurse, in order to save them from contact with colored patients."[50] There was the crusade against the revival of the Ku Klux Klan which culminated toward the end of 1923. *The Crisis* and *Opportunity* shared in the attack, but the peak in condemnatory statement was attained in *The Messenger*, which emphasized the relationship of the Klan to the class struggle and explored its economic roots: "Fascism like Ku-Kluxism is the white guard of plutocracy, two brokers of unspeakable terrorism competing for the lucrative and profitable privilege of serving the kings of dollars, pounds, liras, and francs."[51]

Under the auspices of the N.A.A.C.P., James Weldon Johnson concluded in 1920 his investigation of the occupation of Haiti, and his findings were published in both *The Nation* and *The Crisis*. His report presented an account of the cruelties inflicted upon the natives by the American Marines, and it emphasized the lack of necessity, except for the gratification of imperialistic ambition, for occupation of Haiti at all. "The overthrow of Guillaume and its attending consequences," he writes, "did not constitute the cause of American intervention in Haiti; it merely furnished the opportunity for which this government was waiting." The investigation caused the feeling among Negroes that Haiti's woes were yet other examples of the vicious attack of the white world upon the rights and abilities of the Negro. That the status of American Negroes was involved was clearly indicated in the Johnson report in *The Crisis*:

> The United States has failed in Haiti. It should get out as well
> and as quickly as it can and restore to the Haitian people their
> independence and sovereignty. The colored people of the United
> States should be interested in seeing that this is done, for Haiti is
> the one best chance that the Negro has in the world to prove that
> he is capable of the highest self-government.[52]

All of these incidents are indications of the intense consciousness among Negroes that the race was being attacked. Political rights were not the only issues concerned. The description of the violation of a right in the work of a Negro controversialist was accompanied with a probing of the incident in an effort to discover what principles and values deemed indispensable to the Negro might be affected. The James Weldon Johnson report on Haiti was an excellent example of the application of this technique. Johnson's concern was with the construction of a practical reply in Haiti to the unstated question: Is the Negro worthy of self-government, or of citizenship? Johnson attempted to gather in his article all evidences of good native government in Haiti; these constituted the necessary demonstration for a refutation of the question which Johnson assumed an antagonistic white world had raised in regard to the Negro race. This is a sample of what an incident became in the hands of the Negro controversialist. Exposition of the overt was accompanied by a concern for the erroneous assumptions which formed underlying causes for attack by the white oppressors. Extreme dexterity in probing suspicious actions for assumptions and causal factors, which might upon examination be considered injurious to the Negro, entitled a writer to be called by the black populace a "defender of the race."

The National Urban League was organized in 1910, the year in which the publication of *The Crisis* began. In January 1923, the League began to publish a monthly magazine, *Opportunity: Journal of Negro Life,* with Charles S. Johnson as its editor. A clear statement of the purposes of the organization is to be found in the remarks of Eugene K. Jones in the first issue of *Opportunity.*

> It [the League] has sought to make its contribution toward
> elevating the Negro in the social scale. The motive being to make
> it easier for the Negro to assimilate the cultural advantages of
> American civilization and to aid more Negroes of capacity and
> talent to emerge from the mass of their fellows of less promise.

The League functioned practically in helping to absorb shocks which the migrant suffered with the violent change in environment. It aided laboring, dependent, and delinquent classes in the large cities. It pioneered in social work in urban centers among Negroes. Jones insisted that

> They [the leaders of the Urban League] have revolutionized social work among Negroes, which has changed from the street corner missionary type of work to the up-to-date scientific social service.[53]

It was helpful in discovering and opening employment opportunities, and it endeavored to secure improvements in laboring conditions for Negro employees. Housing was also one of the League's problems, and the League was particularly useful in the hectic days when migration was at a peak. Its officers in the Northern cities functioned as housing bureaus assisting in the location of living quarters for newly arrived migrants.

The emergence of the Urban League was an indication that an attempt was being made to articulate the demands of a new and growing group in Negro life—the black industrial worker. The League was only partially successful in forming an organization which adequately, in the mind of the Negro laborer, voiced his needs and desires. He had ultimately two counts against the League. Primarily, he was to disapprove of the League's continual adherence to racial uplift and defense propaganda which was to be found in its purest form in the utterances of Du Bois. It obscured the necessity for a broad-visioned policy in regard to the organization of Negro labor. The League tended to think of Negro labor as a separate entity for which, by conference with employers and vested-interest groups, it sought special dispensations, pointing toward a betterment of conditions. It was reluctant to thrust across racial lines boldly and urge unreservedly black and white labor combinations. The second count which the black laborer was to hold against the League was its reactionary social philosophy. Eugene Kinckle Jones's statement concerning the function of the League is revealing. This kind of talk was not likely to be agreeable to black labor leaders. There were objections both to the assumption of the essential "rightness" of the social order, which is embodied in the concern for "assimilation," and to the frank

admission of an interest in encouraging "superior" people for the
privileges and advantages that they would receive, rather than in
training "superior" people for leadership of the black masses.
The laboring masses, for the new labor leaders of the twenties,
possessed the only hope for a better world, and the future did not
rest in the social accomplishments and success of isolated individuals. Chandler Owen and Philip Randolph wrote boldly in language differing greatly from that of the League leaders:

> We cynical mortals may not yet live to see the white and black
> toilers marching arm in arm, heedless of the hypocritical incan-
> tations to the fetish of "white supremacy." But the white workers
> are not alone responsible for the failure of the two groups of
> workers to unite. Negro leadership is also blameable.[54]

The dream of the building of a better society which would
come to America by the combination of black and white labor to
form a united and belligerent front was not original with the
radical Negro thinkers coming to prominence in the early twenties.
As early as 1868, William Sylvis conceived of the organization of
Negro and white workers against moneyed aristocracy on the
platform of the newly organized National Labor Union.[55] Actually,
between the National Labor Union Congresses of 1868 and 1869,
conventions of Negro workers began to occur; the first national
convention of colored labor was held in Washington, D.C.,
January 13, 1869. Difficulties arose at the National Labor Union
Convention in 1870. It was evident that Negro workers were
willing to fraternize with friendly whites but not willing to give
up their autonomy. Abram Harris and Sterling Spero note four
specific reasons for failure of Negro working-class action:

1. the decreasing importance of the Negro in industry
2. the growth of craft unionism, excluding the Negro
3. the mutual antagonism between black and white laboring
   classes
4. the social outlook of Negro leadership.[56]

At the close of the Civil War, over 97 percent of the Negro
working class was unskilled; this meant that any developments
up to that time in organization along craft union lines automati-
cally excluded Negroes. The American Federation of Labor,
founded in 1886, broached the doctrine of pure and simple craft

unionism; and since there was still a heavy proportion of unskilled black workers as compared with the skilled workers, its development and progress did not affect the Negro favorably. Moreover, many unions had a racial policy. The Knights of Labor had offered a fleeting hope of betterment to Negro labor. Its democratic spirit and vigorous attempt to organize all workers had caused an estimated 60,000 members to affiliate.[57] Neither its eclipse nor the emergence to dominance in the field of organized labor of the A.F.L. was welcomed by the Negro. To the black labor leader, it meant the triumph of craft interests over industrial brotherhood, of a job-conscious labor movement over a cooperative antimonopolistic one.

It was the custom of the radical labor thinkers of the twenties to add to the condemnation of Booker T. Washington's influence the fact that he retarded the organization of Negro labor. The feeling was that the Washington philosophy taught that labor organizing was inimical to white friendship and inimical to the employer. The emphasis upon the cultivation of good will was deplored, since, to the new thinkers, this was a cowardly compromise with Bourbon aristocracy and moneyed interests. Hampton and Tuskegee were important sources at the turn of the century for skilled Negro labor and for instructors training others in dexterity in the trades. Washington founded the National Negro Business League in 1900 in order to foster Negro business and encourage the development of the business virtues of thrift, enterprise, and tact. Radical thinkers on the labor question were to ask two questions of this kind of development: why a league for the fostering of Negro business was established if the purchasers were not concerned with the maker or the seller of the goods; and how any organization stressing only the virtues of a successful competitor in a shopkeeper world was relevant in an economic world of highly capitalized combines and monopolies.[58]

In 1900, the policy was inaugurated of issuing separate charters to unions of exclusively Negro workers, where it was deemed necessary and where national and international unions refused their entrance. Negro unions consequently possessed weak bargaining power. They were not connected with the white locals; the executive committee only was permitted to request the white local to take up the cause of the Negro unions. It was not until after the Negro migrations of 1912–17 began that the A.F.L. leaders felt the necessity of quickening somewhat the union activity among Negroes. The increased interest in Negro affiliation resulted when the unskilled Negro workers and the skilled Negro mechanics debarred by the unions formed an industrial labor reserve for Northern industrialists. The widespread introduction of Southern Negro labor into Northern industries during 1916–20 witnessed a marked increase in unionization. This was the period of great federal influence over much of basic industry, and a stimulus was provided for unionization. There was a sharp decline in the interest in securing Negro affiliation immediately thereafter.

Independent Negro unions arose in occupations where the Negro was substantially represented, but excluded from unions. This was especially true of the railroads. In 1919, a new movement, the National Brotherhood Workers of America, attempted to federate all Negro unions.[59] The movement collapsed in 1921, but the failure of the Brotherhood did not prevent continual emergence and subsequent eclipse of Negro unions. It is interesting to note that the emergence of the Brotherhood coincided with the most intense period of nationalistic thinking among Negroes, when the U.N.I.A. was attaining huge proportions and Du Bois and his followers were indulging in utopian dreams about reclaiming Africa for black culture.

In 1920, 825,321 Negroes were employed in manufacturing, 16 percent of them skilled laborers, 68 percent unskilled, and 15 percent semiskilled laborers. The problem was still a dual one. There was no organization articulating the needs of the unskilled worker, and the skilled black worker was mainly barred from participation in the craft union movement in spite of several feeble gestures on the part of the A.F.L. As early as 1910, the National Council of the A.F.L. passed resolutions admitting all races, but nothing further was done until 1916 when the fear of Negro invasion forced some unionization. In 1919, the A.F.L. lifted the ban completely, but the problem remained with the locals, which were generally antagonistic to Negro unionization.[60]

The Messenger was in the heart of the movement to recognize Negro labor. In political conviction, it was Socialist. Its editors, Chandler Owen and Philip Randolph, were not only radical thinkers on the labor problem but were practical leaders as well. Randolph organized the National Brotherhood of Sleeping Car Porters and has remained the president of that union. *The Messenger* called loudly for the combination of black and white labor groups to oppose the oppression of capital, and it assailed violently other Negro organizations—particularly the U.N.I.A. and the N.A.A.C.P., which, it thought, functioned to prevent the black populace from appraising and acting upon essential issues. The policy of *The Messenger* was more complicated than an elaboration upon the simple assumption expressed by Ben Fletcher, articulating the magazine's attitude to the economic betterment of the race: "organized labor can bring about a different situation, one that will speed the dawn of industrial freedom."[61] It represented a synthesis of doctrine and opinion in rebellion against the positions of the accepted leaders of the Negro race—Du Bois, Washington, Moton, Garvey, Eugene Kinckle Jones, and Charles S. Johnson—and against the conventions of what were conceived to be the foolishly imitative upper and middle classes of the race. The magazine attacked the comfortable black bourgeoisie with malicious enthusiasm. The men who formed the working nucleus publishing *The Messenger* and who were the ones most successfully articulating the opinions of their group were Chandler Owen, Philip Randolph, Abram Harris, George Schuyler, and Theophilus Lewis.

The intense social ferment of the time offered a ripe field of exploitation for contemporary essayists. Social incidents vastly affecting the Negro were many, and the tendency to resolve difficulties and misunderstandings by violence was stronger during this period than at any time since Reconstruction days. The feeling among the masses of Negroes was that this was a period of flux which called for new and vitalized Negro leadership; and leaders appealed to their followers by indulging often in threats and desperate speech and a rare extravagance in utopian thinking. Upon every social incident the Negro leader felt obligated to take a stand to determine whether or not the honor or the security of the Negro was involved. The intimate relation between the series of provocative incidents filling the years from 1917 to 1924 and contemporary controversial literature has necessitated an exhaustive outline of the period's social history; a background is furnished of the time, much of which is as dependent for complete illumination upon an understanding of contemporary social forces as is a Garvey polemic.

The Negro Essayist and His Problems

A portion of the meaning of the articles of the contemporary Negro essayists on social problems arose from the timelessness of their subjects. In this period of great flux, literary accounts, however meagerly descriptive, dealing with the migration, the War and the Negro, the race riots, or commenting upon any outstanding social phenomenon, were certain to be welcome. Even in the most straightforward descriptive articles there were evidences of principles of selection which precluded complete objectivity and which established the conclusion that the purposes of the article (parts of it at least) were to produce a change of attitude in the reading audience as well as to provide reportorial accuracy. In the work of the major Negro essayists, the operation of the selective principle to be defined was a conscious process, and there is adequate statement to be found justifying and explaining its application. Graham R. Taylor, Executive Secretary, Chicago Commission on Race Relations, recorded his exposition of the peculiar problem of the essayist dealing with a subject concerning the Negro:

> The big problem is the problem of the white mind.
> I wish only to emphasize the fact that among whites at least the conceptions about Negroes are too frequently generalized from inadequate and unrepresentative experience.[62]

The article revealed also what were considered to be the sources behind the perverted functioning of the white mind. It stated that the Commission studying the race situation in Chicago immediately after the riots had discovered this fact:

> That much of the current literature and pseudo-scientific treatises concerning the Negroes are responsible for such prevailing misconceptions as: that Negroes have inferior mentality, that Negroes have inferior morality, that Negroes are given to emotionalism, that Negroes have an innate tendency to commit crime, especially sex crimes.[63]

In an article, "Public Opinion and the Negro," Charles Johnson, editor of *Opportunity* and also a member of the Chicago Commission, endeavored further to define the function of the Negro writer.

> . . . we are dealing with three important and highly sensitive elements: the facts upon which this opinion rests, the theories about these facts, and most important of all, the actions based on those theories.[64]

Many of the Negro essayists, although unable to express their aims as clearly as did Johnson, had come to the realization in the wave of racial conflict in 1919 and in the early twenties of how extremely dangerous were the fictions in the minds of the white masses. Literature became for them a defense medium by means of which a writer, by an illumination of basic misconceptions, destroyed the seeds of further violence. This was evident in the material produced by this school of thought. A primary result of this pattern of thinking was the elevation of the position of the Negro essayist. It was his belief that the false theories of Lothrop Stoddard and Madison Grant, current advocates of racial theories of progress and culture, had articulated deep-seated convictions held by the white populace, convictions which had been mainsprings for mob violence. The Negro essayist became at once the carrier of new "truth" and a crusader taking part in a propaganda program essential for the existence of the black man in America.

Two tendencies were noticeable in literary material produced by this school of thought. There was a new concern for fact-finding, for scientific investigation and reportorial accuracy. A glance at *Opportunity* for the years 1923 and 1924 justifies the claims that Negro contributors had a fascination for regimenting statistics and sociological and psychological analysis to prove conclusions, and that the expression of conclusions at times assumed the manner of the revelation of newly discovered truth. A second important trend was a frontal attack upon misconception and false theory. An elaborate program of counterpropaganda was initiated in which justification was constructed for the accomplishments and potentialities of the race and for the traits and characteristics of the individual Negro. What was to be attempted was a reconstruction of the Negro for the white man; an emphasis was to be placed upon extolling the virtues of the race. The theme of justification of the black man constituted an important organizing principle; it was applied so universally by Negro essayists that the reading audience tended to expect that point of view. The members of the audience were disappointed when material descriptive of social phenomena was written without the assumption that it was necessary to protect the Negro from destructive criticism. How acutely the need for the "peculiar" organization of literary material was felt by Negro intellectuals is indicated by this comment of W.E.B. Du Bois's in his article on "The Negro and the American Stage":

> Any mention of Negro blood or Negro life in America for a century has been occasion for an ugly picture, a dirty allusion, a nasty comment or a pessimistic forecast. The result is that the Negro today fears any attempt of artists to paint Negroes.[65]

That Negro literary material, particularly that portion of it which is descriptive of or interpretive of social event, should function as counterpropaganda effecting change in the minds of the white audience is only one of the desirable reactions sought by Negro essayists. A change also was sought in the Negro's thinking. This is an older stimulus for propaganda writing. The Negro had written since the Civil War a voluminous amount of material urging increased race pride. It debunked slavish admiration of white ideals and base capitulation to white authority. It was belligerent in tone and designed almost exclusively for Negro consumption. The need had not presented itself as it did in the early twenties to complement special talk, urging self-respect and self-development so that the race might progress, with propaganda, which was expressed in terms understandable to both whites and Negroes and designed to defend the race from malicious and unscientific attack. The former and older tradition of rhetorical expression is well illustrated by this statement of Du Bois's in *The Crisis* in 1920:

> It is not that we are ashamed of our color and blood. . . . Black is caricature in our half conscious thought and we shun in print and paint that which we love in life. . . . A mighty and swelling human consciousness is leading us joyously to embrace the darker world, but we remain afraid of black pictures

because they are the cold reminders of the crimes of Sunday "comics" and "Nigger" minstrels.

Off with these thought-chains and inchoate social shrinkings, and let us train ourselves to see beauty in black.[66]

One rhetorical tradition was not replaced by another. The stress of the times increased the pleas for action for racial improvement and for the assumption of a manner of living and behavior befitting the possessor of a long and illustrious racial tradition. What happened to the writing of the Negro essayist producing in this vein was a complete change of assumption in regard to the attitude of whites toward Negro progress. Until 1916, there was frequently the assumption in Negro literary material that the white man would ultimately approve and accept Negro progress, once the ability to make progress as a result of the race's own initiative was demonstrated. The Washington school of thought was largely responsible for the conviction that the white world would welcome the improved and cultured Negro, and it profoundly influenced Negro expression. Argument and encouragement for self-development and an interest in achieving self-respect were advanced often on the basis of eventual acceptance of the Negro as a recognized element of importance in the society. It was stated that a portion of the white world was always sympathetic, an enlightened few, and the remaining majority was to be won over by active demonstration of racial ability.

That assumption and hope had disappeared in the violence of the early twenties for the majority of the Negro intellectuals. An embittered Du Bois wrote after the Fountainebleau School of Fine Arts had refused to accept Augusta Savage as a student:

The ignorant and poor may lynch and discriminate but the real deep and the basic hatred in the United States is a matter of the educated and distinguished leaders of white civilization. They are the ones who are determined to keep black folk from developing talent and sharing in civilization.[67]

Frequently, the construction of an essay incorporated both approaches. The Negro writer attempted to stress the urgency of self-development as well as striking at fictions in the minds of white Americans. Such an attempt is Du Bois's editorial on "Sensitive Liberia" which appeared in *The Crisis* in 1924. The article attacks the fictions that Liberia symbolizes the deficiency of the Negro in the faculty for culture-making and that Liberia represents an example of the incapacity of Negroes to fulfill the obligations of citizenship. The latter assumption had been the reason most frequently articulated for the denial of equal rights to the American Negro. These two misconceptions are the basis for what Du Bois calls "propaganda, continuous, persistent, irresponsible and lying propaganda." There is present also in the article an appeal for progress and a reconstruction of attitudes on the part of Negroes in regard to Liberia. There is a demand for serious thought and interest in the progress of the Negro state; the necessity for contributing to the success of the black democracy is established. The article thus represents a synthesis of two tendencies in the writing of the controversial essay. Evidences of the nature of its organization are revealed in this quotation from it:

> If Liberia falls this justifies slavery, serfdom, autocracy and exploitation of a race "incapable" of self rule.
>
> If Liberia succeeds why should not the Negro succeed in self rule and democratic development and decent industrial organization in Sierra Leone, the Gold Coast, French Africa, South Africa, East Africa, Kenya, the Sudan and Abyssinia?
>
> What is the result? Propaganda, continuous, persistent, irresponsible and lying propaganda. . . .
>
> And we American Negroes have swallowed this propaganda whole.[68]

It is important to notice the two categories into which the misconceptions fall. The primary misconception was a general assumption about the inability of the Negro to function in culture-making. The second is a more specific assumption, stating the worthiness of the Negro for participation in the government of a democratic state. The former has to do with an assessment of racial traits, characteristics, and potentialities; the latter is based on an assessment of individual virtues and vices manifested in the adjustment to a particular pattern of government. These categories will get added meaning in the discussion and analysis of the whole body of literature of "defense" written during the period.

For most of the Negro essayists of the period, the war against malicious fictions in the mind of the American white man was a means of averting violence, an opening which would lead to a

fuller acceptance of the Negro as a participant in American culture-making. Only a few of the more radical Negroes envisaged
the class struggle as the origin of offensive mythology. The conviction was that the myth functioned as a divisive factor effecting
the separation of the great masses of the disaffected. Claude McKay
wrote in the first of his two articles on "Soviet Russia and the
Negro," published in *The Crisis*:

> Misinformation, indifference and levity sum up the attitude
> of western Europe towards the Negro . . . it may be compara-
> tively easy for white American propagandists— whose interests
> behoove them to misrepresent the Negro—to turn the general
> indifference into hostile antagonism. . . .
>
> As American influence increases in the world and especially
> in Europe, through the extension of American capital, the more
> necessary it becomes for all struggling minorities of the United
> States to organize for the world wide propagation of their
> grievances.[69]

The Messenger group, Socialist in political philosophy, was
an endorser of the belief that the class struggle was responsible for
racial misrepresentation. There is a revealing editorial comment
appearing in June 1923 on a news item quoted from the Federated
Press stating that the controlled press had used the word "Nigger"
in referring to the black troops in the Rhineland and in the Ruhr
Valley. The comment ran as follows:

> The German junkers like the French Jingoists, the English
> militarists and the American money-changers, know how to
> capitalize the prejudice-producing power of epithets when the
> occasion arises. The German socialists condemned the policy.[70]

That Du Bois was at one time not so far from this mode of
thinking is indicated amply in a series of articles in *The Crisis*
entitled "The Black Man and the Wounded World," which is an
attempted analysis of the black man's situation internationally in
the postwar world. The structure of thought in the first of the
series of articles is revealed in the following quotation:

> But freedom is always restrained by the fear that the de-
> throning of the Dominant wills at any time—that is, the refusal
> of a large number of persons to submit to a particular opinion

or set of opinions—will result in the partial or total overthrow
of civilized society. . . .

The income-receiving persons form a small but intelligent
and highly specialized minority of men, while the mass of men
are wage-earners or community workers in organized industry.

In other words the Dominant wills proposed to share some
of their economic power with the laborers in return for the
political conquest of the laborer to the policy of conquest,
slavery, monopoly and theft in Western Europe, Asia, Africa,
and Central and South America.

This New Imperialism has widely prevailed and its way has
been cleared by a new propaganda. This propaganda bases itself
mainly on Race and Color—human distinctions long since
discarded by Science as of little or no real significance.[71]

The Messenger, because of its sensitivity to all new currents in
the intellectual world, was the only periodical to indulge in
psychoanalytic explanations for the construction of derogatory
fictions by a hostile white world. Perhaps the most complete
exposition of this point of view is an article by William Pickens,
"Color and Camouflage." There is no evidence that Du Bois, who
was adept at utilizing many frames of reference for rhetorical
reasons, was sufficiently radical at this time to speak in terms of
Freud and his disciples, while expressing himself vigorously in
language strikingly influenced by Marxian dialectic. Pickens explained that an elaborate mechanism had been constructed by the
white man to keep repressed and forbidden desires from entering
the conscious out of the unconscious. Fictions of white superiority
justify "false and unnatural associations" of white Americans
with black Americans, and as a result whites "have their Unconscious stored full of repressed desires and feelings respecting
people of color." This is the reason given for the potential for
violence existing in black and white relations in America. Also
this condition is considered the cause of periodic welling of
sentiment for selected symbols of Negro culture or selected Negroes
or Negro types:

. . . the tired Censor presumably "the gatekeeper" barring forbidden desires from filtering into the conscious from the unconscious gets off the job and there is sometimes a "gushing
over" toward color, when any thing or situation presents itself

which the white individual can consciously (and more or less unconsciously) consider a "good reason" or an "exception" for breaking away from the soul-enslaving custom.[72]

The majority of the Negro essayists did not seek explanation for racial superiority fictions either from interpretation of the class struggle or from the adaptation of psychoanalytic techniques. The existence of the fictions and their vicious influence was recognized; and the Negro essayists were content merely with disproving the myths and contracting their influence. The stimulus for rhetorical counterconstruction was the conviction that success meant the prevention of violence between races and insured racial security to the Negro. A brief exposition of this point of view, commendable for its clarity, is a statement by Herbert Adolphus Miller, Professor of Sociology at Oberlin, in an article in *Opportunity* entitled "The Myth of Superiority":

> Hundred per cent patriotism and confidence in Nordic superiority are the two most dangerous ideas in the world today, because they lead in exactly the opposite direction from that which civilization must take if it is to survive. . . .
> We are being artificially trained into prejudices which are not natural. Individuals of different races or nations may have cordial relations, but when the group prejudice is released, relations that were cordial become hostile.[73]

Thus, the Negro essayist was concerned not so much with the revelation of underlying causes for misconception in the white mind as he was with the identification of misconception and its annihilation by vigorous rebuttal. A change was to occur, then, in the mind of the white man which would make for more satisfactory relations between the black and white races in America. Simultaneously, alterations were to be striven for in the thinking of the Negro, both along the line of the cultivation of a more intense passion for self-development and toward the goal of a greater consciousness of living as a self-respecting citizen, sensitive to and belligerent about encroachments on individual rights and privileges. The formulations of direction toward which a change of mind was desired constituted selective principles, invading even articles devoted presumably to description or objective comment.

Myths of Inferiority: Physical and Mental

The defense of the race was not merely the process of denying the validity of misconceptions in the white mind. It was concerned with disproving false myth, and this necessitated the use of both factual data and elaborate rhetorical construction.

Perhaps one of the most persistent of the misconceptions was the conviction that the Negro had little survival value in an urban society, that the health of the race would prevent its taking any vigorous part in contributing to American culture. The Negro was thought to be a vanishing race. His fate was to be that of the Indians—eventual physical extinction growing out of unsatisfactory assimilation into modern patterns of living.

This was not a myth peculiar to the 1920s. It originally received scientific blessing in the modern world with the publication of Frederick Hoffman's work "The Race Traits and Tendencies of the American Negro,"[74] published in 1896 and based on the census of 1890. The census indicated a significant increase in mortality as compared with births among Negroes and established a kind of scientific basis for the conclusion that the Negro was diminishing in importance as a population factor.

The violence of the twenties and the resurgence of Negro inferiority myths brought the revitalization of Hoffman's conclusions. Accompanying the general assumption of the Negro's greater physical frailty was the conviction that the race was more susceptible than other races to certain diseases, namely, social diseases and tuberculosis.

There were two essential reactions by Negro essayists to the reexpression of this old myth. Primarily there was an attempt to disprove the conclusion upon the grounds upon which it was most convincingly stated, namely by Hoffman: on the basis of population and mortality statistics. Secondly, the urgency was emphasized for the establishment in the large cities of comprehensive health programs. The latter appeal indicates that Negro essayists were admitting that the hostile conclusions were perhaps based upon half-truths at least, and action should be undertaken to destroy any valid basis for derogatory statements.

A statement of the myth concerning Negro health and the rebuttal is to be found in an editorial entitled "Urbanization and Negro Mortality" in the November 1923 issue of *Opportunity*:

> Both biology and anthropology, expostulates Imperial Wizard H.W. Evans, prove that the Negro cannot attain the Anglo-Saxon level. . . . No new environment can more than superficially overcome this age-old hereditary handicap. With the ever increasing exodus from country to city, it is an undoubted fact that another generation will be marked by regression. Equally certain is Dr. W.C. Wilcox of Cornell University, that the drift toward Northern cities spells the solemn doom of the race. Such also was the opinion of Dr. Frederick Hoffman, twenty-five years ago.[75]

Just as much of the factual evidence for the position that the race was retrogressing physically was derived from the 1890 census, much of the rebuttal statement received factual justification at this time from a single source—the publication in 1923 of vital statistics by the Metropolitan Life Insurance Company on its two million insured Negroes, most of whom were living in urban areas. On the basis of that information, *Opportunity* was able to comment editorially and construct adequate rebuttal for the charge of the Imperial Wizard of the Ku Klux Klan:

> Their figures show that in the two years, 1911–1912, the life span of the Negroes at the age of ten was 41.32 years. In 1922 the expectation was 49.74 years. An increase of 5½ years or 13.1 per cent in the ten years during which a million Negroes moved North and twice that number into cities north and south.[76]

The same source of information was responsible for a more complete argument in a similar vein constructed by Louis I. Dublin in *Opportunity* in August 1924. He reiterated the statement concerning the increase within twelve years of the Negro's life span by nearly six years. Particular attention was paid to death from tuberculosis and to the reduction in twelve years of the rate of mortality by 41 percent. Perhaps more revealing than the bulk of the statements in the article was Dublin's explanation of the slight increase in the mortality rate in 1922 and 1923. He denied that migration had anything to do with the increase. To state the reverse would be to provide evidence confirming conclusions of the Hoffman school of thought. Dublin indicated that inconsistencies in the mortality rates in large cities in the North—almost a stable rate in New York City, increases in Chicago and Detroit—encouraged doubt as to whether migration had any effects. Dublin's position was rendered even more tenable when he revealed that increases in cities in the Southern states, in Atlanta, Charleston, and Norfolk, were "even more striking than in Chicago and Detroit."[77] The article is a convincing demonstration of the regimenting of facts as rebuttal statements counteracting the myth of the "vanishing Negro."

Evidence abounds indicating *Opportunity*'s absorption in rectifying misstatement. There was an interesting editorial comment in one of the early issues, noting that there had been a reduction in the excessively high mortality rate of Indians, particularly in the number dying from tuberculosis. "The Indians, commonly regarded as a disappearing race, have been halted in their decline through the effort of health agencies."[78] Louis Dublin indicated how the Negro was faring in his battle with tuberculosis: "The most important single achievement in the health condition among Negroes in the last decade has been the reduction in mortality from tuberculosis."[79]

In other ways, Negro essayists wished to prove the physical equality of the Negro. There is an account in *Opportunity* of the comparison of the physical condition and comparative development of 100 colored women teachers of West Virginia with that of 1600 women at Oberlin College and 1500 women each at Wellesley College and the University of Nebraska, and the Negro women emerged favorably from the critical appraisal. The writer added that the "current interest in physical development according to race was stimulated by the anthropometric records of the War Department [and] has prompted several comparative studies."[80] This is significant given that the publication of Army statistics or tests set off also a wave of discussion about the mental abilities of the Negro American as compared with the white American; moreover, there is revealed here an additional source of information utilized by the Negro controversialist in refuting charges of greater physical frailty. *The Messenger* participated vigorously, though not so intensely as did *Opportunity*, in the debate, and J.A. Rogers, author of "From 'Superman' to Man,"[81] approached the rhetorical question with the same attention to statistics noted in the writing of Louis I. Dublin, with this difference—Rogers relied on the Army records, not the Metropolitan report, for statistical information:

> This time it is the Ku Kluxish, 100 per cent American, "World's Work."
> The editor brings up the three-hundred year old argument that the Negro is physically inferior to white people, that this is not his climate, that he will soon die out. He says:
> That Negroes as people are much frailer physically than the white population will probably not surprise most observers.

Rogers indicated that the Second Report on the Operations of the Selective Service System to December 20, 1918, issued by the federal government, stated differently:

> For every 100 men examined physically the ratio of colored men found qualified for general military service was substantially higher than the ratio for white men by just five per cent. . . .[82]

The second type of reaction to the charges of white propagandists was displayed plainly in the article "The Negro's Struggle for Health," by Eugene Kinckle Jones, guiding head of the National Urban League. There is the original contention that historically the Negro has been superior in health, which is followed by the frank admission: "In fact, for Negroes the record shows an excess of deaths over births." Part of the general trend, it is stated, is "toward the equalization of births and deaths." The first of the quoted statements expresses the fact which prompted Hoffman's conclusions in "Race Traits and Tendencies of the American Negro." Changes for the better, however, were noted by Jones, and he expressed the urgency for still further improvements in health.

> . . . the Negro has actually improved in health and is capable of improving further. . . . Most of the improvement that has come about in Negro health has been the result of the Negro population's seeking an adjustment to the requirements of this environment that they might survive.[83]

Absorbing even more completely the attention of the Negro essayist than the controversy on the survival value of the Negro was the discussion of the comparative native intelligence of the white man and the Negro. Argument concerning the relative mental abilities of the races centered on two points of evidence. First, there was the question whether or not brain size could be interpreted as an indicator of intelligence; second, there were the Army intelligence tests—Alpha and Beta—for the literate and illiterate given to all men inducted into the service during the War period, and a similar question as to a determination of what the tests actually meant. It is difficult to understand the appeal to the popular mind of highly technical discussion on brain sizes or intelligence tests, but the Negro mass mind was turned to follow any discussion refuting a suggestion of myths claiming white superiority. The great amount of printing space devoted to the technical discussion of mental characteristics in popular magazines such as *The Crisis, Opportunity,* and *The Messenger* is an indication of the subject's importance to the Negro and the magazines' few white readers.

The brain-size controversy lost its force during this period. *Opportunity* printed relevant material by Alexander Soldenweizer documenting this problem:

> In the first place, the general correspondence in the range and weight and size of brain between the two races ensures their comparability for all practical purposes whatever the weight of brains at the two extreme ends of the curve may be. In the second place, the relation between what we call intelligence and size and weight of brain is not by any means a direct one.[84]

There are two points of significance in *Opportunity*'s conclusions. First, the accumulated data did not indicate important differences in size; the size criterion in any case was questionable. The situation was altered in the squabble about Alpha and Beta tests. There was a substantial and measurable disparity in the data differentiating the Negro from the white. The problem became, then, for the Negro controversialist, one of defining the meaning of the tests. Almost without exception, the Negro writer established the difference between analysis designed to test the subject's native intelligence and analysis designed to test the influence of the subject's environment. It was concluded generally that the Army tests revealed information relative to environment rather than to native intelligence. Foremost of the rhetoricians coming to the defense of the Negro was Charles S. Johnson, who constructed the following explanation in "Mental Measurements of Negro Groups," which appeared in the second issue of his magazine:

> Over eighty per cent of the Negroes of the South, for example, live in the country isolated from the elaborate paraphernalia of modern city life. . . . The generation of age and eligible for Army Service in 1918 had little schooling and as a consequence read very little, thus further increasing their isolation.
>
> If they are fundamental [differences], distinctly and definitely racial, the fact that Negroes live in Ohio instead of Georgia would not alter the relation of difference; neither would the total number when converted into percentages seriously affect the relation. But this is distinctly not the case.[85]

There is a reference to a statistical demonstration expressed in an editorial in a later issue of *Opportunity*, which documents conclusions formulated above by editor Johnson:

> In the November *Pearson's Magazine*, for example, Hobart B. Alexander groups the scores of the United States Army Alpha and Beta tests for northern Negroes and southern whites and finds that the northern Negroes, in the average, received ratings superior to those of the southern whites. None of the scholarly volumes dared consider such a comparison. It would have confounded a theory of essential racial differences which many regard too sacred to question.[86]

One of the most complete refutations of arguments in defense of white superiority fictions based on mental characteristics was the article "What the Army 'Intelligence' Tests Measured," by Horace Mann Bond. It was important because the usual arguments based on a detailed analysis of the nature of the Army tests were complemented by information stating the effects of the tests upon the American public. The complementary refutation was made, then, in terms of the public welfare. The following statements sought to establish the viciousness of the false conclusions if allowed to influence the thinking of the general public:

It is on the basis of these tests that the Nordic races have been granted the heaven-sent mental superiority over South Europeans which entitles them to entry into this country; that a prominent college president and pulpit orator in the East justifies the policy of segregation in the public schools. . . .

They have given to the professional race-hatred agitator a semblance of scientific justification for his mouthings, and, in the writings of popular and ill-informed publicists, they are rapidly moulding a public opinion in the support of the most reactionary and inequable measures of general policy and public welfare. . . .

There is but one answer to those who would have theories of racial inequality upon the results of the Alpha Army Tests; and that is the indisputable truth that Alpha measures environment and not native inherent capacity.[87]

Dr. W.E.B. Du Bois assimilated and expressed in an idiom peculiar to him the essential points of refutation in the controversy. His editorial on racial intelligence was significant because of its excellent picture of the defensive attitude of the Negro intellectual in this period. It was a revelation of the thinking of a somewhat weary crusader against deliberately concocted misconceptions in the white mind—falsifications which the possessor of truth was obligated continuously to destroy. The destruction of one meant only a temporary victory for the Negro essayist, since others rose always to supplant annihilated myths. This is an extract from Du Bois's article "Race Intelligence," which appeared in *The Crisis*:

Today scientists acknowledge that there is no warrant for such a conclusion and that in any case the absolute weight of the brain is no criterion for racial behavior.

Measurements of the bony skeletons followed and great hopes of the scientific demonstration of race inferiority were held for a while. But they had to be surrendered when Zulus and Englishmen were found in the same dolicocephalic class.

Then came psychology, the children of the public schools were studied, and it was discovered that some colored children ranked lower than white children. This gave wide satisfaction even though it was pointed out that the average included most of both races and that considering the educational opportunities and social environment of the races the differences were measurements simply of the black child's surroundings.

Today, however, all is settled. "A workable accurate scientific clarification of brain power" has been discovered and by none other than our astute army officers.

Du Bois stated that comparative results were obtained from tests of "4,730 Negroes from Louisiana and Mississippi and 28,052 white recruits from Illinois." He indicated that upon this evidence H.H. Trabue, Director of the Bureau of Education, Columbia University, concluded that:

> The intelligence of the average southern Negro is equal to that of a nine-year old white boy and that we should arrange our educational program to make waiters, porters, scavengers, and the like of most Negroes.[88]

Theories of the mental inferiority and physical frailty of the Negro buttressed more comprehensive mythology, stating that the Negro had not participated and could not participate on the level of the white man in the whole process of culture-making. The reaction to the conception that race functioned as the cultural determinant was the root of the most significant portion of black literature of refutation and defense in this period.

Myths of Inferiority: Cultural

The question of the relative importance of the Negro as a contributor to the culture of the world was one which agitated Negro essayists profoundly during these years. A new intensity in racial antagonism complemented by outbreaks of physical violence between whites and Negroes stimulated, among a minority of white intellectuals, the articulation of new theories seeking to restate the old conclusion that culture is merely, if not entirely, the product of the ingenuity of the white (sometimes called Caucasian) race only. The basis for this kind of thinking was the racial theory of history which Madison Grant expressed in contemporary times in "The Passing of the Great Race":

> We must, first of all, realize that race pure and simple, the physical structure of man, is something entirely distinct from either nationality or language, and that race lies today at the base of all the phenomena of modern society, just as it has done throughout unrecorded eons in the past.

A further assumption was made by exponents of this school: the existence of patterns of racial characteristics sufficiently distinct to construct a racial type, a complete racial personality. Madison Grant stated:

> These races vary intellectually and morally just as they do physically. Moral, intellectual, and spiritual attributes are as persistent as physical characters, and are transmitted unchanged from generation to generation.[89]

There were other writers in the period who shared Grant's frame of reference; perhaps most influential of the group, Grant excepted, were Lothrop Stoddard, author of *The Rising Tide of Color*,[90] and Earnest S. Cox, author of *White America*. There was unanimous agreement among them upon this conclusion, as formulated by Cox: "Civilization's every pulse beat is Caucasian. Its source is in the white race, and it cannot continue apart from the white race." These principles were enunciated as inviolable truths:

1. The white race has founded all civilizations.
2. The white race remaining white has not lost civilization.
3. The white race become hybrid has not retained civilization.

Cox's attitude toward the Negro took this form with consistency on the basis of assumptions established: "The Negro has never produced civilized culture, has never proved himself capable of sustaining it."[91] Confirmation of this point of view was to be found in *The Passing of the Great Race*: "Negroes have demonstrated throughout recorded time that they are a stationary species, and that they do not possess the potentiality of progress or initiative from within."[92]

These formulations in terms of racial theories of culture were not the inventions of the period. The Reconstruction period had been preoccupied with the construction of theories of culture based on essential racial differences. Arguments in this vein antedated Reconstruction and are to be found elaborated in the writings of the proslavery authors. Of particular significance in this regard were the works of Thomas Dew and George Fitzhugh. Theorizing of this type represented a vital tradition; it had existed, however, less vigorously from the time of Thomas Dixon[93] to the time of Stoddard. There was a flurry of literary productions giving racial angles and interpretations of culture toward the beginning of World War I and in the first years of the 1920s. Alain Locke indicated the pendulum swings in the interest of writers of controversial literary matter on racial problems in his introduction to Kelly Miller's *Everlasting Stain*: "They register first of all the shift from the purely theoretical discussion of the late Reconstruction period to the practical analysis and statistical comparison of today." This statement is complemented by the observation: "Oddly enough the discussion of today finds itself back to a theoretical phase."[94]

The convictions of Stoddard, Grant, and Cox, though certainly not universally held by the white American world, were not, nevertheless, the futile mouthings of a small coterie of misled intellectuals. Their beliefs were common tender of a good portion of the masses of American whites; they formed the mythological background for a resurgent and revitalized Ku Klux Klan. New strength for racial theories arose from the antagonism and violence characteristic of postwar adjustment; also, new nationalistic inclinations, the world over, infecting the Negro as well as the white man, carried in their train overtones of racial self-determination and an emphasis on cultural construction upon vigorous racial roots, generally accepted ideas establishing a receptive milieu for the spread of belief in the racial interpretation of history.

The reassertion of principles of racial superiority in regard to cultural contributions and the adoption of those principles by masses of American whites were not accepted without comment by the Negro intellectual. Reaction and defense were constructed along those lines. There was, primarily, an immediate counterattack. Essayists satirized and sneered at presumably progressive white America, and particularly deprecated the civilization in the South, from which, traditionally, racial superiority myths were assumed to generate. The tenor of the attack was indicated by an editorial in the March 1917 issue of *The Crisis*, which is a bitter and resentful diatribe:

> What sort of culture is it that cannot control itself in the most fundamental of human relations, that is given over to mobs, reactionary legislation, and cruel practices?
>
> Is it not rather true that the former slave states stand today at least three hundred years behind the civilized world in all essential social and economic thought? And that outside of a very few progressive whites, their only really modern, forward-looking class is the educated Negro?[95]

Quite often the indulgence of more conservative essayists was the trick of demonstrating that the hostile white American shares to even a greater degree than does the Negro a trait considered as indicating the primitive and uncultivated state of a people. The fiction that the Negro is superstitious and, by consequence, primitive was answered in an editorial in *Opportunity* in this fashion. The editorial began with a quotation from an article published in the *American Journal of Psychiatry* by Dr. E.K. Bevis: "All Negroes have a fear of darkness and seldom venture out alone at night unless on mischief bent." The editorial continued with a series of accusations incriminating the American white race. Phenomena mentioned were the grip of terror which Friday the Thirteenth held on the American public, the blood-curdling stories about the Antigonish Ghost, the popularity of mediums, dream books, love potions, and charm rings with the general public, and a front-page announcement in the New York *Times* of a book by Camille Flammarian listing 5,600 haunted houses.[96]

Satirical possibilities were fully exploited by the more radical writers, and the white American's claims to superior culture became the butt of cleverly conceived irony. An editorial in *The Messenger*, "Lawlessness of the 'Hire Learning,'" combined invective with a debunking of American educational and scientific methods, and consisted of a demonstration that progressive methods, of which America was proud, led to chaotic oppression rather than to cultural advancement. An indication of the kind and the construction of the attack is supplied by the following extract from the editorial:

> Neither Russia nor Mexico promotes lawlessness through schools and colleges, still our pious fraternity of 100 per centers hurl anathemas upon their sinful heads, deploring and berating

their waywardness from the approved paths of the righteous
and the holy. . . . Besides the Slavic and Latinic tribes do not
possess scientific minds. They are deucedly sentimental. They
are making serious attempts, as it were, to practice that which
we merely profess and preach in the fields of religion, politics,
and industry. . . . Our minds are severely practical and scientific. We test things. For instance, in the absence of a laboratory,
we improvised one and caused our mob psychology to appre-
hend and lynch a "nigger" for a pragmatic study in the applied
sociology of lynching by the students of the respectable people
of the University of Missouri.[97]

The thesis of the more radical writers, as indicated by the
above literary fragment, was that cultural regression or lack of
progress is measurable by the amount of oppression to the people
who are not dominant in the society. This thesis had a clear
exposition in *Darkwater*, by W.E.B. Du Bois. The categorical
statement was made that "no modern nation can shut the gates of
opportunity in the face of its women, its peasants, its laborers, or
its socially damned." It is interesting that woman is included in
the outcast group as the Negro's fellow sufferer of the oppression
of a hostile white world. And Du Bois deplored "the present low
estate of the outcasts of the world, peering with bloodshot eyes at
the gates of the industrial heaven."[98]

The essence of the radical attack upon the culture of white
America resembled closely in nature the argument for granting
legal justice to the Negro, which was expressed also in *Darkwater*:

> If a race, like the Negro race, is excluded, then so far as that race
> is a part of the economic and social organization of the land, the
> feeling and the experience of that race are absolutely necessary
> to the realization of the broadest justice for all citizens.[99]

The vicious, destructive attack upon white American civilization was only a partial answer by the Negro essayist to claims of
white cultural superiority. A second method was a new interpretation of history designed to give the Negro for the first time his just
importance as a moving and contributing force. There was a
particular interest in rewriting American history. The spirit
which moved the new scholarship is expressed lucidly in the
foreword of Du Bois's *The Gift of Black Folk*:

> Its thesis is that despite slavery, war and caste, and despite our present problem, the American Negro is and has been a distinct asset to this country and has brought a contribution without which America could not have been; and that perhaps the essence of our so-called Negro problem is the failure to recognize this fact and to continue to act as though the Negro was what we once imagined and wanted to imagine him—a representation of a sub-human species fitted only for subordination.[100]

The desire for the reexamination of American history in an effort to determine what had been the role of the Negro developed into an impulse stimulating much creditable scholarship. The major Negro historians of this period were Benjamin Brawley, Carter G. Woodson, and W.E.B. Du Bois. The quotation from *The Gift of Black Folk* summarizes the nature of the approach. The application of the approach and the consequent interpretation of American history by Negro scholars produced certain common important divergencies from orthodox interpretations by white scholars working in the same field. Analysis of the most widely divergent points of difference, the conception of the Negro in the institution of slavery and that of the Negro in Reconstruction, is of value at this point because the expositions of the new conceptions represent, apart from their historical value, excellent tracts defending the cultural status of the Negro.

The new historical research constructed a picture of the African slave varying sharply from that which appeared in the fictions of Thomas Nelson Page and Thomas Dixon at the turn of the twentieth century. It was a picture which differed sharply also from the one emerging in the historical research of contemporary white historians. There the conception was fixed of the rebellious Negro slave, of the resentful black man who was ever resisting white oppression, representing the direct antithesis of the ideal character type of the "before the War" Negro which was popularized in Thomas Nelson Page's *In Ole Virginny*. Du Bois redefined in *The Gift of Black Folk* the attitude and the significance of the black slave:

> It is usually assumed in reading American history that whatever the Negro has done for America has been passive and unintelligent. . . . This is not true. On the contrary, it was the rise and growth among the slaves of a determination to be a free and an

active part of American democracy that forced American democracy continually to look into the depths; that held the focus of American thought to the inescapable fact that as long as there was a slave in America America could not be a free republic.

Along with the emphasis upon the slave type of the belligerent and resentful Negro, there was evidence of increased absorption of the Negro historian with the subject of slave insurrections in the Old South. A vigorous affirmation of this conviction was found in *The Gift of Black Folk*:

> . . . there is no doubt of the continuous and abiding fear of them [slave insurrections]. The slave legislation of the Southern states is filled with ferocious attempts to guard against this.[101]

Similarly, Benjamin Brawley indicated in *A Social History of the American Negro* the restlessness of the Negro under the yoke of slavery. He provided detailed accounts of the Vesey, Gabriel, and Turner insurrections, as well as full reports on the "Amistad" and "Creole" cases. He devoted a chapter to the relationship between the Seminole Indians and the Negroes, and gave credit to ex-slaves for aiding in resisting the advance—often treacherously attempted—of the white man. Brawley took the position that the attitude of the neighboring whites concerning the pursuit of fugitive slaves and the kidnapping of the slaves either belonging to or amalgamated with the Indian tribes helped to precipitate war between the United States and the Seminoles. This statement of Brawley's was important in light of the development of the type of the "rebellious" slave:

> This very close connection of the Negro with the family life of the Indian was the determining factor in the resistance of the Seminoles to the demands of the agents of the United States, and a reason stronger even than his love for his old hunting ground, for his objection to removal to new lands beyond the Mississippi.

Brawley shared Du Bois's position that the rebelliousness of the Negro slave contributed heavily to the antislavery stimulus in the North rather than undergoing a development as a result of antislavery propaganda, which is the conviction of most historians of the South. Brawley stated that the Nat Turner insurrection "focussed attention in the North, and thus helped with the formation of anti-slavery organization.''[102]

In Carter G. Woodson's *The Negro in Our History*, there was to be discovered a similar concern for the exposition of the character type of the "rebellious" slave and an absorption with an explanation of the slave uprisings. The statement was made that the chief source of the uprisings came from refugees from Santo Domingo and free Negroes, and a minimal amount of emphasis was placed on the vigor of antislavery propaganda. Du Bois's idea—that the original impetus toward struggle for emancipation came from the underprivileged Negro himself, and was not a matter of indoctrination or growing popularity of a new ideology—was, thus, buttressed here. Woodson indicated the Southern whites' fear of slave uprisings and cited the creation of numerous defense laws as evidence of a feeling of insecurity among the members of the master group. Cited legislation included the restriction of immigration of free Negroes, the restriction of travel and the right of assembly of all Negroes, the prohibition of the circulation of bills and pamphlets, the creation of more serious penalties for those instructing Negroes in reading and writing and for preachers who spoke to groups of slaves assembled socially without the permission of the masters, and finally the expulsion from some Southern states of the free Negroes.[103]

Negro historical writers attacked in the above manner more orthodox conceptions of the Negro in the institution of slavery. The figure of the resentful serf supplanted other notions varying from the fictional "contented slave" to a more scientific appraisal of the black man, which contended that the attitude and the condition of the Negro slave were variables—that they took one form in a community in Mississippi one generation from the frontier, and another in the border state where the plantation system was in the 1850s undergoing a transformation.

A second area of research where there was significant divergence between the points of view of Negro scholars and white students in the field was the Reconstruction period in American history. That they were writing against orthodox interpretations was a fact of which Negro historians were intensely aware, and there is the consciousness that the new truth is being revealed in the face of flagrant falsehood. The conviction they were opposing was the position the majority of the white historians of the period have taken—that Reconstruction was, in terms of the economic and social development of the South, a mistake, resulting in much wanton destruction of property and the disregard for property rights, misgovernment by white carpetbaggers and ignorant Negro aides, and the growth of ill-feeling and distrust between former masters and slaves.

The evidence presented by Negro scholars was intended to disprove, first, that the Negro generally was hopelessly ignorant and incapable of carrying intelligently the responsibilities of citizenship; second, that giving the vote to the Negro was the gravest of mistakes; third, that Negro civil officers were inefficient and corrupt, participating fully in the wave of violence to property rights which accompanied Reconstruction; and finally, that the responsibility for the failure to evolve a satisfactory postwar adjustment rested upon the carpetbaggers, scalawags, radical reconstructionists, and Negroes who wished to humiliate and complete the conquest of the South.

These were the charges which Negro historians wished to refute, and they proceeded with the understanding, moreover, that contemporary scholarship in Southern history tended to support conclusions which they were unwilling to accept. Brawley's analysis of the behavior of the Negro in this period was a revealing polemic defending the Negro's cultural status:

> Within recent years it has become more and more the fashion to lament the ills of the period, and no representative American historian can write of Reconstruction without a tone of apology. . . . In the first place ignorance was by no means so vast as has been supposed. Within the four years from 1861 to 1865, thanks to the army schools and missionary agencies, not less than half a million Negroes in the South had learned to read and write. Furthermore, the suffrage was not immediately given to the emancipated Negroes; this was the last rather than the first step in Reconstruction.

Brawley added a general conclusion which summarized briefly his point of view: "On the whole the race bore the blessing of emancipation with remarkable good sense and temper."[104]

There were two divergent attitudes on the part of Negro historians concerning the confiscation and attack upon property. Du Bois took the more radical view:

> The chief charge against Negro governments has to do with property. The governments are charged with attacking property and the charge is true. . . . The ex-slaves must have land and capital or they would fall back into slavery. The masters had both; there must be a transfer.[105]

Confiscation, in this frame of reference, was a necessary expedient to attain the freedom of the Negroes and consolidate the gains of the War. Other historians were inclined to shift the odium of loose attitudes toward property rights onto the period rather than onto Negroes participating in the reorganized Southern governments. Brawley felt that in a decade of unparalleled political corruption "it is not just to fix upon a people groping to the light the peculiar odium of the corruption that followed in the wake of the War."[106] And Woodson reiterated that corruption was the theme of the time and added that there was no government more corrupt than that which followed the Reconstruction governments.[107]

The Negro historians did not write apologetically about the Negro's exercise of voting power or of officeholding during the Reconstruction period. The feeling existed among them that the provision of the ballot to the black man saved the Union from defeat and the North from an ignominious surrender. Brawley's interpretation of the passing of the Fifteenth Amendment contains a vigorous affirmation of this position:

> The alternative finally presented Congress, if it was not to make an absolute surrender, was either to hold the South indefinitely under military subjection or to place the ballot in the hands of the Negro. . . . The Union was really restored—was really saved by the force of the ballot in the hands of the black men.[108]

This was precisely Du Bois's position, except for an emphasis upon an economic justification, which maintained that the ballot in the hands of the Negro "diverted the energy of the white South from economic development to the recovery of political power and in this interval—small as it was—the Negro took his first steps toward economic freedom."[109]

Woodson granted that many Negroes were not prepared to vote, but he insisted upon the integrity of most Negroes in finding the best candidates for important positions. He was absorbed to a greater extent than Du Bois or Brawley with the defense of the Negro officeholder. It was his contention that most of the offices were not held by Negroes but by Southern white men and by Northern whites possessing little sympathy for the South, and that most Negro officers served with honorable records. Much of the section on the period dealt with details of the educational qualifications of Negro Reconstructionists, Elliot, Cain, Bruce, and others, and comment upon the creditable careers in public life of F.L. Cardozo of South Carolina, H.B.S. Pinchback and Chester of Louisiana, and fellow Negro officeholders.[110]

There was complete unanimity of opinion among Negro historians regarding the source of the defective spirit causing the failure of Reconstruction policies to evolve a satisfactory and stable society. One historian wrote that the failure was in large part due to the antagonism of former slaveholders, and that the poor whites were moved to resort to terrorism, assuming organized form eventually in the Ku Klux Klan, by the slaveholders' attack upon the policies of the carpetbag governments and by their own unwillingness to accept Negro citizenship.[111] To Brawley, the source of troublesome action was attributable to failure of the Southern states to accept the Fourteenth Amendment.[112] Du Bois deplored the "counter revolution" engineered by the unreconstructed white Southerners but maintained that it came too late, since "the Negro had stepped so far into the new economic freedom that he could never be put back into slavery."[113]

A summary of the overall view of the Negro historian in regard to the Reconstruction period would approach Du Bois's concept that it was a purgation period for a developing American democracy, with the Negro functioning as a moving force toward the attainment of democratic idealism.

> In a peculiar way, then, the Negro in the United States has emancipated democracy, reconstructed the threatened edifice of freedom and been a sort of eternal test of the sincerity of our democratic ideals.[114]

The project of rewriting American history was ambitious even for scholars as able as Brawley, Woodson, and Du Bois. Motivation for the task was not merely to further scholarly research but also to supply a vigorous defense against the arguments of those wishing to decry the Negro's part in the formation of American democracy. These historical studies were rhetorical pieces concerned with the problem of the cultural status of the race, as the whole of American culture progressed into greater complexity. Du Bois resented the assumption that the role of the Negro had been a passive and unintelligent one. He and his fellow historians would not tolerate the implication that the Negro was not sufficiently sensitive to the impetus for cultural contribution to be a positive and constructive force in American history.

A final technique by which cultural justification of the race was sought was the development of conviction and elaborate thought patterns around the idea of the Negro's peculiar genius or individual gift to higher civilization. There were numerous references in contemporary literature to the singularity of this racial gift and to its strength in the members of the racial group. Statements of its exact nature were inclined toward vagueness, but always included in an attempted analysis was an emphasis upon the ability of the Negro in the fine arts:

> Every race has its peculiar genius, and so far as we can at present judge, the Negro with all his manual labor, is destined to reach his greatest heights in the field of the artistic.

Not content with prediction, Brawley wrote in the preface to his *The Negro in Literature and Art in the United States* that "any distinction so far won by a member of the race in America has been almost always in some one of the arts. . . ."[115] The strength of the racial leaning toward cultivation of the arts was repeatedly affirmed; its power was such that the Negro, it is said, was not easily drawn into the "new prosaic, and materialistic society, encompassing him."[116] The peculiar genius of the Negro was a leavening agent, overcoming the handicaps of an alien culture. This position had significance in terms of the conception of the mind of the mulatto: "the element of genius that distinguished the Negro artist of mixed blood is most frequently one characteristically Negro rather than Anglo-Saxon." Brawley documented his conclusion by referring to the "romantic and elemental sculpture of Meta Warrick Fuller and the mystical religious paintings of Henry O. Tanner."[117]

There was much elaborate theorizing about the Negro's "element of genius," and the aspects of the problem receiving the most attention were analysis of the element, its origin, and its manifestations in racial attainment. Figuring prominently in descriptions of the Negro's flair for the artistic was the conception of the importance of the African tradition, of the primitive adjustment of the Negro to a hostile tropical environment. This was an essential point in Brawley's explanation:

> But there is something deeper than the sensuousness of beauty that makes for the possibilities of the Negro in the realm of the arts, and that is the soul of the race. . . . There is something very elemental about the heart of the race, something that finds its origin in the African forest, in the sighing of the night wind, and in the falling of the stars.[118]

Explications of Negro genius had an inescapable overtone of romance. The simple, poetic life of the primitive black man opposed the mechanistic, prosaic white culture; the coming of the Negro meant an infusion of color and song. Evidenced also was a new unconcern for the conventional moral codes of the white man and freedom from inhibitions binding personal enjoyment and vigorous expression.

> As a tropical product with a sensuous receptivity to the beauty of the world he was not as easily reduced to be the mechanical draft-horse which the northern European laborers became. He was not easily brought to recognize any ethical sanctions in work as such but tended to work as the results pleased him and refused to work or sought to refuse when he did not find the spiritual returns adequate; thus he was easily accused of laziness and driven as a slave when in truth he brought to modern manual labor a renewed valuation of life.[119]

Out of this set of convictions affirming the presence of a residuum of African characteristics contributing to the Negro personality grew the concept of the "tropical nonchalance."[120] The phrase was Alain Locke's, and the idea became an essential myth current in the work of the writers of the Negro Renaissance.

It became one of the leading motives in the original synthesis of ideas popularizing Renaissance convictions, a synthesis which was the handiwork of Locke, appearing first as an article in the Harlem (March) issue of *The Survey Graphic* of 1925, and later as a prefacing essay to *The New Negro*, an anthology of selected essays and imaginative productions of the modern Negro.

The ideas were originally formulated in this pre-Renaissance period; they became common currency in the Negro literary world with the growing stature of the poets Jean Toomer, Claude McKay and Countee Cullen, and with the flowering of the Garvey and other pan-African movements in the early twenties. Vivid poetic expressions of what came to be known as the "tropic nonchalance" can be found as early as 1920; this was the year in which McKay published in London *Spring in New Hampshire*. A few lines from "North and South" indicate a successful transmutation of the idea into poetic symbols:

> There time and life move lazily along
> There by the banks of blue and silver streams
> Grass-sheltered crickets chirp incessant song
>
> A breath of idleness is in the air
> That casts a subtle spell upon all things
> And love and mating-time are everywhere
> And wonder to life's commonplaces clings.[121]

A significant aspect of the development of the conviction about the Negro genius and its peculiar cultural offerings was the tendency of Negro writers to flirt with theories of distinctive characteristics inherent in the race itself. The temptation existed always to reduce the basis for conviction to an exposition of fundamental racial physical and mental traits. This meant a serious divergence from the argument of more conservative writers interested also in the Negro's special talent in the arts, but inclined to seek evidence from cultural environment alone, refusing to place trust in theories of inherent racial or African traits. Wallace V. Jackson, dramatic critic of *The Messenger*, articulated this position:

> Whatever traits reminiscent of African ancestors he may have
> brought out of the span of over two hundred years were only

negative and did not take the lead in shaping his actions or artistic faculties.[122]

The statements of doubters did not restrain the ardor of Negro writers insistent upon finding the roots of the cultural gifts of the Negro within the bounds of inherited characteristics and disclaiming any influence of the white man upon the development of black culture. The argument in outline followed this pattern: From his African ancestors the Negro has inherited a body with physical characteristics and peculiarities designed by nature to meet the needs of a tropical environment. From the same ancestors, he inherited a "temperament, mind, spirit, designed for the expression of a deep-seated aesthetic and religious nature in a vitalized, well-regulated and age-old society in which he has formed an integral part, rather than mental and social tendencies conducive to adjustment and resignation in the new, prosaic and materialistic society." In spite of the temptations of the strange machine world, the American Negro has, nevertheless, refused to be persuaded that in American urban art forms he is to find the highest expression of his inner life, and he has created a culture-world of his own.

> The social history of the American Negro is essentially the expression of reflexes and complexes elaborated and refined and handed down to him in the fiery blood of his African ancestors who played their part well in this mighty world that now has persisted.[123]

All contributions of the Negro are, thus, related to African beginnings and characteristics, plastic, though sufficiently strong to erect within crass materialism a vital romantic world.

These patterns formed the substructure of most contemporary Negro art and literary criticism. Brawley was a fellow-traveler of the Negro theorists, but he did not proceed to the extreme conclusions arrived at by both Locke and Du Bois. He was content in the preface of *The Negro in Literature and Art in the United States* to indicate the reflection in Negro art production of what he called the "soul of the race," which he defined as "something that finds its origin in the African forest."[124] Brawley's description of the distinctive "African quality" in American Negro production is vague; it is a general statement giving evidence of the direction only of Negro critical thinking, and indicating none of its complexity. Brawley's remarks were concerned, as was most Negro criticism of the period, with explicating the peculiar "faculty" of the artist—this he did with less elaboration and with less documentation than either Locke or Du Bois. The issue of inherited characteristics received little attention, though it absorbed the energies of other critics.

The position of Locke and Du Bois reflected an adherence to more radical opinion as to the nature of the Negro's faculty for artistic expression. Neither scholar hesitated to flirt with theories of inherited characteristics or to indulge in the kind of romantic utterance previously outlined and indicated as the property of the radical art critic. The approach which Du Bois made to the consideration of Negro art and literature in *The Gift of Black Folk* was interesting in this respect:

> The Negro is primarily an artist. The usual way of putting this is to speak disdainfully of his "sensuous" nature. This means that the only race which has held at bay the life destroying forces of the tropics has gained therefrom in some slight compensation a sense of beauty, particularly for sound and color, which characterizes the race. The Negro blood which flowed in the veins of many of the mightiest of the Pharoahs accounts for much of Egyptian art. . . .
>
> Beyond the specific ways in which the Negro has contributed to American art stands undoubtedly his spirit of gayety and the exotic charm which his presence has loaned the parts of America which were spiritually free enough to enjoy it.[125]

It is important to notice that Du Bois makes "the sensuous nature" and the faculty for the arts racial traits which can be discerned in the cultures of the world just as the student would discover prominent Negroid physical characteristics (nose shape, hair texture, etc.) in the people forming the society from which the culture derives. This statement was made without reservations as to the structure of the society from which the Negro might come, or about the type of adjustment the Negro might have to make in entering an alien society. Du Bois's remark was, indeed, an ambitious generalization.

Locke's statements were nearly as comprehensive. It is evident from his comments on African art that he believed that the black man's peculiar perception for design and organization in art would enable the American Negro to achieve complete understanding of the intricacies of African art.

> . . . we must believe that there still slumbers in the blood something which once stirred and will react with peculiar emotional integrity toward it [African art]. If by nothing more mystical than the sense of being ethnically related, some of us will feel its influence at least as keenly as those who have already made it recognized and famous.[126]

Some Negro critics, though subscribing to the myth of racial genius, were hesitant about attributing the credit for its manifestation to the survival of African characteristics. Brawley was willing enough to accept belief in a certain spiritual joyousness, "a sensuous, tropical love of life, in vivid contrast to the cool and cautious New England reason; a slow and dreamful conception of the universe, a drawling and slurring of speech. . . ." He insisted upon adding:

> There is something grim and stern about it all, too, something that speaks of the lash, of the child torn from its mother's bosom, of the dead body riddled with bullets and swinging all night from a limb by the roadside.[127]

Brawley's reference to the difficulties experienced by the Negro in slavery revealed the second important element of the Negro genius. The strength to bear suffering and the aptitudes which the Negro acquired during serfdom constituted a part of the black man's faculty for the arts, a part considered by many critics as more significant (certainly more authentic) than the more publicized myth of the survival of an African impulse in the Negro artist. A white playwright, Ridgeley Torrence, referred to and defined the relationship existing between the Negro's experience of slavery and the racial strength and power evident in Negro creative expression:

> Its [the race's] life under slavery, with its intense but seemingly hopeless longings for liberty, produced in it a certain epic spirit, unconscious, of course, which is reflected in the tremendous sweep of its camp meeting songs.[128]

Discussion of aptitudes and characteristics which were deemed survivals of an antebellum adjustment was the concern of Wallace Van Jackson, dramatic critic of *The Messenger*:

> Slave life left him [the Negro] with certain leanings in emotional expression, a litheness of movement in the dance, a facility in songs and music and a peculiar aptness at mimicry—slavery will lead any people with such tendencies, witness the Russian serf.

Though Jackson denied the possibility of African survivals of any importance in the Negro,[129] his catalogue of distinguishing characteristics did not differ greatly from the series of traits which his fellow Negro critics stoutly maintained as possessing African origins. Thus, a double interpretation was possible of the advice of the eminent dramatic producer Max Reinhardt, intended for aspiring Negro dramatists:

> My last word is, be original—sense the folk spirit, develop the folk-idiom, artistically, of course, but faithfully; and above all, do not let that technique of expression which is so original, so potential, get smothered out in the imitation of European acting, copied effects.
>
> With such control of body, such pantomime, I believe I could portray emotion, as it has never been portrayed—pure emotion, almost independent of words or setting. It is really marvelous.[130]

The statement would be accepted as valid by both the critics believing in African survivals and those giving more credence to the influence of characteristics acquired during antebellum days.

Frequent references to the statements of white critics reveal an interesting sidelight on the evolution of critical dogma concerning Negro art. Speculation about the black man's talent was not confined to Negro critics; eminent white artists and critics indicated their interest in the artistic contributions of the Negro and explained its importance in similar terms. Paul Guillaume, a French art critic, affirmed the idea that the peculiar gift of the Negro artist was to bring lightness and new beauty to a prosaic modern American world.

> Negro art has a spiritual mission; it has the great honor to develop the taste, to stir the depths of the soul, to refine the spirit, to enrich the imagination of this very Twentieth Century. . . .[131]

Raymond O'Neil, dramatic critic and producer, reiterated familiar patterns of thought about the Negro artist.

> He, too, is gifted with a sensuous nature. He loves life and he lives life with the sensuous and the emotional parts of him constantly exposed to it. As with the Russians these sensuous qualities are the springs of the Negro's creative potentialities.

Entirely consistent with the new criticism, O'Neil deplored the plight of the non-Negro American.

> Being mostly Anglo-Saxon, hence possessing sensuous and emotional qualities none too robust at best, he surrendered to assault upon him with scarcely a protest. The result has been a nation of individuals who receive less fun, pleasure and inspiration from clouds, flowers, and birds than any other group of civilized beings.[132]

While the Negro critic was engaged in the formulation of dogma and the determination of origins, he was concerned with yet another extension of the general problem of examining the race's peculiar faculty for the arts. He demonstrated and illustrated the operation of that "talent" in the modern world. Many of the race's artistic accomplishments were especially congenial for treatment. Receiving perhaps more attention than other of the black man's attainments was his music. The discovery of the "natural" Negro artist led to a quickened interest in Negro folk music—in the spiritual and in the "blues"; enthusiasm about the art forms was followed by theoretical explanations of the uniqueness of the form and eulogies stressing that the evolved art form was free from the taint of foreign racial cultures. One critic wrote in *The Messenger*:

> Blues is recognized, always, by its characteristically weird melody. Its most unique possession is one of longing. . . .
> Blues music is yet undeveloped, but time will prove that it is more capable of great works such as song classics, sonatas, operas and symphonies, than many other crude works.

The desire of this critic to indicate that "blues" music is worthy enough to provide excellent material for older and more sophisticated art forms should be noted; evidently he wished to make certain that the "blues" received consideration as "serious" music.

Also emphasized in the article were the distinctive qualities of the "blues": rhythm "characterized chiefly by syncopation," harmony "weird and unconquerable,"[133] employing both the major and the minor modes.

Du Bois was interested also in arriving at distinguishing qualities to be found in the folk music of the American Negro.

> The great difference between music of Africa and the music of Europe lies in rhythm; in Europe the music is accented in the regular beats of the music while in Africa the accents fall on the unstressed beats.[134]

This singular musical feature had been retained in the Negro folk song and was producing what in the contemporary idiom was known as "ragtime."

The dance was another field in which the touch of Negro genius was thought to be easily demonstrable. The "cake walk," "clog," and "turkey trot" were pointed to as Negro creations. Moreover, the peculiar aptness of the race in the art of mimicry received attention.

African art products were as important for illustrative purposes as American Negro folk music. There was much current criticism detailing the new differences in art forms, particularly those appearing in the African plastic arts; moreover, this was supplemented by commentary on the extension of the interest of the intellectual world in African plastic expression to a general absorption in African cultural patterns. Locke cited this virtue in the uniqueness of African plastic art:

> The discovery of African art happened to come at a time when there was a marked sterility in certain forms of expression in European plastic art, due to generations of the inbreeding of idiom and style.[135]

He quoted from Roger Fry's *Vision and Design*[136] an opinion which attempted to locate the special excellence of the Negro's work in the visual arts: "So far from clinging to two dimensions, as we tend to do, he [the Negro artist] actually underlines, as it were, the three-dimensionalness of his forms." Locke did not limit the interest of modern art criticism to African expression in the plastic arts alone. The flair for things African began shortly to express itself in poetry. He indicated that a recognized school of modern French poetry, including Apollinaire, Reverdy, Salmon, Fargue, and others, professed the inspiration of African sources. In music H.A. Junod, Bernard, Satie, Poulenc, Honegger, and Milhaud were credited with having been affected by African traditions.[137]

The cause of the defense of race culture was served nobly by the Negro art and literary critics. The authority in art criticism was Alain Locke, who was an analyst both of the newly discovered African art works and of attempts of contemporary Negroes in the plastic and visual arts; in literary criticism, Benjamin Brawley, William Stanley Braithwaite, W.F.B. Du Bois, and Jessie Fauset joined Alain Locke in making outstanding contributions. Central to all critical expression was the assumption of the theory of the "special tradition" or of the "special faculty" for the arts, which, as the foregoing analysis has indicated, originated at least partially from a desire to construct a defense counteracting attacks upon Negro culture and the general ability of the race to make cultural contributions. The initial stimulus, giving rise to the primary theories concerning the race's cultural distinction, was strong, but it was largely responsible for their elaborate development into the important myths of the Negro Renaissance.

The full tide of the Renaissance, reached during the mid-twenties, found these familiar cultural myths without much of the negativity which came from their functioning merely as defense mechanisms. They had become blueprints for creative productions. The Negro artist exploited consciously his "special tradition," either through his American folk or his African heritage; the poetry of Countee Cullen, Claude McKay, Jean Toomer, and Langston Hughes, the prose of Cullen, McKay, and Toomer, and the drama of Willis Richardson and John Matheus stand as significant evidence of the production in the new direction. The Negro critic interpreted the works of art in light of the established theory maintaining that Negro art was the expression of a race gifted with extraordinary facility and perception. Thus, cultural myths, which had served an important rhetorical function, became to a greater extent toward the mid-twenties principles stimulating creative production.

Braithwaite was articulating in 1919 familiar critical dogma:

> While we have no traditions in the art, we have a rich and
> precious tradition in the substance of poetry: vision, intense
> emotionalism, spiritual and mystical affinities, with both ab-
> stract and concrete experience, and a subtle natural sense of
> rhythmic values. All these are essential folk qualities. . . .

But this utterance, consistent with the patterns of thought in the
literature of cultural defense, was complemented by talk of new
creative productions stimulated by racial consciousness. Braithwaite wrote that Claude McKay, whose poems had been published
in the October 1918 issue of *The Seven Arts*, "may well be the
keystone of the new movement in racial poetic achievement."
Braithwaite's optimism about the future of Negro artistic production was underlined in this comment written in highly figurative
language: "there is power and beauty in this pristine utterance—
wood notes wild that have scarcely yet been heard beyond the
forest of their own dreams."[138] Du Bois talked even more particularly of a dawning literary movement, and it is interesting to
note that as early as 1920, reference was made to "renaissance."

> A renaissance of American Negro literature is due: the material
> about us in the strange, heart-rending race triangle is rich
> beyond dream and only we can tell the tale and sing the song
> from the heart.[139]

Renaissance dogma appeared, primarily, in the rhetoric of the
prose stylists writing controversial material immediately after
World War I. Not only were convictions sharpened in the heat of
producing a literature of defense, but they were made currency in
the Negro intellectual world. An understanding of how the key-
words of the mythology became the vocabulary of the Negro
leader requires an indication again of how generally and how
intensely the Negro world felt the attacks which a hostile white
civilization directed against it. In 1920, Brawley wrote of the
rising tide of ill-feeling between the races:

> A great war was to give new occasion and new opportunity for
> discrimination; defamatory propaganda was to be circulated on
> a scale undreamed of before, and the close of the war was to
> witness attempts for a new reign of terror in the South.[140]

What has been undertaken in the preceding material is the definition of the attacks upon the Negro, and the description and analysis of the rhetorical literature answering those attacks. Something of the complexity and great scope of the reply of the Negro intellectual has been indicated. Du Bois, stoutest champion of the cause of racial defense, revealed in vivid language in *Darkwater* the assumptions which he and his fellow-travelers were seeking to destroy; and he disclosed also what technical analysis had brought to light previously—that the Negro essayist has drawn copiously from the amazingly varied areas of knowledge to supply the material for his rhetoric. Du Bois defined the argument of the opposition as:

> A world campaign beginning with the slave trade and ending with the refusal to capitalize the word "Negro," leading through a passionate defense of slavery by attributing every bestiality to blacks and finally culminating in the evident modern profit which lies in degrading blacks—all this has unconsciously trained millions of honest, modern men into the belief that black folk are sub-human. This belief is not based on science, else it would be held as a postulate of the most tentative kind, ready at any time to be withdrawn in the face of facts; this belief is not based on history, for it is absolutely contradicted by Egyptian, Greek, Roman, Byzantine, and Arabian experiences; nor is the belief based on any careful survey of the social development of Negro blood today in Africa and America.[141]

1942

Notes

1. Alain Locke, "The New Negro," *The New Negro*, ed. Alain Locke (New York: Albert and Charles Boni, 1925), p. 4.
2. Claude McKay, *Harlem: Negro Metropolis* (New York: Dutton and Company, 1940), p. 177.
3. Marcus Garvey, "The Negro's Greatest Enemy," *Current History*, 18 (September 1923), 951–957; W.E.B. Du Bois, "Back to Africa," *Century*, 105 (February 1923), 539–548.

228   THE AFRO-AMERICAN LITERARY TRADITION

4. Louise V. Kennedy, *The Negro Peasant Turns Cityward* (New York: Columbia University Press, 1920), p. 23.
5. Benjamin Brawley, *A Social History of the American Negro* (New York: Macmillan Co., 1921), p. 345.
6. Carter G. Woodson, *A Century of Negro Migration* (Washington, D.C.: Association for the Study of Negro Life and History, 1918), p. 135.
7. Joseph A. Hill, "Recent Northward Migration of the Negro," *Opportunity*, 2 (April 1924), 102.
8. Kennedy, p. 30.
9. Emmett J. Scott, *Negro Migration During the War* (New York: Oxford University Press, 1920), p. 3.
10. Kennedy, p. 367.
11. Ibid., pp. 33, 34.
12. Scott, *Negro Migration During the War*, p. 14.
13. Ibid., p. 17.
14. Ibid., p. 21.
15. Ibid., p. 24.
16. Ibid., pp. 24, 40.
17. *Opportunity*, 2 (October 1924), 303.
18. Ibid.
19. *Opportunity*, 2 (October 1923), 290.
20. Woodson, *A Century of Negro Migration*, pp. 186, 189.
21. Hill, p. 105.
22. Scott, *Negro Migration During the War*, p. 101.
23. Chicago Commission on Race Relations, *The Negro in Chicago* (Chicago: University of Chicago Press, 1922), p. 15.
24. William H. Holtzclaw, *The Black Man's Burden* (New York: The Neale Publishing Company, 1915); William J. Edwards, *Twenty-Five Years in the Black Belt* (Boston: Cornhill Co., 1918); Robert R. Moton, *Finding a Way Out* (Garden City, N.Y.: Doubleday, Page and Co., 1920).
25. Emmett J. Scott and Lyman B. Stowe, *Booker T. Washington* (New York: Doubleday, Page and Co., 1918).
26. Brawley, *A Social History of the American Negro*, p. 364.
27. Walter F. White, "Chicago and Its Eight Reasons," *The Crisis*, 18 (October 1919), 297.
28. *Opportunity*, 1 (January 1923), 3.
29. Emmett J. Scott, *Scott's Official History of the American Negro in the World War* (Chicago: Homewood Press, 1919), p. 32.
30. Carter G. Woodson, *The Negro in Our History*, 4th edition, rev. (Washington, D.C.: Associated Publishers, 1927), p. 819.
31. Scott, *American Negro in the World War*, p. 97.
32. Woodson, *The Negro in Our History*, pp. 520, 523.
33. Moton, p. 251.
34. Addie W. Hunton and Kathryn H. Johnson, *Two Colored Women with the American Expeditionary Forces* (Brooklyn, N.Y.: Brooklyn Eagle Press, 1920), p. 42.

35. Brawley, *A Social History of the American Negro*, p. 365.
36. Alain Locke, "Apropos of Africa," *Opportunity*, 2 (February 1924), 37.
37. Kelly Miller, *The Everlasting Stain* (Washington, D.C.: Associated Publishers, 1924), p. 102.
38. W.E.B. Du Bois, "Third Pan-African Congress," *The Crisis*, 26 (October 1923), 248.
39. McKay, *Harlem: Negro Metropolis*, pp. 147, 146.
40. Charles S. Johnson, "After Garvey What?" *Opportunity*, 1 (August 1923), 231.
41. McKay, *Harlem: Negro Metropolis*, p. 155.
42. Ibid., p. 181.
43. Woodson, *The Negro in Our History*, p. 441.
44. Booker T. Washington, "Industrial Education and the Public Schools," *The Annals of the American Academy of Political and Social Science*, 49 (September 1913), 227.
45. Scott and Stowe, pp. 66, 72.
46. Woodson, *The Negro in Our History*, p. 443.
47. Scott and Stowe, p. 108.
48. Woodson, *The Negro in Our History*, p. 443.
49. *The Crisis*, 20 (May 1920), 5.
50. *The Crisis*, 26 (July 1923), 106.
51. *The Messenger*, 5 (June 1923), 733.
52. James Weldon Johnson, "The Truth About Haiti," *The Crisis*, 20 (September 1920), 220, 224.
53. Eugene K. Jones, "Cooperation and Opportunity," *Opportunity*, 1 (January 1923), 4, 5.
54. *The Messenger*, 5 (June 1923), 735.
55. Sterling D. Spero and Abram L. Harris, *The Black Worker* (New York: Columbia University Press, 1931), p. 22.
56. Ibid., p. 31.
57. Ibid., pp. 39, 40.
58. Ibid., pp. 117, 51.
59. Ibid., p. 117.
60. Woodson, *The Negro in Our History*, p. 541.
61. Ben Fletcher, "The Negro and Organized Labor," *The Messenger*, 5 (July 1923), 759.
62. Graham R. Taylor, "Race Relations and Public Opinion," *Opportunity*, 1 (July 1923), 197.
63. Ibid., p. 199.
64. Charles S. Johnson, "Public Opinion and the Negro," *Opportunity*, 1 (July 1923), 201.
65. *The Crisis*, 27 (June 1924), 55.
66. *The Crisis*, 20 (October 1920), 266.
67. *The Crisis*, 26 (August 1923), 153–154.
68. W.E.B. Du Bois, "Sensitive Liberia," *The Crisis*, 28 (May 1924), 10.
69. Claude McKay, "Soviet Russia and the Negro," *The Crisis*, 27 (December 1923), 62–63.

70. *The Messenger*, 5 (June 1923), 736.
71. W.E.B. Du Bois, "The Black Man and the Wounded World," *The Crisis*, 27 (January 1924), 110, 113.
72. William Pickens, "Color and Camouflage—A Psychoanalysis," *The Messenger*, 5 (July 1923), 773, 774.
73. Herbert Adolphus Miller, "The Myth of Superiority," *Opportunity*, 1 (August 1923), 223.
74. Frederick Hoffman, "Race Traits and Tendencies of the American Negro," *Publications of the American Economic Association*, 11 (August 1896).
75. *Opportunity*, 1 (November 1923), 323.
76. Ibid.
77. Louis I. Dublin, "The Effect of Health Education on Negro Mortality," *Opportunity*, 2 (August 1924), pp. 232, 234.
78. *Opportunity*, 1 (July 1923), 194.
79. Louis I. Dublin, "Recent Improvement in the Negroes' Mortality," *Opportunity*, 1 (April 1923), 6.
80. *Opportunity*, 1 (May 1923), 22.
81. J.A. Rogers, *From "Superman" to Man* (New York: Lenox Publishing Co., 1924).
82. *The Messenger*, 6 (February 1924), 49.
83. Eugene K. Jones, "The Negro's Struggle for Health," *Opportunity*, 1 (June 1923), 4, 7.
84. Alexander Soldenweizer, "Racial Theory and the Negro," *Opportunity*, 1 (August 1923), 230.
85. Charles S. Johnson, "Mental Measurements of Negro Groups," *Opportunity*, 1 (February 1923), 25.
86. *Opportunity*, 2 (January 1924), 4.
87. Horace Mann Bond, "What the Army 'Intelligence' Tests Measured," *Opportunity*, 2 (July 1924), 198, 201.
88. W.E.B. Du Bois, "Race Intelligence," *The Crisis*, 20 (July 1920), 119.
89. Madison Grant, *The Passing of the Great Race* (New York: Charles Scribner's Sons, 1916), pp. 17, 197.
90. T. Lothrop Stoddard, *The Rising Tide of Color Against White World-Supremacy* (New York: Charles Scribner's Sons, 1920).
91. Earnest S. Cox, *White America* (Richmond, Va.: White American Society, 1923), pp. 299, 23, 299.
92. Grant, p. 69.
93. Thomas R. Dew, *Review of the Debate in the Virginia Legislature of 1831 and 1832* (Richmond, Va.: T.W. White, 1832); Dew, *An Essay on Slavery* (Richmond, Va.: J.W. Randolph, 1849); George Fitzhugh, *Sociology for the South* (Richmond, Va.: A. Norris, 1854); Fitzhugh, *Cannibals All! or, Slaves Without Masters* (Richmond, Va.: A. Norris, 1857); Thomas Dixon, *The Clansman: An Historical Romance of the Ku Klux Klan* (New York: Doubleday, Page, & Co., 1905); Dixon, *The Leopard's Spots: A Romance of the White Man's Burden, 1865–1900* (New York: Doubleday, Page, & Co., 1903).
94. Kelly Miller, pp. 10, 11.
95. *The Crisis*, 12 (March 1917), 216.

96. *Opportunity*, 2 (July 1924), 196.

97. *The Messenger*, 5 (June 1923).

98. W.E.B. Du Bois, *Darkwater* (New York: Harcourt, Brace, Howe Co., 1920), pp. 154, 117.

99. Ibid., p. 144.

100. W.E.B. Du Bois, *The Gift of Black Folk* (Boston: The Stratford Co., 1924), pp. ii–iii.

101. Ibid., pp. 138, 147.

102. Brawley, *A Social History of the American Negro*, pp. 92, 148.

103. Woodson, *The Negro in Our History*, pp. 185–187.

104. Brawley, *A Social History of the American Negro*, pp. 270, 288.

105. Du Bois, *The Gift of Black Folk*, p. 224.

106. Brawley, *A Social History of the American Negro*, p. 271.

107. Woodson, *The Negro in Our History*, p. 400.

108. Brawley, *A Social History of the American Negro*, pp. 270–271.

109. Du Bois, *The Gift of Black Folk*, p. 217.

110. Woodson, *The Negro in Our History*, pp. 407–408, 406–407, 408.

111. Ibid., pp. 489, 413.

112. Brawley, *A Social History of the American Negro*, p. 270.

113. Du Bois, *The Gift of Black Folk*, p. 249.

114. Ibid., p. 257.

115. Benjamin Brawley, *The Negro in Literature and Art in the United States* (New York: Duffield and Co., 1918), pp. 8, 4.

116. William L. Hansberry, "The Social History of the American Negro: A Review," *Opportunity*, 2 (June 1923), 20.

117. Benjamin Brawley, *Your Negro Neighbor* (New York: Macmillan Co., 1918), p. 78.

118. Brawley, *The Negro in Literature and Art in the United States*, pp. 7–8.

119. Du Bois, *The Gift of Black Folk*, p. 53.

120. Alain Locke, *The New Negro*, p. 15.

121. Claude McKay, *Spring in New Hampshire* (London: Grant Richards, 1920), p. 20.

122. Wallace V. Jackson, "The Negro Stage," *The Messenger*, 5 (June 1923), 747.

123. Hansberry, pp. 20, 21.

124. Brawley, *The Negro in Literature and Art in the United States*, pp. 7, 8.

125. Du Bois, *The Gift of Black Folk*, pp. 287–288.

126. Alain Locke, "A Note on African Art," *Opportunity*, 2 (May 1924), 138.

127. Brawley, *The Negro in Literature and Art in the United States*, p. 8.

128. *The Crisis*, 14 (June 1917), 80.

129. Jackson, pp. 746–747.

130. Alain Locke, "Max Rheinhardt [sic] Reads the Negro's Dramatic Horoscope," *Opportunity*, 2 (May 1924), 146.

131. Paul Guillaume, "African Art at the Barnes Foundation," *Opportunity*, 2 (May 1924), 142.

132. Raymond O'Neil, "The Negro in Dramatic Art," *The Crisis*, 27 (February 1924), 186.

133. Astor Morgan, "Blues Music," *The Messenger*, 6 (February 1924), 58–59.

134. Du Bois, *The Gift of Black Folk*, p. 233.

135. Locke, "A Note on African Art," p. 135.

136. Roger Fry, *Vision and Design* (London: Chatto and Windus, 1920).

137. Locke, "A Note on African Art," pp. 135, 137, 137–138.

138. William S. Braithwaite, "Some Contemporary Poets of the Negro Race," *The Crisis*, 18 (April 1919), 275, 277.

139. *The Crisis*, 19 (April 1920), 290.

140. Brawley, *A Social History of the American Negro*, p. 341.

141. Du Bois, *Darkwater*, pp. 72–73.

On Nathan Irvin Huggins's
Harlem Renaissance

Harlem Renaissance by Nathan Irvin Huggins (New York: Oxford University Press, 1971; 343 pp.) does not live up to the pretensions found on the flyleaf. This study is not the "first full assessment of . . . black artists [of the Renaissance] and of their intellectual and cultural efforts in the decade following the first World War." Indeed, it is doubtful that Huggins believes that there was a Renaissance at all. He thinks, rather, that what passed for a movement was a vast promotional scheme, based on innocent black aspirations and corrupting white money. Assuming such a perspective, Huggins does not and cannot provide a full assessment of any black artist of the period, one extending roughly from 1920 to the early 1930s.

The assessment of the major writers of the time, the core of the book, actually, reflects a confused critical approach. Huggins is appreciative of the poems of Langston Hughes because they resemble the spirituals in their simplicity and in their closeness to ethnic roots, but he is critical of Zora Neale Hurston's attempts in fiction to use folk sources, partly, one suspects, because of Miss Hurston's dependence during much of her creative life upon white godmothers. Huggins justly praises the art of Jean Toomer, but fails to see the innovative power in the fiction of Claude McKay, though the works of both writers rely upon the shrewd inversion of conventional black stereotypes, suggesting a black reality more intense and more sensually rich than mundane existence. A harsh judgment is passed upon Countee Cullen, the black poet, because of his continuing allegiance to the conventions of genteel English Romanticism. At the same time, the conventional novelist Nella Larsen merits approval, oddly, even though she, like Cullen, has depended upon the shopworn devices of an earlier day. Plagued by such inconsistency and arbitrariness, one comes to the reluctant conclusion that Huggins has neither the literary background nor the critical skills to accomplish his important task.

Huggins has strengths, though they are not literary. There is merit in his exploration of the relationship between the Harlem

Renaissance and American Progressivism. He sees correctly that provincialism is a disease that afflicted black American artists as well as white American artists. His comparison of the emergence of black culture in America with the culture of recently arrived immigrant groups is valuable. No doubt, a future historian of the Renaissance will profit from his political and psychological speculation. The best chapter in this loosely organized and poorly edited volume is not about the Renaissance at all, but about the minstrel tradition as it moved from the tents and the small-town halls of the nineteenth century to the stages of the most prominent New York theaters of the twentieth.

Huggins makes the point that the Renaissance was a misguided effort to create a "serious high culture" and that this attempt was doomed to failure because black art was removed from the people, from authentic ethnic roots, and from a true view of social and political reality. The same criticism can be made of any primarily artistic movement, certainly of the art of an earlier renaissance, the American, in the years from 1830 to 1860. What is badly needed (and what Huggins has not provided) is a serious history of the Harlem Renaissance, revealing its sources, defining its leading ideas, covering adequately the interrelated contributions of music, the visual arts, folk material, and experimentation in language and literature, tracing in an orderly fashion the development of the movement, and assessing, finally, its permanent impact upon American life. Wallace Thurman's brilliant parody, *Infants of the Spring*, is not a correct estimate of this important phenomenon, though Huggins thinks it is; that is a little like saying that all that wonder that came from Concord in the earlier renaissance is best viewed through the eyes of Miles Coverdale.

1973

Jean Toomer and the South: Region and Race as Elements within a Literary Imagination

If we are to take the word and trust the memories of those who participated in the Negro Renaissance in the 1920s, the most exciting single work produced by the movement was *Cane* by Jean Toomer.[1] *Cane* appeared in 1923,[2] the work of an author not entirely unknown. Portions of *Cane* had appeared in *The Crisis* and in an impressive number of little magazines, known for their commitment to revolutionary ideas and experimental writing. The list reads like the index of the study by Hoffman, Allen, and Ulrich, *The Little Magazine: Broom, Double Dealer, Liberator, Little Review, Nomad, Prairie,* and *S4N*. It suggests that Toomer was a part of a lively intellectual world that considered with great seriousness the cultural situation of America at the time.[3] And it suggests too that the publication of *Cane* was an event of national consequence, not a local or provincial phenomenon or simply a racial one, the case, indeed, if Toomer's achievement were simply the satisfaction of being another Negro who had managed to publish a book. After all, just a year before, T.S. Eliot had published *The Waste Land* in another of these little magazines, *The Dial,* and we have just barely recovered from that event. Toomer arrived with a bang, with a set of qualifications that could hardly be more impressive.

Though Toomer's achievement is not limited, finally, by reference to either region or race, it exploits in an unusual way both of these elements. Technically, Toomer was not a Southerner. Or to put it better, his connection with the South was not direct; it resembles Frost's association with New England. Robert Lee Frost was born in San Francisco, of parents originally from New England; Nathan Eugene Toomer, later called Jean, whose parents were originally from the South, with family ties to the state of Georgia, was born in Washington, D.C. For both writers the connection with the region was a form of recovery of a lost heritage. Gorham Munson, who wrote a book about Frost as well as participating vigorously in the organization and the direction

235

of little magazines concerned about the future of modern machine culture, put the point plainly when he said in a review of *Cane* that Toomer "desired to make contact with his hereditary roots in the Southland."[4] For both writers, then, the return was a passionate involvement with countercultural implications; that is to say, Frost and Toomer deliberately turned their backs upon contemporary urban culture to seek a more satisfying reality in rural surroundings. In a loose sense their attitudes can be called pastoral. Munson sketches the typical background for the pastoral quest, probably without an intimate knowledge of Toomer's early life: ". . . one infers a preceding period of shifting and drifting without settled harborage. Weary of homeless waters he turns back to ancestral soil. . . ."[5]

"Shifting" does accurately describe much of what we know of Toomer's early career, which displays an excessive movement from place to place and a rapid change from one intellectual commitment to another. After graduation from Dunbar High School in Washington, D.C., Toomer enrolled in 1914 at the University of Wisconsin, moved to the Massachusetts College of Agriculture in 1915, and stopped for a while in Chicago in 1916. Later there were brief sojourns in Milwaukee and New York. Always in between there was a return to Washington. Not until 1920 did his movement about the country stop, when Toomer settled in Washington, convinced then that he should devote his time and energy fully to reading and writing.

The outline of Jean Toomer's autobiography,[6] a work projected but never apparently completed, reveals an active and wide-ranging mind. The attraction to agriculture and physical culture seemed to be uppermost at Madison, Wisconsin; the exposure to socialist and materialist thought occurred in Chicago, and to the writings of Bernard Shaw in Milwaukee. Working as a clerk in New York City and later as a general manager for Acker and Company in 1919 in Ossining made possible the cultivation of a whole range of new interests, music among them. But meeting new people was just as important to him as the authors whom he read, Goethe, Whitman, Ibsen, and again Shaw, or the lectures that he attended. Though Toomer met at this time Lola Ridge, the American editor of *Broom*, E.A. Robinson, Witter Bynner, Scofield Thayer, and other literary figures prominent in the New

York scene, no one had a greater impact upon him than did Waldo Frank, whose *Our America* he had read with care. It is the New York adventure that seemed to be decisive in turning Toomer's attention to art. When the inevitable return to Washington came in 1920, Toomer was prepared to commit himself to more systematic reading, addressing not only all of the works of Waldo Frank, but books by Tolstoy, Flaubert, Baudelaire, Dostoyevsky, Sinclair Lewis, Dreiser, Sherwood Anderson, Frost, and Freud. He read the little magazines too, absorbing from Frank and others a critical attitude toward an American society which had become warped by the demands of modern technology and unchecked urbanization. Toomer was ripe for a sweeping commitment of some kind in 1920, one that would affirm man's basic emotional life rather than his intellectual achievement, one, as Frank put it graphically later, that would protect him from the stink of the marketplace and keep him "warm underneath, in the soil, where the throb is."[7]

The specific form of Toomer's commitment was determined by a factor beyond his control, by his ancestry, which involved intimately both region and race, both the recognition of the South as home and the affirmation of an allegiance to the black race. Jean was the grandson of P.B.S. Pinchback, who was at one time during Reconstruction days Lieutenant-Governor, then Acting Governor of the state of Louisiana. He was the son of Pinchback's daughter Nina, who had married briefly Nathan Toomer, a union that actually terminated in 1895 after a year of marriage and was formally dissolved in 1899. Jean was especially close to his grandparents, with whom he lived after Nina's death in 1909. The strong emotions that swept through Toomer's consciousness while he was writing *Cane* were deeply intertwined with his concern for his grandfather's declining health. Indeed, Toomer recalled in the notes for an autobiography that Pinchback died the day after he had finished the first draft of "Kabnis." The suggestion of the end of an era, so strong in *Cane*, may owe something to the feelings and the sympathies of the young artist as he observed the last moments of a man, once so powerful and vigorous, reduced to a broken and pathetic figure.[8] The journey to New Orleans to place Pinchback's body in the vault already occupied by Toomer's mother must have reenforced the intimation of an imminent conclusion, aroused the echoes in his ears of a "swan-song"[9] that was personal as well as cultural.

The event that provoked Toomer's emergence as an artist had preceded Pinchback's death; it had, no doubt, psychic reverberations of great consequence. This was the period of three months in 1921 which Toomer spent in Georgia. He had accepted an offer to replace a principal of a school in Sparta who had gone North to raise funds for the school, a necessity familiar to the administrators of many Southern black educational institutions at the time. For Toomer, going to Georgia was a return. Both grandfather Pinchback and father Nathan Toomer had come from Georgia. Jean recalls the impression that the new Georgia scene made upon him: "The setting was crude in a way, but strangely rich and beautiful. . . . There was a valley, the valley of *Cane*, with smoke-wreaths during the day and mist at night. . . ."[10]

The discovery of the physical characteristics of the region was only a part of Toomer's total response. Another part had more to do with what was heard than with what was seen. The artist was moved by the spirituals sung by the blacks in Georgia. He was touched not merely by their beauty but by the sense that they represented a dying folk-spirit, a creative impulse doomed to be destroyed by the small town and then the city, by the inevitable encroachment of industry, commerce, and the machine. What occurred, of course, was the coalescence of two quite divergent drives in Toomer. One certainly, as Munson suspected, was the desire to stop the drift in his life, to find a home, even though a temporary one. The second was the expected reaction of a talented but disciplined student well trained in the curriculum promoted by Waldo Frank and Sherwood Anderson. In discovering his heritage Toomer rejected contemporary culture with its emphasis upon urbanization and a machine technology.

The touchy point about Toomer's return is race or, rather, allegiance to a race. The problem is more complicated than it appears to be. In Georgia, Toomer identified with the life of blacks and he acquired in this way a deep appreciation for the richness and strength that came from the intimate connection existing there between man and soil. Arna Bontemps, in his "Introduction" to a reissue of *Cane*, quotes from a letter written by Toomer to the editors of *The Liberator* magazine in the summer of 1922 which offers matter that has a direct bearing on this point. In it Toomer describes his racial background: ". . . I seem to have (who knows for sure) seven blood mixtures: French, Dutch, Welsh, Negro, German, Jewish, and Indian." Then he adds, in what must have seemed at the time an amazing piece of heresy: "Because of these, my position in America has been a curious one. I have lived equally amid the two race groups. Now white, now colored." American society in 1920, perhaps less so now, was pathologically sensitive to racial attachments. It was bad enough for Faulkner, early in the next decade, to create a character in *Light in August* who was a Negro by sociological definition alone,[11] but here from young Toomer, in life, not in art, we have the assertion that he could choose his racial identity. He adds in the letter to *The Liberator*: "Within the last two or three years, however, my growing need for artistic expression has pulled me deeper and deeper into the Negro group. And as my powers of receptivity increased, I found myself loving it in a way that I could never love the other. It has stimulated and fertilized whatever creative talent I may contain within me. A visit to Georgia last fall was the starting point of almost everything of worth that I have done."[12]

Toomer chose to be black. His stance was artistically useful because he allowed himself maximum freedom in defining his heritage. It was not something that he had to accept because he was trapped, as many Americans were, by history or family or caste or race. It was something that he discovered, or, since the discovery was essentially a matter of consciousness, something that he made. Toomer brought rare objectivity and sensitivity to his task, and in his time perhaps only he was equipped to create his form of the South, preeminently a black South, one just as strongly projected as the old forms, but more beautiful in the description of the land, more complicated in revealing the tangled, half-articulated emotions of its people, and more deeply human.

Making something new demands a rejection of what is at hand. As a black American in 1920 Toomer had available to him at least three forms of the South, none of which he accepted.

There was the world created by the Plantation Tradition, especially by the dialect poems of Paul Laurence Dunbar, which had appeared originally in the late nineteenth and early twentieth centuries and had been reprinted, subsequently, in special editions, sometimes lavishly illustrated.[13] This was a black South full of memories of good times on the old plantation, demonstrations of the efficacy of Christian piety, and antics of collapsible, indestructible comedians in black face. What is referred to here is the popular impression of Dunbar's verse, reinforced by faithful and frequent recitation by blacks and whites all over America. A study of the whole Dunbar canon reveals a troubled poet deeply sensitive especially to the materialist and mechanistic thought at the turn of the century. But Dunbar's South, for most Americans, was not to be distinguished from that projected by the minstrel stage and created nostalgically in sentimental fiction. By 1920 blacks had ceased to take it seriously, if they ever had, except for those enterprising artists who sought to extract from it profitable theatrical or musical formulas.

A second South was linked to the name of Booker Washington, who offered it to the world in the pages of *Up From Slavery*.[14] These presented a picture of improving relations involving blacks and whites and an improving economic status for blacks. Patience, Christian virtue, and hard work would result in prosperity soon; but civil rights, the vote, and full citizenship would take longer. Survival demanded the compromise of manhood, perhaps, but Washington had the Social Darwinist's faith that all good things would come in time to those best equipped to have them. Washington's South was real enough, but by 1920 it had lost credibility with most black intellectuals. His reality seemed to be restricted to those oases in the South that tended to justify his convictions. Meanwhile, the masses of blacks in the South lived poor, desperate lives unleavened by the force of Booker's rhetoric.

The design of the South that inspired greatest conviction among intellectual blacks was that sketched by W.E.B. Du Bois in *The Souls of Black Folk, The Crisis* magazine, *Darkwater*, and elsewhere.[15] Certain salient features stand out. Du Bois claimed that a condition of naked oppression existed in the South, which was not improving as a place for blacks to live and to work. The people who seemed to be most oppressed lived in rural areas where law and sharp business practices combined to exploit them. Du Bois asserted that Washington's optimistic predictions about economic progress for blacks in the South was empty, if not absurd, when blacks lacked the basic rights of citizenship to protect their property. The hope for an improved life rested with the leadership of the Talented Tenth, the educated members of the black middle class to be found largely in the towns and the black schools. At issue for Du Bois always was manhood, which could not be sustained by anything other than a broad and liberal education (rather than industrial training) and could not survive the daily humiliations imposed by a segregated society.

The South that Toomer made succeeded in reversing nearly all of Du Bois's conclusions, without echoing Dunbar's pious sentiments or referring to the necessity for a pragmatic accommodation with whites in Southern communities. What supported the new view was not facts, as Du Bois would define them, not statistical surveys coming out of Atlanta University, but an emotional response, a young man's impression of the black heritage he had returned to discover.

Toomer saw a beautiful land of pine trees, mist, and red soil (not the red clay that Du Bois despised so thoroughly that he refused to bury his infant son in it),[16] a land in which fertility was finally stronger than terror, though moved by a threat of violence that seemed all-pervasive. He admired the black "peasants," the strong people who lived close to the soil and reflected in their preoccupation with sex and mystical religious experience the fertility of the land. "Peasants"[17] is Toomer's term, with a meaning far removed from the "peasants" of Faulkner's *The Hamlet*, descriptive there of farmers who had been exploited and humiliated by ruthless predators. The weak people in Toomer's South (Esther is one of them) were the shopkeepers, the light-skinned Negroes of the middle class, the potential members of the group that Du Bois had labelled the Talented Tenth. They lived in the towns and they were both attracted and repelled by the crude black energy they saw in the peasants. Life was the issue here, and middle-class conventions and aspirations denied life and, incidentally, love. Black manhood survived in the South as a response, in part, to a more powerful force. But only in part. Fred Halsey, a pillar of strength in the dramatic narrative "Kabnis," has other sources of power: pride in his profession as a master craftsman and an owner of a wagon-shop, and delight in using his mind in debating with the professors, Lewis and Kabnis. The signs of degeneration are present everywhere—in the lack of coordination of body and spirit, in sexual excess, and in mystical hysteria. They are external as well as internal, with the menace of physical violence, with death by lynching always close. The forces of degradation may kill the body but not destroy the integrity and the spirit of the truly strong: Barlo, the black preacher; Tom Burwell, Louisa's black lover in "Blood Burning Moon"; Fred Halsey. Toomer's Southern exposure produced a wholly new way of looking at Southern life, one that is related clearly to the position of the Nashville Fugitives, as Bontemps notes in his "Introduction,"[18] but one quite different, finally, because the controlling point of view is black, not white.

The invaluable documentation of Toomer's approach to the South found in his letters and in his notes toward an autobiography throws light upon the poem, "Song of the Son," which functions really as a form of preface to the whole of *Cane*. We are introduced to the consciousness of a poet-speaker who imposes unity upon the verses, sketches, narratives, and symbolic signs that make up the body of the work.

"Song of the Son" describes a return to a scene from which the poet has been long separated. The initial lines suggest an amount of detachment. In much the way that Whitman often did, in "Crossing Brooklyn Ferry," for example, the poet requests the landscape to arrange itself for his pleasure:

> Pour O pour that parting soul in song,
> O pour it in the sawdust glow of night,
> Into the velvet pine-smoke air to-night,
> And let the valley carry it along,
> And let the valley carry it along. (p. 21)

What is at stake is not merely the desire for physical delight, though this is strong; the poet realizes that he is responding to "that parting soul," the spirit in the land. The reference to "parting" introduces the problem of time. The poet has returned "just before an epoch's sun declines," at that moment when the land is losing a value that it has long possessed. This is one that the speaker was either not aware of or not appreciative of when he was present at this scene before. The value itself is the culture of "A song-lit race of slaves," a culture that was unique and rich.

For one thing, it was intimately tied to the land, so deeply intertwined that the slaves can be referred to as organic growths— "dark purple ripened plums." For another, the culture is sad, "plaintive," because the slaves are under pressure, suffering, indeed, from oppression and because, further, it is disappearing, dying. The two characteristics form the basis for song, for the spirituals sung by the slaves and other forms of artistic expression that flow naturally from a unified existence. What is being lost, as the poet looks and ruminates, is song, along with other vestiges of the slave culture, not simply the music itself but the ability to make music. We are not told what the hostile forces are that oppose song, though we are led inevitably to speculate about them—perhaps, freedom from suffering, or the city, or education, or modern society. The poet has returned in time to secure possession of one vestige of the old culture, one "plum" providing the seed that would enable him to reconstruct the earlier civilization. This is important to do because of the ancient beauty that becomes now available to him and because the new awareness forms a basis for new songs, to be created, no doubt by the poet. The double emphasis cannot be missed: "What they [souls of slavery] were, and what they are to me" (p. 21). The conclusion of the poem resembles the dramatic end of "Out of the Cradle Endlessly Rocking," when Whitman says, after at least a partial reconciliation with death, symbolized by the sea: "The sea whisper'd me."[19]

"Song of the Son" presents the consciousness that stands behind the varied verbal structures in *Cane*. In the poem it is a sophisticated intelligence yearning for completion and adequate expression and finding the means for achieving these ends in contact with the South and with a newly discovered black culture. It plays multiple roles elsewhere in *Cane*. It is responsible for the sympathy and understanding expressed by the narrator of "Karintha" and "Carma," for that need to explain the actions of the characters in the stories, to place their behavior within an appropriate intellectual context. On occasion the consciousness becomes embodied in characters, in the curious "I" figures in "Becky" and "Fern" who seek to penetrate the deeper mysteries and contradictions of Southern life. Always one of the important functions of the brooding intelligence which invests *Cane* is projection, as significant characters, despite differences in race and station in society, share the desire for a fuller life, one in which their half-understood and half-articulated impulses may have a place.

The preoccupation with the problems of consciousness is responsible for the design in *Cane*. Toomer is not content simply to explore the situations in which an alien Northern intelligence confronts Southern realities; he is as much concerned with analyzing the factors that have shaped the Northern mind. He sees the necessity for regional connection, for the Northern black to acquire the emotional strengths that black Southerners still possess, though they may be rapidly losing them. What haunts Toomer's mind is a circle based upon regional relationships, or, more accurately, a broken circle, since the author does not reach the point in *Cane* of successful prefiguration, the anticipation of the full existence for man, what would be called later the "all around development of man," involving the "constructive functioning" of body, emotions, and mind.[20]

Toomer's own comments on the structure for *Cane* are invaluable and offer a beginning for any discussion of the organization of the whole work. In December 1922, Waldo Frank received a letter from Toomer announcing the completion of *Cane* and defining the principles which were intended to give unity to his achievement:

> From three angles, *Cane*'s design is a circle. Aesthetically, from simple forms to complex ones, and back to simple forms. Regionally, from the South up to the North, and back into the South again. Or, from the North down into the South, and then a return North. From the point of view of the spiritual entity behind the work, the curve really starts with Bona and Paul (awakening), plunges into Kabnis, emerges in Karintha, etc., swings upward into Theater and Box Seat, and ends (pauses) in Harvest Song.[21]

Toomer's first comment on form is plain enough and requires little explanation. The Georgia tales and "Kabnis" are reasonably straightforward narratives, with intensities that are either lyric or dramatic. They are without the symbolic complexity of the middle section of *Cane*, the one devoted to the North. We find here the experimental sketches "Seventh Street," "Rhobert," and "Calling Jesus," presenting a level of abstraction not discovered elsewhere.

Moreover, in the narratives "Theater" and "Box Seat" symbolic devices and distortion are employed with subtlety and effectiveness. The dance in "Theater" represents the ideal of a fulfilled relationship between Dorris and John, who come from different classes in the highly stratified black society of Washington, D.C. In "Box Seat" the seats in the Lincoln Theater are "slots," "bolted houses" (p. 117), cutting Muriel off from rewarding connection with anyone else, especially from her desperate, would-be lover Dan. In both stories the emphasis is placed upon what the characters think rather than upon what they do. "Box Seat" relies more heavily upon distortion than does "Theater," a fact particularly evident with the use of the dwarf to stand for the revulsion which the conventional Muriel feels toward any life existing outside of her cherished middle-class patterns. There is a deliberate correspondence between the complexity of Toomer's literary technique and the complexity of the Northern urban environment. What is magnified, thereby, is the struggle of the human spirit, bound by dehumanizing conventions and mechanical restrictions, to achieve freedom and satisfaction.

The more puzzling part of Toomer's statement of intention involves the reference to regions. We have an apparent contradiction: we begin *Cane* either in the South or in the North, and we conclude the work either in the South or in the North. What seems to be apparent nonsense becomes rewardingly clear only when the element of consciousness is considered, what Toomer calls "the spiritual entity behind the work."[22] The external order for *Cane*, recorded simply as it appears, establishes the first background in Georgia, the second in Washington and Chicago, and the third again in Georgia. It is South, North, South.

But if the action is viewed organically, we take our cue from the form of the consciousness as defined by "Song of the Son." Toomer suggests that we begin with "Bona and Paul," a story in which Paul discovers that he is not like Bona. The racial difference, felt deeply first in the Crimson Gardens, a nightclub in Chicago, is the basis for Paul's rejection by Bona; at the same time Paul experiences something less painful and equally important, the need to explain his attraction for Bona to the huge black man who opens and shuts the door of the nightclub. Frustration, then, is accompanied by the intimation of a new connection, "awakening,"[23] Toomer called it. "Kabnis," looked at this way, is the direct confrontation with what it means to be black in the South. The trial for the Northern Kabnis is disturbing, humiliating, and apparently futile, with only infrequent suggestions of black strength. The affirmation of difference and the tribute to black emotional power are to be found in the Georgia stories, especially in the portraits of sensual black women. The progress of consciousness moves next to the North where city realities are weighed against Southern black strength. Dorris's dance and Dan's plea to the prim Muriel grow from the same impulse that moves Karintha and Carma. This is stated most explicitly in "Box Seat," when Dan sits beside a portly black lady in the Lincoln Theater. Her fragrance arouses racial memories in Dan: "Her strong roots sink down and spread under the river and disappear in blood-lines that waver South. Her roots shoot down. Dan's hands follow them. Roots throb. Dan's heart beats violently. He places his palms upon the earth to cool them. Earth throbs" (p. 119). The center of the resistance to the frigid and mechanical North is located in racial memories that linger, shards and vestiges of an old black culture.

"Harvest Song" in this context is the conclusion of *Cane*. It is a poem that denies its title, since it is not the celebration of work done well and the grain collected. What is missing is enjoyment, the ability of the poet to taste and to receive nourishment from the product that has demanded so much sweat and toil:

> I am a reaper whose muscles set at sundown. All my oats are
> cradled.
> But I am too chilled, and too fatigued to bind them. And I
> hunger. (p. 132)

Nourishment and enjoyment demand friendship with others, a sense of brotherhood and community. The poet, though he is reluctant and too timid to attempt the unexpected, moves to a point that he cries out to his fellow laborers:

> O my brothers, I beat my palms, still soft, against the stubble
> of my harvesting. (You beat your soft palms, too.)
> My pain is sweet. Sweeter than the oats or wheat or
> corn. It will not bring me knowledge of my hunger.
> (p. 133)

There is no sign that the cry is responded to, as it is, say, in another harvest poem, Frost's "The Tuft of Flowers."[24] And without response there is not satisfaction for hunger, not even the knowledge of what hunger is. "Harvest Song" offers a strong plea for human values, for the virtues of emotional connection, one that relates immediately to Toomer's description of Northern society, in which mind, work, and propriety have crushed soul.

The central movement of *Cane*, interpreted in terms of a developing consciousness, is then North, South, North. The curve ends, Toomer writes, in "Harvest Song," but the term that he uses as a substitute for "ends," that is to say, "pauses," is a better one.[25] The poet stands poised at the end of "Harvest Song," waiting for the responding cry that does not come. The progress of the curve stops, short of completion, the fulfillment of a design that might be viewed as a rounded circle. Toomer is not prepared to explore completion or to celebrate a triumphant ending—nor was this his intention—because completion would mean nothing less than the promise of a redeemed America, a fusion of North and South, a region that for him is emotional and black.

Curveship has another meaning for the structure of *Cane*. In the same letter to Frank in which he suggested various ways of reading his newly completed work, Toomer wrote: "Between each of the three sections, a curve. These, to vaguely indicate the design."[26] It is useful to consider what this means when we look at the relationships between the sections. What may be promised is a substantial connection in materials and problems. We discover with close examination that that kind of correspondence does exist in fact, with significant differences separating the sections resting, rather, in the way the familiar questions are resolved.

The first two sections, one devoted to the Georgia scenes and the other to urban episodes, connect in this fashion, and, indeed, seem to balance each other. The same problems thread their way through both divisions of the book. Karintha and Avey suffer from excessive, undirected, almost unconscious sexuality. But there is a difference: men are still awed by Karintha's mysterious beauty, but some cynics, not the narrator, consider Avey to be a common whore. "Fern" and "Calling Jesus" are comments on the attempted invasion of the body by the soul, with vastly different consequences. Fern welcomes the descent of the spirit that startles her more worldly city-admirer. On the other hand, the unnamed girl of "Calling Jesus" rejects the possibility of a larger and more deeply mystical experience because she is content with her "large house" and absorbed in shallow dreams. Only Jesus can bring a change. Esther in the story given her name and Dan in "Box Seat" share a common urge for freedom and love and are reduced to near madness by the insensitivity and lack of understanding in their love objects. Esther's pathetic proposal to Barlo seems ridiculous and absurd to those who frequent Nat Bowle's place because the pattern of her sterile existence is far removed from that of ordinary black people. Dan's cry causes disruption in the Lincoln Theater partly because he sees accurately, as others do, that Muriel's impulse to reject the gift of the dwarf performer is based upon a conventional distaste for what is considered in life crude, deformed, and black. "Blood-Burning Moon" and "Bona and Paul" present interracial affairs that end in failure, but with a difference. White Bob Stone, despite his family tradition and his inherited contempt for blacks, makes a total commitment to his love for the black Louisa to the point of willing his own death. The black Paul loses the white Bona as a consequence of a moment of distraction. The fine words which state Paul's passion reveal also a lack of integration in his personality and his inability to give himself wholly to love in the way that Stone or his black rival, Tom Burwell, do. In Toomer's world the pulse of life beats more slowly in Chicago.

"Kabnis," in one sense, is a fitting conclusion for *Cane* because it gives expression to nearly all of the themes developed in the two earlier sections. We find the intense resentment of middle-class restraints, the undirected sexuality, the attempt to achieve a mystical knowledge of some kind, and the awesome gap between the races. "Kabnis" is also an effective demonstration of the inconclusiveness of *Cane*, offering a most thorough exploration of the unhappy disjunction between mind and emotion that has haunted the black characters of the urban section. But "Kabnis," as Toomer suggested, falls earlier within the development of the central consciousness informing the whole book, at some point before the discovery of the energy of black folk to be found in "Karintha" and "Carma." There are suggestions of that power in

Kabnis's futile effort to extract wisdom from Father John, the old black man who is a vestige of the slave civilization. Viewed within the perspective of the organic cycle, "Harvest Song" offers a more appropriate termination. Frustration is not localized. There the long lines of free verse and the repetitive elements recall Whitman's poems of celebration, but the American harvest is sterile. Unhappiness, pain, fear, and hunger are incongruously present with the sources of the good life immediately at hand. And all paths in *Cane*, whether in the North or South or whether pursued by blacks or whites, lead to this disturbing end.

Cane owes everything to the symbolic representation of region and race. Toomer discovered his blackness in Georgia, and armed with this revelation he was able to construct a pattern of life which contrasted with what he had seen about him in the cities of the North. Neither pattern was to be satisfying finally. The writing of *Cane* occurred at a very special moment in Toomer's life. This time came when his awareness of his own heritage was heightened by the impending death of grandfather Pinchback, when his sense of the corruption of modern urban society was keen as a result of a close intellectual association with Waldo Frank and Sherwood Anderson, and when the exposure to black rural life in Georgia resolved momentarily his own ambivalent and uncertain feelings about racial identity. This moment was enough to link him to other writers of the Harlem Renaissance, who were at the time struggling to conquer feelings of uncertainty and inadequacy of a different kind in an effort to achieve an expression of that which was most authentic in their lives.

Toomer was correct when he commented in retrospect that *Cane* was a "swan-song."[27] It was the end not only of a way of Southern black life, as he saw it, but of his own commitment to place that life in art. Even during the year of *Cane*'s publication, 1923, Toomer's attention turned to problems that he considered to be more fundamental than the challenge of producing another work modelled on *Cane*. When he looked at his friends and acquaintances, many of whom were committed in some way to the world of art, he was compelled to say: "Most of the men and women were growing into lopsided specialists of one kind or another; or, they were almost hopelessly entangled in emotional snarls and conflicts. And neither literature nor art did anything for them. In short, my attention had been turned from the books and paintings to the people who produced them; and I saw that these people were in a sorry state. What did it really matter that they were able by talent to turn out things that got reviews?"[28] Toomer continued to write, but he was not destined to produce anything that matched *Cane*'s power. His primary concern became experimentation in life rather than in art, an endeavor to be heavily influenced by contact with Gurdjieff's ideas, occurring for the first time in 1923. Before we deplore the loss to art as a consequence of this decision, we should recall that it was the aftermath of another experiment in life, Toomer's brief period of existence as a black in Georgia, that brought us *Cane*.

1974

Notes

1. For example, Countee Cullen wrote: "I bought the first copy of *Cane* which was sold, and I've read every word of it. . . . It's a real race contribution, a classical portrayal of things as they are." Letter to Jean Toomer, September 29, 1923, in Jean Toomer Collection, Fisk University Archives, Nashville, Tenn., Box 1, Folder 12, No. 386. Charles S. Johnson, editor in 1923 of *Opportunity: A Journal of Negro Life*, recalled in later years his reaction to the emergence of Jean Toomer: "Here was triumphantly the Negro artist, detached from propaganda, sensitive only to beauty." Arna Bontemps, "The Awakening: A Memoir" in *The Harlem Renaissance Remembered*, ed. A. Bontemps (New York: Dodd, Mead and Co., 1972), p. 9.

2. Published by Boni and Liveright, Inc. The edition cited throughout this study is a Perennial Classic paperback edition published by Harper and Row (New York, 1969). Subsequent references to *Cane* will appear parenthetically in the text of my essay.

3. Sherwood Anderson's interest in *Cane* is to be measured by this generous offer: "I hoped to write something about Cane for Freeman but it had been given to some one else. If your publisher knows of any place I can write of it I'll be mighty glad to do it. My admiration for it holds." Letter to Jean Toomer, January 14, 1924, in Toomer Collection, Box 1, Folder 1, No. 51.

4. "The Significance of Jean Toomer," *Opportunity*, 3 (September 1925), 262.

5. Ibid.

6. Toomer Collection, Box 14, Folder 1.

7. Letter to Jean Toomer, April 25, 1922, in Toomer Collection.

8. Toomer Collection, Box 14, Folder 1, No. 59.

9. Ibid.

10. Ibid.

11. Joe Christmas in *Light in August* (New York: Random House, 1932).

12. Letter to *The Liberator*, 1922, quoted by Arna Bontemps in his "Introduction" to *Cane*, pp. viii–ix.

13. Dunbar's poems appeared originally in six volumes during his lifetime: *Oak and Ivy* (1893), *Majors and Minors* (1895), *Lyrics of Lowly Life* (1896), *Lyrics of the Hearthside* (1899), *Lyrics of Love and Laughter* (1903), *Lyrics of Sunshine and Shadow* (1905). In addition there were special editions like *Poems of Cabin and Field* (New York: Dodd, Mead and Co., 1899), with photographs by the Hampton Institute Camera Club and Decorations by Alice Morse.

14. Doubleday, 1901.

15. *The Souls of Black Folk* (Chicago: A.C. McClurg and Co., 1903); *Darkwater: Voices from Within the Veil* (New York: Harcourt, 1920).

16. In "Of the Passing of the First-Born," *The Souls of Black Folk* (New York: Fawcett, 1961), p. 155.

17. Letter to *The Liberator*, "Introduction," *Cane*, p. ix.

18. Bontemps, "Introduction," *Cane*, p. xvi.

19. *Leaves of Grass*, ed. H.W. Blodgett and Sculley Bradley (New York: Norton, 1968), p. 253.

20. Outline for an autobiography, Toomer Collection, Box 14, Folder 1, pp. 63–64.

21. Letter to Waldo Frank, December 12, 1922, Toomer Collection, Box 3, Folder 6, No. 800. Toomer supplies no punctuation for the titles.

22. Ibid.

23. Ibid.

24. Robert Frost, *Complete Poems* (New York: Holt, Rinehart and Winston, 1949), pp. 31–32. The terminal lines are: "'Men work together,' I told him from the heart,/ 'Whether they work together or apart.'"

25. Letter to Frank, December 12, 1922.

26. Ibid.

27. Outline for an autobiography, Toomer Collection, Box 14, Folder 1, p. 59.

28. Ibid., p. 63.

Robert Hayden's
Use of History

History has haunted Robert Hayden from the beginning of his career as a poet. In 1941, when a graduate student at the University of Michigan, he worked on a series of poems dealing with slavery and the Civil War called *The Black Spear*, the manuscript of which was to win for him a second Hopwood Award.[1] This effort was no juvenile excursion, to be forgotten in the years of maturity. Though some of the poems have not been reprinted in *Selected Poems* (1966),[2] *The Black Spear* survives in a severely altered form in Section Five of that volume. What remains is not simply "O Daedalus, Fly Away Home" and "Frederick Douglass," but a preoccupation with a continuing historical ambition. This was the desire to record accurately the yearnings, the frustrations, and the achievement of an enslaved but undestroyed people. "Middle Passage," "The Ballad of Nat Turner," and "Runagate, Runagate," all written later, share this concern. In these poems noble blacks, Cinquez, Nat Turner, and Harriet Tubman, rise from oppression and obscurity.

An extended period of study and research, as well as correspondence in theme, links these later poems with *The Black Spear*. Hayden had intended "Middle Passage" to be the opening work of *The Black Spear*, but the poems in 1941 would not assume a shape that would satisfy a meticulous craftsman.[3] "The Ballad of Nat Turner" and "Runagate, Runagate" come from poring over journals, notebooks, narratives, and histories dealing with the slave trade, plantation life, slave revolts, and the Underground Railroad, reading begun about 1940 and continued for perhaps a decade, judging from his recollection of the activity of composition.[4]

A generation later Hayden displays an attachment somewhat less strong to historical themes. In 1966 "Frederick Douglass" closed Section Five of *Selected Poems* and the book, a sign of a surviving commitment. "El-Hajj Malik El-Shabazz (Malcolm X)" opens Section Three, "Words in the Mourning Time," of Hayden's most recent book of poems, bearing the title of the section and published in 1970.⁵ Though the commitment to interpreting history is still present, the emphasis has changed. The poems of *The Black Spear* emerge from the suffering of black people before Emancipation and record their assertion of manhood, more than the simple ability to survive, but those in "Words in the Mourning Time" describe the agony undergone by Malcolm and others to achieve spiritual liberation in our own day and the search for meaning in history upon which that liberation depends. What has endured through the years is the central importance of history in Hayden's poetry—not history as the poet would like it to be, but history as he has discovered it.

The birth of the historical impulse in Hayden is not easily described. He seems to have nourished always a sense of the past. Hayden said in conversation with Paul McCluskey, his editor at Harcourt Brace Jovanovich: "For some reason, I don't know why, I seemed to have a need to recall my past and to rid myself of the pain of so much of it."⁶ The poet, then, was discussing poems written in the 1950s, but the statement applies with equal force to his work at any stage in his career. The activity of truth-telling from memory, of reconstructing the past, is purgative—at least in part, and it is intimately connected with the necessity to write poems.

Hayden's predisposition acquired quite early a formal reinforcement. The record of this is bound up with the writing of the poems in *The Black Spear*. Though W.H. Auden, his mentor at Michigan, looked on when Hayden received a prize for *The Black Spear*, the British poet was not the dominant influence shaping the work. That, rather, was Stephen Vincent Benét, whose long historical narrative *John Brown's Body* (1927) moved Hayden to think of approaching slavery and the Civil War "from the black man's point of view."⁷ Indeed, Hayden has acknowledged that the title of his sequence of historical poems, *The Black Spear*, comes from Benét and has pointed to a passage appearing late in *John Brown's Body*,⁸ in which the reaction of the newly emancipated slaves to Sherman's march through Georgia is described. Benét, in this passage, commented upon his failure to register in verse the full range and depth of the black response to the trauma of freedom:

> Oh, black skinned epic, epic with the black spear,
> I cannot sing you, having too white a heart,
> And yet, some day, a poet will rise to sing you
> And sing you with such truth and mellowness,
>
> That you will be a match for any song
> Sung by old, populous nations in the past, . . . (p. 308)

Hayden aspired to become the poet called for by Benét, one with a heart sufficiently black. Indeed, he told Benét, several years after reading *John Brown's Body* and a year or so before the commencement of serious work on *The Black Spear*, that he intended to write a poem on the materials pointed to by the white poet,[9] though possibly not the "black skinned epic" so solemnly predicted.

Benét was a hindrance as well as a help, as every major influence must be for a poet struggling to find his own voice. The story of the writing of "Middle Passage" documents the point. This poem, in many ways the most impressive achievement of Hayden's early career, was completed in some form by the time that *The Black Spear* was submitted to the Hopwood judges. But Hayden refused to include it in his volume, even though he had planned it as the inaugural piece of the whole sequence. And his reasons for delay are good ones: "Actually I had tried writing the poem in blank verse—unrhymed iambic pentameter—but, then, it was too much like Benét, not only in form, but in diction and narrative organization also."[10] The statement prepares us for differences in the final form of the poem, published originally in *Phylon* in 1945,[11] but it also requires us to look for correspondences with *John Brown's Body*, because Benét's influence has been so powerful and pervasive.

The section of *John Brown's Body* which is closest to Hayden's "Middle Passage" is the one that appears immediately after the "invocation," "Prelude—the Slaver."[12] Benét presents here the captain of a slave ship who is moved to comment on a profession in which he is skilled, while actually transporting a cargo of black ivory from Africa to America. The impulse toward self-revelation is aroused by the questions, often not stated but implied, posed by a young mate, who is inexperienced and innocent. The bulk of the narrative consists of exchanges between the two. The Captain is firm in his piety: he reads his Bible regularly and sees no contradiction between practicing Christianity and ferrying blacks for profit to a life of enforced and unending servitude. The Mate is less certain; he recoils from what he sees—the blacks in chains, the threat of the plague, the hatred of the enslaved—and he yearns for his and the Captain's native New England. Most of all, he is upset by what he calls the Blackness, the stench that is everywhere, the stain that will not wash out. His own emotions approach a mystical terror that seems to deny the Captain's pieties, a terror more appropriate for the sinning than for those who take comfort in the fact that they are adding heathen black souls to Christ's kingdom.

Hayden takes over the problem of reconciling Christianity and slavetrading in "Middle Passage,"[13] though the machinery of his narrative is much more complicated. The first of three parts offers the log entries, the prayers, and the ruminations of a pious member of the crew of a slaver. The conflict, however, is internal rather than external. The spur toward self-revelation is not an innocent youth on a maiden voyage, but the consciousness of the speaker, as he feels the threat to body and soul in the hazards and the emotional excesses that come from participation in the slave trade. Once again we find black resistance, rebellion and implacable hatred, and the threat of the plague. To these familiar difficulties, Hayden adds a new trial—the temptation to lust with black wenches, the giving up wholly to sex and alcohol so that ship, slaves, and self are all lost.

Hayden's addition points to one of the differences separating Benét's poem from his own—the richness of his documentation. The accurate touches that come from Hayden's wide reading are impressive. His wealth of information is to be seen in Part One in the names of the slave ships, the form of the ship's log, the description of the creeping blindness (Ophthalmia), and the graphic account of the drunken orgy aboard *The Bella J*. Parts Two and Three, almost untouched by the example of Benét's poem, display evidences of extensive research in the slave trade in the library of the University of Michigan.[14] The recollections of the bluff slave trader, undistorted by qualms of conscience, describe the slave factories, the collection methods, the corruption of black kings, and the good times on the West African coast. Following this straightforward statement, we hear in Part Three the testimony of a Spanish slaver, who supplies from his own point of view the details of the *Amistad* Mutiny in 1839. Now, the sources of Hayden's knowledge are many, but he recalls two as being especially rewarding, *Adventures of an African Slaver*[15] and Muriel Rukeyser's biography *Willard Gibbs*,[16] which presents an accurate description of the *Amistad* Mutiny and the trial that followed.

Though Benét's poem might have suggested to Hayden the technique of handling the poetic problems of "Middle Passage" through the use of voices, it could not provide a model for the subtle use of the technique which Hayden's poem displays. Benét's "Prelude" has three voices—the skipper's, the mate's, and the poet's. Actually the poet intrudes very little, only to utter prophecy in a brief section toward the end of the poem. According to the poet, the black seeds "robbed from a black king's storehouse" (p. 12) would fall on American earth, "lie silent, quicken" (p. 12) and then grow. A seed would become "A black shadow-sapling, a tree of shadow," and the tree, the poet promises, would ultimately blot out "all the seamen's stars" (p. 12). An ominous prediction, then, is offered, one that identifies the shaking of the leaves of the shadow tree with the trampling of the "horses of anger," the "Beat of the heavy hooves like metal on metal" (p. 12), the signs of war. The poet of the "Prelude" engages, then, in the necessary prefiguration of the Civil War that he will describe in later books.

The poet of "Middle Passage" has a good deal more to do. His is the central consciousness of the poem, providing a frame in Part One for the description of the painful voyage from Africa to America and, at the beginning of the poem, extracting meaning for the journey: "voyage through death to life upon these shores" (p. 65). A crew member of a slave ship provides the actual description of the middle passage itself. His narration is not simple because it is made complex by the fact of his piety. On the one hand, there is the sailor's prosaic voice, instructing us in entries in ship's logs and, finally, in a legal deposition, of the hazards of a rebellious cargo, disease, and lust. On the other hand, there is the voice praying for "safe passage" to bring "heathen souls" to God's "chastening" (p. 65). What the sailor tells has so much cruelty and depravity that it seems finally to overwhelm the teller of the tale. The secure sense of accomplishing God's design departs, and there is only the cry, despairing, now, rather than confident: "Pilot Oh Pilot Me" (p. 67).

The poet echoes, clearly, the cry of the sailor. He has been moved deeply by the prosaic account in rather different ways. For one thing, he is aware of the irony present in the crewman's piety, and he comments, in the language of Shakespeare's Ariel and with a precedent provided by *The Waste Land*:[17]

> Deep in the festering hold thy father lies,
> of his bones New England pews are made,
> those are altar lights that were his eyes. (p. 65)

The allusion to Shakespeare's sea-change mocks a less spiritual transformation, though Hayden's too has a claim to religious motivation. The "altar lights" in a church in New England are vulgar consequences of an investment in black gold. Moreover, the poet speculates quite openly on the destiny of the Yankee slave ship, with the benefit of a greater perspective and more knowledge than the sailor:

> What port awaits us, Davy Jones'
> or home? I've heard of slavers drifting, drifting,
> playthings of wind and storm and chance, their crews
> gone blind, the jungle hatred
> crawling up on deck. (p. 66)

The poet's historical perspective appears more clearly in subsequent parts. In Part Two the poet becomes the "lad," who listens to the recollections of a hardened and unrepentant slaver, reconstructing the beginnings of the wretched trade in Africa in greed, vanity, war, deception, devastation, and disease. In Part Three the historical perspective acquires an important spiritual dimension. Here the slave ships become "shuttles in the rocking loom of history" (p. 68) and the pattern from the loom itself emerges. The ships, though they may bear "bright ironical names like 'Jesus,' 'Estrella,' 'Esperanza,' 'Mercy'" (p. 65), contribute to "New World littorals that are/ mirage and myth and actual

shore" (p. 68). The poet promises the "actual shore," and the
journey to it, the middle passage, becomes a descent into death
resembling the dark night of the soul. The "shore" is life at the
end of death, but first blacks must experience death, a "voyage
whose chartings are unlove" (p. 68).

Cinquez, the leader of the *Amistad* Mutiny, assumes especial
prominence in the poet-speaker's vision of "Middle Passage."
The Spanish slaver considers Cinquez "that surly brute who calls
himself a prince,/ directing, urging on the ghastly work" (p. 69).
But in the enlightened historical perspective of the poet, Cinquez
is an expression of "The deep immortal human wish,/ the timeless
will" (p. 70). He is seen as an early sign of "life upon these
shores," a "deathless primaveral image,/ life that transfigures
many lives" (p. 70). Hayden describes, then, a second sea-change,
one more genuine than the transformation of the "festering hold"
into pews and altar lights in New England because this change
transfigures blacks. Cinquez, on the bloody deck of the *Amistad*
and beyond the "butchered bodies" (p. 69) of the slave crew,
points to the discovery of manhood and human dignity, even to
recognition by law (thanks to "the august John Quincy Adams,"
p. 70).

Nothing resembling this historical vision appears in *John
Brown's Body*. Benét sees the Civil War as the "pastoral rebellion
of the earth/ Against machines, against the Age of Steam"
(p. 334), and out of John Brown's body grows "the new, mechanic
birth,/ . . . the great, metallic Beast/ Expanding West and East"
(p. 335). Hayden is not concerned with these problems, but rather
with the transformation of slave to man, a transfiguration frequently touched with mystical overtones in his poems.

All of the poems of Section Five of *Selected Poems* have this
preoccupation of Hayden's. Nat Turner in the darkness of the
Dismal Swamp has a vision of bright angels in fiery combat, and
he rises from his dream "at last free/ And purified, . . ." (p. 74),
and committed to holy war. He knows, then, that the "conqueror
faces" (p. 73) of his dream were like his. Harriet Tubman, in
"Runagate, Runagate," rises above the impulsive, headlong flight
of slaves to the North to insert steel in the spines of the timid, to
provide light and direction to the bewildered, and threaten death
to the faltering and craven. She is "woman of earth, whipscarred,/

a summoning, a shining" (p. 76), asserting a single objective, "Mean to be free" (p. 76). Indeed, only she, "alias The General/ alias Moses Stealer of Slaves" (p. 76), knows that one must be "mean" to be free. The spiritual justification of her purpose comes in lines echoing the language of a Negro spiritual toward the conclusion of the poem:

> Midnight Special on a sabre track movering movering,
> first stop Mercy and the last Hallelujah

Though the mystical transformation of the desire to be free, to assert manhood, links all of Hayden's historical poems of this period, "The Ballad of Nat Turner" and "Runagate, Runagate" point to the importance for Hayden of another kind of source material. Behind these poems, indeed, lies the research of the 1940s that supported "Middle Passage" as well, an accumulation of materials so rich that Hayden was moved to write a play about Harriet Tubman, *Go Down, Moses.*[18] He recalls, in reviewing formal sources, that *The Negro in Virginia*, a study completed in 1940 by the Writer's Program of the Works Projects Administration and supervised by Roscoe E. Lewis of Hampton Institute,[19] had especial value for him as he prepared to write "The Ballad of Nat Turner." But this familiar pattern of research and rumination received support from a knowledge of a type of source material not found in "Middle Passage." This was the Negro folk tradition.

Nat Turner is struck by the cessation in the turning of the wheel within a wheel, an image that recalls the spiritual celebrating Ezekiel's illumination. The details of the celestial combat have the vividness and the primitive power of a folk sermon. Nat's account in a moment of intense excitement tends to employ the repetition found so frequently in the words of a folk preacher, suggesting with its incantatory rhythms the chant that accompanies traditionally God's direct influence upon his mortal instrument:

> But I saw I saw oh many of
>   those mighty beings waver.
> Waver and fall, go streaking down
>   into swamp water, and the water
> hissed and steamed and bubbled and locked
>   shuddering shuddering over. (p. 73)

There is a folk basis too for the references to Africa, for those intimations of the mother land that come to blacks frequently in darkness and in the forest:

> where Ibo warriors
> hung shadowless, turning in wind
> that moaned like Africa. (p. 72)

"Runagate, Runagate" has linguistic touches that suggest a strong folk inspiration, with "jack-muh-lanterns" (p. 75), "pat-terollers" (p. 76), an "a-murbling" (p. 76) fear, a "movering" (p. 77) train, "jaybird-talk" (p. 76), and "oh Susyanna" (p. 76). The invitation to get aboard the coach to the North is extended to enslaved blacks in accents that show dialect roots:

> Come ride-a my train
> Mean mean mean to be free. (p. 77)

The language is just a sign of the rich reliance upon the materials that come ultimately from the folk imagination. We have the vision of the free North as the "star-shaped yonder Bible city" (p. 75), the association of the journey to freedom with the "North star and bonanza gold" (p. 76), the identification of the flight itself as "crossing over" (p. 75) or as the freedom train, and the assumed connection between the calling of the hoot-owl and the "hants in the air" (p. 77). Not the least of these evidences of the pressure of folk culture intimately known are the snatches from the spiri-tuals. Though these are mostly echoes rather than direct quota-tions, there are two lines, indeed, that come without change from the great spiritual that begins with the phrase "Oh-h freedom":

> And before I'll be a slave
> I'll be buried in my grave.

Hayden relies upon folk materials almost exclusively in only one poem in Section V of *Selected Poems*—"O Daedalus, Fly Away Home." Like the others, this poem transforms mystically the desire for freedom. In the interview with Paul McCluskey, Hayden has identified the source of the poem as "a legend common among the Georgia Sea Island Negroes—the legend of the Flying African."[20] He adds that it was their belief that certain slaves had the magical power to fly to freedom in Africa. The poetic machinery that supports this central idea uses other elements in a folk culture. The metrics of the poem suggest the rhythm of a folk dance called "juba," widely performed by slaves in the antebellum South. The instruments providing the musical background are a "coonskin drum" and a "jubilee banjo" (p. 71). The only touch in the poem that does not show the influence of Negro folk history is the reference to Daedalus in the title and the resonance that is achieved throughout from the comparison with an earlier and better-known historical flight.

History, formal and folk, serves Hayden's purpose, and that purpose in the early historical poems is to describe the mystical emergence of freedom from circumstances that appall and degrade, and the making of a man, a black man in America. No better description of the poet's objective exists than the first lines of the justly famous tribute to Frederick Douglass:

> When it is finally ours, this freedom, this liberty, this
> beautiful
> and terrible thing, needful to man as air, usable as
> earth; . . . . (p. 78)

Contributing to Douglass's eminence is his own "middle passage," his painful exposure to death in various forms—physical violence, humiliation, and ostracism:

> this man, this Douglass, this former slave, this Negro
> beaten to his knees, exiled, visioning a world
> where none is lonely, none hunted, alien, ... (p. 78)

Following death comes life, not simply for Douglass, whose image survives in our memories, but for us all. In a voice touched with awe at the transformation, the poet concludes his tribute in this way:

> Oh, not with statues' rhetoric,
> not with legends and poems and wreaths of bronze alone,
> but with the lives grown out of his life, the lives
> fleshing his dream of the beautiful, needful thing. (p. 78)

The end of the Douglass sonnet echoes, then, the theme of "Middle Passage":

> Voyage through death
> to life upon these shores

and offers again the great theme of the historical poems of Hayden's early period.

Hayden's poems published in 1970, *Words in the Mourning Time*, reveal a persistence of an interest in historical materials, but they do not have the focus or the concentration which the ideal of *The Black Spear* provided. No doubt, the poet's own soul has yielded to "migratory habits" (p. 64),[21] which the poet represents as being the theme of Socrates at his "hemlock hour." Like Socrates, Hayden faces a world not entirely reassuring to the firmness of his early vision. The startling carcasses, "death's black droppings" (p. 64), strewn about the Fisk University lawns are bad enough, but they suggest, with their troublesome presence, the existence of more serious challenges elsewhere.

The consequences of "middle passage" are not all good, nor all life. The poet travels to Lookout Mountain,[22] the site of a great Civil War battle, where the agony of suffering, struggle, and death was most acute, and finds himself among "Sunday alpinists" who "pick views and souvenirs" (p. 26). The Union victory seems "dubious," to say the least, when from the perspective of "A world away" the poet is moved to say:

> . . . the scions of that fighting climb
> endless hills of war, amid war's peaks
> and valleys broken, scattered fall. (p. 26)

The Roman rhetoric heard at the *Amistad* trial in "Middle Passage" has become the song of the "stuffed gold eagle" (p. 26).

Confusion comes from something other than the failure of the time to live up to its brightest vision; it occurs in the minds of those who stand to benefit most from the realization of the dream—the oppressed blacks. Hayden's dramatic poem "The Dream" deals with this problem. Old Sinda remains behind in the slave quarters after "Marse Lincum's soldier boys" (p. 12) have brought freedom to the plantation. This "ragged jubilo" (p. 12) does not accord with Sinda's expectations, and she hides in the quarters rather than follow, rejoicing, in the wake of the army. Her dream of emancipation is infinitely more attractive, and Sinda sees the

faces of her sons Cal and Joe, and that of Charlie, possibly their
father, who was sold to the ricefields many years before, on "the
great big soldiers marching out of gunburst," and she will not
accept "those Buckcras with their ornery/ funning cussed commands" (p. 12). These are not "the hosts the dream had promised
her" (p. 12). Sinda fails to understand that war is prose, recorded
in Cal's letters to her about the "Kernul" and the "contrybans,"
the rain, the hardtack and the bullybeef, the "ficety gals," and the
constant worry about the "Bullit" with his name "rote on it."
And liberation is prose too. But Sinda will cling to her vision
until she dies, until the very end of her waning, "brittle strength"
(p. 13).

"On Lookout Mountain" and "The Dream" are comments on
history that have especial value in light of *The Black Spear*, since
they deal with the pain and the expectation attached to the Civil
War, but they do not confront directly the problems of recent
history. "El-Hajj Malik El-Shabazz (Malcolm X)" does this. Certain prefigurations come from "On Lookout Mountain" and
"The Dream" that prepare us for Hayden's approach to the career
of Malcolm X. One is the poet's objection to the vulgar and
materialistic limitations in contemporary American culture;
another is the poet's sense of the possibility of distortion, even
corruption, in the mind of the holder of the dream. Both are
related to the epigraph of "El-Hajj Malik El-Shabazz": "O masks
and metamorphoses of Ahab, Native Son" (p. 37).

Malcolm, like Douglass, is a folk hero. What is required to
measure the man is an understanding of the folk milieu out of
which he came as well as his position in history as a charismatic
leader of black people. The two kinds of historical knowledge
which Hayden displayed in "The Ballad of Nat Turner" and in
"Runagate, Runagate" are present here as well. The folk mores
that rest behind Malcolm's emergence are urban, however, not
rural. No doubt, the poet's memory of his own childhood in black
Detroit gives especial poignancy to the reconstruction of Malcolm's early years. There is no question about the authority of his
description of "Dee-troit Red" on the street:

> He conked his hair and Lindy-hopped,
> zoot-suited jiver, swinging those chicks
> in the hot rose and reefer glow. (p. 37)

Hayden is equally prepared to face the thorny problem of Malcolm's place in history. His consideration must begin with Malcolm's sense of his role, with the facts of the *Autobiography*.[23] The reliance seems to be especially clear when the poet refers to the tragic end of Malcolm's father and mother, to his reputation in prison ("'Satan' in The Hole" [p. 38]), and to his intimations of his own violent death. But Hayden moves beyond the *Autobiography* to comment on Malcolm's Black Muslim faith. What stirs the poet is something other than a casual interest in Islam; it is the concern of a man deeply touched by the power of an Eastern religion, a devoted Bahaist who can sympathize with a conversion to a faith that many think exotic. Personal factors as well as the passion for accuracy combine to describe the historical phenomenon that is Malcolm.

The documentation of Malcolm's commitment to Islam has impressive economy. Important to his faith is the narrative attributed to Elijah Muhammad, the leader of the Nation of Islam among black Americans, about the creation of the white man. "Yacub's white-faced treachery" (p. 38) refers to the original mistake in genetic experimentation that led to the ultimate suppression of blacks by upstart and diabolical whites. In this version of creation there is no doubt about the color, rather the lack of it, of Ahab, the unholy king. Arabic phrases in Hayden's poem are fortunate and functional additions. Something of the evangelical character of the faith and of the excitement that thrills the faithful is conveyed through these exclamations. The poet describes with precision Malcolm's role in the movement:

> He X'd his name, became his people's anger,
> exhorted them to vengeance for their past;
> rebuked, admonished them,
>
> their scourger who
> would shame them, drive them from
> the lush ice gardens of their servitude. (p. 59)

Malcolm becomes Christ in this passage, angrily driving the money changers from the temple. There is accuracy in this comparison, and there is irony, too, if we consider Christ something other than Calvin's creation, with the "hellward-thrusting hands" (p. 38) that so repelled Malcolm. The irony becomes explicit rather than potential when the poet adds: "Rejecting Ahab, he was of Ahab's tribe" (p. 39).

The presence of ironies ties "El-Hajj Malik El-Shabazz" to "Middle Passage." In the earlier poem the play upon "sea-change" adds dimension to Hayden's statement; in the poem about Malcolm the "dawn" functions in much the same way. A "false dawn of vision" precedes a true awakening. Malcolm is first converted, through the offices of Elijah Muhammad, to a faith in a "racist Allah," one whose "adulterate attars could not cleanse/ him of the odors of the pit" (p. 38). His pilgrimage to Mecca sparks a "final metamorphosis," a truer revelation that eliminates hate as a necessary component of faith. Malcolm moves from neo-Islam to orthodox Islam, and Hayden celebrates the second conversion:

> He fell upon his face before
> Allah the raceless in whose blazing Oneness all
> were one. He rose renewed renamed, became
> much more than there was time for him to be. (p. 40)

Hayden's tribute to El-Hajj Malik El-Shabazz, formerly Malcolm X, renamed after the Hajj rituals or the rites of the pilgrimage to Mecca, expresses a view of what the movement in history should be. The early poems record Hayden's vision of a black man who has acquired freedom and humanity. The later poems, dealing with history after Emancipation, describe the confused wanderings and the tormenting frustrations of the liberated man, but they still maintain that modern man must become more human. The first part of the long poem "Words in the Mourning Time," a lament for the deaths of Martin Luther King and Robert Kennedy, sketches this necessary development in our culture, upon which our survival depends. The destruction of King and Kennedy—and of El-Hajj Malik El-Shabazz—represents for us a "middle passage" to "life upon these shores":

> the agonies of our deathbed childbed age
> are process, major means whereby,
> oh dreadfully, our humanness must be achieved. (p. 41)

The heroes of history in this time of mourning are different from those in The Black Spear. They are more fallible, more vulnerable, more confused, and more easily destroyed, but El-Hajj Malik El-

Shabazz matures to share a vision that Douglass has seen and which Hayden still enunciates with eloquence:

> a human world where godliness
> is possible and man
> is neither gook nigger honkey wop nor kike
>
> but man
>
> > permitted to be man. (p. 49)[24]

1973

Notes

1. Robert Hayden discusses the genesis of *The Black Spear* in the third section of a series of exchanges with his editor, Paul McCluskey, recorded in New York in January 1971. The whole series was subsequently published in five sections in *How I Write/1* (New York: Harcourt Brace Jovanovich, Inc., 1972). Hayden is one of three literary artists discussed in the book; the others are Judson Philips and Lawson Carter. The third section, "The Black Spear," of "Robert Hayden—The Poet and His Art: A Conversation" is to be found on pp. 169–193.
2. *Selected Poems* (New York: October House Inc., 1966). Subsequent references to *The Black Spear* poems and other early poems will be to this volume.
3. *How I Write/1*, p. 175.
4. Ibid., pp. 175–180.
5. *Words in the Mourning Time* (New York: October House Inc., 1970). Subsequent references to "El-Hajj Malik El-Shabazz" and other late poems will be to this volume.
6. *How I Write/1*, p. 143.
7. Ibid., p. 170.
8. Stephen Vincent Benét, *John Brown's Body* (New York: Farrar and Rinehart, Inc., 1927). Subsequent references to this poem will be to this edition.
9. *How I Write/1*, p. 170.
10. Ibid., p. 176.
11. "Middle Passage," *Phylon*, 6 (Third Quarter 1945), pp. 247–253. The poem was revised and shortened by the omission of an introductory section before republication in *Selected Poems*.
12. *John Brown's Body*, pp. 8–13.
13. *Selected Poems*, pp. 67–70.
14. *How I Write/1*, p. 175.
15. Brantz Mayer, *Adventures of an African Slaver* (New York: A. and C. Boni, 1928).

16. Muriel Rukeyser, *Willard Gibbs* (Garden City, N.Y.: Doubleday, Doran and Co., 1942).

17. Ariel's famous song in *The Tempest* begins:

> Full fathom five thy father lies,
>   Of his bones are coral made,
> Those are pearls that were his eyes,
>   Nothing of him that doth fade
> But doth suffer a sea-change
> Into something rich and strange. (I.ii.397–402)

One reference in *The Waste Land* (T.S. Eliot, *The Complete Poems and Plays, 1909–1950* [New York: Harcourt, Brace and World, Inc., 1952]) appears in Part II, "A Game of Chess" (p. 41):

> I remember
> Those are pearls that were his eyes. (II.124–125)

18. *How I Write/1*, p. 188.

19. *The Negro in Virginia* (New York: Hastings House, Publishers, 1940).

20. *How I Write/1*, p. 180.

21. In "A Plague of Starlings." The poem has this final stanza:

> And if not careful
> I shall tread
> upon carcasses
> carcasses when I
> go morning now
> to lecture on
> what Socrates,
> the hemlock hour nigh,
> told sorrowing
> Phaedo and the rest
> about the migratory
> habits of the soul. (p. 64)

22. "On Lookout Mountain" (p. 26).

23. Malcolm X, *The Autobiography of Malcolm X* (New York: Grove Press, Inc., 1966).

24. The final lines of Part IX in "Words in the Mourning Time."

III
On Wright, Ellison, and Baldwin

Richard Wright:
The Artist as Public Figure

It is useful, perhaps, to resurrect once again the squabble between Richard Wright and James Baldwin about the central issue of protest in literature. After very nearly a quarter of a century the opinion of most critics remains unchanged. It is one, essentially, that affirms Baldwin's position but deplores his manners. The uneasiness about manners has been reinforced by Baldwin's inept attempts at explanation. Perhaps everyone does know that it is perfectly natural to kick one's father and to consider this liberating act a subject for celebration, but many of us do not like to read about it. I revive the memory of the argument not because I wish to comment on the decorum appropriate for a disciple but because I must consider once again the difference in substance separating Wright and Baldwin. I am forced to do this because of the special relationship existing between Wright the artist and Wright the public man, one that demands a perspective rather different from the one imposed by Baldwin.

Wright was a public man throughout his career. That is to say, at crucial points when his life changed direction he made statements that have defined his political position. These were not private confessionals intended to clarify his own ideas and to assist him in discovering a proper orientation for his art. They were rather pieces of rhetoric written for the purpose of persuading a knowing audience of the rectitude of his new stand.

It is possible to establish four clearly defined positions during the course of Wright's life. The first, of course, is the Communist period, too well known to require documentation. Wright's emergence as a writer is inextricably connected with his commitment to communism. This is true even though he never seemed comfortable as a Communist, as Daniel Aaron has carefully pointed out. From the very beginning of his connection with the Party, Wright guarded his freedom as an artist and resisted the advice of Party hacks who offered literary criticism in light of what was likely to increase the membership in Cell 15. Indeed Wright said as much to Mike Gold, when the Party, after a hesitation that was long enough to be embarrassing, finally responded officially to the publication of *Native Son*: "There is a proneness on the part of many Party officials to believe that the novel ought to be used in the units with the directness of an organization letter."* Despite serious and continuing reservations Wright remained loyal to the Party in most essential ways, covering political problems of interest to the Party, performing necessary editorial chores, and subscribing to the Marxist theory of history, which, by the way, he never relinquished.

Authoritarianism, exhibited in a most primitive form, made Wright's life miserable during 1941 and 1942 and ultimately forced a formal break. "I Tried to Be a Communist," which appeared in the August and September issues of *The Atlantic* in 1944, stresses the terrorist methods employed by the Party to whip into line its undisciplined members. It was not the great shift in that line that so much disturbed Wright, the reversal that confused and dismayed Communists committed to consistency in theory. Wright complained about the spying, the insults, the systematic efforts to discredit him, and the complete absence of a respect for individual liberty, not the flip-flop in the approach to the Third Reich, not really the abandonment of blacks in the cities of America, a matter of deep concern for his friend Ralph Ellison. When Wright left the Party, he joined one of the most distinguished clubs in America, that of libertarian ex-Communists, a club that was never organized, but one that had a profound influence upon shaping attitudes toward the outstanding problems in American life. Preparing in the early 1940s for his defection, Wright explored with a new intensity black life in America, and he relied more heavily upon his study of psychoanalysis and sociology. He saw his function as that of providing an education for the white middle class, which could be persuaded to regard racist thought as a pathological reaction to the American industrial society. He wished to expose the truths about that society, to exhibit as sick fabrications the myths of democracy and happiness. He went so far as to propose the publication of a new magazine, "American Pages," to be issued monthly and to follow the format of the daily newspaper *PM*. The projected periodical never

*Michel Fabre, *The Unfinished Quest of Richard Wright* (New York: William Morrow, 1973), p. 185.

acquired the necessary financial backing, but it was to have offered a wide variety of pieces illuminating black life—articles on black folklore and black humor, reports on race relations, portraits of whites masquerading as blacks and blacks masquerading as whites, and biographies of blacks who achieved success as well as failure in the society. Already, Wright was developing the theory that the life of the American black provided a useful way of looking at the problems of America as a whole and that the American black, a creature of two cultures, was uniquely equipped as a marginal man to undertake such an investigation.

Wright's third position was related to his new residence in France and was moved perhaps by an effort to find a sustaining organizational connection. He associated himself with Jean-Paul Sartre in the attempt to make the Rassemblement Democratique Revolutionnaire, an organization of the Non-Communist Left, a powerful movement. Wright was useful to the R.D.R. and to its periodical, *Les Temps Modernes*, because he was able to articulate certain objections to American policy with an authority possessed only by a native American. Unfortunately the new involvement exposed Wright once again to the factionalism of leftist politics. He shared Sartre's hope, no doubt futile, that R.D.R. would amount to something more than an organization held together by an implacable hatred for the Soviet Union. For this reason, both the French intellectual and the American were forced to disassociate themselves from positions taken and activities assumed by R.D.R., an organization destined for a short career. Though the attacks by French Communists were not as unsettling, perhaps, as those of their American counterparts, Wright experienced a new tension in his life. How diligently might he pursue political activity in a country which had accepted him as an honored guest? Michel Fabre, who has written the definitive record of Wright's French years, has assured me that this was a problem which caused continuing concern.

Wright's fourth position was worked out in connection with his developing interest in Africa, an interest extended subsequently to the emerging nations in Asia as well. The year 1953 is identified by Fabre as marking Wright's "spiritual departure" from Paris and Europe. This is not overstatement. Wright boarded the Elder Dempster line ship *Accra* at Liverpool on June 4, and reached the

Gold Coast at dawn twelve days later. The new approach, which the experience in Africa led him to, resembled in many ways his second position, his stand as an ex-Communist in America during the years before his European exile. Wright saw himself as a marginal man, one drawn by sentiment and race to the land of his ancestors yet one tied irrevocably to the West through education and immediate background. The role that he assumed was that of an intermediary, of an informed, rational interpreter. In 1944, he sought to educate a white middle-class audience in America about the reality of life in a black subculture with the hope that there would be a reduction in prejudice and race hatred. In 1954, with the publication of *Black Power*, Wright sought to inform a largely ignorant Western world of the staggering problems faced by Nkrumah in Ghana. On the one hand, there were the vestiges of colonialism lingering in a British-trained black elite and elsewhere, and, on the other hand, there were ancestral tribal loyalties which threatened to disintegrate any form of combination or cooperation of people within the nation. It is important to emphasize the word "rational." Again and again, Wright affirmed the values of the European Enlightenment; no disillusionment with the politics of contemporary Europe or America ever touched this allegiance. He deplored religion in Africa wherever he saw it—in forms Christian and pagan. He considered the industrialization of Ghana necessary and desirable, and he hoped that that goal could be accomplished without ransoming the lifeblood of the nation to either of the two great powers. Africa, to Wright, was an emerging third force with the chance to develop a modern society without the blights that industrialism had produced elsewhere. And Wright sought to persuade his audience to permit Nkrumah and other African leaders to exploit that chance, even if they must wink at the temporary curtailment of political liberties Wright himself had cherished so deeply in America. It was a dangerous compromise that Wright supported—resembling the proposition, offered in 1944, that Americans, black and white, should face the realities of black life in a society trained to ignore them.

The report on the Bandung Conference in 1955 revealed Wright again in the role of the sympathetic Western intermediary, the observer with Western rational values equipped to face highly charged issues in a world divided now not only into two parts but potentially three, with the emergence of China as a great power. Wright prepared with more than usual thoroughness for the meeting of the Asian leaders. The early pages of *The Color Curtain*, the report published in 1956, were given over to the results of a questionnaire prepared for Wright by the American sociologist Otto Klineberg. Posing the questions to compliant Asians and Eurasians in Europe before his departure must have reminded Wright of the old days in Chicago, twenty years before, when the South Side fairly teemed with interviewers, all bent on determining racial attitudes or resolving problems of social structure. Race and religion, Wright discovered, were high on the hidden agenda at Bandung. Resentment against racial superiority displayed by the Western nations was the common bond, more than anything else, that linked the newly independent nations. Wright, predictably, appealed to the West to revise its narrow colonial attitudes and to encourage these emerging countries to seize their chance to develop industrialized economies. For, Wright added, it was the last chance. Not merely for half a billion human beings, but for the West itself.

We must make one observation about Wright's political behavior before relating his politics to his more imaginative writing, what I have called his art. We no longer hear now the charge that was once made about Wright, that he quit politics when he left America. This was simply the voice of our provincialism, a convenient device to mask our ignorance. He became, if anything, more political when he resided in Europe. More, in the sense that he ceased being a follower of a hard though vacillating party line and sought to assume the responsibility of political leadership. More, too, in his widened conception of audience, extended quite consciously now to the whole Western world, for whose essential tradition Wright expressed the deepest appreciation.

This unique political odyssey in Europe occurred at the expense of art. *The Outsider*, the novel that Wright struggled so hard to complete, remains essentially an intriguing philosophic exercise. Though memories of the hard days in the Party, of the cynicism, the insincerity, and the terror, touch episodes and character, what concerns the author primarily is the intellectual problem posed by a man who succeeds in liberating himself from all human ties and who plays God with disastrous consequences. The most moving sections owe more than a little to an earlier, then unpublished, novel, *Lawd Today*, with its memorable picture of the United States Post Office as a middle-class trap. Elsewhere, there is little of the blazing sense of social and economic injustice that supplied an electric charge to the relationships among his characters in the earlier works. Without it, violence seemed gratuitous, even capricious, only marginally entertaining for an American taste fed on human butchery, private and public.

More touching is *The Long Dream*, Wright's last novel. His fictional skill was never more sophisticated. We find in it an impressive use of symbol, dream sequence, and a strong narrative line. Fishbelly learns the facts about his Southern community in a way that is thoroughly convincing. It is an education that mixes delight and terror, the rough pleasure of a rural excursion and the numbing fear of town law. There is present in *The Long Dream* something which Baldwin missed so keenly in Wright's art, the background of a complicated and functioning black community. But Fishbelly does not leave town with the urgency that moved Big Boy. Despite the care and the grace (we must call it that) of Wright's art, we sense an amount of flabbiness in the record of the action, an amount of arbitrariness and artificially imposed willfulness in Fishbelly's decision to go to France.

The fact is that Wright was best when he mixed politics and art. The mixture was often uneven, depending upon how much of the political needed to be absorbed and whether or not politics was consistent with character and background. There is no doubt that the vision on the part of blacks in the South of a life of security and dignity was something that Wright acquired from his Communist teachers. This is the large view that informs and integrates the stories in *Uncle Tom's Children*. What prevented the achievement of the vision was the pathological society dominated by a corrupt Southern white morality almost invariably associated with the town. Silas, in "Long Black Song," kills the white salesman who has violated his wife and succumbs in a blazing holocaust rather than compromise his honor. The hero of "Down by the Riverside" does what a man of conscience should do—he saves the family of the white man he has killed in a moment of justifiable desperation, knowing full well that his own destruction is paired with the family's salvation. Black violence seems in both instances to be a matter essentially of reaction, stimulated by white perversity. We can argue that the vision itself is naive in the 1930s, affording a prospect held only by a political group capable of projecting as a realistic alternative the plan for a black forty-ninth state. Though we are moved deeply by what occurs in these stories, the action itself challenges credibility, standing at the edge of our acceptance.

"Big Boy Leaves Home" is another matter. It too is touched by the same vision which I have attributed to Wright's Communist instruction; that is to say, the naive illusion that security and happiness are possible for blacks once the distorting pressure of the white society is removed. But the story has older and more primitive elements. These emerge in the gaiety and the play of Big Boy and his companions. We sense in their gamboling, haunted by fear of reprisal, a living contact with the land, in their songs a musical heritage extending back to slavery, and in their banter the authentic voice of a submerged black subculture. Wright is in touch with a folk tradition rarely visible elsewhere in *Uncle Tom's Children*, and the touch leaves a mark of distinction, making "Big Boy Leaves Home" the most memorable of the tales.

Credibility is violated in "Fire and Cloud" and in "Bright and Morning Star." "Fire and Cloud" suffers less from political distortion because of Wright's serious effort to reconcile Reverend Taylor's Christian principles with the demands for a more militant resistance to entrenched white injustice. We are amazed still that within the space of a few pages the black minister can be exposed both to the scourge of the wicked and the temptation of the mighty (that is to say, to a beating by the town rowdies and a visit from the mayor), and we suspect that Taylor's commitment to march with the workers excludes more likely alternatives. His decision seems to be something less than inevitable.

"Bright and Morning Star" is a demonstration of the operation of political ideas unchecked by an adequate concern for art. We are introduced to a number of surprising human relationships involving blacks and whites without sufficient preparation. The pattern of the action offers a movement from the improbable to the impossible. The climax that offers the heroic action of a traditional black mother in the interest of the Party seems to be drawn directly from any proletarian potboiler. The mother of a black organizer shoots a white traitor just as the vital information about membership in the local cell is about to be revealed. Wright's style, especially his superior command of the language describing action, is all that saves this story from becoming yet another saint's biography in the forward progress of the Communist faith.

The political stand, then, is a potent but tricky ingredient. Wright's art would not exist without it. The art flourishes when politics is held in balance, when it is restricted to determining the general approach to reality, to describing the large landscape against which the action occurs. The political commitment becomes destructive when probability in action and character is warped, and when language becomes the tool for drilling home a point. Such is the perversity of the reader that when the rhetoric becomes obvious in a work of high art, doubt is cast upon the sincerity of the artist. Does he really believe the flat things that he tells us? Is he troubled, more deeply than he is willing to admit, by accepting a position essentially foreign to his nature?

It is possible that Wright did not realize completely what he was about in *Uncle Tom's Children*, why a work of such rare power should be so uneven. This claim cannot be made about *Native Son*, as the third book of the novel, "Fate," richly demonstrates. A familiar approach to urban reality dominates the first two books of the novel. That is to say, Bigger Thomas is more or less the product of a defective environment, of a black ghetto in which the potential for violence is considerably heightened by the near presence of a well-to-do white district. I say more or less, because brilliant as Wright's portrayal of this connection is, the environment so described fails to account for all of the elements in Bigger's personality—not, say, for his innocent affection for the symbols of power (resembling the delight with objects of nature found in "Big Boy Leaves Home"), his disproportionate fear of an exposure to sophisticated white society, and his sense of a dim connection with other blacks. These qualities supply an individuality beyond the predictable product of the streets. When the time comes for the humanization of the black ape that Bigger has become, Wright refuses to permit his protagonist a share in Max's vision of the good society that communism would bring into being. Wright does so because he will not violate Bigger's total nature. The artist will make no further concessions to the demand of his public position. No doubt, Wright considered it sufficient to grant Max an opportunity to develop fully the Communist perspective on Bigger's problem. Bigger finds the talk helpful, but concludes, much to the dismay of Wright's comrades, that his salvation lies elsewhere. Though resurrection through the affirmation of one's crimes, a discovery of human identity through murder, seems unlikely and overambitious finally for a young black with Bigger's credentials, it is infinitely preferable to facing with a sense of partial compensation the dawn of a Communist millennium.

Black Boy, as Stanley Edgar Hyman and others have pointed out, owes much to Wright's disillusionment with communism. It is a product of what I have identified as the author's second position. The fact of the dependence upon his new public stand tends to be hidden by the reduction of the original work to the chapters describing life in the South. *American Hunger*, an early title of the work, was sent to Harper's with a conclusion supplying details on Wright's struggle within the Party and his ultimate separation from it. Though *Black Boy* is essentially autobiography, the work offers problems of selection, organization, and language that link it closely to the fiction. We find a strength of commitment in *Black Boy* that we do not discover anywhere else in the Wright canon. The commitment is to the controlling principle of a new reality, primarily political or, at least, political in origin. This is the equation of liberty with life, physical and imaginative. The desire for freedom functions as a metaphor does in imposing unity upon the materials of the book. We observe a shift in the form of the vision. No longer are security, simple happiness, and basic dignity ideals creating frustration and stimulating desperate action. Instead, we have an impressive conjunction of an expanding consciousness and a mounting need to leave the South. We experience none of the uneasiness about the awkward introduction of the political commitment that is inspired by *Uncle Tom's Children*. Wright has found a way to mobilize his deepest instincts and emotional drives, and the result is a work of rare power.

A comparison of *Black Boy* and the slave narratives of the nineteenth century is not an idle one. Like Douglass in the

Narrative, Wright offers a convincing picture of the growth of intelligence. Beyond this, there are the elemental qualities which we have seen before in "Big Boy Leaves Home" and which appear also in the most sensitively written slave autobiographies. We think of the rich use of sense experience, the reaction to the land, the knowledge of the rituals of communication and instruction that link the members of a submerged race. Wright seems to be immediately in touch with his black past.

At the same time, Wright imposes a structure upon his narrative which is distinctly modern. Though action is important, what counts more is the internal exploration that gives significance to the act. We are reminded constantly of Joyce's *Portrait of the Artist as a Young Man* as Richard struggles to escape from the pitfalls placed before him by family and society and to achieve liberation of body and imagination.

We should recall that the break with communism is the final political act that gives definitive shape to the work of art. Wright's role as a public figure supplies the climate for art, indeed, the organizing principle for the artistic achievement itself.

Wright was right, then, about what was good for Wright when he said that literature was a form of protest, and Baldwin was wrong. We wonder if Baldwin's own flirtation with political leadership in the late 1950s and early 1960s has altered his position any. He too has had to put up with ill-mannered offspring with cannibalistic appetites who have based their attacks upon a form of the higher law. Alas, poor James. From latest reports, he too lives in exile, as Wright did before him, and in another country.

1978

From Experience to Eloquence: Richard Wright's *Black Boy* as Art

Native Son[1] is the work for which Richard Wright is best known, but *Black Boy*,[2] an autobiography more or less, may be the achievement that offers the best demonstration of his art as a writer. This idea is not so startling given Wright's special talents—the eye of a skilled reporter, the sensibility of a revolutionary poet, alert to varied forms of injustice, and the sense of symbolic meaning carried by the rituals of ordinary life. The problem up to the present time is not the lack of attention the work has received. Like *Native Son*, *Black Boy* was selected by the Book-of-the-Month Club and was thus assured a wide distribution and a serious if somewhat skewed reading from many critics. In 1970 Stanley Edgar Hyman, in reviewing Wright's entire career, assigned *Black Boy* to a period in which Wright's "important writing" occurred—according to his definition, Wright's last years as a resident in America, from 1940 to 1945.[3] But *Black Boy* by itself failed to acquire as an original work of art the reputation it deserves.

It appears now, from the perspective of a generation, that a measure of distortion was unavoidable, given the political temper of the time. The history of the publication of the manuscript entitled *American Hunger*,[4] of which *Black Boy* was a part, encouraged a violent political response. It was well known that "I Tried to Be a Communist," which appeared in the August and September issues of *The Atlantic Monthly* in 1944,[5] were chapters of an autobiographical record to be published the following year, even though they were excluded finally with the rest of the matter dealing with the years in Chicago and New York. When *Black Boy* did appear, knowing critics read the book in light of the much-publicized account of Wright's difficulties with the Communist Party. Baldly put, the situation for the critic encouraged a form of outside intrusion, a case of knowing too much, of supplying a frame of reference which a reading of the basic text does not support. The board of the Book-of-the-Month Club or Edward Aswell or both,[6] in suggesting a restriction of autobiographical matter to the period before migration to Chicago, exercised a judgment that displayed something more than the good sense of successful editors; indeed, that judgment pointed up the artistic integrity of the work. Someone concluded accurately that the intensity of *Black Boy* came from a concentration upon one metaphor of oppression, the South, and prevented the diffusion of power that would be the consequence of the introduction of a second, the Communist Party.

If the political reaction created one kind of distortion in the eye of the examiner, more normal literary expectations created another. *Black Boy* baffled W.E.B. Du Bois, the most impressive black intellectual of his time. His review in the New York *Herald Tribune* states his dilemma: ". . . if the book is meant to be a creative picture and a warning, even then, it misses its possible effectiveness because it is as a work of art so patently and terribly overdrawn."[7] By 1945 Du Bois had published three major works with outstanding autobiographical elements, one of which, *Dusk of Dawn*, was a fully developed autobiography of considerable intellectual distinction,[8] and he could not be accused of responding merely to a sense of affront to his middle-class sensibilities. Du Bois was not prepared to accept Wright's bleak Mississippi; he was appalled not so much by the condition of terror there as by a state of mind that denied the possibility of humanity for blacks and frustrated all black efforts to achieve satisfaction beyond the minimal requirements for life. After all, Du Bois had vivid memories of his experience as a young teacher in rural Tennessee, where he encountered aspiring, sensitive pupils who, though often defeated or betrayed by their environment, were not totally crushed by Southern oppression.[9] Moreover, Du Bois joined, no doubt, a group of critics of *Black Boy* best defined by Ralph Ellison as consisting of readers who complained that Wright had "omitted the development of his own sensibility."[10] But this is to define sensibility in a way generally understood by the nineteenth century, which is to hold that sensibility is an orderly accretion of the mind and heart within an environment recognizably human, and not to accept Wright's radical equation of the existence of sensibility with survival.

Du Bois did not doubt that autobiography could be art, though more naive critics might. He could not accept the principles of an art as austere as Wright's was, one in which many of the facts of

Southern life, so familiar to him, were excluded and in which generalization had been carried to such extreme lengths. After all, the book's title was *Black Boy*, not "A Black Boy,"[11] with an appropriately limiting modifier. Viewed superficially, Richard's odyssey was unique primarily because it had a happy ending— the escape from the hell of the South, where, apparently, all of his black associates (he had no friends in the narrative) were destined to spend the rest of their days. Wright's generalizations about the dehumanizing relationships between whites and blacks and the almost equally unsatisfying connections between blacks and blacks shaped his South, and these assumptions Du Bois thought to be distorted. One sweeping statement by young Wright in Memphis, where he lived from his seventeenth to his nineteenth year and where he committed himself formally to becoming a writer,[12] would certainly extract from Du Bois an expression of disbelief, if not annoyance: "I knew of no Negroes who read the books I liked and I wondered if any Negroes ever thought of them. I knew that there were Negro doctors, lawyers, newspapermen, but I never saw any of them. When I read a Negro newspaper I never caught the faintest echo of my preoccupation in its pages."[13]

Not only Du Bois, but also other blacks, even those lacking the knowledge of black life in America which Du Bois had acquired from his surveys and research projects at Atlanta University,[14] would be appalled at Richard's confession of his cultural isolation. This is a moment when generalization approaches fiction, when we must say that a statement may be acceptable within its context, but that it is questionable as a fact standing on its own, as something that might be supported by the confessions of other black boys, especially those emerging from families with middle-class aspirations and pretensions like Wright's.

Editing the raw matter of life is necessary, of course, to write an autobiography with any claim to art. No one has described this activity better than Ellison has in his critical examination of *Black Boy*: "The function, the psychology, of artistic selectivity is to eliminate from an art form all those elements of experience which contain no compelling significance. Life is as the sea, art a ship in which man conquers life's crushing formlessness. . . ."[15] What Ellison did not say is that such editing requires the use of controlling principles that are invariably fictional. This is to say that the organizing ideas are assumptions that are not strictly true according to the most objective criteria. Operating from a strict conception of the truth, we have every right to question the emotional basis for *The Education of Henry Adams*, an especially intense form of self-pity coming from the most widely cultivated American of his time, who, nonetheless, constantly reminds us of his lack of preparation for the nineteenth century, not to mention the twentieth. And in *Black Boy* we are asked to accept Richard's cultural isolation as well as his vulnerability to all forms of deprivation—physical, emotional, social, and intellectual.

Some critics, carried off by the impact of *Black Boy*, tend to treat the autobiography as if it were fiction. They are influenced by the fact that much great modern fiction, Joyce's *Portrait of the Artist as a Young Man*, for example, is very close to life. And the tendency here is reinforced by the fact that the author himself, Wright, is a creator of fictions. Yielding so is a mistake because many of the incidents in *Black Boy* retain the sharp angularity of life, rather than fitting into the dramatic or symbolic patterns of fiction. Richard's setting fire to the "fluffy white curtains" (p. 4), and incidentally the house, is not the announcement of the birth of a pyromaniac or a revolutionary, but testimony primarily to the ingenuity of a small black boy in overcoming mundane tedium. We must say "primarily" because this irresponsible act suggests the profound distress and confusion an older Richard would bring to a family that relied heavily upon rigid attitudes toward religion, expected behavior, and an appropriate adjustment to Southern life. Richard's fire is not Bigger's rat at the beginning of *Native Son*, when the act of killing brings out pent-up violence in the young black man and foreshadows, perhaps, the events of Book Two, "Flight," when Bigger's position becomes that of the cornered rat.[16] Nor does Richard's immodest invitation to his grandmother during his bath (p. 49) offer disturbing witness of the emergence of a pornographer or a connoisseur of the erotic; rather, it points to something more general, the singular perversity in Richard that makes him resist family and the South. In *Black Boy* we exist in a world of limited probability that is not life exactly, because there is an order to be demonstrated, and it does not display the perfect design of a serious fiction. We occupy a gray area in between. The patterns are here on several levels. Though they may not be so clear and tight as to permit the critic to predict, they do govern the selection of materials, the rendering of special emphases, distortions, and the style.

We seldom raise questions about what is omitted from an autobiography, yet if we wish to discover pattern, we must begin with what we do not find. The seasonal metaphor in *Walden* (we move from spring to spring) becomes all the more important once we realize that Henry Thoreau lived on the shore of Walden Pond more than two years.[17] Franklin's few "errata"[18] point up the strong aridity of an autobiography that touches so little on the traumas of the heart. Franklin's education, his achievements in business and science, and his proposals for the benefit of society seem at times supported by an emotional substructure far too frail. But the purposes of both autobiographies—in *Walden*, to offer the model of a renewed life; in the *Autobiography of Benjamin Franklin*, to sketch a convincing design of a successful life in the new world, one that emphasizes the practical values that most Americans admired and many Europeans envied—were achieved in part because of the shrewdness in excluding truthful, though extraneous, matter. So, too, *Black Boy* profits from rigorous and inspired editing.

One function of the omissions is to strengthen the impression in our minds of Richard's intense isolation. This is no mean achievement given that Wright was born into a large family (on his mother's side, at least) which, despite differences in personality, cooperated in times of need. The father, because of his desertion of his mother, was early in Richard's mind, perhaps in the sentiments of other family members, too, an object of hate and scorn. There are no names in the early pages of *Black Boy*, not even that of Richard's brother, Leon Allan, just a little more than two years younger than Richard. When the names begin to appear in *Black Boy*, they tend to define the objects of adversary, often violently hostile relationships—Grandmother Wilson, Aunt Addie, Uncle Thomas. Two notable exceptions are Grandfather Wilson, an ineffectual man capable only of reliving his past as a soldier in the Civil War, and Richard's mother, Ella, a pathetically vulnerable woman of some original strength who, because of continuing illness, slipped gradually into a state of helplessness that became for Richard symbolic of his whole life as a black boy in the South.[19]

The admirable biography of Wright by Michel Fabre suggests another dimension for Richard's opponents in his embattled household. The climax of the violence in the family occurred with the confrontation with Uncle Tom, portrayed as a retired and defeated schoolteacher reduced at the time to earning a living by performing odd jobs as a carpenter. Richard resented being the victim of Uncle Tom's frustrations, and he responded to orders from the older man by threatening him with razors in both hands and by spitting out hysterically, "You are not an example to me; you could never be. . . . You're a *warning*. Your life isn't so hot that you can tell me what to do. . . . Do you think that I want to grow up and weave the bottoms of chairs for people to sit in?" (p. 140). A footnote from Fabre adds more information about the humiliated uncle:

> The portrait of Uncle Thomas in *Black Boy* is exaggerated. After living with the Wilsons, he moved next door and became a real-estate broker. In 1938, he was a member of the Executive Committee of the Citizen's Civic League in Jackson and wrote a book on the word *Negro*, discussing the superiority complex of the Whites and its effects on the Blacks. At this time Richard put him in contact with Doubleday publishers and the uncle and the nephew were completely reconciled.[20]

Wright includes in *Black Boy* a touching description of meeting his father again after a quarter-century. As the newly successful author looked at a strange black sharecropper in ragged overalls holding a muddy hoe, the old resentment for past neglect faded: "I forgave him and pitied him as my eyes looked past him to the unpainted wooden shack" (p. 30). But *Black Boy* contains no softening reconsiderations of Uncle Tom, or of Aunt Addie, who, like her brother, seems to have possessed some redeeming qualities,[21] or of Granny Wilson for that matter. Their stark portraits dominate the family and define a living space too narrow, too mean, and too filled with frustration and poverty for an imaginative youngster like Richard.

A growing boy, when denied the satisfactions of a loving home, looks for emotional support at school or at play, and if he is lucky, he finds something that moderates domestic discontent. But there is little compensation of this sort in *Black Boy*. The reality of the life away from the family seems to be less bleak than Wright represents it, though his schooling was retarded by early irregularity because of the family's frequent moves, and his play restricted, perhaps, because of the family's desperate need for money and Granny's Seventh Day Adventist scruples. Once again we are struck by the absence of names—of teachers like Lucy McCranie and Alice Burnett, who taught Richard at the Jim Hill School in Jackson and recognized his lively intelligence,[22] or Mary L. Morrison or the Reverend Otto B. Cobbins, Richard's instructors in the eighth and ninth grades of the Smith-Robinson School,[23] to whose dedication and competence, despite personal limitations, Wright paid tribute elsewhere.[24] There was no question about his marginal status in these institutions, since Richard stood regularly at the head of his class.

Black Boy is singularly devoid of references to rewarding peer associations. There is no mention of Dick Jordan, Joe Brown, Perry Booker, or Essie Lee Ward, friends of this period and so valued that Wright was in touch with several of them ten years later when he was living in Chicago.[25] The fact that a few of Wright's childhood associates did succeed in making their way to Chicago has an amount of interest in itself, serving, as well, to break the isolation that Wright has fabricated so well. Among the childhood activities that went unrecorded were the exploits of the Dick Wright clan, made up of a group of neighborhood boys who honored in the name of their society, no doubt, their most imaginative member. The clan included Dick Jordan, Perry Booker, Joe Brown, and also Frank Sims, a descendant of a black senator during the Reconstruction period, Blanche K. Bruce.[26] What is amply clear, then, is that Wright had a childhood more than a little touched by the usual rituals and preoccupations of middle-class boys growing up in America, but what is also apparent is that reference to them would modify our sense of Richard's deprived and disturbed emotional life, a necessity for the art of the autobiography, rather more important than any concern for absolute accuracy.

Wright has little to say directly about sex. Richard's most serious temptation for sexual adventure comes toward the end of

Black Boy in Memphis, when he is taken in by the Moss family.
Richard succeeds in resisting the opportunity to take advantage of
a cozy arrangement with Bess, the daughter whom Mrs. Moss
seeks to thrust upon him, with marriage as her ultimate objective
(p. 185). There are some indirect references to frustrated, subli-
mated, or distorted forms of sexual energy—in Miss Simon, certainly, the tall, gaunt, mulatto woman who ran the orphan home
where Richard was deposited for a period (pp. 25–28). And there
were exposures to white women, all calculated to teach Richard
the strength of the taboo prohibiting the thought (not to mention
the fact) of black-white sexual relations in the South. But Richard
never takes an aggressive interest in sex; the adventures that he
stumbles into create traumas when they are serious and unavoidable, or are embarrassing when he can resist participation and
control his reactions. Wright, indeed, seems to be even more
discreet than Franklin was; by comparison, Claude Brown is a
raving sensualist in *Manchild in the Promised Land,* though
roughly the same period of growth is involved. It is strange that
so little space is given to sexual episodes and fantasies in the
record of the gradual maturing of an adolescent—unbelievable,
given the preoccupations of the twentieth century. We face the
problem of omission again. Wright deliberately seeks to deprive
his hero, his younger self, of any substantial basis for sensual
gratification located outside his developing imagination. The
world that *Black Boy* presents is uniformly bleak, always ascetic,
and potentially violent, and the posture of the isolated hero, cut
off from family, peer, or community support, is rigidly defiant,
without the softening effects of interludes of sexual indulgence.

Richard's immediate world, not that foreign country controlled
by whites, is overwhelmingly feminine. Male contacts are gone,
except for occasional encounters with uncles. The father has
deserted his home, and the grandfather is lost in the memories of
"The War." The uncles tend to make brief entrances and exits,
following the pattern of Hoskins, quickly killed off by envious
whites in Arkansas, or the unnamed new uncle, forced to flee
because of unstated crimes against whites (pp. 48–49, 57–60).
Thomas is the uncle who stays around somewhat longer than the
others do, long enough to serve as the convenient object for
Richard's mounting rebellion. The encounter with Uncle Tom is

the culminating episode marking a defiance expressed earlier against a number of authority figures, all women—Richard's mother, Miss Simon, Grandmother Wilson, Aunt Addie. Women dominate in Richard's world, with the ultimate authority vested in Granny—near-white, uncompromising, unloving, and fanatical, daring Richard to desecrate her Seventh Day Adventist Sabbath. The only relief from feminine piety is the pathetic schoolteacher who, in a happy moment, tells an enraptured Richard about Bluebeard and his wives (p. 34). But even this delight, moved in part, no doubt, by Bluebeard's relentless war against females, is short-lived. Granny puts a stop to such sinning, not recognizing, of course, the working out of the law of compensation.

Richard's odyssey takes him from the black world to the white—from the problems of home and family to new and even more formidable difficulties. The movement is outward into the world, to confront an environment that is not controlled by Granny, though it provides much that contributes to an explanation of Granny's behavior. Richard's life among blacks emphasizes two kinds of struggle. One is simply the battle for physical existence, the need for food, clothing, shelter, and protection that is the overwhelming concern of the early pages of *Black Boy*. The second grows out of Richard's deeply felt desire to acquire his own male identity, a sense of self apart from a family that exerts increasing pressure upon this growing black boy to behave properly, to experience Christian conversion, and to accept guidance from his (mostly female) elders. Survival in two senses, then, is the dominant theme, one which does not change when he leaves the black community. The terms are the same, though the landscape is new. Richard desperately seeks employment in white neighborhoods and in the downtown business districts in order to contribute to the support of his family. He discovers, when he does so, that the demand to accommodate becomes even more insistent and less flexible than that exerted by his own family.

The difference is that the stakes are higher. Richard thinks he must find a job, any job, to earn a living. This awareness represents a step beyond the simple dependence that moves a small boy to complain, "Mama, I'm hungry" (p. 13). If he does not find work, Richard feels that he has failed his family in an essential

way and made its survival precarious. Though his independence
in the black world leads to harsh sanctions—threats, bed without
supper, whippings—he is not prepared for the infinitely greater
severity of the white world. It is cruel, calculating, and sadistic.
Richard never doubts that he will survive the lashings received
from his mother, Granny, and assorted aunts and uncles, but he
does question his ability to endure exposure to whites. The ways
of white folks are capricious and almost uniformly malignant.
Richard understands that the penalty for nonconformity, down to
the way a black boy walks or holds his head, is not simply a sore
body, but death. When Richard gives up a good job with an
optical company, with a chance, according to his boss, to become
something more than a menial worker, he does so because of the
opposition exhibited by whites who think he aspires to do *"white
man's work."* Richard confides to his boss when he leaves the
factory: "I'm scared. . . . They would kill me" (p. 168).

From the woman who inquires of Richard, looking for yet
another job, "Boy, do you steal?" (p. 128) to the two young men
who attempt to arrange for Richard to fight another black boy for
the amusement of an assembly of whites (pp. 209–210), we witness
an unrelieved set of abuses. Certainly omission of some mitigating
circumstances and artful distortion are involved in this bitter
report. Richard is gradually introduced to a white world that
grows progressively more dominant, divisive, and corrupting
concerning the black life that serves it. Richard understands fully
what is expected of him:

> I began to marvel at how smoothly the black boys acted out the
> roles that the white race had mapped out for them. Most of
> them were not conscious of living a special, separate, stunted
> way of life. Yet I know that in some period of their growing
> up—a period that they had no doubt forgotten—there had been
> developed in them a delicate, sensitive controlling mechanism
> that shut off their minds and emotions from all that the white
> race had said was taboo. (p. 172)

In Wright's South it was unthinkable for a black boy to aspire to
become a lens-grinder, much less to harbor the ambition to become
a writer. When Richard is thoughtless enough to reveal his true
aim in life to one of his white employers, the response is pre-

dictable: "You'll never be a writer. . . . Who on earth put such ideas into your nigger head?" (p. 129). Given his difficulties in adjusting to an oppressive Southern system, Richard sustains his interest in writing through a monumental act of will. We are led to the inevitable conclusion that Richard must flee the South if he is to remain alive, and the desire to achieve an artistic career seems less important in light of the more basic concern for life itself.

We have every reason to suspect that the treatment of whites gains a certain strength from artistic deletion, too. Michel Fabre points out that Wright's relationship with a white family named Wall does not fit the pattern of abuse and brutal exploitation that emerges from the autobiography: "Although *Black Boy* was designed to describe the effects of racism on a black child, which meant omitting incidents tending to exonerate white persons in any way, there is no doubt that the Walls were liberal and generous employers. For almost two years Richard worked before and after class, earning three dollars a week bringing in firewood and doing the heavy cleaning."[27] Fabre adds, with reference especially to Mrs. Wall and her mother, "Since they respected his qualities as an individual, he sometimes submitted his problems and plans to them and soon considered their house a second home where he met with more understanding than from his own family."[28] This is not matter that reinforces a design displaying increasing difficulty for Richard as he moves outward and into contact with white society. Nor does it support Richard's growing conviction that his survival depends upon his escape from the South. The design of *Black Boy* offers an accelerating pattern of confrontations, taking into account both an increase in danger for Richard and a mounting seriousness in terms of society's estimate of his deviations. Like Big Boy, Richard must flee or die.

The narrator of *Black Boy* has three voices. The simplest records recollected events with clarity and a show of objectivity. We may be troubled by an insufficient context surrounding or an inadequate connection linking these episodes until we become aware of the suggestion of a psychological dimension for them. The incidents illustrate basic emotions: the discovery of fear and guilt, first, when fire destroys Richard's house; the experience of hate, directed this time toward the father, in killing the kitten; the satisfactions of violence, in defeating the teenage gang; the dangers of curiosity about the adult world, in Richard's early addiction to alcohol. The psyche of a child takes shape through exposure to a set of unusual traumas, and the child goes forth, as we have seen, into a world that becomes progressively more brutal and violent. Style in this way reinforces the first theme of the autobiography, survival.

It is in hearing the more complicated and lyrical second voice of the narrator that we sense for the first time another theme in the autobiography. This is the making of the artist. The world, we have been told, is cold, harsh, and cruel, a fact which makes all the more miraculous the emergence of a literary imagination destined to confront it. The bleak South, by some strange necessity, is forced to permit the blooming of a single rose. Wright expends upon the nourishment of this tender plant the care that he has given to describing the sterile soil from which it springs.

A third, didactic voice offers occasional explanations of the matter recorded by the other two. It comments at times upon the lack of love among blacks in the South, the distortions in human relationships involving blacks and whites, and corruption in the social and economic systems. At other times it advises us of the necessity for secrecy when a black boy harbors the ambition to write, and explains the difficulties which he confronts when he seeks to serve an apprenticeship to his art. Despite formidable opposition and the danger of complete isolation, this ambition lives and forces the growth of Richard's imaginative powers.

We do not begin simply with the statement of the intention to become an artist. We start, rather, as Joyce does in *A Portrait of the Artist*, with the sense experience that rests behind the word. Richard's memory offers rich testimony of the capacity to feel objects of nature, small and large. Not only these. We note that accompanying the record of sensations is the tendency to translate sensation into an appropriate emotion—melancholy, nostalgia, astonishment, disdain. All of the senses achieve recognition in Richard's memory, and all combine to emphasize memories of violent experiences: the killing of the chicken; the shocking movement of the snake; the awesome golden glow on a silent night (pp. 7–8).

Apart from this basic repository of sensation and image, we sense early in Richard two other qualities just as essential to the budding artist. One is detachment, the feeling of being different from others. In two worlds to which he is exposed, that of the family and then the more muddled arena of affairs, he rejects all efforts to moderate his apartness. Though conversion and subsequent baptism apparently point to joining the company of the saved, viewed in the conventional way, damnation is assured by the refusal to deliver the right kind of valedictory at the graduation exercises of his grammar school (p. 153). Barely passing one ritual, he flunks another. He maintains under pressure his status as an alien, so ultimately he will be free to exercise the imagination that faces the cold world.

The second quality is curiosity. His mother tells Richard that he asks too many questions. Our young hero is apparently undaunted by the fact that his insistent prying has led to one of the earliest addictions to alcohol recorded in literature. But another addiction is more serious, to the truth in the appearances about him. "Will you stop asking silly questions!" his mother commands (p. 42)—about names, about color, about the relationship between the two. Curiosity constantly leads Richard to forbidden areas more menacing than the saloon, to the mysterious privileged province of whites in Mississippi and the equally mysterious restriction of the blacks.

A neat form of inversion is involved in the development of Richard's artistic talent. We note that the qualities supporting and sustaining the growing boy's imagination are just those preventing a successful adjustment to life in the South. To achieve a tolerable existence, not even a comfortable one, Richard must have firm relationships with the members of his family and with his neighbors and peers; to survive in the larger, white-dominated society he must accept without questioning the inflexible system of Southern mores and customs. Richard, rejecting these imperatives, responds to the demands of his own imagination.

Richard's sensations in nature anticipate a discovery just as valuable and far reaching. This is literature itself. Of the encounter with *Bluebeard* Richard says, "My sense of life deepened. . . ." He recalls, further, a total emotional response, emphasized, no doubt, by the background of an unresponding family, and he realizes that he stands on the threshold of a "gateway to a forbidden and enchanting land" (p. 36). So, early, the opposition is clear. On the one hand is the bleak environment frowning upon any activity of the imagination, whether passive or active, and on the other a determined Richard who will not be turned aside. His reading would be done in secret, a clandestine activity abetted by delivering racist newspapers and borrowing the library card of a compliant white man. There is no evidence that he discussed his reading with anyone, black or white. In Memphis, when he was able to patronize second-hand bookstores and to buy magazines like *Harper's*, *Atlantic Monthly*, and *American Mercury*, his tastes reflected the shape of his early conditioning (p. 198). He admired the great liberators, the destroyers of provincial and private worlds like the one that oppressed him; Mencken in a *Book of Prefaces and Prejudices*; Sinclair Lewis in *Main Street* and *Babbitt*; Theodore Dreiser in *Sister Carrie* and *Jennie Gerhardt* (pp. 217–219).

It might be said that Richard has the loneliness of a naturalistic hero, of McTeague or of Carrie Meeber. Theirs are worlds in which no one talks to anyone else, worlds entirely given over to the expression of power—one person's drive pitted against that of another—and the consequence of the struggle has more to do with heredity or chemistry than with persuasion. Richard's behavior, much like that of a character created by Norris or Dreiser, though it is not governed by the tight probability of fiction, carries constantly the solemn and overwhelming weight of the universe. He cannot say "sir" without acquiescing to the ever-present power of the white man, and he cannot read Mencken without the satisfaction that he has triumphed over a hostile white South through subterfuge and trickery.

Richard's commitment to write precipitates confrontations. As we have seen, his honest admission of this aspiration to one white lady employer results in bitter ridicule, and Richard feels, despite the pressures of his situation, that his ego has been assaulted. His first publication, "The Voodoo of Hell's Half-Acre," is little more than the crude rendering of the stuff of *Flynn's Detective Weekly*, but Richard discovers that printing it is an act of defiance, further separating him from the world that surrounds him, both black and white (p. 146).

Richard does not intend to restrict his range to any half-acre, though his first is identified as "Hell." His province would be the real world around him. True, it is sometimes not to be distinguished from the subject area defined by his first literary effort. At a very young age Richard sees "elephants" moving across the land—not real "elephants," but convicts in a chain gang, and the child's awe is prompted by the unfortunate confusion of elephant and zebra (p. 52). An inauspicious beginning, perhaps, but the pattern of applying his imagination to his immediate surroundings is firmly set. Later, Richard says more soberly that he rejects religion because it ignores immediate reality. His faith, predictably, must be wedded to "common realities of life" (p. 100), anchored in the sensations of his body and in what his mind could grasp. This is, we see, an excellent credo for an artist, but a worthless one for a black boy growing to maturity in Mississippi.

Another piece of evidence announcing Richard's talent is the compulsion to make symbols of the details of his everyday experience. This faculty is early demonstrated in his tendency to generalize from sensational experience, to define an appropriate emotion to associate with his feelings. A more highly developed example is Richard's reaction to his mother's illness and sufferings, representative for him in later years of the poverty, the ignorance, the helplessness of black life in Mississippi. And it is based on the generalizing process that Richard is a black boy, any black boy experiencing childhood, adolescence, and early manhood in the South.

Richard leaves the South. He must, to survive as a man and to develop as an artist. By the time we reach the end of the narrative, these two drives have merged. We know, as well, that the South will never leave Richard, never depart from the rich imagination that developed despite monumental opposition. We have only the final promise that Richard will someday understand the region that has indelibly marked him.

Richard's ultimate liberation, and his ultimate triumph, will be the ability to face the dreadful experience in the South and to record it. At the end of *A Portrait of the Artist as a Young Man*, the facts of experience have become journal items for the artist.[29] At the conclusion of *Invisible Man*, Ellison's unnamed narrator can record the blues of his black life, with the accompaniment of extraordinary psychedelic effects. Stephen Dedalus is on his way to becoming an artist; Ellison's hero promises to climb out of his hole, half-prepared, at least, to return to mundane life.[30] The conclusion of *Black Boy* is less positive and more tentative. True, Richard has made it; he has whipped the devils of the South, black and white. But he has left us with a feeling that is less than happy. He has yet to become an artist. Then we realize with a start what we have read is not simply the statement of a promise, its background and its development, but its fulfillment. Wright has succeeded in reconstructing the reality that was for a long time perhaps too painful to order, and that reconstruction may be Wright's supreme artistic achievement, *Black Boy*.

1979

Notes

1. (New York: Harper, 1940). Dorothy Canfield Fisher in the introduction writes that the "novel plumbs blacker depths of human experience than American literature has yet had, comparable only to Dostoievski's revelation of human misery in wrongdoing" (p. x).
2. The full title is *Black Boy: A Record of Childhood and Youth* (New York: Harper, 1945). Dorothy Fisher in the introductory note calls Wright's work "the honest, dreadful, heartbreaking story of a Negro childhood and youth . . ." (p. vii), without referring to its art or even its place in an American literary tradition.
3. "Life and Letters: Richard Wright Reappraised," *Atlantic Monthly*, 225 (March 1970), 127–132.
4. *American Hunger* (New York: Harper & Row, Publishers) was published in 1977. It is not the whole autobiography but the second part, the continuation of *Black Boy*. Michel Fabre in the afterword provides an accurate brief history of the decision to publish only the first section in 1945. See pp. 143–144.
5. *Atlantic Monthly*, 174 (August 1944), 61–70; (September 1944), 48–56.
6. Fabre, "Afterword," *American Hunger*, pp. 143–144.
7. W.E.B. Du Bois, "Richard Wright Looks Back," *New York Herald Tribune*, March 4, 1945, sec. 5, p. 2.
8. The three are *The Souls of Black Folk: Essays and Sketches* (Chicago: A.C. McClurg, 1903), *Darkwater: Voices from Within the Veil* (New York: Harcourt, Brace, 1920), and *Dusk of Dawn: An Essay toward an Autobiography of a Race Concept* (New York: Harcourt, Brace, 1940).

9. Chapter IV, "Of the Meaning of Progress," in Du Bois, *The Souls of Black Folk*, pp. 60–74.

10. "Richard Wright's Blues," *Antioch Review*, 5 (June 1945), 202. Reprinted in *Shadow and Act* (New York: Random House, 1964).

11. Wright wrote Edward Aswell, his editor at Harper's, on August 10, 1944, suggesting *Black Boy* as a title for the book. He added, for emphasis, that *Black Boy* was "not only a title but also a kind of heading to the whole general theme" (Fabre, "Afterword," *American Hunger*, p. 144).

12. Wright comments on this commitment in *Black Boy*: "I had once tried to write, had once reveled in feeling, had let my crude imagination roam, but the impulse to dream had been slowly beaten out of me by experience. Now it surged up again and I hungered for books, new ways of looking and seeing" (p. 218).

13. Ibid., p. 220.

14. Between 1897 and 1915 Du Bois edited fifteen studies on the condition and status of blacks in America. These volumes represented the Proceedings of the Annual Conference on the Negro Problem, organized by Du Bois and held at Atlanta University.

15. Ellison, "Richard Wright's Blues."

16. *Native Son*, pp. 4–5.

17. Thoreau is precise about the length of his actual stay, despite the fact that the events of *Walden* fall within the design of a single year: "The present was my next experiment . . . for convenience, putting the experience of two years into one." Henry David Thoreau, *Walden*, ed. Sherman Paul (Boston: Houghton Mifflin, 1957), p. 58.

18. Franklin refers in this way to his neglect of Miss Read, to whom he was engaged, during a period spent in London: "This was another of the great errata of my life. . . ." "Autobiography" in Benjamin Franklin, *Autobiography and Other Writings*, ed. R.B. Nye (Boston: Houghton Mifflin, 1958), p. 38.

19. See Michel Fabre, *The Unfinished Quest of Richard Wright* (New York: William Morrow, 1973), pp. 1–17.

20. Fabre, *Unfinished Quest*, p. 533.

21. Another footnote by Fabre in *Unfinished Quest* suggests an additional dimension for Addie, who, "too, was not spared in *Black Boy*. She reacted rather well to reading the book—she stated that if Richard wrote in that way, it was to support his family . . ." (p. 533).

22. Ibid., p. 39.

23. Ibid., p. 48.

24. E.R. Embree describes, in *Thirteen Against the Odds* (New York: Viking, 1944), Wright's attitude toward his education in Jackson: "He [Wright] remembers the Smith-Robinson school with some gratitude. The teachers tried their best to pump learning into the pupils" (p. 27).

25. Fabre, *Unfinished Quest*, p. 39.

26. Ibid., p. 43.

27. Ibid., pp. 46–47.

28. Ibid., p. 47.
29. See James Joyce, *A Portrait of the Artist as a Young Man* (New York: New American Library, 1955), pp. 195–196.
30. Ellison's narrator states his final position with some care: "Thus, having tried to give pattern to the chaos which lives within the pattern of your certainties, I must come out, I must emerge." *Invisible Man* (New York: New American Library, 1952), p. 502.

The Heavenly Voice of
the Black American

Black people as a group receive credit for occupying both ends of a spectrum that reflects the relationship between man and God. Some critical Americans consider blacks to be especially resistant to religious instruction, and they point to the continued strength of "nature" in Negroes, when "nature" is defined as a life without the restraints of a civilized society. These critics point, with a certain Puritanical pleasure, to the reputation for uninhibited consumption of alcohol, easy love, fighting, and stealing—in short, the elements that make up the stereotype of "Black Sambo" that survives still in the minds of a few unreconstructed Southern politicians. More Americans think that blacks are peculiarly receptive to divine influence, and they invariably cite as evidence to support this claim characteristic themes found in the Negro spirituals: the intense yearning for a spiritual home to replace a material one and the desire to merge with God in an effort to erase the memory of misery and unhappiness on earth.

Though we are not concerned here with the "natural" voice of American Negroes, we should note that the Sambo stereotype was strongly supported by a form of popular art, the minstrel show, that flourished in America in the nineteenth and early twentieth centuries and was exploited, to a lesser extent, by the writers of dialect poems and tales. What the American black is really like, then, has been thoroughly corrupted by an artistic tradition that had, finally, little concern for accuracy of representation. We wonder if the black man's reputation for possessing an affinity for things mystical is based similarly on such a precarious foundation.

Close inspection of the claim suggests that it is the Negro spiritual that is usually cited as supporting the black man's possession of the "heavenly voice." There is no doubt that those "black and unknown bards"[1] who created the spirituals were touched by a mystical fever of some kind, but can we attribute to their descendants, in uncounted generations, the same mystical powers with which the creators were endowed? We should be

299

naïve if we did, and once again art has intervened. Mystical illumination should not be confused with the satisfaction, no matter how pious, of participating in an artistic performance, the singing of the spirituals. Art, high in the case of the spiritual, or low when we think of Mr. Bones and Sambo, taints both claims.

What amounts to a stand-off should discourage the making of sweeping generalizations of any kind about racial characteristics. Though we offer no new rash claims, we must say that most people concerned with the problem rarely consider the best evidence for attributing to the black man the extraordinary experience of communicating directly with divinity. We have heard much about the Negro spirituals; W.E.B. Du Bois,[2] James Weldon Johnson,[3] and Alain Locke[4] have written eloquently about the haunting beauty of these songs, so intensely emotional and so otherworldly. We have heard less of an art form closely linked to the spiritual, the folk sermon. The sermon resembles the spiritual in coming from the same kind of religious experience. That is to say, it is the product of the black man's effort to assimilate and to adapt Christian ideas, an effort that folklorist Bruce Rosenberg dates as far back as the Second Great Awakening in 1800, if not before.[5] The sermon resembles the spiritual in not being entirely the property of black people. There are white spirituals and, of course, white folk sermons, but we hear more about black achievement in these areas possibly for the reason that for many years America has had a higher proportion of illiterate blacks than illiterate whites, or possibly because black accomplishments carry more emotional power and display more imaginative strength.

If we compare the folk sermon and the spiritual as instruments useful in conveying a sense of communication with God, we must insist that the folk sermon is far purer and far more efficient. The spiritual was sung commonly by a congregation or a group, repeating, with widely varying understanding and feeling, words that were remembered. Very seldom do we have the act of creation occurring in conjunction with the singing. Despite the most spontaneous and sincere of performances, we must admit to ourselves that ultimate credit must go to those "black and unknown bards" about whom we know so little. Not so with the folk sermon. In this art form the preacher quite literally begins with the assumption that he *is* the voice of God. "Is" is not quite

correct, perhaps; "becomes" is better because the preacher gradually works himself toward an ultimate identification with God.
That moment occurs when the black spokesman chants in a
strong and rhythmical cadence the words that God has given,
possibly, while leaning backward from the pulpit, with eyes
closed, veins bulging in his forehead, and sweat streaming from
every pore. The black performer, if asked to repeat what he has
said at this moment, may be at a loss to reconstruct the chain of
phrases that have come pouring from his mouth, made sacred for
the short period just passed.

What is being described is by no means a dead art, to be
reconstructed from documents or the memories of aged ministers,
but one that lives still, in store-front churches in the ghettoes of
American cities, in the tents of camp-meetings held on the out-
skirts of cities or in the country, and on the radio, at stations to be
found usually at the extreme ends of the dial spectrum at those
frequencies where the folk sermon must compete with country
music and advertisements for patent medicines. It is possible,
then, for a well-trained critic with a strong background in the
tools and the methods of folklore to describe the art form with
some precision by using contemporary models. And Professor
Bruce Rosenberg has done so in *The Art of the American Folk
Preacher*. He provides a shape for the authentic folk sermon that
is suggestive in many ways. What has been looked at largely as an
emotional or spiritual experience becomes an identifiable art
form subject to analysis and comparison. Immediately invited, of
course, is the chance to examine the artistic reproductions of the
sermons—that is to say, the approximations constructed by literary
artists—in light of an authentic model. *God's Trombones*[6] by
James Weldon Johnson is a collection of poems that imitate the
structure of the folk sermon and convey something, as a consequence, of the authority of the original form. One step removed
from such a comparison is the critical exploration of the use of
the art form of the sermon in another, perhaps more familiar,
literary structure—the novel. James Baldwin, once a child-
evangelist himself, does just this in *Go Tell It on the Mountain*,[7]
giving to the sermon a flexibility and dimension undreamed of by
the often illiterate or semiliterate black exhorter, who would
claim that he was simply about God's work.

Now to describe the form. The first characteristic established by Professor Rosenberg's analysis is rhythm,[8] already alluded to when we spoke of the increased regularity in the phrasing of the preacher as he approached his climax. Indeed, Rosenberg has insisted that a rhythmical pattern transcends words in importance, that is to say, words as an expression of ideas or concepts. A significant part of the training of a neophyte in the art, often a child incapable of grasping much else, would be listening to and responding to an overall rhythmical pattern.[9] Customarily the beginning of a folk sermon would be prosaic, building on a reference to a text or to a situation that has led to the preoccupation with a particular theme. Then the preacher moves through a set of what may be called trial sequences toward increased regularity in phrasing. At the moment of climax we observe that the prosaic syntax and the imagery appropriate to mundane discussion give way, under extraordinary emotional pressure, to the verbal devices of a chanted poem, characterized by a strong beat, and to an imagery made luminous or symbolic by what the speaker takes to be providential intrusion. Then, at the conclusion, the preacher returns to the world of ordinary mortals in supplying a message that might be carried like a handkerchief from the church door.

Rosenberg's sample sermons display a number of easily identifiable devices. Nothing is more marked than the repetition in diction and syntax. We find parallel clusters in which the same phrase occurs or the same or similar grammatical constructions.[10] Then there are the repeated formula phrases, important in the structure of early epics in revealing ties to an oral tradition, which may record breaks in the development of the preacher's thought or represent direct appeals to the congregation.[11]

It is the formula phrase that suggests an important additional characteristic of the art form. We are reminded that the role of the congregation is not passive. Correctly and efficiently exhorted, the congregation responds in formula phrases of its own: "Preach it, brother," or "Yes, Lord," possibly. The reaction of the audience ideally takes the emotional pattern of the preacher's sermon. When the exhorter's chant becomes most regular and most insistent, the members of the congregation reach the climax of their excitement. As the folk preacher feels afterwards that God has spoken directly through him, those exhorted feel afterwards that God has spoken directly to them.

The congregation makes an additional contribution that is somewhat more difficult to define; it concerns the matter of continuity or, to be more accurate, the sense of continuity. A folk sermon may lack elements that provide connection and coherence in other forms. The epic, with oral origins too, would be a case in point; here narrative provides much of what is necessary for continuity. But there is no reason to expect a coherent narrative in a sermon. Story elements may appear, but they tend to demonstrate and to illustrate other points and not to be sufficient in themselves. What is lacking in narrative is seldom balanced by logic. Indeed, it is difficult to avoid the conclusion that much of what passes for continuity comes from the congregation itself, the reaction to the preacher's rhetoric. Continuity may exist when the congregation feels that the rhythmical pattern, or the larger emotional design to which that pattern is related, is fulfilled. This is overstatement, no doubt, for certainly imagery, references to bits of narrative (if not the sense of a developing tale), and repeated allusions to the problem or to the theme supply more concrete evidences of planned organization. But it is not overstatement by much. Baldwin, among the literary artists manipulating the form, realizes most thoroughly the great contribution of the audience, and the structure of *Go Tell It on the Mountain* reflects this fact.

The language and the imagery of the folk sermon derive, in part, from the Bible. Only in part. Perhaps a more significant contribution comes from the infusion of matter from ordinary life. Striking effects are the consequence of this rude juxtaposition of the familiar religious phrase and the homely illustration or elaboration. This point is seen clearly in a sequence, recorded by Rosenberg, of a sermon "The Twenty-Third Psalm," recited by Rev. Rubin Lacy on May 5, 1968, in Corcoran, California:

> David in his old age
> Can say the Lord is my shepherd
> I shall not want
> Devil kept on runnin' after David
> They run him so tired

> Sometime he was hungry
> He had to eat the short bread
> IIe didn't have time to go to the store
> He had to eat the bread ·
> That the trees issued
> God from Zion (ll. 103–113)[12]

As we know, Johnson modeled *God's Trombones* after the folk sermons. Though he has caught with accuracy the spirit of the black preacher, we note some differences. While the tone of Johnson's preacher is undoubtedly the same as that of an authentic black exhorter, it has, at the beginning of a sermon, more authority, the kind of strength reserved for a folk preacher nearer the middle of his sermon. Johnson eliminates the prosaic frame, the commencement and the conclusion, containing matter closest to the mundane world of the congregation. Though the pattern of growing intensity remains, the speaker in one of Johnson's *Trombones* has not far to go. The moment of great excitement is recorded in the same old way—in more regular metrics and with an overwhelming amount of repetition in the phrasing. Johnson's preacher cries out in the sermon entitled "The Crucifixion" at the moment that the nail pierces the flesh of the hanging savior:

> On Calvary, on Calvary,
> They crucified my Jesus.
> They nailed him to the cruel tree
> And the hammer!
> The hammer!
> The hammer!
> Rang through Jerusalem's streets
> The hammer!
> The hammer!
> The hammer!
> Rang through Jerusalem's streets.[13]

We discover formula phrases in Johnson's sermon, terms that represent stops in the development of the preacher's thought or permit time for recovery and redirection and, above all, appeal directly to the assembled congregation. Lacy's "God from Zion" has a counterpart in Johnson's "The Prodigal Son." There "Young man—/ Young man—" serves the same function; we watch helplessly as the wayward youth slips ever more deeply into the sinful ways of Babylon. The marvelous juxtaposition of the conventionally religious phrase and the vulgar action or image, often providing raciness in the folk sermon, appears in Johnson's *Trombones* too, with something less than the vigor of the folk model:

> And God stepped out on space
> And he looked around and said
> I'm lonely—
> I'll make me a world.
>
> And far as the eye of God could see
> Darkness covered everything,
> Blacker than a hundred midnights
> Down in a cypress swamp.[14]

Though the narrative element has increased significance in the *Trombones*, it does not preempt the function of the message, the plain, sometimes rude instruction to the assembled church members about what they should carry from the service. At the end of "The Crucifixion," Johnson's preacher says, "Oh, I tremble, yes, I tremble,/ It causes me to tremble, tremble,/ When I think how Jesus died."[15] Indeed, we are not to forget the awesome magnificence of Christ's sacrifice. The message has a particular poignancy here because it echoes the phrasing of the great Easter spiritual, "Were You There When They Crucified My Lord?" We are reminded that the folk sermon and the spiritual came from the same source.

It is in the attention to the congregation that we sense an important difference between the art sermon and the folk sermon. Though Johnson's preacher in the funeral sermon, "Go Down Death," addresses specific people in his audience, "Heart-broken husband," "Grief-stricken son," and "Left-lonesome daughter,"[16] he is generally less precise. Actually, what is often missing in the *Trombones* is the pressure of an involved congregation actively goading the preacher to attain a more accurate expression of God's Word. Some indication of how that pressure works can be seen in another of Rev. Rubin Lacy's sermons, this entitled "God's Ploughboy," delivered on May 19, 1968, in Tulare, California:

> I'm wondering do ya hear me today
> Somebody here
> Soft-peddlin' the gospel
> Tryin' to soothe somebody
> Twistin' the Word of God
> I'm here to tell ya today
> Preach the Word
> Preach the Word
> Don't care who don't like it
> I don't care who it hit
> Ohh preach the Word
> I don't care who don't like it
> I don't care who get offended about it
> Preach the word (ll. 207–220)[17]

Moreover, Johnson in the art sermon seldom musters at the climactic moment the kind of raw power that the folk sermon has when it is successful. The repeated references to "The hammer," in "The Crucifixion," fail to move even a sophisticated reading audience as much as Lacy's definition of the *Word* at a moment of great intensity in "God's Ploughboy":

> Because the gospel
> Is the saving salt
> That serves the soul
> Umm-hmm
> Preach
> Because the gospel
> Is the power of God
> Unto those of salvation
> To everyone that believe
> Ohh preach the Word
> I'm glad God told me
> A long time ago
> To preach my Word
> Ohh go eat
> Therefore (ll. 231–247)[18]

Perhaps one of the reasons why we are so impressed by Lacy's rhetoric is the fact that the preacher has come very far from "That's the text/ You'll find it in Hebrew thirteen to seventeen/ That's the text."[19] On the other hand, Johnson's preacher strikes an opening note in "The Crucifixion" just slightly below the intensity of his later description of the agony of Jesus:

> Jesus, my gentle Jesus,
> Walking in the dark of the Garden—
> The Garden of Gethsemane,
> Saying to the three disciples;
> Sorrow is in my soul—
> Even unto death[20]

We are never far from the rhythm of the folk sermon throughout Baldwin's *Go Tell It on the Mountain.* The structure of much of the novel is given over to "The Prayers of the Saints" (Part Two), in which the closest relatives of the young black hero, John, offer confessions or testimonials about their own lives. Gabriel, John's stepfather; Florence, Gabriel's sister; and Elizabeth, John's mother, encouraged by the exhortation of the preacher, move toward some sort of ultimate illumination, in much the way the folk preacher struggles with the empty and misleading forms of the world to achieve a perfect statement of the Word. Baldwin is not content with correspondences so general. There are folk sermons incorporated into the testimonial of Gabriel, the deposed preacher. He has been deposed because he had found God's service no shield protecting him from the sins of lust and pride. As part of his recollection of the great turning points of his life, Gabriel recalls sermons of his own, often in their entirety, because they relate closely to and illuminate the action he is on the point of taking. When he is deciding to marry Deborah, the holy fool, the black girl who has been cruelly raped by whites and who has survived to remind the world of its corruption, Gabriel preaches eloquently on the wages of sin.[21] When he is attempting futilely to resist the physical attractions of Esther, after his marriage to Deborah, Gabriel retells the story, in the second book of Samuel, of young Ahimaaz who ran too soon to bring the tidings of battle to King David. Gabriel appeals to the flippant and careless Esther to commit herself to God, by commenting on Ahimaaz's words: "I saw a great tumult but I know not what it was."[22] Gabriel thinks that the statement applies to Esther's situation and in his pride and ignorance does not see that it applies with even more compelling force to himself, to his struggle to ignore or to master the seething sexuality rising within him.

Gabriel's sermon, delivered at the time he was brooding over Deborah's virtues of the spirit and inadequacies of the body, has a structure that is typical of the folk sermon. We see in Baldwin's description of the beginning of Gabriel's sermon a statement that would characterize accurately the first minutes of most folk sermons:

> He did not begin with a "shout" song, or with a fiery testimony; but in a dry, matter-of-fact voice, which trembled only a little, asked them [the congregation assembled for the Twenty-Four Elders Revival Meeting] to look with him at the sixth chapter of Isaiah, and the fifth verse.[23]

As Gabriel warms to his task, we hear the repeated phrase and the chant of the prose poem, with an insistent and inescapable beat:

> Let us remember that we are born in sin, in sin did our mothers conceive us—sin reigns in all our members, sin is the foul heart's natural liquid, sin looks out of the eye, amen, and leads to lust, sin is in the hearing of the ear, and leads to folly, sin sits on the tongue, and leads to murder. Yes! Sin is the only heritage of the natural man, sin bequeathed us by our natural father, that fallen Adam, whose apple sickens and will sicken all generations living, and generations yet unborn![24]

Gabriel's rhetoric lacks the rude juxtapositions of the vulgar and the conventional that enliven Lacy's sermons and occasionally touch the rolling periods of Johnson's preacher in the *Trombones*. Gabriel's sermons resemble Johnson's in avoiding dialect, seldom exhibiting even the colloquial nuances that give a special quality to the *Trombones*. We remember with pleasure the grammatical lapse in "Go Down Death": "But they didn't make no sound."[25] No liberties of this sort exist in the diction of Baldwin's preacher; Gabriel's language is much too close to that of the Old Testament to allow for anything approaching verbal humor. Instead we stagger from the buffeting of a flood of Biblical references and from the cosmic sweep of Gabriel's leaping imagination. Gabriel lives in two worlds—three, if we count the country of memory: the South of his youth and young manhood. But the two worlds that are present at the time of telling the tale are Harlem of the 1930s, in the area of Lenox Avenue and 135th Street, and the valleys and the mountains of Israel, the timeless world of the Old Testament.

There is much evidence of Baldwin's shrewdness in the use of the congregation while the sermon develops. Gabriel, for example, receives assistance from an unidentified woman shortly after he has begun his eloquent condemnation of sin: "'Yes!' cried a woman. 'Tell it!'"[26] And another sympathetic voice cries out shortly afterwards: "Amen! You preach it, boy!"[27] A close reading of the sermon reveals a certain order to these outbursts. As Gabriel approaches his climax, the voices of the inspired intruders tend to be identified. "Oh, yes . . . bless our God forever!"[28] is shouted by one of the elders, one of the twenty-four whom Gabriel, in terms of his professional reputation, wishes to impress most. But it is the cry of "Praise Him!" from Deborah,[29] at the high point of the excitement, that more than anything else convinces Gabriel of his success, for Deborah's approval—acceptance by the holy fool—is the key to the door that leads to high spiritual eminence. She has access to divine authority by right of having experienced ultimate violation. Her shout comes just before Gabriel's most sweeping pronouncement, when with the voice of God's anointed Gabriel says:

> Woe is me, for when God struck the sinner, the sinner's eyes were opened, and he saw himself in all his foulness naked before God's glory. Woe is me! For the moment of salvation is a blinding light, cracking down into the heart from Heaven— Heaven so high, and the sinner so low. *Woe is me!* For unless God raised the sinner, he would never rise again![30]

Gabriel speaks as if he had borrowed the voice of God, and we receive confirmation of this fact from a congregation that has responded with complete sympathy to the divine surge of Gabriel's rhetoric. "Yes, Lord!" shouts a voice, again unidentified, "I was there!"[31] And so have we all been, in intimate touch with divinity.

The most brilliant section technically of *Go Tell It on the Mountain* grows from Baldwin's sensitivity to the reaction of the congregation. This is the third and last part, "The Threshing-Floor," which records John's experience of conversion. The sense of the outside world, of what is happening actually in the Church of the Fire Baptized, is not very clear because we are entirely absorbed with John's inner struggle. There is, without a doubt, a sermon being preached just as John's agony begins. What it is we do not know, though it plainly serves as an exhortation to sinners to join the band of the faithful. John hears an unidentified voice, possibly the voice of the preacher, the cry of conscience, or the appeal in simplified form that comes out of his whole experience. Whatever it is, it is insistent:

> He wanted to obey the voice, which was the only voice that spoke to him; he tried to assure the voice that he would do his best to rise; he would only lie here a moment, after his dreadful fall, and catch his breath. It was at this moment, precisely, that he found he could not rise; something had happened to his arms, his legs, his feet—ah, something had happened to John.[32]

Other voices we hear in the background just before the vision of the Lord occurs. Again we have no identifications. Possibly, these are the words of people who assist the preacher on the occasion of a conversion, but what precedes their statements is invariably some sort of sermon appealing to the sinner to accept Christ. John hears one voice emerge from the background urging, "Yes . . . go through, Go through."[33] Another advises, "Call on Him. Call on Him."[34] Yet another queries, *"Have you been to the river?"*[35] Then comes a more disturbing inquiry, *"Sinner, do you love my Lord?"*[36] These voices linger in his mind and mix with the flood of memories that involve his relationship with his stepfather, more pleasant recollections of his friend Elisha, of his mother and his aunt, and the sounds of the cosmos, from the roaring of the fires of Hell to the softer echoes of the moving feet of the saints in Heaven.

What occurs, at last, is a breakthrough of the kind that we discover in a folk sermon. There the preacher assumes God's voice, but here, on the threshing-floor with John, who has heard the divine summons, the experience of transcendence makes use of sight rather than sound. Earlier, we recall, at the climax of Gabriel's sermon on sin, one of the deeply moved auditors cried, "I was there."[37] And Baldwin records John's exciting moment in similar fashion:

Then John saw the Lord—for a moment only; and the darkness for a moment only, was filled with a light he could not bear. Then, in a moment, he was set free; his tears sprang as from a fountain; his heart, like a fountain of water, burst. Then he cried; "Oh, blessed Jesus! Oh, Lord Jesus! Take me through!"[38]

God's voice does, and no writer of fiction has used that voice more skillfully than Baldwin has. He reproduces the art form of the folk sermon and explores its effects. He is both preacher and congregation, God and sinner, and he uses as a background—as a church, in effect—Harlem, the rural South, and the land of the Old Testament. Though part of the power that is generated in *Go Tell It on the Mountain* comes from Baldwin's own artistry, much of it has a source more widely shared, with James Weldon Johnson and with every black preacher who deplores modern ways and succeeds in making the old form work on Sundays. Surely, much of Baldwin's force in the novel rests upon the expectations that we have of the form of the folk sermon itself, the instrument that comes as close as humanly possible to offering black people the gift of the "heavenly voice."

1971

Notes

1. James Weldon Johnson, "O Black and Unknown Bards," *American Negro Poetry*, ed. Arna Bontemps (New York: Hill and Wang, 1968), p. 1. The first lines read:
       O black and unknown bards of long ago,
       How came your lips to touch the sacred fire?
2. In "Of Our Spiritual Strivings," *The Souls of Black Folk* (Greenwich, Conn.: Fawcett Publications, 1961), p. 22.
3. See "O Black and Unknown Bards" and *The Book of American Negro Spirituals*, ed. J. Weldon and Rosamund Johnson (New York: The Viking Press, 1925).
4. Alain Locke, "The Negro Spirituals," *The New Negro, an Interpretation*, ed. A. Locke (New York: Arno Press and the New York Times, 1968), pp. 199–213.
5. Bruce Rosenberg, *The Art of the American Folk Preacher* (New York: Oxford University Press, 1970), pp. 14–16.

6. James Weldon Johnson, *God's Trombones: Seven Negro Sermons in Verse* (New York: The Viking Press, 1961).
7. James Baldwin, *Go Tell It on the Mountain* (New York: Dell Publishing Co., 1968).
8. Rosenberg, p. 76.
9. Ibid.
10. Rosenberg, pp. 49–51.
11. Ibid., pp. 54–56.
12. Ibid., p. 148.
13. Johnson, *Trombones*, pp. 41–42.
14. "The Creation," in Johnson, *Trombones*, p. 17.
15. Ibid., p. 43.
16. Ibid., p. 27.
17. Rosenberg, p. 184.
18. Ibid., pp. 184–185.
19. Ibid., p. 182.
20. Johnson, *Trombones*, p. 39.
21. Baldwin, pp. 102–105.
22. Ibid., p. 119.
23. Ibid., p. 102.
24. Ibid., p. 103.
25. Johnson, *Trombones*, p. 28.
26. Baldwin, p. 103.
27. Ibid.
28. Baldwin, p. 104.
29. Ibid., p. 105.
30. Ibid.
31. Ibid.
32. Baldwin, p. 194.
33. Ibid., p. 202.
34. Ibid.
35. Ibid., p. 203.
36. Ibid., p. 204.
37. Ibid., p. 105.
38. Ibid., p. 204.

The Mixed Heritage
of the Modern Black Novel:
Ralph Ellison and Friends

Friendship is where we begin. Once upon a time there were three friends, Wright, Ellison, and Baldwin, and Wright, it was, who served as the central person in the relationship, extending the arm of affection to his two younger colleagues, Ellison and Baldwin. They were not friendly at the same time. Ellison was close to Wright until his departure for France and permanent exile in 1947, just at the time that he was beginning to write *Invisible Man*, and Baldwin sought out Wright in Paris during the early years of his residence there. Friendship is not always a pact made in heaven; it resembles at times an insurance policy. That is to say, there are terms, and if the terms are ignored, the friendship is strained, frequently to the breaking point.

Now the accepted element in the Wright–Ellison–Baldwin alliance was that Wright was the dominant father figure, offering advice to his younger associates, directing their reading. As everyone knows, fathers, in the course of things, are destined to be rejected—indeed, in suffering such rejection, some attain unexpected heights. The young associate, seeking distance from an all-embracing arm that has become too confining, can manage his rejection with discretion or with rudeness.

Ellison was discreet. We might expect that he would be, since he was well brought up in Oklahoma and has paid in his autobiographical pieces respect for his elders, especially to a Mr. Randolph, his adopted grandfather, who served as the learned caretaker of the library of the Oklahoma legislature. Ellison, in an interview published in *The Massachusetts Review* in the Autumn 1977 issue, voiced his rejection in a measured way:

> . . . most friendships have their vague areas of mystery and the older member of a relationship between writers might himself project the younger in a role which obscures the extent of his intellectual maturity or the extent and variety of his experience. One of my early experiences with Dick Wright involved such an underestimation, with him assuming that I hadn't read

313

many books with which I was, in fact, quite familiar. . . . Well, among others, he assumed that I hadn't read any of Marx . . . Conrad . . . Dostoevsky . . . Hemingway—and so on. I was somewhat chagrined by his apparent condescension, but instead of casting him in the role of misunderstanding "father," I swallowed my pride and told myself, "Forget it, you know what you know, so now learn what he thinks of in terms of his Marxism and the insights he's gained as a developed writer of fiction." And that was the way it went.

On the other hand, Baldwin was a good deal less discreet. After all, he came from a background charged by evangelical religion, and his long suit, if you forgive the mixed metaphor, was conversion, not cultivation. Baldwin attacked Wright in a famous essay written in the mid-fifties entitled "Everybody's Protest Novel," in which he lumped together *Native Son* and *Uncle Tom's Cabin* and asserted, with some pretension, that both failed to qualify as high art. Baldwin said then that the novel should have to do not with society but rather with "the power of revelation," the "journey toward a more vast reality which must take precedence over all other claims." It matters little now that Baldwin was wrong, fuzzily wrong. He was mistaken about the relationship between the novel and society, about the worth of *Native Son*, even about the artistic value of that extraordinary fusion of sentiment and propaganda that is *Uncle Tom's Cabin*. What does matter in our context is that the Wrights (Richard and Ellen) never forgave him, even though they realized that he was reflecting, simply, the pressures of a singularly smug and complacent decade. I say Wrights, by the way, because Ellen, Richard's second wife, still remembers the assault upon her husband and the objectionable piety that accompanied it. I should add that the last word on this controversy has yet to be printed. There exists now in the Beinecke Library, where the whole Richard Wright Archive now rests, a completed novel, *The Island of Hallucinations*, the second work in a projected trilogy begun by *The Long Dream*, which presents a particularly unpleasant character named "Mr. Mechanical." Some of us, including Michel Fabre, see a striking resemblance between that character and a former intimate associate of Wright's. Ellen Wright, at the moment, will not permit the publication of the novel because it contains matter damaging to the reputations of people still living.

We are not essentially interested really in the flow and ebb in friendship, but in a moment in the history of Afro-American literature when these interests of Wright, Ellison, and Baldwin converged. This would be in the years 1952 and 1953, when *Invisible Man, The Outsider* by Wright, and *Go Tell It on the Mountain* by Baldwin appeared. The dominant force in the literary ferment created by this convergence was exercised by Ellison, not Wright, the distant master.

Ellison is the writer who comes to mind when we retrace the beginnings of a truly modern tradition in black fiction. Indeed, Ellison's is the achievement that black critic Addison Gayle must reject when he wishes to replace a complex and perhaps perverse heritage with a simple art of straightforward expression and black pieties. Happily, such a replacement is impossible as well as unthinkable, and the dream of it is destined to go the way of the philistine complaint against Henry James, that James's fiction would somehow be stronger, healthier, and more American if he had tended the flame of his genius at Washington Square. The fact is that Ellison for all of his readers, his admirers as well as his detractors, created a new thing in the black novel, shaped a new climate, and forced upon his audience a new pattern of expectations for the art of black fiction, and he did so not by denying the Western tradition in a foolish gesture that would cost him half of the resources of his imagination and his language, but by using it and combining an essentially "white" heritage with the matter and the manner of a rich black oral culture.

Though everyone admits that a break of some kind in the continuity of black fiction occurs with Ellison, few critics, especially those so passionately opposed to his malign influence, can say exactly what it is. Certainly, there is nothing unique about stirring into the same pot white art forms and black folklore, soup stock and exotic herbs. Chesnutt had done this with some commercial success in the 1890s, notably in *The Conjure Woman*; but there is a great difference here in both ingredients and cuisine. Chesnutt used the fictional forms from the conservative genteel tradition, the short narrative carefully tailored for the reading audience of *Scribner's, Century, Harper's, The Critic,* and *The Dial,* which respected a cultivated middle-class sensibility that welcomed titillation but not trauma. Nothing ever really changes in the psychic life of the retired couple who listen to the yarns of Uncle Julius in *The Conjure Woman.* It costs the husband a few dollars now and then and rather more time, but the exposure to black folklore is managed at a proper distance and with a display of civilized tolerance that survives quite easily the odd happenings among lesser black folk. True, Chesnutt's style at its best approaches an irony that might unsettle the most sensitive. The folklore center within the genteel envelope of a typical Chesnutt tale has vitality, but this matter is tempered, too. All of the attention to goophering and transformation tended to sustain conventional moral standards and values, if not in blacks directly, indirectly in the whites, punishing excess in human appetites, and rewarding, at times in odd ways, fidelity and endurance. The precedent for handling folk matter in this way was established, no doubt, by George Washington Cable in the decade preceding the emergence of Chesnutt as a writer, when the quaint ways of the Creoles in Louisiana charmed Eastern audiences, not entirely to the satisfaction of the residents of New Orleans, Plaquemines, and Natchitoches.

The comparison of Chesnutt and Ellison is a device for measuring Ellison's achievement, providing the terms for a proper evaluation. Ellison does not rely upon the more conservative models provided by the mainstream of the American narrative, which would be in the late 1940s a still vigorous Naturalism. Now, "conservative" in this context has nothing to do with politics. The reality is that the American political Left applied the formulas of Naturalism with a new rigor and a new intensity, giving to the achievement of James Farrell and Richard Wright an authority not to be lightly dismissed. A writer of this school practiced exact, detailed representation and looked to the social sciences, at times to Marxist notions of history, for ways of structuring human behavior. The emphasis was always upon the society, not upon the rare individual who dropped out of a well-defined place or a well-clocked time; the challenge for the Naturalistic hero was inevitably adjustment, not psychic trauma that might be magnified in proportion to the character or sensitivity of an individual consciousness. The Naturalist was always about the business of Man, with a capital M, and it helped little to make him Common and to claim that his low state came from a pathological environment. The consequence is an art of constraints: more, indeed, for Wright than there were for Dreiser, since Wright bore consciously and deliberately, but with much turmoil, a commitment to the Communist Party.

I suppose that Wright's inner doubts and his frequent questions were as much responsible as his continuing faith in the Party for the fact that he wrote the finest proletarian novel ever written in America, *Native Son.* But a complete break with his Naturalistic models was unthinkable for Wright while he was a Party member and while he remained in America. Not so for Ellison, who stood at the periphery of the New York political scene in which Wright was a central actor, and who came from a background dominated by an interest in several of the arts rather than a single one. He was also Southern in a way that Wright was not. Ellison was prepared, in short, to turn his back on both American Naturalism and the American Left and to welcome aspects of a Southern exposure not recognized by Wright, or Chesnutt either, for that matter.

Ellison tells us that *Invisible Man* had its beginnings on a farm in Vermont in the summer of 1945 when he read *The Hero* by Lord Ragland and speculated on the nature of black leadership in the United States. Ellison never intended to construct an odyssey of a representative man, a standard exercise in Naturalism, given its direction by an inflexible social milieu. From the start, he was concerned with a hero with especially endowed characteristics and possibilities, perhaps even with talents not unlike his own. Ellison had read Conrad, Henry James, and Dostoyevsky, even before Wright in New York guided the younger writer to James's "Prefaces," the letters of Dostoyevsky, and the critical commentary of Joseph Warren Beach. He admits now to "playing possum" with Wright, simulating an innocence of knowledge that he did not possess when they talked in the early forties. After all, T.S. Eliot, whose imprint upon *Invisible Man* is to be seen everywhere, especially on the early pages and in the conclusion, was a Tuskegee discovery like the fine black woman pianist Hazel Harrison. Ellison had a talent for sculpture too, as well as for music, and he was able to recognize a certain naiveté and unsophistication in the sculptor Richmond Barthé, with whom he studied briefly. As a consequence, he adopted a style that was always eclectic, changing to reflect the psychological shifts within his unnamed narrator. He has associated in "The Art of Fiction," an interview published in *The Paris Review* in 1955, a particular and distinctive style with each of the three sections of the novel: Naturalism with the adventures in the South, though it is Naturalism of a highly symbolic kind, when we move away from the well-manicured lawns of the black college; impressionism for the early efforts of the hero to establish himself in the North; and surrealism with the documentation of the hero's fall from grace in the Brotherhood. We may quibble, as I do, with the accuracy of these labels, but not with the presence of a staggering virtuosity in technique that brought into being *Invisible Man*. The point is that Ellison casts off the shackles of Naturalism, both in matter and in manner.

Nowhere is the departure from Naturalism more evident than in the way that environment is rendered, the always richly documented background demanded by that form of the novel extended by Norris and Dreiser, one which devoted attention to the central forces that shape life. Even in the more Naturalistic pages of *Invisible Man*, we find a Melvillian duality, a delight in playing with two equally valid but opposed physical realities—the gleaming and orderly campus of the college, with its suggestions of New England and the triumphs of Christian faith and hard work, and the unsightly cabins of Trueblood and his brothers, sisters, and children, reminding us and Mr. Norton, the trustee from the North, of unattended back alleys of the spirit, unmistakably black and recalling an instinctive life that cannot be forgotten.

This duality is to be found wherever background is sketched in *Invisible Man*; in The Liberty Paint Factory, in the domains of Kimbro and Brockway; in upper Manhattan itself, with a topside of apartments and stores, and a bottom equipped with the most elaborately illuminated basement ever rendered in literature or in life. It is clear that the essentially fictional problem is not adjustment, since no one knows to what he might adjust; rather, the more desperate question is ordering one's tradition, history, and psyche, best put by one of Ellison's favorite authors at the time, Eliot, at the conclusion of *The Waste Land*: "These fragments I have shored against my ruins." No more. And the unnamed narrator confesses that he is only half prepared to emerge from his hole. A little like Louis Armstrong, who would "Open the Window and let the foul air out," knowing all the time that the "Old Bad Air" was responsible for the good music.

Perhaps the plainest indication of Ellison's reliance upon the rich tradition in experimental Western art is the title itself. "Invisibility" is not simply a characteristic first given visual expression by the fine British actor Claude Rains in a horror movie, nor even first used as a metaphor for blackness in 1948 by George Orwell. It is a concept that owes something to European Expressionism, in which the dominant idea in a complex whole of a community of values or of a social system or a culture or a human relationship is extracted, magnified, distorted, and allowed to stand for the whole. For precedents of this kind, we do not need to look to the dramatists Kaiser or Capek with their experiments in Europe, but closer at hand to O'Neill in *The Hairy Ape*, or, indeed, to Eliot, in "The Hollow Men." What is exaggerated, of course, is what some of us still remember from the bad days before the black revolution, the tendency of whites to ignore or to make easy generalizations about blacks; this is not so prevalent since the publication of *Invisible Man* and the parade of liberated individualized black psyches that followed in print.

We are dealing in halves here, since the break with Naturalism constitutes only one half of the meaning of Ellison's achievement. The flip side of the coin that represents his contribution to the modern black novel is all black and connected directly with a black oral tradition. Chesnutt, we must recall, used only that folk matter that could be absorbed with comparative ease by a genteel reading audience. He wrote about conjurers, mostly women, who restricted their practice of the black arts to blacks, in general, and blacks in a reasonably remote community in North Carolina at that. Zora Hurston knew much more than Chesnutt did about the black folk tradition, especially the animal tales, the boasts and jokes, and the rituals in folk medicine, but in her fiction she tended to separate the white world and the black, following Chesnutt's pattern, but often rendering black life with more dignity, fullness, and wonder. It was Ellison who suggested a subversive dimension for the black arts.

Ellison uses the matter and the style of a black folk culture with a new broadness and with an incredible range, from music through the spoken word to the icon. His blackness is much more accessible and much more threatening. Trueblood demonstrates this early on when Norton, the college trustee, has the temerity to stray away from the neatly landscaped grounds of the narrator's institution. But there is much more. Louis's trumpet blues complain eloquently about the unchanging condition of blackness in white America, played off the beat, of course, and making marvelous art from "bad air." The characters from beast fables, Buckeye Rabbit and Jack the Bear, appear as symbols representing the narrator's psychological states, documenting the measure of his submission to or evasion of inhuman white authority. Cryptic folk rhymes stir racial memories that would moderate somewhat the narrator's headlong pursuit of conventional goals within the context of commercial New York. The extraordinary "Prologue" contains, along with snatches of blues and other bits of folk matter, an irreverent folk sermon on the text "Blackness of Blackness," and it offers a summary description of the action which is hard to improve upon:

> "Black will make you . . ."
> . . . .
> ". . . or black will un-make you"

And the response of the assembled congregation in this dream sequence seems wholly appropriate: "Ain't it the truth, Lawd?" An object, not simply a musical line or a phrase, has the power in *Invisible Man* to link past and present. We think of Brother Tarp's leg chain, a device associating two kinds of bondage: chattel slavery in the South and absolute allegiance demanded by the Brotherhood. The chain, though not folk art in any true sense, has the effect of an icon in that it arouses memories of almost unbreakable intensity of the cruelty of black servitude in the South. Illustrations accompanying the slave narratives when they appeared in the North during three decades of appeal to the American conscience just before the Civil War frequently presented a black and his leg chain.

To give a proper estimate for what Ellison has accomplished we must record it in black and white, that is to say, within the framework of a vital and comprehensive black folk culture and within the emerging tradition of the experimental modern novel. He breaks decisively, on both counts, from the practice of his immediate predecessors, and such is the power of his genius that he leaves the impression that by his efforts alone he has prepared the way for the bold achievements in black fiction that are to come.

To believe so would be to attribute too much to Ellison, great as his work is, and to ignore the time. The crucial period of gestation and formation of the modern black novel is the late forties and early fifties. Indeed, the culminating years for these pioneer efforts are 1952 and 1953, a two-year period during which not only *Invisible Man* appeared, leading the way in 1952, but *Go Tell It on the Mountain*, and also *The Outsider* by Richard Wright, which appeared a year later in 1953.

We tend to ignore *The Outsider* in this context, probably because of the false assumption that his self-imposed and widely advertised exile in France had deprived Wright of the nourishment of American society. It is the old provincialism again, underestimating, as it always did, the power of a really strong imagination. In fact, *The Outsider* is a new departure for the old master of Naturalistic fiction, demonstrating that Wright in his own way had shared the same road with Ellison, not too unexpected given that they were firm friends in the early forties.

The Outsider has a protagonist who is also extraordinary and who very early in the action seeks to shape his own life by assuming a new identity: Cross Damon becomes Lionel Lane; the black postal worker in Chicago becomes an important, though unofficial, member of a local cell of the Communist Party in New York. We sense in both Ellison's hero and Wright's that they have the potential for leadership, though circumstances of life are not favorable. What is important, finally, for both is not success but coming to terms with themselves. The Invisible Man must develop, first, an awareness of his needs as a person; Cross makes what he considers, at last, to be the wrong decision about his need, and faces, in his dying moments, the human consequences of a freedom gained by violating accepted moral standards and living outside of society. Both protagonists drop out of time; for Ellison, such an escape is short-term therapy that works, for

Wright it is ultimately disastrous, destroying the connection, the "bridge from man to man," which is, Cross maintains, all we have: "starting from scratch every time is . . . is no good."

Despite a certain identity in theme and in fictional strategies, the two works are remarkably different. Ellison's is a personal odyssey that leads to the discovery of a rich black folk heritage, which accompanies the acquisition of a psychological equilibrium at the end, almost sufficient to face a chaotic and often senseless world. There are few such positive assurances in *The Outsider*, singularly devoid of allusions to a racial heritage or to psychic traumas that oppress the Invisible Man. Wright's novel is, instead, a form of fable in which personal relationships and their exploration count for little. What matters is a philosophical point: the power and the cost of the condition of conscious alienation debated with brilliance by Cross and Ely Houston, the District Attorney of New York City, two outsiders, one a black criminal evading capture and the other a hunchback lawman with the capacity to reconstruct the motivation of the man whom he hunts and about whom he can speak, at his death, with the voice of a brother. Raskolnikoff and Porfiry, we think, in *Crime and Punishment*, and we are not far off. Wright's fable, relying on reason and philosophical discussion rather than upon psychological development, makes a powerful statement about the human condition, which is clear and unqualified: "Alone a man is nothing." The narrative, despite its lean, even ascetic technique, manages to view the future in a hopeful light, assuming, indeed, the presence of an audience that might learn from a well-told lesson. Beyond the horror, Cross's four murders, rests a promising prospect: "Man is returning to the earth finding himself in a waking nightmare. . . . The real men, the last men are coming." Nothing so hopeful as this emerges from *Invisible Man*, though Ellison's hero, despite temptation, is never moved to resort to such violent means to achieve his ends.

One critic has called Wright a birthright existentialist, which is an affirmation that criticism will use any science or pseudo-science to make its point, even dialectics. I prefer to think of Wright as a home-grown existentialist, made so by his traumatic childhood in Mississippi, his reading of the more libertarian Naturalists like Dreiser, who scorned moral conventions and inhibitions supported by religion, and his trials in the Communist Party.

What is inescapable, with both Ellison and Wright, is that the discovery of blackness and its meaning represents a starting point for the artists; Wright's experience, as we have seen, leads to an existential view of reality. Ellison states his notion of what constitutes a beginning best in a remarkable article on the art of his friend Romare Bearden:

> I refer to that imbalance in American society which leads to a distorted perception of social reality, to a stubborn blindness to the creative possibilities of cultural diversity, to the prevalence of negative myths, racial stereotypes and dangerous illusions about art, humanity and society. Arising from an initial failure of social justice, this anachronism divides social groups along lines that are no longer tenable while fostering hostility, anxiety and fear; and in the area to which we now address ourselves it has had the damaging effect of alienating many Negro artists from the traditions, techniques and theories indigenous to the arts through which they aspire to achieve themselves.

Ellison practices what he counsels: he addresses "social imbalance," using the full range of the techniques available to him from contemporary fiction, music and the plastic arts, and the folk tradition.

James Baldwin, like Ellison and Wright, explored in *Go Tell It on the Mountain* the problems of a potential leader, though of a special kind. The intellectual context for the coming of John, to echo Du Bois for a moment, is religious and psychological, not political or philosophical. John, Baldwin's protagonist, has the talent and the temperament to become a preacher, a wise and compassionate shepherd for a black congregation; but he lacks the spirit, the sense of mission that comes from the experience of conversion. John's difficulty rests not with the attraction to sin, which he resists without real conflict, but in the hatred of his stepfather, Gabriel, once a powerful preacher in the South, now brought low because he has yielded to lust and pride. John must moderate his antipathy for Gabriel before he can join the community of the saints of the Temple of the Fire Baptized in Harlem. He does so by absorbing the testimonies, "prayers" Baldwin calls them, of his aunt, his stepfather, and his mother. We know that John in this way has acquired an understanding of, if not a complete sympathy for, the adults of his family, because snatches from their statements, their responses to the call of the preacher to come to God, appear in the remarkable record of his conversion. The family's collective guilt, as well as its collective memory, weighs him down as he approaches the agony and the light on the threshing-floor. This necessity to reckon with a black past, to learn it and to accept it, follows the pattern of Ellison's nameless hero who eats a yam in public as a step toward establishing his racial identity.

Though the essential fictional problem owes little to Naturalism, the description of the background in Harlem, with its dirt, smells, rats, and harlot cries, displays an indebtedness that is quite clear. It is firm until John slips off into Central Park and we discover ourselves suddenly upon a hill in Judea with a view of a sinful city below. Baldwin's South has even less the shape of a readily identifiable land; the terrain is rather the mountains and the valleys of the Old Testament prophets. By the time we reach the threshing-floor, the landscape is wholly surrealistic.

Certainly one of the great triumphs of *Go Tell It on the Mountain* is the imaginative use of a folk art form, specifically the folk sermon. Ellison was ingenious, too, in the way that he absorbed folk materials within the structure of *Invisible Man*, but he did not take Baldwin's longer step in this respect. The entire novel is a response to a folk sermon, culminating indeed in a conversion scene. The black preacher's call to "Come" results first in "Telling," the testimonies of members of the Grimes family and then the descent of God's grace upon John. At the end of the narrative John is saved, but he has yet to be tried. His faith will be tested when he himself goes forth to spread the Word, risking the hazards to the psyche that will afflict him when he struggles to ascend the steep side of the mountain, as Gabriel had attempted to do. I can think of no other example in modern fiction in which a form derived from folk art exercises such commanding authority.

It is time now to take stock, to sum up the most visible consequences of this artistic revolution in the early fifties. We know now that it is not simply Ellison that we must thank or damn, but Wright and Baldwin too, whose more modest participation must be counted. This new literature is a record of an exceptional sensibility as it copes not so much with a hostile world but with the terrors of its own creation. What is prized more than anything else is an understanding of one's black self, and this requires a reconciliation of some sort with the black heritage, family and folk, in America. Almost in his dying words, Cross Damon warns: "Starting from scratch every time is . . . is no good." No good it is for any of these writers.

Ellison, Wright, and Baldwin depart from Naturalistic techniques to render the turmoil of the psyche. Ellison uses dream sequences and violent distortions of reality, both clocked to a remarkable sense of place and of pace. Wright constructs a morality tale, a modern fable permitting a naked and a full discussion of such issues as freedom, power, and human connection. Baldwin fashions what might be called a counter-sermon, fleshing out what rests behind the audience's "Amen" and ending in a description of a convulsive transcendence that is one of the extraordinary achievements in modern literature. For all three, the old verities no longer work. Theirs are now the realities beyond success, freedom, and salvation, and we inherit a house of black fiction that has yet to settle securely on a foundation so recently reclaimed from the marshes of the psyche.

If we look more closely at *Native Son*, we can observe that the signs of change are already in the air in 1940. I refer to the third book of the novel, still often criticized for being inconsistent with the brilliant Naturalism of the first two books. We recall that Bigger, after his conviction for murder, throws the crucifix out of his cell when he is visited by a black preacher bringing the chance to repent and to acquire, at the last moment, divine grace, and we listen with astonishment to the rejection of the Marxist vision of his lawyer, Max, when Bigger insists that his murders were not the consequence of society's pathology but the result of his own will. And to Max's dismay, Bigger asserts that the murders were good since they gave him a human dimension that he never possessed before. Bigger, after his resurrection in the final act, may be a phenomenon that is premature; but with the perspective of literary history, we can say that he has brothers in the heroes of novels published more than a decade later, in the fifties.

1979

IV

A Bibliography of
the Writings of
Charles T. Davis

with G.W. Allen. *Walt Whitman's Poems: Selections with Critical Aids.* New York: New York University Press, 1955.

(ed.). *E.A. Robinson: Selected Early Poems and Letters.* New York: Rinehart, 1960.

(ed.). *A New England Girlhood* by Lucy Larcom. New York: Corinth Books, 1961.

"Image Patterns in the Poetry of Edwin Arlington Robinson," *College English* (March 1961), 380–386.

"Letters from the Old Hawk," Review-article of *The Correspondence of Walt Whitman,* I and II, ed. E.H. Miller, *The Nation,* 193 (July 15, 1961), 34–35.

"Walt Whitman and the Problem of an American Tradition," *CLA Journal,* 5 (September 1961), 1–16.

with G.W. Allen. "The World of Primal Thought," *Whitman, the Poet,* ed. J.C. Broderick. Belmont, Calif.: Wadsworth Publishing Co., Inc., 1962, pp. 130–132.

"The Art of Teaching English," *The Journal of General Education,* 14 (October 1962), 175–184.

"Impressionism as a Cultural Impulse," *School Arts,* 63 (February 1964), 12–15.

"Humanistic Imperatives in an Age of Technology," *Pennsylvania Library Association Bulletin,* 20 (August 1964), 7–11.

"Poetry: 1919–1930," *American Literary Scholarship: an Annual! 1963.* Durham, N.C.: Duke University Press, 1965.

Review of *Anne Bradstreet* by J.K. Piercy, *Seventeenth-Century News,* 25 (Winter 1967), 75–76.

"Image Patterns in the Poetry of Edwin Arlington Robinson," *Appreciation of Edwin Arlington Robinson,* ed. R. Cary. Waterville, Maine: Colby College Press, 1969, pp. 191–199.

"Robinson's Road to Camelot," *Edwin Arlington Robinson: Centenary Essays*, ed. E. Barnard. Athens: University of Georgia Press, 1969, pp. 88–105.

with D. Walden (eds.). *On Being Black: Writings by Afro-Americans from Frederick Douglass to the Present.* New York: Fawcett Publishers, 1970.

"The Heavenly Voice of the Black American," *Anagogic Qualities of Literature*, ed. J. Strelka. University Park and London: The Pennsylvania State University Press, 1971, pp. 107–119.

with R. Corrigan (eds.). *Richard Wright: His Work, His World and His Influence.* 4 vols. Publications of the Third Annual Institute for Afro-American Culture. Iowa City: University of Iowa, 1971.

"A Poet's Language," *Studies in "Leaves of Grass,"* ed. G.W. Allen. Columbus, Ohio: Charles E. Merrill Publishing Co., 1972, pp. 46–60.

with R. Corrigan (eds.). *W.E.B. Du Bois.* Publication of the Fourth Annual Institute for Afro-American Culture. Iowa City: University of Iowa, 1972.

Review of *The Harlem Renaissance* by Nathan I. Huggins, *American Literature* (March 1973), 138–140.

"Robert Hayden's Use of History," *Modern Black Poets*, ed. D. Gibson. Englewood Cliffs, N.J.: Prentice-Hall, Inc., 1973, pp. 96–111.

"Introduction," *Richard Wright: Impressions and Perspectives*, ed. D. Ray and R.M. Farnsworth. Ann Arbor: The University of Michigan Press, 1973, pp. 1–6.

"Jean Toomer and the South: Region and Race as Elements within a Literary Imagination," *Studies in the Literary Imagination*, 7 (Fall 1974), 23–37.

"From Experience to Eloquence: Richard Wright's *Black Boy* as Art," *Chant of Saints: A Gathering of Afro-American Literature, Art and Scholarship*, ed. R.B. Stepto and M.S. Harper. Urbana: University of Illinois Press, 1979, pp. 425–439.

"Paul Laurence Dunbar," *American Writers: A Collection of Literary Biographies*, ed. A. Walton Litz. Supplement II. New York: Charles Scribner's Sons, 1981, pp. 191–219.

with Michel Fabre (eds.). *A Bibliography of the Richard Wright Canon.* Boston: G.K. Hall, Inc., 1982.

Black is the Color of the Cosmos, ed. H.L. Gates, Jr. New York: Garland Publishing, Inc., 1982.

"The Slave Narrative: First Major Art Form in an Emerging Black Tradition," *The Slave's Narrative,* ed. C.T. Davis and H.L. Gates, Jr. New York: Oxford University Press, 1982.

The Shaping of the Afro-American Literary Tradition, ed. H.L. Gates, Jr. 2 vols. New Haven: Yale University Press (forthcoming).

V
Appendix

William Roscoe Davis
and His Descendants

[*My grandfather, William Roscoe Davis, died at the age of ninety-two, three days before I was born. I have always been sorry that I arrived too late to know the patriarch of my family. He was evidently a striking personality. I have talked with many persons who knew him, and they have all spoken glowingly about the warmth, the essential dignity, and the downright strength of his character. Fascinated by the colorful anecdotes about him that have come to me through the years, I have attempted here a brief biographical sketch of him. My grandfather was in no sense a national figure; but as he lived in stirring times and as his life in several respects was different from that of the ordinary slave and freedman of his era, I feel that this sketch will be of some interest to the student of the pre–Civil War and Reconstruction periods.*]

In the Ante Bellum Times

William Davis was born a slave on Todd's Farm, near Norfolk, Virginia, about the year 1812. I say "about" because he himself was never quite certain concerning the exact year. Slaves seldom were; they usually determined their age by counting *up to* and *from* some outstanding event which occurred during their early lives. My grandfather used the War of 1812 as his "marker." He was the son of a sea captain, white, of course, and a slave woman of mixed blood. His mother must have had a considerable amount of Indian blood because the high cheek bones, the hawklike features, and the distinct copper coloring which he had all gave evidence of Indian as well as Negro-white ancestry.

My grandfather was reared at Todd's Farm, staying there until he became a "good-sized" boy. He was then sent over to Shield's Farm, on the Hampton side of Hampton Roads—a farm which was owned then by a Mr. Westerly Armistead. Whether both farms belonged to the same family, I don't know, but he was evidently not sold. In any case, when he came to Shield's Farm, he was a tall, strapping, handsome and intelligent young slave. He had been taught to read and write by his young master on Todd's Farm. Of this fact, he was always very proud and with good reason. Even though slavery at its worst was quite mild in Tidewater Virginia, it was certainly unusual to find a master teaching his slave to read and write.

But Grandfather Davis was also a high spirited young lad, and like many another slave of his type, he soon ran afoul of the "poor white" overseer. His story except for the ending is like a thousand others in slave memoirs. To use his phraseology, he "took" the overseer's brutality for a long, long time, and then one day, for no apparent cause, just simply decided that he wasn't going to "take" any more. He had a "corn knife" in his hand when he made his decision to become a man. If a fellow slave had not intervened he would have murdered the overseer. As it was, he treated the fellow pretty roughly.

The aftermath of this attack was unusual, and I am still puzzled by it. In such cases, the Negro was customarily given a terrible punishment and then sold "down South." But in this instance, the master got rid of the white man and subsequently made my grandfather overseer of the farm. The Armisteads must have been definitely unconventional slave-owners, or else there must have been some "blood" tie-up in the whole business which has not come down to me. I also note that by the time of the Civil War, the mistress of Shield's Farm (the master evidently having died) and my grandfather were on excellent terms. For many years prior to the War, she had allowed him freedom to work as a pleasure-boat operator at Old Point Comfort. He had not only made money for her but had saved up a considerable sum for himself, as we shall see.

During his years of early manhood, my grandfather was "called to preach." Concerning this call, I know nothing whatsoever. In his later years, he was a very highly puritanical and "fundamentalistic" Baptist. I imagine, therefore, that his call must have followed the usual pattern of such conversions. In any case, he became a very popular and influential "exhorter" and a definite leader among the slaves of the Peninsula.

As an up-and-coming slave leader and exhorter, Father Davis (as he was called by the whole family) began courting Nancy Moore, a mulatto slave owned by a well-known family in the town of Hampton. Nancy had one child when my grandfather married her in 1837, and that child became in all respects save blood relationship Father Davis's oldest son. The two loved and respected each other throughout the years, and the two different families lived in the same house as one family, united not only by the same grandmother but also by the impartial treatment of my grandfather.

Nancy Moore had been left free by her master, but the latter's son, claiming that his father had been of unsound mind when he wrote the will, refused to let her go. My grandfather had saved eighteen hundred dollars from his pleasure-boat work; he took this money and hired lawyers to sue for her freedom. It took a lot of courage for a slave to sue a planter in those days; moreover, it was an unheard-of proceeding, and the lawyers, I am told, were so handicapped by lack of precedent and by adverse public opinion that they tried to persuade my grandfather to drop the case. But he was a determined man and doggedly refused to give up the fight. The case dragged on for over a decade. Father Davis won a verdict in 1859, but because of the attitude of the judge, he had to wait until 1861, when the Yankees came to Hampton, to get his wife and children.

When the Union Army came to the Peninsula in '61, my grandfather had intelligence enough not to believe the lies which the Southerners spread concerning the Yankees. Not only did he refuse to leave the town with his mistress, but he also persuaded many other Negroes to stay. On August 7, 1861, the Rebels under General Magruder burned the town of Hampton. Father Davis, seizing opportunity by the forelock, moved his family to Wood's Farm (the present location of Hampton Institute) and took up residence in Wood's Mill. The building still stands on Hampton's campus and is now known as Griggs Hall. My uncle, somewhat more ambitious, took over the "Great House" of Wood's Plantation, the house which is now the presidents' home at Hampton Institute. During the whole of the Civil War, my people lived on this plantation. The farm faced Hampton Roads, and from it my father, although he was too young to remember it, saw the battle of the *Monitor* and *Merrimac*.

There is an interesting picture of my grandfather at this period to be found in the *Atlantic Monthly* for November, 1861. In an article entitled "The Contrabands at Fortress Monroe" (pp. 626–40), one finds the following comment:

> The more intelligent the slave and the better he had been used, the stronger this desire [to be free] seemed to be. I remember one such particularly, the most intelligent one in Hampton, known as "an influential darky" ("darky" being the familiar term applied by the contrabands to themselves). He could read, was an exhorter in the Church, and officiated in the absence of the minister. He would have made a competent juryman. His mistress, he said, had been kind to him, and had never spoken so harshly to him as a Captain's orderly in the Naval Brigade had done, who assumed once to give him orders. She had let him work where he pleased, and he was to bring her a fixed sum, and appropriate the surplus to his own use. She pleaded with him to go away with her from Hampton at the time of the exodus, but she would not force him to leave his family. Still he hated to be a slave and talked like a philosopher about his rights. No captive in the galleys of Algiers, not Lafayette in an Austrian dungeon, ever pined more for free air. He had saved eighteen hundred dollars of his surplus earnings in attending on visitors at Old Point [vacation spot before the war], and had spent it all in litigation to secure the freedom of his wife and children, belonging to another master, whose will had emancipated them, but was contested on the ground of the insanity of the testator. He had won a verdict, but his lawyers told him they could not obtain a judgment upon it, as the judge was unfavorable to freedom.

The author of the above article is not named, but we learn from his own statement that he was a lawyer from Massachusetts, then serving as a private in the Union Army. He must have been amused at my newly-freed grandfather's insistence upon his rights and particularly with his attitude toward the "Captain's orderly." That attitude, however, was a perfectly natural one for an "aristocratic" slave to take. To my grandfather, the orderly, in all probability, was just another "poor white." Superior slaves always looked down upon and resented poor whites. My grandfather never lost that contempt, and he passed it on to his son, my father.

The story of Butler's first contrabands of war is too well known to repeat here. My grandfather was among those hundreds of refugees who gathered at Fortress Monroe. Because of his intelligence and reputation as a leader among the Peninsula slaves, he was put in charge of distributing supplies to the contrabands. During my boyhood, there were several persons living who had received on the ration days meal, flour, meat, and hardtack from Br'er Billy Davis, as he was called by his fellow Christians.

Feeding and clothing the contrabands, however, became a real problem for Butler's army. Fortunately for the military, the American Missionary Association offered to help in the emergency, and in September of 1861 sent the Reverend Mr. Lewis G. Lockwood to Fortress Monroe to find out what the Association could do to relieve the army. Lockwood was highly impressed with my grandfather and wrote glowingly about him to the *American Missionary*, the official organ of the Association.

The following entry, appearing in the issue for October, 1861 (p. 248), praises his ability as an exhorter:

> The afternoon meeting was one long to be remembered. After I had finished my discourse, several of the exhorters spoke. One of them, Mr. Davis, is an Apollos. I spoke of his eloquence, etc., in former letters, but his address yesterday was a masterpiece. It melted every heart. He appealed to the soldiers present who were in rebellion against God striving to put down rebellion in this land, and asked them how they, who had been taught to read the Bible, and learned the Lord's Prayer in infancy from a mother's lips, could stand in judgment, when a poor despised and inferior race, who, though denied the Bible, had been taught of God and found their way to Christ, should rise up and condemn them. He then turned to his fellow contrabands and entreated them to embrace thankfully, and improve, the boon already given. He considered the present a pledge of the future— the virtual emancipation of fifteen or eighteen hundred, the promise of the emancipation of four million. The Lord works from little to great.

Another entry (p. 244, the same issue) speaks again of him as being "very able in exhortation, resembling Frederick Douglass in appearance, and like him remarkable for native talent."

In still another (p. 246), one finds a long account of my grandfather's analysis of his learning to read and what it meant to him:

Brother Davis, a leader among them, of whom I have made mention in my last, told me to-day something of his feelings in reference to learning to read and write. He expressed to his master's son his strong desire to read the Bible, and he replied "You shall know." So he got him first an elementary book, and then a Bible. Within a year, by constant application, at leisure intervals, he learned to read the New Testament very well, and the Old Testament by spelling out some hard words. "Oh," said he, "when he gave me a lesson in the Testament to get familiar with, so that I could read it readily, I would go alone and pray that God would help me learn His word, and He did help me. And then, how I thanked Him that I could read the Bible for myself, and teach others to read it. I was accustomed to make the love I had for my wife and children the standard of my best feelings, but when I was seeking religion, I enquired of myself whether I loved Christ more than them, so that, if need be, I could give them up for Him. And so, when learning to read the Bible, I felt that though it would be like taking life to part with them, I could let them go rather than not know how to read God's book."

Such is the value an intelligent, pious slave puts upon the word of God, which is denied to seven-eighths of them by the laws and customs of slavery. The man of whom I have spoken, stated to me that the year he learned to read, he gave better satisfaction in his work, and his own family were better provided for, than during any previous years. Yet, it must be confessed, as he stated, that the reading of that freedom-inspiring book gave him an increased longing after liberty, and expectation that the day of deliverance would soon come.

Sensing the excellent propaganda possibilities in my grandfather, Lockwood, when he returned to the North, took Father Davis with him to beg money and clothing for the contrabands at Fortress Monroe. The mission was successful, and, according to the AMA reports, an appreciable amount of money and clothes came to Fortress Monroe as a result of my grandfather's efforts in the North.

Father Davis evidently remained in the North for a considerable length of time; so long in fact that my grandmother, becoming alarmed, began to fear that he would never return to her. Even though he still sent money home, she was not satisfied with the tone of his letters. My grandmother was a quiet woman, I am told, but a strong one. Although she had never traveled anywhere in her life; although the Civil War was being fought and ordinary transportation was not easily obtained, she made up her mind to go to New York and have an understanding with her husband. Her oldest son was now a grown man, and he owned a sloop. Taking two of her youngest children, my father and my aunt, she and her son sailed in this open boat from Hampton Roads to New York City! Once there she found that her fears were groundless, but she didn't regret the trip. It was the only one she ever made during her sixty-eight years of life. Moreover, the bringing of her two children made it possible for my grandfather to conduct an "auction sale" in the church of the great Henry Ward Beecher.

Beecher's auctions, as we know, were a sensational feature of the anti-slavery movement. On this occasion my grandfather dramatically "sold" his two children to a large and enthusiastic assembly in Beecher's church—sold them for the benefit of the contrabands in Virginia. My father, who took a reluctant role in this historic experience, remembers no part of it; but my aunt, who was several years older than he, told me that my parent acted rather disgracefully. When Henry Ward Beecher took him up in his arms, my father alarmed the church with screams of protest.

In New York, my grandfather met Mr. Whipple, the head of the AMA. Whipple, like Lockwood, was impressed with the ability and Christian sincerity of this ex-slave and gave him a position as lecturer for the Association. In this office, my grandfather travelled throughout the North. He was paid an excellent salary for that day, sixty dollars a month and expenses. The following entry in the *American Missionary* (April 1862, p. 83) gives some idea of his travels at the time:

> William Davis, one of the freedmen at Fortress Monroe, who came to this city last January, with Rev. L.C. Lockwood, and addressed several meetings here and in the vicinity so acceptably, has been for several weeks in Massachusetts, where, in company with our agent, Mr. W.L. Coan, of Boston, he has labored on behalf of his kindred and friends in Virginia, from whom he has been separated awhile that he might awaken such an interest in their favor that their temporal and spiritual wants could be more adequately supplied.

Mr. Davis has spoken, we understand, at Chelsea, Boston, Malden, Worcester, Newburyport, West Newton, Newton Corner, Dover and Nashua (N.II.), Lynn, Salem, Fitchburg, Lowell, Reading, Roxbury, Brookline, etc. Although his health has not been good he has spoken very satisfactory. His natural abilities and uncommon eloquence (considering his disadvantages as a slave) have surprised and gratified his numerous hearers, and inspired in them new feelings in relation to American slaves. Collections have been taken up, at the different meetings, moderate in amount, and a quantity of clothing has been given, to be sent to the ex-slaves. This lecturing tour will long be remembered by the friends of humanity, who have had the opportunity, to listen to this gifted representative of the bondmen of his country; and the lecturer, on his return to Virginia, will be able to inspire his people with new hopes, when he relates the kind reception given to him, and the generous response given to his appeals, by the friends of liberty in Massachusetts.

During Reconstruction

After the War, Father Davis returned to Hampton. My Aunt Emma told me an interesting anecdote about the meeting of my grandfather with the master whom he had formerly sued. Father Davis, she said, lined his whole family up in front of Wood's Mill to receive the former slave-owner, but he warned each of them: "If you call him *master*, I'll whale you good." When the master came up, he extended his hand and said: "Well, William, I guess we can bury the hatchet now." My grandfather was not to be outdone in graciousness. "Yes, Mr. Banks," he said, "let bygones be bygones; we are all men now!" As for my aunt, she admits that she said nothing when her former master greeted her. She was afraid to call him just plain *mister*, and she knew her father would have smacked her down if she had disobeyed him. She therefore hung her head and said nothing. Somehow, I have always liked the scene. There was a quiet but real drama in it.

For a short while after the Civil War, Father Davis was pastor of a small church on Lincoln Street in the town of Hampton—a church which the AMA built for him. He was a good preacher in every respect save one; he was inclined to be too "bossy" and exacting for his congregation. Essentially puritanical himself, he brooked no backsliding in his members. As a result he tended to run them away by his rigid and uncompromising attitude. [Incidentally, he was just as sternly moral with his own family. None of his grown sons or daughters-in-law or grandchildren dared let him know that they attended dances or even went to a theatre. And all had to take part in the morning and evening prayers held daily in the home.] He was not a glum or sour puritan, but he was a puritan nevertheless and expected far too much from a congregation composed entirely of persons who had just come out of slavery.

Seeing his congregation dwindle, Father Davis decided to give up the church and establish an elementary school in the building. His interest in education had always been strong, and even as a slave he had surreptitiously taught his fellow bondsmen to read the Bible. Ignorance he considered the greatest curse which slavery had placed on the Negro, and his favorite term of reproach and of condemnation whether applied to his parishioners, his deacons, his fellow clergymen, or to his own family was *ignorant*. He of course had no patience with those Negroes who didn't try to educate themselves, when slavery was abolished. To him as to many of his type and generation, education was the Balm of Gilead that would cure all of the social and economical ills of the Negro. It was only natural therefore that he should wish to start a school in place of his church. It was just as natural that he should have, as he did, an intense and life-long interest in another educational experiment in the community—Hampton Institute.

Grandfather Davis always took credit for the founding of Hampton Institute in that he was the cause of Armstrong's coming to Virginia. And the story is quite plausible. When Father Davis returned to Hampton after severing his connection with the AMA, he found that the Negro children of Hampton were being taught as a temporary expedient in the courthouse by a Yankee who used the rod a bit too freely in his instruction. Though the man was a Northerner, he was still white, and my grandfather was too recently released from bondage to relish the idea of any white man whipping Negroes. Although he didn't like this beating business, he didn't take any action against it until one day the teacher whipped one of his nieces. My grandfather immediately wrote a letter of protest to his AMA friends, requesting them not only to send a new and more humane man down to Hampton but also a man who would start a *real* school for Negroes. As a result of his request, the American Missionary Association sent General Samuel Chapman Armstrong, who founded Hampton Institute in 1868.

Although General Armstrong and Grandfather Davis later became quite good friends, the two at first didn't hit it off too well together. My grandfather was disappointed in Hampton's curriculum; he considered it too elementary. The idea of teaching Negroes who had been in slavery all of their lives *how to work* seemed to him the height of foolishness. "If Negroes don't get any better education than Armstrong is giving them," he used to say, "they may as well have stayed in slavery." Above all else, he wanted Latin and Greek taught. If they were the subjects the whites learned, then the Negroes ought to have them too, he reasoned. And, frankly, he was quite right. The Negroes of that generation were unconsciously fighting against the idea of a "peculiar" education for their children. Whether they were totally "practical" or not was, we see now, a matter of no great importance. Their spirit was right. It is too bad they lost the fight.

It was inevitable that a man of grandfather's type should go into Reconstruction politics. As a matter of record, he was very reluctant about the whole business, and the only purely political job he ever took was that of Door Keeper in the Virginia Constitutional Convention of 1867. I think my grandfather's attitude toward the Negro and politics was of the you-must-crawl-before-you-can-walk kind. In any case, he absolutely refused to run for Congress himself because he knew that his education was inadequate. Always a plain and forthright man, he used to criticize his fellow politicians on the score of *their* educational preparation, and what is worse, he criticized them in open public meetings. This practice didn't increase his popularity among his fellow citizens and on occasions it was positively dangerous. My father, a "wild" young man at the time, used to attend the political rallies to act as a sort of official bodyguard for my grandfather. The political meetings of those days were often quite rough, and my father had to go into violent action on several occasions to protect his outspoken parent.

My grandfather felt that if the Negroes didn't have an educated candidate of their own, they shouldn't hesitate to pick a qualified white man, provided of course the latter was an "all right" person. Carrying out this policy, my grandfather chose Arthur Segar, a white lawyer in the town (he was a Northerner), and by his personal effort and influence sent Segar to Congress. The two men—Segar and my grandfather—were not simply political allies; they were friends—friends in a way impossible for the two races in the South today.

I should add here that my grandfather did get another job as a result of his political activity. For a decade or more, he was the lighthouse keeper at Old Point Comfort. A very efficient workman at all times, he used to boast that on one inspection his charge was designated the best kept lighthouse on the Atlantic Coast. My father, of course, did most of the actual work because he was the youngest son and the only one to live at home during this period. One anecdote from this period illustrates the character of my grandfather. On one occasion the inspector-general of all the lighthouses in America visited the Old Point light. A bluff retired admiral, he strode into my grandfather's house, his hat on, and began to give instructions and advice concerning the running of the lighthouse. Before he had completed his first sentence, my grandfather stopped him. "Just a minute, Admiral," he said; "this may be a government lighthouse, but it is also my home and you must respect it as such." The admiral looked at this ex-slave with amazement. He then slowly removed his hat and apologized.

There is an interesting sidelight on my grandfather's stay at Old Point Comfort. During his residence there, many of the better-class Negroes throughout Virginia used Old Point Comfort and my grandfather's house as a vacation spot. There were no colored beaches on the Peninsula in those days, but there was an excellent beach in front of the lighthouse. Moreover, the "old" Hygeia, a fashionable hotel for rich whites, was also at Old Point, just a few yards from the lighthouse. Negroes staying at my grandfather's home therefore had the opportunity of using the same beach as the guests of the swanky Hygeia. The late Mrs. Rosa K. Jones, the mother of Eugene Kinckle Jones, told me that she used to come down from her home in Lynchburg quite frequently to visit my aunts at Old Point, and of course to use the beach there.

Incidentally, there has been no Negro lighthouse keeper at Old Point Comfort since the Reconstruction. My grandfather lost his job when his political faction went out of power. He moved from Old Point to the family home on Lincoln Street in the town of Hampton, and for the rest of his life made his living largely through a truck garden which he kept in the yard. He was an excellent gardener, raising the best vegetables in town; but he was also a better manager or "driver," because he made everybody in his house—sons, daughters, in-laws, grandchildren—work in the garden. The little girls picked the bugs from the plants and gathered the vegetables, the adults prepared them for sale, and the little boys peddled them through the streets or delivered them to special customers. It was truly a cooperative enterprise with Father Davis acting as a stern coordinator of the whole business.

A typical Victorian father in every sense of the word, he ordered the lives of his grown children and their wives and spanked the grandchildren at will. Although his house contained only seven rooms, he kept most of his family with him, including my parents' flock, of whom there were seven before my advent.

His friends outside the family were few, his closest a white real estate owner, J.B. Lake, an old Hamptonian, and Henry Schmelz, also white, the town's banker. He used to go daily to Lake's office, and the two of them would spend each morning talking religion. He attended the First Baptist Church (colored) for a long while and was a distinguished member of the congregation and, of course, an exhorter. But when the group, after the way of all good Baptists, got into what my grandfather called a "nigger mess" and split the church, he withdrew from both factions and attended the white First Baptist Church. A strict fundamentalist, knowing his Baptist doctrine, he made it his duty to "jack up" the white minister on Monday morning if the latter had strayed the least bit from the orthodox interpretation of God's Word.

Although he had white friends, he was no "handkerchief-head." He felt that he was the superior of most people and the equal of any man that walked; he therefore demanded respect from everybody. My cousin told me of an incident that occurred during my grandfather's last years. The two of them were walking down Queen Street, the town's main thoroughfare, when they met one of the town's distinguished white ladies. "Good morning, Uncle Billy," she said to my grandfather; "How are you?" The old man looked sternly at her for a moment and then said, "Madam, I am not your father's brother! The name is Davis— William Davis."

During his last days, he became a patriarch of the town, respected by black and white alike. A tall, spare, erect and distinguished-looking bronze man, he could be seen daily, with a basket of food on his arm and a small Bible in his pocket, visiting the sick and the needy of the town. He considered this his Christian duty, and only illness prevented his daily visits.

"It was a pleasure to see him coming down the street," my cousin said in describing him. "He was always very neat in his black or dark blue cloth suit, white shirt, black tie, and well-blacked shoes. He was one of very few colored men who could walk downtown *dressed up* every day. We were all very proud of him."

In his last years, he walked the streets of Hampton everybody's friend and also everybody's critic. Unfortunately, he had a wee bit of that first generation disillusionment often possessed by successful ex-slaves; that is, he tended to criticize too harshly the shortcomings of many of his fellow-Negroes. He felt that most of them were not grasping the opportunities which were before them, and he probably told them so too bluntly and too frequently. In spite of this forthrightness, however, he never lost the respect of the town. There are old persons living in Hampton who still pay me a left-handed compliment when talking about my grandfather. "You are doing all right, Boy," they tell me, "but you will never be the man your grandpappy was."

And I like to think of him as a real man. In spite of his slave background and his lack of training, he walked through the world with a confidence and an at-homeness that would do credit to any human. In spite of his slave background and his lack of training, he was more of a typical American and a typical Virginian, more a part of his community, more deeply rooted in the soil of his native section than his grandson can ever be.

His Descendants

The descendants of William R. Davis are legion, and they are now scattered from Alabama to Massachusetts. The mere listing of all their names, though necessary for a complete picture, is practically an impossible task, because relatives have a strange way of getting lost, and even those who stay put have an irritating way of not answering one's letters. I can say, however, that I have got in touch with most of the living members of my family; and I of course have some general information concerning even those whom I could not reach. Because the family has so many branches, I feel that the simplest and fairest way of treating them is to present in chronological order each one of Father Davis's children, tracing his line down to the present generation, or as far as it goes. Needless to say, *I shall make all entries and comments as brief as possible.*

William R. Davis had six children to reach adulthood, and they were born in the following order: John, William, Fannie, Thomas, Emma, and Andrew. Although they were all born in slavery, my grandfather, profiting by his own experience, saw to it that there would be no uncertainty concerning the ages of *his* offspring, because he recorded in his Bible the exact date of each birth. To find such accurate information in a slave family is unusual, to say the least.

John Davis, the eldest surviving child, was born May 20, 1840. John was a chef by trade. He was twice married—first, to Nora Chisman of Hampton and after her death to Mary (Pinkie) Billups. From this second marriage, which took place in 1877, there were three children—Mamie, Bessie, and Fanny—only one of whom, Bessie, is now living. Bessie Davis married Sumner Boteler of Philadelphia. They now live in New York City and have two grown children. Sumner (Jr.), the younger child, is a post office employee in that city. Frances, who was an honor graduate of Hunter College, is now employed as a social investigator in the New York City Department of Welfare. She is married and has one child, a girl, Judith Lewis, aged 6.

William Davis, the second child, was born 1843. A butler by trade, he left home shortly after the Civil War and settled in

Providence, Rhode Island, where he died in 1880 at the age of 37. He was never married.

Fannie B. Davis, the third child, was born September 10, 1847. She married Dallas Lee, a carpenter, in her native town. A sort of tragic Nemesis pursued this branch of the family, and no member of it is now living. Fannie died at the age of 37, leaving two children—William and Emma. After attending Hampton Institute, William married and started out in his father's trade. But the marriage, for several unpleasant reasons which I need not detail here, soon went on the rocks; and the two children of the union, Dallas and Theresa, were placed in the two Catholic boarding schools at Rock Castle, Virginia. There Dallas died while still in his teens. Theresa died childless during the late thirties. She was living and working at Tuskegee at the time of her death. Her husband was a teacher in that school. Emma, the younger child of Fannie and Dallas Lee, inherited her mother's good looks and her beauty is still talked about by "old-timers" in both Hampton and New York. The older people also remember the romance and the tragedy of her first marriage to W. Henry Bonaparte. Supposedly related to Jerome Bonaparte, Henry was a handsome and brilliant orator and political leader in his native town. Because of an affair, which I need not report here, Henry got into serious trouble. But the thing which the townsfolk still remember vividly is the faithfulness of Emma to this unfortunate man, how she stuck with him and nursed him to the bitter end—and it was a most bitter end. After Bonaparte's death, Emma moved to New York. There she met and subsequently married Charles Anderson, the well known Republican leader and Collector of Revenue for the Second District of New York. In the days when Negro society life centered in 53rd Street, Emma was admittedly the most beautiful woman in her set, and, according to Teddy Roosevelt (who was Charlie's close friend), the most beautiful woman in all New York. She entertained in her home during those years many of the finest persons—white and Negro—in the political and social life of New York. Emma and Charlie Anderson both died during the thirties, leaving no descendants.

Thomas Davis, the fourth child, was born April 21, 1850. He became a prosperous and highly successful business man in his native Hampton. For many years he owned a trading schooner which plied the waters of the Chesapeake Bay. He also acquired a considerable amount of property and was the last Negro in Hampton to own oystering grounds. In addition to these "outside" enterprises, he was for many years the custodian of the Hampton post office. In reality he was more than mere custodian; he was the "unofficial postmaster," the one who "broke in" each new white appointee. Though not formally educated, Thomas had a great deal of natural business acumen and was oftentimes far shrewder in his foresight and in his analysis of business trends than those who were formally trained. A staunch Republican all of his life, he was a leader in the "mixed" Republican Club of the Peninsula. He died in 1929. Thomas Davis was twice married. His first wife, Millie Wilson, died childless in 1904. On February 21, 1905, he married Undine Wiggins of Plymouth, North Carolina, by whom he had three children: Undine, Thomas, and William. A most promising lad, William, the youngest child, died when he was twelve years old. Thomas Peake Davis, a graduate of Hampton and of Fisk and Meharry, is now a dentist, living in Washington, D.C. Undine, a graduate of Hampton and of Oberlin, is a librarian by profession but is at present engaged in newspaper work on her husband's paper. She married P.B. Young, Jr., editor of the Norfolk *Journal and Guide*. They have three children: P.B. Young III, Thomas Young, and Davis Young, aged 18 months.

Emma Jane Davis, the fifth child, was born June 30, 1853. After attending Hampton Institute, she taught school for a short period, and then married John Mealey, one of the most highly successful contractors in the state. Although he was not formally educated, John Mealey was an expert plasterer and builder with large projects in both Virginia and Pennsylvania. In the latter state he did a lot of work for Frick, who was then beginning his rise to the financial dominance he later attained. And Emma Jane was in her own right an unusual personality. Inheriting much of her father's will power and determination, she was a strong and resourceful person through all of her eighty-odd years. When her husband died, she supported her children by opening the Hoffman House, one of the first Negro hotels in Virginia. In the days before the Peninsula beach resorts were established, the Hoffman House was a famous vacation spot for the "better" Negroes of the state; it was also the headquarters for several national fraternal conventions during the years when these orders were still small enough to convene in the town of Hampton. Emma and John Mealey had five children: Eva, William, Fanny, Edna, and Arthur. With the exception of Eva, who now lives in Baltimore, all of these children are now dead. I should add here that Emma Jane moved her family to Boston at the turn of the century, and most of the present-day Mealeys live in or near that city. All of the Mealey children married, but only two of them—Eva and William—had descendants who are now living. Eva Mealey had two daughters. One of them—Helen—married John Jackson of Cambridge, Massachusetts; the Jacksons, in turn, have four children, two sons and two daughters, who are now married and living in Boston. William Robert Mealey started out learning his father's trade, but ran away from home at the age of 14 to join the Navy in the Spanish–American War. At the close of the war, he settled in Boston, where he subsequently married Maude Armstrong, a native of that city. William and Maude Mealey had three children. Leonard, the eldest, is married and is now the father of a married daughter— Gloria Mealey Davis. And Gloria has two charming daughters of her own—Renee and Marcia Davis. (Incidentally, they are the great-great-great-grandchildren of William R. Davis.) Robert William, the younger son, a sergeant in the army during the late war, is also married and has one son, Robert William Mealey, Jr., aged 4. Dorothy Mealey, the only daughter of William and Maude Mealey, has been for several years a civil service worker for the Department of Public Welfare in the city of Boston. She has studied art and professional photography; she has done special work at Boston University; and at the present time, she is enrolled in the Liberal Arts College of Northeastern University.

Andrew Davis, the youngest child of William R. Davis, was born August 19, 1856. He was one of the earliest graduates of Hampton Institute, having finished in 1872, as salutatorian of the school's second class. After his graduation, he went to Pennsylvania and learned the plastering trade under John Mealey, his brother-in-law. He became a "master mechanic" in every sense of that term, and he had the kind of fierce pride in his work which is seldom seen nowadays. The leading plasterer and plastering contractor in Hampton, he did practically all of the first-class work in his field on the Peninsula and was, in addition, the only Negro "head mechanic" on the two government reservations in the community. A reserved, almost anti-social person, he was warmly devoted to his family and had few interests outside of his home and his work. A stern disciplinarian, he was yet an excellent parent—one who had at all times his children's respect and affection. Though born in slavery and reared in the South, he had grown up in that period immediately following the Civil War when the South grudgingly and briefly awarded the Negro equality. He never outgrew his early conditioning in freedom; as a result he walked through life as a *full* man, making few if any concessions to race. He died in 1935. In 1884, Andrew married Frances S. Nash of Hampton, who incidentally is very much alive at the present time and has just celebrated her eighty-third birthday. From this union there were nine children: Oma (who died in infancy), William, Thomas, Don, Harry, John, Nancy (who died in 1924 at the age of 26), Collis, and Arthur.

William Roscoe Davis, named for his grandfather and the latter's favorite, was born in 1886. He graduated from Hampton Institute as a painter and interior decorator and continued his training at Pratt Institute, Brooklyn. For many years he was a teacher of his trade at South Carolina State College and at Claflin, both in Orangeburg. Having been a star player at Hampton, he was also football coach at these two schools respectively. In later years, he moved his family to New York to secure a Northern education for his children. When he was killed by a hit-and-run driver in New York during the early thirties, he was foreman-in-charge of all the painting work on Governor's Island. William was twice married. His first wife was Fannie E. Johnson of Orangeburg, South Carolina, by whom he had four children: William R. (Jr.), Rowena, Andrew, and Harry. After her death, he married Fay L. Hendley of Huntsville, Alabama, a teacher of home economics, by whom he had one child, a daughter, Fay E. Davis. All five of these children are now married. William Roscoe (Jr.), the oldest, took his B.S. at Hampton and is now principal of a high school in Councils, North Carolina. He is also the owner of two successful businesses—a dress shop and a chicken farm. Anna Rowena, a graduate of Hunter College, was a YWCA worker before her marriage. She is now the wife of John H. Morrow,

Professor of French at Talladega College, where she makes her home. The Morrows have two children—Jean Rowena, aged 12, and John H. (Jr.), aged 5. Andrew H. Davis, a veteran of World War II, is now a postal clerk in New York. He has one child, Marilyn, aged 11. Harry L. Davis, also a World War II veteran, lives in Orangeburg, South Carolina, and has one daughter, Harriet, aged 6. Fay Elizabeth Davis, like her sister a Hunter graduate, married Henry Boulware, a mail carrier in New York. They have one child—William H. Boulware, aged 6 months.

Thomas Henry Davis, the third child of Andrew and Frances Davis, was a railroad employee who lived in Washington, D.C., at the time of his death in 1934. He attended Hampton Institute but was "sent home" in his junior year because of some minor infraction of the rules. Though he never returned to school himself, he contributed unstintingly to the education of his younger brothers. A soldier in the first World War, Thomas won the Distinguished Service Cross on September 30, 1918, for extraordinary heroism at Binarville, France. According to the citation, he "voluntarily left shelter and crossed an open space fifty yards wide, swept by shell and machine gun fire, to rescue a wounded comrade." This act was typical of him; it was in essence the kind of thing he did in his everyday association with his family and his fellow workers. Generous to a fault, happy-go-lucky, and possessed of a glorious sense of humor, Tom refused at all times to take life too seriously; and when he saw death approaching in the form of a dread disease, he faced that too with his characteristic good nature and high spirits.

Don Andrew Davis, the fourth child, is the Business Manager and Comptroller of Hampton Institute, his alma mater. A leader in the civic, business, and religious life of his community, Don has also been for many years the Chairman of the Executive Committee of the National Business League. A pioneer worker among Negro college business officers, he is considered by many the "unofficial dean" of this group. In 1912, he married Ethel Dunning of Norfolk, Virginia; they have three children: Don (Jr.), Charles, and Elizabeth. Don (Jr.), the oldest, is a graduate of Dartmouth College and is at present the Secretary-Manager of the People's Building and Loan Association, a very sound and highly successful Negro business in Hampton. He is married to Lennie

Smith of Newport News, Virginia, and has one child, a daughter, Joan Eileen, aged 2. Charles T. Davis, the second child, also attended Dartmouth College where he had a most brilliant record in scholarship. Elected to Phi Beta Kappa in his junior year, he graduated as ranking scholar of his class. Although he was not chosen, he had the honor of representing the state of New Hampshire as a Rhodes Scholar candidate. (Rhodes Scholars are not selected through competitive examinations. The final choice is made on the basis of an interview. Charles was one of six New England candidates from whom two were selected.) He took his M.A. at the University of Chicago, leaving there to enter the Army. Before the war ended, he had become a captain in the Adjutant General's Office, one of two Negroes in that service. He is now an Instructor in English at New York University. Charles is married to Jean Curtis, the only daughter of Dr. and Mrs. Maurice Curtis of Paterson, New Jersey.

Harry Winfred Davis, the fifth child, is a railroad employee now living in Washington, D.C., but he has been in turn a house painter, a restaurant owner, and an undertaker. He married Elizabeth Levy of Camden, South Carolina, in 1917; they have three grown children: John, Ella, and Nancy. John D. Davis, the oldest child, a government employee in Washington, married Martha Louise Steele of Milledgeville, Georgia, by whom he has two children: Diane, aged 7, and Jon, aged 2. Ella Davis, the second child, married Thomas Augustus Jordan, a government employee, and they also have two children: Gregory, aged 2, and Cassandra, aged 1. Nancy Davis, the youngest child, is a graduate of Howard University and of Traphagen Institute in New York City. She is an interior designer by profession and is at the present time a teacher in Letcher's Art School, Washington, D.C.

John Andrew Davis, the sixth child of Andrew and Frances Davis, is a physician in New York City with a very large and lucrative practice. After a brilliant career at the Howard Medical School, from which he was graduated in 1925 at the top of his class, he interned at Freedman's Hospital. After his internship he opened his practice in New York City, joining there the staff of Harlem Hospital, where he continued his work in surgery. In 1926 he married Melissa Thomas of Washington, D.C. They had one daughter, Barbara, who died in 1945 at the age of eighteen. A beautiful and charming girl, Barbara was a junior at Hunter College at the time of her untimely and tragic death.

Collis Huntington Davis, the eighth child, is the Dean of Students and Professor of Chemistry at Hampton Institute. One of two Negro students chosen by the late Julius Rosenwald for an "interracial" experiment at Grinnell College, Iowa—please note that this experiment was tried prior to the establishment of the Rosenwald Fund—Collis graduated from that school in 1923, winning a Phi Beta Kappa key for excellence in scholarship. He is an M.A. in chemistry from Columbia University and has done advanced work in his field both at Harvard and at the University of Pennsylvania. In 1930, he married Louise Barbour of Kansas City, a graduate of Sargent who was at the time a teacher of physical education at Hampton. They have four children: Louise, a freshman at Colby College in Maine; Jennie, a junior in Fryburg Academy (also in Maine); Collis, aged 7; and Barbara Neal, aged 5 months.

Arthur Paul Davis, the last child of Andrew and Frances Davis, is now Professor of English at Howard University. A Phi Beta Kappa graduate of Columbia College, he is also a Ph.D. in English from the same university. He is the author of *Isaac Watts: His Life and Works*, a scholarly work which has recently won critical acclaim in England, and is the co-editor (with Sterling A. Brown and Ulysses Lee) of *The Negro Caravan*, a popular anthology of Negro literature published in 1942. In addition he is the author of numerous reviews, stories, newspaper columns, and scholarly articles. In 1928, he married Clarice E. Winn, who was then a librarian in the New York Public Library. Clarice Winn is the daughter of Dr. and Mrs. Malcolm Winn of Columbus, Ohio. [Her mother, Mrs. C.A. Winn, now retired, was for many years connected with the National Board of the YWCA, and her aunt, the late Eva D. Bowles, was the founder of Negro work in that organization.] The Arthur P. Davises have one son—Arthur Paul (Jr.)—who is now in Dunbar High School, Washington, D.C.

Although this account deals primarily with William Roscoe Davis and *his* descendants, I feel that I ought to mention briefly the members of my family stemming from my grandmother's side. As I have noted above, Nancy Moore had one son, Henry Servant, before she married my grandfather. This son, as I have also pointed out, became in everything save blood relationship Father Davis's child. Two of Henry Servant's daughters are still living, and each has a fine family. Mrs. Lillie Servant Rivers, the youngest of the Servant children, now lives in Phoebus, Virginia. She has three grown children: Eva Rivers Thomas, the wife of the Head of the Music Department at Florida A. and M. College; Lillie Rivers Hill, the Librarian of St. Philip's Hospital, Richmond, Virginia; and Robert Rivers, Supervisor of Physical Education in the Negro schools of Greensboro, North Carolina. The next daughter, Nannie Servant McGuinn, recently retired, was for many years the Dean of Women at Florida A. and M. College. She too has three grown children: Robert P. McGuinn, a well-known and successful attorney in Baltimore, Maryland; Dr. Henry J. McGuinn, Director of the Department of Social Sciences at Virginia Union University; and Callie McGuinn Harris, a public health worker in Washington, D.C., and the wife of Dr. Abram Harris, Professor of Economics at the University of Chicago.

My grandfather, as I have stated above, was intensely concerned about the education of his race; and though born and reared a slave, he had a supreme confidence in the Negro's intrinsic "equality." This belief was the main theme of many of his speeches. "Some say we have not the same faculties and feelings with white folks," he used to tell his audiences, and then he would add in thunderous tones: "Only educate us and we will show ourselves capable of knowledge."

With such a background, it is but natural that a large number of Father Davis's descendants (by far the largest number for any one calling) should be engaged in educational work. Moreover, it is interesting to note that most of these descendants, whether or not in school work, have realized the importance of education and have attended some of the best schools in America. A list of the institutions to which they have gone reads like a "Who's Who" of top flight American colleges. Among the schools attended by them are the following: Harvard, Columbia, University of Chicago, Dartmouth, Oberlin, New York University, Colby College, City College of New York, Grinnell College, University of Pennsylvania, Boston University, Fordham, Hunter College, Pratt, Howard, Virginia Union, Fisk, and Hampton.

I know that it is bad taste to "parade" degrees, but since one is allowed a little leeway on that score in an article of this sort, I wish to point out that the descendants of William R. and Nancy Moore Davis have earned the following degrees: two Ph.D.'s, one M.D., one D.D.S., one Ll.B., five M.A.'s, and fourteen A.B.'s. *There are three Phi Beta Kappas in the family.* This record, though by no means sensational, is certainly not a bad showing for a family whose first *two* generations were actually born in slavery!

I have stressed this educational side for one reason only: I believe that Father Davis's implicit and enthusiastic faith in the efficacy of learning has been in some measure a spur to those of us who have come after him. And I am sure, were he alive today, that he would be proud of the educational status of his numerous descendants.

Arthur P. Davis
1950

Robert W. Mealey, Jr.

Gregory Jordan

Cassandra Jordan

Jon and Diane Davis

John H. Morrow, Jr.

Barbara Davis

Capt. Charles T. Davis

Arthur P. Davis, Jr.

Georgia Louise Davis

Nancy Davis

Jennie C. Davis

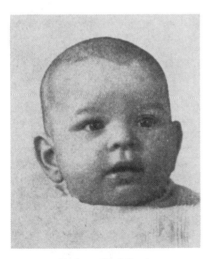

Barbara Neal Davis

Andrew Davis

Frances Davis

Emma Jane Mealey

Capt. Thomas Davis

Collis H. Davis, Jr.

Ella Davis Jordan

Sgt. Robert Mealey

Elizabeth Davis

Don A. Davis, Jr., and daughter

Grandsons of William Roscoe Davis and sons of Andrew and Frances Davis: (seated) Thomas, Collis, William; (standing) Don, Arthur, Harry, and John. (This picture was taken in 1924 immediately after the funeral of Nancy E. Davis, their sister.)

William Roscoe Davis and his daughter Fannie

Nancy Moore Davis (1822–90), wife of William Roscoe Davis and mother of the Servant and Davis families. A member of the well-known Peake family, she was related by marriage to Mrs. Mary Peake, the first Negro school teacher in Virginia. By nature quiet and retiring, Nancy Moore was nevertheless a very strong woman. Though born and reared a slave, she stubbornly and courageously refused to let her master "correct" any of her children. A very human and understanding wife and mother, she gave through her quietness and reticence a much needed "balance" to a household whose members were decidedly high spirited. And her influence on the family, though not so obvious as that of William Roscoe, was just as vital.

Dr. Thomas P. Davis

Undine D. Young

Arthur P. Davis

Great-great-great-grandchildren Renee and Marcia Davis and their parents

Index

DEMCO